The Contours of

Christian Education

The Contours of
Christian Education

Edited by
Jeff Astley and David Day

McCrimmons
Great Wakering, Essex

First published in Great Britain in 1992 by
McCrimmon Publishing Co Ltd
10-12 High Street,Great Wakering, Essex SS3 0EQ, England

© 1992 the editors and authors

ISBN 0 85597 495 8

Typeset in New Baskerville by McCrimmon Publishing Co Ltd
Printed by BPCC Wheatons Ltd, Exeter

Contents

Foreword

STEPHEN SYKES

Bishop of Ely

It is no doubt true that growth in faith is a mystery. Jesus himself is said to have grown 'big and strong and full of wisdom' (Luke 2:40) and to have 'advanced in wisdom and favour with God and men' (Luke 2:53). Dr Alfred Plummer (a Durham theologian), writing a major commentary in 1910, insisted in contemporary psycho-biographical vein, that such assertions implied a process of moral and spiritual growth. Contemporary scholars are more reticent about the light these conventional words shed on Jesus's own personal development. Even so we may take them to be evidence at least for the contemporary assumption that growth in faith is part of the lives of many. That it is predicated of Jesus merely emphasizes the fact that its taken-for-granted character conceals its mysteriousness.

But the Christian response to mystery is not, and never has been one of intellectual passivity. All the more puzzling and regrettable, therefore, has been the slowness of the English theological establishment to pursue and to appropriate the insights of educationalists into how people learn. As with so much in English theology this neglect can be attributed to nothing more profound than the accidents of the history of various institutions. In contrast to the situation in the United States, English churches have never taken full professional responsibility for the education of children and young people in the Christian faith. As a consequence our seminaries and the theological colleges have not offered Christian education as a major discipline for degree-level study. As compared with Germany, on the other hand, the university faculties and departments of theology have lacked the scale of intellectual incentive, such as that provided by Friedrich Schleiermacher's still impressive contribution to pedagogics (posthumously published lectures of 1826, reissued as *Pädagogische Schriften I,*

Frankfurt: Ulstein Buch, 1983). Theology and educational theory in England have pursued separate and unrelated courses.

There have also been intellectual alibis, one of which is the double uncertainty concerning the security of the intellectual foundations of educational theory, and the terms of the relations between psychological and spiritual maturation. But if the practice of Christian education has been fearful of 'trendy educational theories', ignorance has not proved a potent defence. In fact, of course, the churches have been vulnerable to fashion precisely because of their lack of a tradition of thorough critical reflection. The psychological and sociological ideas undergirding modern educational theory are so generally pervasive in the culture that the choice before the churches is, in practice, between being critically or uncritically, reflectively or unreflectively, influenced by them.

Students of educational theory quickly discover that the discipline sustains disputes, some of which are very far-reaching. As a consequence there is not one, but a plurality of theoretical structures on offer. When this bears upon the existing variety of perspectives, traditions and practices in Christian theology and church life, the consequences can seem discouragingly diverse, and even self-contradictory. Two things become immediately necessary — a map, to plot out the territory, and a community of scholars willing to reflect on the issues and to debate them with one another, so that the variety of perspectives and observations can be explored and tested.

The achievement of this collection is not merely to have gathered a fascinating group of essays from major contributors to the discipline; it is also to have provided a mapping of the field from a variety of angles of vision. The reader will find both theoretical perspectives and studies from within the differing contexts of church, school and general culture. To these are added the fruits of empirical investigations of very great interest, particularly for those concerned with the reasons why teenagers persist in, or disappear from, the churches.

The work marks the first ten years of life of the North of England Institute for Christian Education, the first Chairman of whose Council I had the privilege of being. I warmly welcome these investigations. Their range and quality show how greatly needed is the stimulus of NEICE's existence, and it is my belief that the churches will, in time, demand still more of it.

10 March 1992   Stephen Ely

Preface

All of these papers are associated with the North of England Institute for Christian Education. Many of them were delivered at meetings of NEICE's ecumenical and multi-disciplinary Christian Education Seminar. This brings together on six or seven occasions each year a group of educationalists, theologians and others with an interest in and responsibility for Christian education for the purpose of discussing papers from members of the Seminar and from visiting scholars — sometimes from overseas. Other papers in this collection were presented as part of our occasional series of 'Hild/Bede Lectures' in Newcastle or Durham, and were given to a wider audience of clergy, ministers, teachers and interested lay Christians. Some were prepared for NEICE's conferences or study days. A number of the more empirical studies illustrate NEICE's policy of collaborative research with others outside the Institute.

As editors we wish to express our gratitude to all those who made their papers available for this volume, now published to mark the first decade of NEICE's work. In drawing together all these essays we have attempted to achieve some measure of consistency between them in the matter of references etc (while permitting both the 'humanities' and the 'Harvard' systems), but we have done nothing to flatten the variety of the collection, or the individuality of the separate pieces. We acknowledge with thanks the support of the Management Committee of the Institute and of its funding body, the Trustees of St Hild and St Bede. Our greatest debt of gratitude, however, must go to Mrs Dorothy Greenwell, Secretary of NEICE, for all her patient hard work in preparing this text for publication.

February 1992   Jeff Astley
Durham   David Day

1

The Contours of Christian Education

JEFF ASTLEY AND DAVID DAY

MAPPING THE FIELD

On embarking on any journey it is important to be clear about your position and the direction in which the road leads. For the pilgrimage that is Christian education we need something to show us what is what and where, as well as the connections between this, that and the other feature of the landscape. We need to know where we are, and where we should be going. We need a map of the contours of Christian education. It is the purpose of this volume to help those who want to find their way about this difficult theoretical and practical terrain.

In country like this, perhaps we need more than one sort of map. For some maps are strong on physical features, but they do not mark the youth hostels; whereas population density maps are useless for geological surveys, although they do indicate that it may prove fairly expensive to dig the mineshaft in the middle of a housing estate. And it is useful to have maps of very different scales: those that provide an overview from a great height, as it were, as well as those on which you can almost see the whites of their net curtains. The true student of geography will want several maps. Likewise with the Christian educator. So this book offers many different, overlapping frameworks and perspectives on the practice of Christian education. Together they bring, we trust, a little more clarity, and perhaps a little extra by way of depth of understanding. Approaching the same area in very different ways, and mapping it on very different scales, our various contributors together provide a more comprehensive survey than could anyone on his or her own.

Further, it may be argued that maps — like essays — can and should be selective, partial, even idiosyncratic. Maps reflect the interests and 'worldview' of the cartographers, as well as the terrain that they confront. Features that are immensely salient to one mapmaker will be unmarked by another. It may be that, as map-readers, we share their interests and perspectives. But even when we do not, their views can illuminate our own. 'I hadn't noticed that before.' Sometimes another person's viewpoint, or mental map, can be more illuminating precisely for being partial, even partisan — perhaps especially when 'we don't see things that way'.

But it is time to drop the metaphors, and speak more plainly. And once we are in plain speaking mode, one question above all clamours for an answer. What is this 'area' of Christian education? What is Christian education?

CHRISTIAN EDUCATION: A CARTOGRAPHER'S NIGHTMARE?

There is some danger that the phrase may become, like St Paul, all things to all people. 'Christian education' is a phrase that can be applied either to processes of Christian formation or to the intellectual development of a critical evaluation of the Christian faith. Some restrict it to particular ways of learning Christianity: especially learning-with-understanding. Others use the phrase to designate teaching people in a 'non-confessional' way about Christianity. For many it denotes a critique of general education (or a 'philosophy of education') undertaken from a Christian perspective, or labels those educational processes in home, school, college or elsewhere that they regard in some sense as (at least) congruent with the values and insights of the Christian gospel.

Hence John Hull has claimed that the use of the phrase 'Christian education' usually conceals a confusion among: (a) 'the processes and means whereby Christians bring up their children'; (b) 'a Christian approach to, or philosophy of, general education'; and (c) 'Christianity as curriculum content'.[1] Altogether, we shall argue, five distinct understandings may be discerned.

Christian Formation
Most authors and readers understand the phrase Christian education in Hull's sense (a): ie as Christian 'nurture' or 'formation'. Some of them would expand his definition, however, to include
(i) people over their entire lifespan (ie not just children); and
(ii) conversion to, as well as the nurture/formation of individuals and groups in, the Christian worldview, character and identity. To quote a section from the objectives of the North of England Institute

for Christian Education, Christian education includes 'how people of all ages understand the concepts and participate in the experiences of the Christian faith'. More will be said about this type of Christian education later in this chapter. Suffice it to say at this point that Christian education as formation is, in some sense at least, a matter of making disciples.

Christian Self-criticism

The development of critical *(in a neutral sense)*, evaluative and analytical skills in the Christians formed by the above processes is regarded by a number of educators as an important complement to Christian formation, at least for many learners. These learners can then evaluate for themselves, from and within a Christian standpoint, the Christian culture and self-understanding into which they have been nurtured. Some argue that the fostering of this ability is an *essential* element in anything that is to be properly designated Christian *education*. This critical Christian education (or 'critical openness' within Christian education) leads to that which may also be designated 'Christian criticism'.[2] It includes what has been traditionally described as 'faith seeking understanding', and (in educational circles) as 'reflection upon experience'. If it were to take place from a perspective wholly *outside* the Christian ideology and form of life it may become indistinguishable from what is described in the next section as 'secular evaluation of the Christian religion'.

Curriculum Christianity

Hull's category (c) — 'Christianity' as curriculum content — represents 'education about Christianity' in the sense of a secular, scholarly elucidation and evaluation of the Christian religion. The objective here is solely that of (critically) understanding the Christian tradition. This is in contrast with Christian education as formation, which also includes among its objectives growth (with understanding, or so most commentators insist) in the faith, and — for many — conversion (with understanding) to it. It may be argued that education about Christianity is a proper and important aim of any complete secular education.[3]

The Christian Mind

This, slightly odd, phrase — taken from the title of Harry Blamires's well-known book — may serve to denote one aspect of Hull's category (b): Christian education as an approach to, or (more generally) a perspective on, general education. Hull's category covers two interrelated areas, the first of which is the Christian critique of education. We include here understandings of education that are developed with conscious and particular reference to the Christian viewpoint and which function, positively or negatively, as critiques of other (for example more secular) accounts of education and educational activities.[4] Such critiques often operate with criteria that are only characteristic of Christianity rather than distinctively Christian (ie specific to, and distinctive of, Christianity). Thus Christian 'philosophies of education' may oppose indoctrinatory methods in education or espouse certain goals in moral education, but they often do so on grounds that are shared by those viewing education from other standpoints. Occasionally, however, the Christian perspective may be a distinctive one that is not shared by other critiques of education. This 'Christian mind' may widen its purview, of course, to take in issues and problems that are not restricted to explicitly educational contexts or processes, but have educational implications. (Examples of this widening are to be found in this volume.)

The Christian Curriculum

The Christian critique of education outlined above may lead to a general education of a Christian kind, what has been described as a 'Christian scheme of education'.[5] This phrase denotes general educational activity that is not directly focused on Christianity, but which is influenced by a Christian understanding of education. Again, in most cases, the Christian input will be in those areas that are characteristically, rather than distinctively, Christian — for instance concern for the value of the individual or concern for truth.[6] Such an 'implicitly Christian education' (eg loving, caring education) will not necessarily differ in content or method, but only in motivation, from other species of education that lead to personal growth. Some have argued, however, that the Christian teacher's 'mode or manner' of teaching will have a particular effect that distinguishes such education from at least some other educational endeavours.[7] Others have reached the more radical conclusion that, as 'Christian presuppositions do provide an interpretative framework for all the forms of knowledge', 'there must be a unique content to Christian education in all areas of study'.[8] How all this is worked out will vary from Christian to Christian, particularly from liberal Christian to conservative Christian. In certain ways a 'Christian curriculum' may operate in secular educational institutions, as well as in the more obvious contexts of 'church schools' or 'Christian schools'.[9]

THE DIVERSITY OF CHRISTIAN EDUCATION

There are clearly important differences in aim, content and method between these different understandings of Christian education. In fact, the majority of papers in this collection understand Christian education in the sense of, or as involving, the formation and nurturing of Christian commitment, and therefore as a 'confessional' activity.[10] Many theorists and practical educators prefer to use the term 'Christian nurture' for this activity; some (especially Catholics) retain the hallowed term 'catechesis', others describe it as 'confessional RE'.[11]

Even within this genus of 'confessional' Christian education, of course, many different species are found. For those practitioners and scholars who take 'education' in its broad sense as the intentional facilitation of learning, or even more broadly simply to mark any process that leads to learning, Christian education covers any and every (structured) learning experience that gives rise to the adoption or deepening of a person's Christian beliefs, attitudes, values, or dispositions to act and experience 'in a Christian way'. On this definition evangelism and formation are indeed species of education. Chapters 3 and 10 in this collection illustrate this understanding. Others — see chapter 4 below — prefer a more restrictive, normative definition of education, on which to be educated in anything necessarily involves a growth in cognitive understanding of a morally acceptable kind (and by morally acceptable means). Christian 'education' will then be distinguished from any Christian evangelism/formation that takes place in a indoctrinatory fashion (or with an indoctrinatory intention, or leads to closed learning outcomes). On this definition Christian formation/evangelism may then be a type of education, or it may not: we shall have to look and see.

The reader may be inclined to ask tentatively at this point why we do not just legislate for the use of the phrase Christian education, and throw out of the Christian education club all those who do not share the particular definition that the club committee has adopted. 'Ladies and Gentlemen, the motion before the meeting today is that Christian education is a phrase only to be used according to Professor Hull's definition (a), amended according to your agenda. Those in favour...'. Well, that would be *one* way of ensuring a small membership, and restricting discussion to an in-group. As editors of this volume, however, we have decided to allow into the debate discussion on all types and conditions of what people call 'Christian education', as well as some papers that are concerned with secular RE but have implications for Christianity and Christian learning. All we ask is that each debater who uses the phrase 'Christian education' should know what he or she means by it, and that they should tell the rest of us. We think that is only fair, and hope that it contributes to a broader, and more far-reaching, discussion.

The diversity that this book, and similar reflections on Christian education, accommodates includes the *diversity of standpoint and perspective* mentioned earlier. There is a great deal to be said for bringing general overviews alongside detailed examinations of particular situations. But other examples of diversity are to be found here. Thus we consider *diverse forms* of Christian learning. Some Christian education envisages intentional activity and explicit 'courses' that express its aims in practical strategies; but we need to recognize also that Christian learning may depend on a hidden curriculum, or may even be the unexpected and unplanned effect of chance, unscripted encounters. A *diversity of focus and context* may also be remarked. There are the traditional contexts of congregation, Sunday school and liturgy: places and occasions where you would expect Christian learning to happen. But some of our authors also speak of 'evangelizing the media' and of Christian education as contributing to political and social unity on a European scale. Similarly both the context of the secular school and that of the church school may be addressed; and we may find ourselves critically scrutinizing aspects of Christian faith and practice at one moment, and training our evaluative skills on that which is outside the church (society, television, etc) at the next.

The Study of Christian Education

As so many of our essayists have chosen to incorporate some notion of Christian formation into their understandings of Christian education, with or without an element of Christian self-criticism, we feel it appropriate to offer here an *apologia* for the study of this particular activity.

Christian education, understood in this way, is a practice that provides an area or field of study to which various disciplines can contribute. A *diversity of methodology* is essential here. At both the theoretical and the practical levels, Christian education links the worlds of theology and education — ie of theological studies and educational studies.[12] Education is an activity that can properly be studied by the scholarly and empirical disciplines of philosophy, history, psychology and sociology; their sub-disciplines (eg linguistic analysis, cultural anthropology, empirical psychology) and offspring disciplines (curriculum theory, learning theory, social psychology etc). There is therefore a scholarly and empirical literature on the study of education: education has a 'researchable base'. The study of Christian education can draw on this literature, and can generate its own reflective and empirical studies related to its own particular practice. It may also take into account relevant research from the major disciplines of theology and religious studies. These might include the philosophy of religion, psychology of religion, sociology of religion, critical-historical studies (eg on the teaching methods of Jesus and the nature of the early church's *kerygma*) and theological reflection (eg on the nature of conversion or the nature of Christianity).

Clearly Christian educators disagree as to the extent to which the different disciplines contribute helpfully to the theory and practice of Christian education. The major disagreement is with regard to the respective contribution of the discipline-groupings of 'theology' and those of the 'social sciences' (see chapter 7 in this volume). Some argue that theology has a normative role in advising the Christian educator as to the nature of the Christian religion, but that it is unhelpful (to say the least) as a contributor to any account of the means whereby people learn, and can be taught, to be Christian. In these latter areas, it is said, only the social sciences can provide us with appropriate theories and methods. Others wish to claim a much greater role for theology. Some may even wish to deny altogether the relevance of the claims of psychologists and sociologists to illuminate the teaching of religion. Most Christian educators recognize, however, that they need to take at least some account of *both* sets of disciplines. For them the Christian educator stands at the cross-roads between theology and the social sciences. She needs to look and listen all round — and to learn from every direction. She must therefore be able and willing to see the relevance of apparently disparate data, methodologies and theories; to discern and explore the connecting links between the disciplines; and to capitalize on all these insights in practical ways.

All of which explains why the task of the student of Christian education is no easy one. There are so many relevant disciplines and subject areas with their own methods, facts and theories, vying for his attention. Those who have been trained primarily as theologians, having struggled with New Testament Greek, mediaeval philosophy or contemporary theology, may be unwilling — and feel unprepared — to take on educational psychology and the sociology of religion as well. Or, if trained as a teacher, the Christian educator may feel quite at home in the disciplines of education, but all at sea when reading what the systematic or philosophical theologians have to say about

Christianity. The compartmentalization of study that results in such a disabling of the Christian educator is unfortunate. There is nothing wrong, however, in having an amateur status vis-à-vis one or other of the contributory discipline-sets, provided that we recognize how little we know, and retain our critical skills for sifting what other people claim to know, in these subjects. It is always a risky business to try to make sense of someone else's subject. But when it is a subject that seems to be saying things to which we need to listen, the risk is worth taking. Here, as elsewhere, if we never run the risk of getting things wrong, we shall never succeed in getting them right. Certainly we should not dismiss whole areas of research and scholarship as irrelevant to our concerns as Christian educators unless we have first made some effort to discover what those researchers and scholars are saying. Ignorance is inevitable; but as it can be remedied (at least partially), it is no excuse.

A full and proper training as a Christian educator should involve, therefore, both theological and educational (including social scientific) study. Speaking very broadly, the former will provide part of, and appropriate reflection on, the subject-matter *content* of Christian education; the latter will fulfil similar roles for its *method*. There will be some overlap, for theologians should provide a theological critique of method (which itself teaches us particular things, and has been called 'structural content') and the work of social scientists can illuminate theological debate about the nature of the Christian religion (Christian education's 'substantive content').

However, this diversity and (often) disagreement raises a pertinent question. Is there any unity here at all? Or is the quest for this particular holy grail a waste of time?

THE UNITY OF CHRISTIAN EDUCATION

Whatever we take Christian education to be, it must be part of the teaching activity of the church, understood in as generous a sense as possible. Thus if it is to be authentically Christian, it will stand in some relation to the person of Christ. If that is the case, then certain features of Christian education follow.

First, its content will be ultimately personal. What is to be communicated and learned, understood and applied, is the truth as it is in Jesus. Such a truth is not finally to be expressed in concepts or propositions but only in personal — and inter-personal — terms.

Secondly, its processes or methods will reflect the character of Christ. If they do not, if they are out of harmony with or distort the ways God seems to have chosen to work with his creation, then we have every right to reject them.

Thirdly, its goals or ends will be capable of being harmonized with the ends that we have come to recognize as Christian 'maturity': the measure of the stature of the fullness of Christ. Goals are good: any practical education needs to acknowledge them and specify them. 'Assessment' is not necessarily the product of utilitarian educational systems, whittling square pegs down to fit round holes. But the ends of Christian education must be congruent with the ends of Christianity, with the end that *is* Christ.

All this is to say no more than that Jesus is both truth, way and life. The study of Christian education — not least in this book — may seem to be thoroughly centrifugal, flying off in all directions (and sometimes 'flying off the handle', too). But to qualify as Christian education it must retain some contact with its centre. The enterprise, in its furthest reaches, must somewhere bear the imprint of *his* touch, something of the whorls and configurations of his mark.

Which is to say that Christian education, like maps, must have a purpose. It, and they, must lead to action. Parents of young children need town plans on which the public toilets are marked. Colonial administrators and business people need map-makers of whom they can request, 'Colour in the bits we own, Fortescue'. Those who bury a treasure of great price need to leave for those who come after a note of a practical route whereby they can discover it for themselves, and avoid the dragons. All travellers need a clear route to a safe haven, or at least a map that shows where other vessels are wrecked. The end is to travel with purpose and direction, to seek with reasonable hope of success, to see more clearly in order to act more surely (and, no doubt, love more dearly and follow more nearly). Hence, we dare to argue, the urgency of the task before us, and the inexcusability of its neglect.

THE URGENCY OF CHRISTIAN EDUCATION

If Christian education is as significant and omni-relevant an activity as the authors in this volume often imply, it is perhaps surprising that it is not taken more seriously by the churches. Courses in the study of Christian education exist in seminaries and elsewhere in the United States, but much ministerial education in the UK still largely ignores the subject except where it can find a hearing among the proponents of its apparently sexier sister 'pastoral studies'. Teachers in secular and church schools *are* often interested in the area, but (quite properly) in ways that are appropriate to the contexts in which they teach. Even in the States, however, Christian education does not have the status it deserves either in the seminary or in the church. It is not often regarded as a 'serious study', as is doctrine or Biblical studies. Everywhere it shares some of the prejudice suffered by educational research, theory — and practice.

Clergy and ministers are, on the whole, more persuaded of their pastoral and preaching roles than of their broader role as Christian educators. If the study, and indeed the practice, of Christian education has sometimes in the past seemed superficial and unprofessional, that may be partly explained by the fact that it is difficult to do good work if you know that you are not taken seriously. The church has often ignored Christian education, and regrettably Christian education has often responded by giving the church a good excuse for ignoring it.

We believe that this vicious circle may now be beginning to be broken. In Britain as elsewhere there are now signs of a new recognition by the churches of their educational responsibilities, which is matched by a new depth of thinking and research taking place within Christian education. The traditional neglect of the subject is perhaps coming to an end. It is imperative that it should; for the neglect of Christian education is a tragedy for the church, and that for two different reasons. First, because what is actually going on when people embrace and live a religion (as children and adults) is technically largely a learning process, and the role of a Christian minister (lay or ordained) in that process is technically largely that of a teacher or educator.[13] And secondly, because the study of how Christian education proceeds 'in the context of all the influences that bear upon [Christian learners] in contemporary culture' (to quote again from the NEICE Trust Deed) raises some of the most urgent and most difficult of theological issues. These include questions not only about the relationship of human beings to God, but also about the nature of Christianity itself and of the foundations of religion.[14] Both these claims, if they can be substantiated, should lead us to see that some study of the theory and practice of Christian education is central and crucial for the theological and professional formation of the Christian minister, and indeed for all Christians who have a responsibility for the Christian learning of others in home, school, college, church or workplace. It is critical to the continuing life and health of the church in general.

As we have said, there are hopeful signs of a new interest in the practice and theory of Christian education. But in England at any rate this new interest has still not permeated very far into some of our theological colleges and seminaries.[15] Until it does, there is the danger of Christian education being done in a haphazard and unreflective way and (if the phrase be allowed) 'without benefit of clergy'. It will also be subject to the vagaries of fashion. What is needed is a developing serious study of the aims and implications, content and methods of Christian education. Much of this work will need to be done by social scientists and by theologians; some of it will have to be done by philosophers. If anyone else can help, they would be most welcome. Sometimes — often — all these fellow labourers should meet, and try to think and work together.

This particular journey needs the best map-makers, and it needs lots of them.

NOTES

1. John M. Hull, *Studies in Religion and Education*, Lewes: Falmer, 1984, p 39, also p 206. See also his *School Worship: An Obituary*, London: SCM, 1975, pp 73-74. Douglas Hubery is one author who applies the phrase 'Christian education' to (his own understanding of) all three: see his *Christian Education in State and Church*, Redhill: Denholm House, 1972, p 30 and *passim*. Compare also E. Orteza y Miranda, 'Some Problems with the Expression "Christian Education" ', *British Journal of Religious Education*, Vol. 8, No. 2, 1986.

2. The literature on the various contexts, processes and understandings of *formative* Christian education is vast. Some reference to it may be found in chapters 7 and 10 of this volume. See also Jeff Astley (ed), *Christian Education: A Select Bibliography*, third edition, Durham: NEICE, 1992. On 'critical Christian education', and the notion of 'critical openness' (the latter is often applied to RE in schools), see Leon McKenzie, *The Religious Education of Adults*, Birmingham, Ala.: Religious Education Press, 1982, pp 36f, 64ff; Karl-Ernst Nipkow and Stewart Sutherland in M. C. Felderhof (ed), *Religious Education in a Pluralistic Society*, London: Hodder & Stoughton, 1985, pp 31, 140; John M. Hull, *What Prevents Christian Adults from Learning?*, London: SCM, 1985, pp 71ff, 121ff; Leon McKenzie, 'The Purposes and Scope of Adult Religious Education', in Nancy Foltz (ed), *Handbook of Adult Religious Education*, Birmingham, Ala.: Religious Education Press, 1986, p 12 and *passim;* Hull, *Studies in Religion and Education*, pp 190ff, 197ff, 207ff; Arthur J. Rowe, 'Critical Openness and Religious Education', *British Journal of Religious Education*, Vol. 8, No. 2, 1986; Brenda Watson *et al., Critical Openness*, Oxford: Farmington Institute, no date. We should stress that 'critical' here implies only reflective judgement, and not negative, censorious fault-finding.

3. On teaching about Christianity, see Owen Cole, 'What about Christianity?', in Cole (ed), *World Faiths in Education*, London: Allen & Unwin, 1978, and 'Christian Studies in Schools', in Robert Jackson (ed), *Approaching World Religions*, London: John Murray, 1982; David V. Day, 'Christianity in our Multifaith Community', *Spectrum*, Vol. 15, No. 2, 1983; Trevor and Margaret Cooling, 'Christian Doctrine in Religious Education', *British Journal of Religious Education*, Vol. 9, No. 3, 1987; Clive Erricker,

Teaching Christianity: A World Religions Approach, Cambridge: Lutterworth, 1987. The distinction between 'teaching about' Christianity (or any religion) and 'teaching Christianity' is explored, and criticized, in R. M. Rummery, *Catechesis and Religious Education in a Pluralistic Society,* Sydney: Dwyer, 1975, pp 156-161; John Sealey, 'Teaching "About" and Teaching "What is" in Religion', *British Journal of Religious Education,* Vol. 2, No. 2, 1979; Gabriel Moran, *Interplay: A Theory of Religion and Education,* Winona, Minnesota: St Mary's Press, 1981, ch 5; and Moran, *Religious Education as a Second Language,* Birmingham, Ala.: Religious Education Press, 1989.

4. As examples of such an approach see Spencer Leeson, *Christian Education,* London: Longmans, Green, 1947, lecture V; M. V. C. Jeffreys, *The Aims of Education (Glaucon),* London: Pitman, 1972, pp 151-167; Patricia English, 'A Christian Perspective on Classroom and School Discipline', *Journal of Christian Education,* Vol. 60, 1977; Michael Hinton, 'A Theology for the Classroom', in *Christianity in the Classroom,* London: Christian Education Movement, 1978; William K. Kay and Fred Hughes, 'Christian Light on Education', *Religious Education,* Vol. 80, No. 1, 1985; Edward Hulmes, 'Christian Education in a Multi-cultural Society', in V. Alan McLelland (ed), *Christian Education in a Pluralist Society,* London: Routledge, 1988, pp 89, 91-92; Brian V. Hill, *That They May Learn: Towards a Christian View of Education,* Exeter: Paternoster, 1990; and various articles in Leslie J. Francis and Adrian Thatcher (eds), *Christian Perspectives for Education: A Reader in the Theology of Education,* Leominster: Fowler Wright, 1990.

5. See John M. Sutcliffe and Philip Lee-Woolf, 'Christian Education and RE', in Sutcliffe (ed), *A Dictionary of Religious Education,* London: SCM, 1984, p 67. The works cited in note 4 above often make a contribution here as well. See also Edmund Fuller (ed), *The Christian Idea of Education,* New Haven: Yale University, 1957, p viii and *passim;* and Witold Tulasiewicz and Colin Brock (eds), *Christianity and Educational Provision in International Perspective,* London: Routledge, 1988, *passim.*

6. See Gabriel Moran, 'Of a Kind and to a Degree', in Marlene Mayr (ed), *Does the Church Really Want Religious Education?,* Birmingham, Ala.: Religious Education Press, 1988, pp 21-22.

7. Jacques Maritain, 'On Some Typical Aspects of Christian Education', in Fuller (ed), *op. cit.,* p 180.

8. Elmer J. Thiessen, 'A Defense of a Distinctively Christian Curriculum', *Religious Education,* Vol. 80, No. 1, 1985, p 50.

9. On 'Christian schools' see John Vriend, *To Prod the Slumbering Giant,* Montreal: Wedge Publishing, 1972; Brian V. Hill, 'Christian Schools — Issues to be Resolved', *Journal of Christian Education,* Vol. 75, November 1982; Alan Peshkin, *God's Choice: The Total World of a Fundamentalist Christian School,* Chicago: University of Chicago Press, 1986; Noel Weeks, *The Christian School,* London: Banner of Truth Trust, 1988; Ruth Deakin, *The New Christian School,* Bristol: Regius Press, 1989. On the traditional (English) 'church school', see *A Future in Partnership* (1984) and *Positive Partnership* (1985), both London: National Society; Joanna Yates (ed), *Faith for the Future,* London: National Society, 1986; Bernadette O'Keefe, *Faith, Culture and the Dual System,* Lewes: Falmer, 1986; Leslie J. Francis, *Religion in the Primary School: A Partnership between Church and State?,* London: Collins, 1987.

10. 'Confessionalism' in British discussions of RE does not refer to a denominational emphasis, but more broadly to religious 'instruction in particular beliefs to the exclusion of all others'. Robin H. Shepherd, 'Confessionalism', in Sutcliffe (ed), *op. cit.,* p 94. The use of confessional language in this context has been criticized, see Hull, *Studies in Religion and Education,* p 180.

11. This understanding of Christian education is similar to that adopted in the United States, although there 'Christian education' has historically been a Protestant term, whereas Catholics have traditionally preferred 'catechesis'. In the United States — readers (and librarians!) should note — 'religious education', whether Jewish, Christian or whatever, is the generic term for any activity that is sponsored by the

religious community and is intended to lead to the development of religious commitment. Religious education does not (for legal, historical and practical reasons) refer there to any teaching about religion in secular ('public') schools, a practice of which many Americans are still suspicious. On the different uses of some of these terms in the United States and Britain see Gabriel Moran, 'Religious Education', in Mircea Eliade (ed), *Encyclopedia of Religion*, Vol. 12, New York: Macmillan; London: Collier Macmillan, 1987; 'Religious Pluralism: A US and Roman Catholic View', in Norma H. Thompson (ed), *Religious Pluralism and Religious Education*, Birmingham, Ala.: Religious Education Press, 1988; and *Religious Education as a Second Language*, p 85, ch 4 and *passim*. On the background to the situation in US schools, see N. Piediscalzi, 'Public Education Religion Studies since the *Schempp* Decision', in Marvin J. Taylor (ed), *Foundations for Christian Education in an Era of Change*, Nashville, Tenn.: Abingdon, 1976.

12. James Michael Lee writes of religious instruction (the intentional facilitation of the learning of religion) as a 'mediator', uniting religion ('substantive content') and instruction (method, or 'structural content') in a new entity that is different from both. See his 'The Authentic Source of Religious Instruction', in Norma H. Thompson (ed), *Religious Education and Theology*, Birmingham, Ala.: Religious Education Press, 1982, pp 165ff. This book is a useful collection of papers on (primarily formative) Christian education, and its relationship to theology.

13. Cf J. M. Lee 'Towards a New Era: A Blueprint for Positive Action', in Lee (ed), *The Religious Education We Need*, Birmingham, Ala.: Religious Education Press, 1977, p 141.

14. 'Education is a matter of practice. As such there will be a peculiar advantage for theology, albeit perhaps a painful one, in engaging in dialogue with or reflection upon the processes of education. Educational practice thrusts upon theologians questions which otherwise and mistakenly they might "leave till the end". Each demands a response from theologians and each raises matters of fundamental substance about the very nature of theology itself.' Stewart Sutherland, 'Education and Theology', in Yates (ed), *Faith for the Future*, p 37.

15. Scotland does things better, as is often the case educationally; and there are hopeful developments in Wales. Catholics (and to some extent the Free Churches) are much better in these matters than Anglicans. Perhaps the authors, two Anglicans, might be allowed to comment that too often the English Anglican situation, which is shared by some Protestants on the Continent, presents as a paradigm for Christian education the model that operates in the increasingly secular university departments of theology and/or religious studies with which they are familiar. In some seminaries and 'theological colleges' (note the name!) religious thinking and scholarship is expounded as if these institutions had almost exactly the same objectives as publicly-funded bodies for higher education that have to justify their existence to a secular world. Even where this is not the case, a brief visit will show the interested outsider what subjects, educational experiences and outcomes are given *real* status by the teachers and (therefore?) by many of their students. Christian education will not usually appear among them. It is our view that to adopt the university theology syllabus and its methods as all, or nearly all, that is required for the religious — not to say professional — formation of Christian ministers is to fail the church badly.

PART ONE
'The Satellite Picture':
Theoretical Reflection in
Christian Education

INTRODUCTION

Stephen Barton's study of 'Jesus — Friend of Little Children?' investigates how far it is legitimate to give a positive answer to this question from a straight reading of the gospels. A detailed examination of the relevant passages leads him to ask whether the contemporary investment in children may not distort our perceptions, ensuring that we find in the gospels the reflection of our own needs. He shows, in fact, that the evangelists were more interested in childlikeness as a metaphor for discipleship than in Jesus's actual treatment of children *per se*. Nevertheless the claim that Jesus is the children's friend may be justified on grounds that are primarily theological and christological.

In 'Tradition and Experience: Conservative and Liberal Models for Christian Education', Jeff Astley takes up the popular metaphor that describes Christian education as passing on 'not the painting but the paintbox'. He subjects this to critical analysis and discusses the strengths and weaknesses of didactic and experiential Christian education, and the importance of utilizing both models in a complete programme of facilitating Christian learning. The paper includes some discussion of the dangers of an 'ideals-and-principles-only' Christian education.

Kevin Nichols's paper, 'The Logical Geography of Catechesis', attempts a logical analysis of a number of terms used in discussion in Christian education. The author begins by training the philosophical searchlight on the words 'education' and 'socialization', so as to achieve some measure of clarity about the proper use of these terms. Moving on to discuss the language of 'catechesis', he notes the ways in which it both resembles and differs from education. He argues that for catechesis 'faith is a primary criterion, understanding a secondary one' (though still a definitive one). He concludes with a defence of catechetics as a field of study.

In 'Christian Nurture, Indoctrination and Liberal Education', the Canadian scholar Elmer Thiessen discusses in depth the notion of 'indoctrination'. He argues that 'we are by no means clear as to what is really meant when the charge of indoctrination is made', and analyses the key problems associated with the concept and the assumptions that underlie it, as well as the difficulties involved in the ideal of a 'liberal education'. He concludes that 'the charge of indoctrination as applied against Christian nurture is much weaker than is generally assumed', and offers what he believes to be a more defensible account of the ideals of liberal education (including both 'initiation' and 'liberation') and of ('normal rational') autonomy, together with a new definition of indoctrination. He adds some practical implications for Christian nurture.

'Can Christianity Avoid Enculturation?' by W. S. F. Pickering tackles the vexed issue of the place of culture in religion. Pickering distinguishes that component of religion that 'relates to an order of existence beyond the present', which he calls the transcendental (or divine) element, from the 'material' element — such as language and ritual — through which it is expressed. The former appears to be protected and non-negotiable, and is often held to be without cultural mediation. Yet many argue that the unchangeable does change, albeit very slowly, and that 'the alleged eternal truths...were not given to Christians cultureless'. The implications of these arguments for Christianity and its communication are reviewed, with particular reference to the symbols of the Christian faith and the role of missionaries.

David Heywood's article on the theoretical basis of Christian education, entitled 'Theology or Social Science?', attempts to mediate between the champions of these two causes. Heywood surveys the criticisms commonly made of the theological and social science approaches to Christian education and finds faults on both sides. To help resolve the dispute he focuses directly on the relation between theology and the social sciences, with particular reference to their understandings of the learner. Examining the role of interpretation in science, and of the conceptual framework of the scientific community, the paper discusses the relation between fact and theory and the interdependence of science (as empirical investigation) and philosophy (as conceptual analysis and revision). This leads to a discussion of the 'image of human life' in psychology and in theology, and thus to a framework for resolving disagreements over the parentage of Christian education.

2

Jesus – Friend of Little Children?

STEPHEN C. BARTON

INTRODUCTION

According to the popular Sunday school chorus, Jesus is 'the friend of little children'. And, of course, from the viewpoint of the Christian believer, who could complain about that? Very properly the words convey the sense that the gracious love of God revealed in Jesus is not exclusive, that fellowship with God through Jesus is open — even, and especially, to children, who serve as a kind of 'focal instance' of the breadth of the divine mercy. Nevertheless, a survey of the gospels shows that the picture of Jesus as the children's friend cannot be arrived at straightforwardly.[1] To put the matter more precisely, the claim that Jesus is 'the friend of little children' may be a theological and christological *intuition of Christian faith* which is perhaps only tenuously linked to the gospels' stories of Jesus's actual dealings with children or teaching about them.

Among the grounds for caution are the following considerations. First, it is important not to come to the gospels expecting too much. Like the Bible as a whole, the gospels are — in some sense at least — products of their time and patriarchal social setting. Note, for instance, Matthew's ending to the story of the miraculous feeding: 'And those who ate were about five thousand, *not counting women and children*' (Matt 14:21; cf also 15:38). The additional mention of the women and children in Matthew's version doubtless expresses the evangelist's conviction that women and children belong to the people of God and are recipients of the divine grace revealed in Jesus. At the same time, however, the way they are mentioned presupposes a patriarchal social structure in which the male household head held precedence and the identity and roles of women and children were defined in relation to him.[2]

Second, like the Bible as a whole, the gospels were written by male adults for male adults and their dependants, who included children.[3] This helps to explain why much of the biblical (and gospel) material on children in relation to morality has to do with the obligation upon children — including adult children — of *obedience* to their parents, in accordance with the fifth commandment (eg Mk 10:19). As Duncan Derrett puts it: 'After a child reached the age of 5 he began to learn that society was duty-orientated, not right-orientated'.[4] Elsewhere, as we shall see, the child and children are used in metaphorical ways to express what is incumbent, religiously and spiritually, upon *adults*. Only in one or two instances is attention drawn to children in their own right. It is difficult to escape the general conclusion — unappealing to liberals perhaps — that biblical morality works 'from the top down';[5] and therefore that Jesus's friendship of children (the sick, the poor, etc) is an act of *condescension*.

Third, it is worth pointing out that two of the four canonical gospels have no material whatsoever on Jesus as a child. For Mark and John it is Jesus's adult, public ministry, culminating in his death and resurrection, which constitutes 'the gospel'. And in none of the gospels does the adult Jesus refer to his own childhood in his teaching. Matthew and Luke contain birth and infancy narratives, and in Lk 2:41-51 there is a story about 'the boy [*ho pais*] Jesus' at the age of twelve attending the Passover with his parents in Jerusalem and revealing in the temple signs of his great wisdom. But it is impossible to be confident about the value of this material as historical evidence pertaining to Jesus as a child.[6] Its value lies, rather, in the testimony it bears to the post-resurrection faith of the respective evangelists that Jesus, the son of Mary and Joseph, was also the Son of God (cf Matt 1:18-23; Lk 1:30-35; 3:23-38). Only later, from the mid-second century onwards, do we have *apocryphal* stories about Jesus's 'hidden years' prior to his baptism, the earliest and most important of which are the so-called *Protevangelium of James* and the *Infancy Gospel of Thomas*. But these stories are pious fictions produced, in the absence of controlling, canonical tradition, for the purpose of satisfying curiosity and defending christological dogma.

Fourth, the claim that Jesus is the children's friend has to cope with certain rather uncomfortable facts about Jesus himself. One is that Jesus himself apparently did not marry and so had no children of his own. Like Paul after him, and contrary to the prevailing social expectations of the time, Jesus understood his vocation as requiring the renunciation of marital and family ties (cf Matt 19:11-12; 1Cor 7:7).

Another is that Jesus called on his disciples to subordinate their own familial obligations for his sake.[7] This included obligations to children: 'If anyone comes to me and does not hate his own father and mother and wife and children [*ta tekna*] and brothers and sisters...he cannot be my disciple' (Lk 14:26 par Matt 10:37; cf Mk 10:29-30). Yet again, Jesus warned his disciples of serious enmities between parents and their children on his account (Mk 13:12 par Matt 10:21; Lk 21:16). Further, Jesus is nowhere depicted as a teacher of children,[8] except insofar as they were present in the crowds of men and women who thronged to hear him. Children at play provide the stuff of just one of Jesus's parables (Matt 11:16-19 par Lk 7:31-35) — but the parable itself is addressed to adults, and depiction of the fickle, immature children in the parable itself is hardly flattering. In sum, children *per se* were not at the heart of Jesus's message. What *was* central was the prophetic summons of *the people of Israel* to repentance and to a renewed obedience to the will of God in view of the imminent coming of God. In response to this summons, children are expected to obey their parents, in accordance with the commandments (eg Mk 7:9-13; 10:19). Similarly, the various accounts of the miraculous healing of children (eg the healing of Jairus's twelve-year-old daughter, in Mk 5:21-43) are expressions of the power and character of God's coming rule over all people already at work through Jesus.

A fifth and final reason for caution has to do, not with the setting of Jesus and the gospels, but with the setting of *the readers* of the gospels in the modern period. The 'discovery' of childhood, as a recognized developmental stage of importance in its own right, is a modern phenomenon, as Philippe Ariès and others have shown.[9] And Robert Raikes's Sunday schools for children were not begun in England until the late eighteenth century. In other words, the modern, western fascination with children and the sentimentalizing of childhood ought not to be read back into the gospels. It is possible, of course, that this modern 'discovery' of childhood leads us quite properly to ask questions and to make discoveries of Jesus and the gospels which it was not possible to do before, when the readers' (and writers') conceptual and experiential horizons were different. On the other hand, it is possible that the psychological, social and institutional *investment* in children so characteristic of modernity may lead us to see in the gospels little more than the reflection of our own needs and to interpret them only in ways which justify our prior investment. To what extent, for example, is the Jesus who is the friend of little children a coded way of *idealizing* children (by associating them with Jesus) the consequence of which is, by so distancing ourselves from children, to avoid acting responsibly toward them as actual human beings? Or is it a way of idealizing *Jesus* (by associating him with 'little children') in order to keep at a distance the claims that he makes upon our lives as adults? Alternatively, does the picture of Jesus as the children's friend express a desire to find in Jesus the friend of the child *in us?* Such possibilities are no less real for being hidden. Potentially they are part of what we bring as readers to the gospel material about Jesus and children.

JESUS AND CHILDREN

There are two noteworthy gospel traditions relevant to the study of Jesus's attitude to children: Mk 9:33-37 and Mk 10:13-16 (and parallels). These have received attention in the commentaries and in the works of, among others, Simon Légasse and Hans-Ruedi Weber.[10] Commentators agree that the sayings of Jesus about children have a complex tradition history. In general, the tendency of the tradition is to develop the metaphorical potential of the child for teaching about Christian discipleship. As Hans-Ruedi Weber says, with not a little exasperation: 'Already Mark, Matthew and Luke seem to have been more interested in what a child symbolizes than in Jesus's attitude to actual children'.[11] But it may be that Weber is looking for something which is not there, and that for Jesus, as well as for the evangelists, it was the child as metaphor which was most important in his teaching.[12] Nonetheless, several findings about Jesus's attitude to children are highly probable.

First, Jesus held that children have a share in the kingdom of God. The saying of Jesus in v 14 of Mk 10:13-16 makes this clear: 'Let the children [*ta paidia*] come to me, do not hinder them; for to such belongs the kingdom of God'. In this episode Jesus angrily countermands the disciples (who show their characteristic obtuseness), welcomes the children and, as a sign of blessing — reminiscent, perhaps, of the blessing of Ephraim and Manasseh by Jacob in Genesis 48[13] — lays his hands upon them. We would be surprised to discover otherwise concerning the attitude of Jesus. The covenantal religion of Israel embraced children. The teaching of the rabbis did likewise.[14] And the Qumran community augmented its ranks by adopting male children.[15] Fundamentally, therefore, Jesus's attitude to the children is in strong continuity with that of his confrères in Judaism. Children belong in the people of God. God's eschatological grace, proclaimed by Jesus, is an inclusive grace, open to the 'little people' of all kinds, including children.

Second, Jesus taught that the kingdom of God was to be received 'as a child [*hos paidion*]' (Mk 10:15 par Matt 18:3; Lk 18:17; cf Jn 3:3,5). Here, in a surprising and powerful simile, Jesus makes the child the model for receiving or entering the kingdom. Many suggestions have been made as to precisely *how* the child is a model.[16] For Matthew it meant humility, for he adds: 'Whoever humbles himself like this child, he is the greatest in the kingdom of heaven' (Matt 18:4). But the very quality of the saying as metaphor suggests that a variety of meanings is possible and legitimate. Nevertheless, it is most unlikely that the Gnostic interpretation in terms of sexual innocence, in *Gospel of Thomas* 22 (cf 37), bears any resemblance to the understanding of Jesus. The interpretation of Matthew is much more likely to be closer to the mark. Differences of status or rank have no bearing on membership of the kingdom. That is what marks off the kingdom of God from normal patterns of social organization, including even the family!

Third, Jesus placed special importance on receiving hospitably and with kindness the least important members of society, including the children: for in the kingdom of God even children can serve as divine representatives, just as Jesus is the representative of God. This seems to be the sense underlying the heavily reworked tradition of Mk 9:33-37 and parallels. According to E. Best: 'The so-called *shaliach* principle is employed here to suggest that Jesus is encountered and helped when the child, who is the least important of all humans, is encountered and helped.'[17]

These three aspects of Jesus's attitude to children are important. Above all, they provide a firm basis in history and the tradition for the Christian theological and ecclesiological claim that Jesus *is*— now, in the present — the friend of little children. Note that debates about baptism are not the point so far as Jesus and the gospels are concerned[18] — which is not to say that such debates may not benefit from reflection upon the gospel stories. The point, rather, has to do, on the one hand, with the inclusiveness of the grace of God revealed in Christ, of which Jesus's acceptance of the children is a marvellous focal instance; and, on the other hand, with the challenging novelty of the values of the kingdom of God over against the values of normal social patterns and structures, such that a child can be used as a type of the model disciple.

THE GOSPELS

Study of the history of the gospel tradition shows that these few stories and sayings about children were important for the first followers of Jesus in their various attempts to work out what it meant to be God's new covenant people in the period after Jesus's death and resurrection. Invariably the child becomes a metaphor of discipleship, a way of talking about God and the shared life of faith in the light of Christ.

(i) The Gospel of Matthew
The material on children in Matthew is understood best in relation to the evangelist's emphasis in his theology on God as the heavenly Father, on Jesus as the Son of God, and on believers as both children of God and brothers and sisters of one another. It relates also to the priority in Matthean ethics of the virtue of humility as the basis for life together as the people of God.

The birth and infancy narratives (Matt 1-2) are a good case in point. Here (in 1:18-25) Jesus is portrayed as the divinely begotten Son (*huios*). But he is also the vulnerable child (*paidion*) who, with his equally vulnerable mother (2:11,13,14,20,21), is threatened from the beginning by the powers-that-be, and watched over by his heavenly Father working through angelic intermediaries. So the coming of Jesus the Son is in weakness and humility, the very qualities which mark him out as the true king of Israel (cf 2:2,6,8,11) and which, subsequently, form the centre of his teaching (eg 5:3ff; 11:29) and lifestyle (cf 21:5).

In that teaching, the figure of the child is prominent. First, it expresses a doctrine of revelation and election. The Father and the Son are made known to the least likely, to 'babes' (*nepioi*) (11:25-26): those, that is, who recognize their weakness and utter dependence upon divine grace and accept the invitation of Jesus as the wisdom of God (11:27-29). Second, it expresses a requirement of membership of the kingdom of God: radical humility (18:2-4; cf 5:3-5). Third, it provides a way of talking about pastoral care in the Christian brotherhood (18:5-14): the leaders of the church are to avoid at all costs (antinomian) teaching or behaviour which would lead the 'little ones' (*mikroi*) to stray from the narrow path of righteousness. Fourth, it expresses a concern for persecuted followers of Christ and, in particular, early Christian missionaries. This seems to be the sense of the reference to 'these little ones' in 10:42, as also of the reference to 'the least [*elachistoi*] of these my brethren' in 25:40 (cf v 45).

When Jesus comes to the temple after his triumphal entry into Jerusalem it is not surprising, therefore, that those who rejoice at the arrival in Zion of the Son of David are children (*paidia*) (21:15). It is they who represent God's new covenant people and inherit the kingdom of God.

(ii) The Gospel of Mark

In partial contrast with Matthew, the theology of Mark is less anthropomorphic and the gospel of Mark is less explicitly ecclesiological and ethical in its orientation. The picture of God as the loving heavenly Father who cares for his Son and for his children on earth as they are obedient to him, is much more muted in Mark. Prominent instead is an emphasis on the sovereignty and transcendence of God, the mystery of the divine purpose especially in relation to suffering, and the imperative of faith and watchfulness in the midst of darkness (eg Mk 4:13). Nevertheless, God is depicted as Father and Jesus as the Son (eg 1:11; 9:7; 13:32; 14:36; 15:39), while those who do God's will are identified as the spiritual family of Jesus (3:35).

It is significant that the main teaching about children in Mark's gospel (ie 9:33-37; 10:13-16) comes in the central section, 8:27-10:45, where the focus is on the nature of discipleship of the Christ who is to be crucified and raised. Here the child is a metaphor of discipleship (cf 10:24b!), and this is appropriate in a gospel which emphasizes so strongly that divine power is revealed in weakness and that true greatness lies in becoming last of all for Jesus's sake (eg 8:34-35; 12:41-44). It is hardly coincidental that Mark has two stories in which Jesus heals children (5:21-43; 9:14-29), and that both take the form of a raising from death in response to the power of Jesus. For Mark, death and resurrection constitute 'the way' (*hodos*) of Jesus himself and of all who would follow him.

In 9:33-37, as E. Best points out, several sayings have been brought together and placed at the head of a longer block of teaching of the disciples 'in the house' (9:33-50).[19] In this context the Jesus of Mark seems to be saying that true greatness is shown in being a servant of all, even to the point of being able to welcome low status outsiders — an itinerant missionary, represented by a child (vv 36-37), or an anonymous exorcist (vv 38-41) — into the fellowship.

The material in 10:13-16 is also part of a larger block of tradition relevant to Christian discipleship (10:1-31), dealing successively with marriage and divorce (vv 2-12), children (vv 13-16), and property (vv 17-31). The second section clearly affirms the legitimate place of children in the Christian fellowship. As with the anonymous exorcist, they are not to be 'forbidden' (cf *koluein* in 9:39 and 10:14). Rather, Jesus welcomes them in the most demonstrative way by 'taking them in his arms' (cf *enkalizesthai* in 9:36 and 10:16) and blessing them. Particularly important for Mark, though, is the saying in v 15, where child-like receiving is a metaphor of faith.[20]

(iii) The Gospel of Luke

Traditions about children play an important part in expressing what Luke believed about God, the good news of salvation, and how to live the life of Christian faith. These traditions are suggestive of a Christian community ethos which, in partial contrast to the Marcan ethos, is more optimistic and world-affirming.

First, the stories of the two miraculous births in Lk 1-2 show that the God of biblical faith is at work again bringing salvation to his people. In a dramatic and powerful narrative, the birth of sons to Elizabeth and Mary is a new beginning in salvation history and the fulfilment of God's covenant promise. Hence their arrival is marked by prophetic and angelic witness, miraculous signs, and outbursts of joy. Even the unborn infant (*brephos*) John leaps for joy at the coming of Mary (1:41,44), the one who is to give birth to the Son of God (1:32, 35).

Second, the stories of Jesus's presentation at the temple (2:22-40) and his pilgrimage to the temple as a boy of twelve (2:41-51) fulfil an important apologetic function, showing that, even as a child, Jesus revealed those divine qualities which marked him out as the fulfilment of Israel's hopes and as the saviour of the world (2:40,52). The latter episode not only highlights Jesus's divine sonship (2:49), but also its potential cost for Jesus's natural kin (2:48-50; cf 14:26-27).

Third, children in Luke exemplify the evangelist's emphasis on the gracious mercy of God towards the poor, the weak and the marginal. Witness the birth of a son to a barren woman (1:7,25) and to a lowly 'handmaiden' (*doule*) (1:48); the revelation of the babe (*brephos*) to shepherds from the countryside (2:8-14); the identification of the children (*tekna*) of wisdom as including 'tax collectors and sinners' (9:34-35, and cf vv 29-30); the miraculous healing of a man's 'only [*monogenes*, so Luke] son', which moves everyone to wonder at 'the majesty of God' (9:37-43); and the parable of the two sons in 15:11-32.

Finally, Luke's theology of divine grace towards the poor has an ethical and social corollary.[21] It is noteworthy that in Luke's version of the tradition about true greatness (in 9:46-48) Jesus identifies closely with the child (*paidion*) by putting him 'by his side' and, in a more concrete way than Mark and Matthew, says that 'Whoever receives this child [*touto to paidion*]...receives me'. Similarly in Luke's redaction of Mk 10:13-16 it is not children (*paidia*) but 'even infants' (*kai ta brephe*) who are brought to Jesus and whom he calls (18:15-17). God's mercy towards the weak is conveyed in Jesus's mercy towards the weak also, and this is the example which disciples of Jesus are to follow (cf 22:26).

(iv) The Fourth Gospel

Even more than in the Synoptics, child-related material in John is almost entirely metaphorical. It is also distinctly scarce, as the word statistics in H. R. Weber's study show.[22] Missing is the Q parable about the children playing. Missing, likewise, are the stories of Jesus blessing the children and teaching his disciples to 'receive' children and to become 'like a child'. There are no birth or infancy narratives. Stories of children being healed by Jesus are reduced to one (Jn 4:46-54).

This is not to suggest that the fourth evangelist deliberately omits material about children, only that his principal concerns lie elsewhere and that his conceptual framework is distinctive. So, for instance, John's interest is more in Jesus's revelatory discourses in Samaria and Judaea than in his public ministry among the people (including the children) of Galilee. Again, the teaching of the Johannine Jesus is predominantly about himself rather than about entry into the kingdom of God or the ethics of the kingdom of God, where (from a Synoptic viewpoint) sayings about children — or, better, childlikeness — are particularly important.

Oepke makes the important observation that in the Fourth Gospel a consistent linguistic distinction is maintained between Jesus as 'the Son of God' (*ho huios tou theou*) and believers as 'the children of God' (*ta tekna tou theou*) (as in Jn 1:12; 11:52; cf 1Jn 3:1,2,10; 5:2).[23] The strong Pauline eschatological and ecclesiological doctrine that 'sonship' is something which believers share with Christ (eg Gal 4:6-7; Rom 8:14-17,23,29; 9:4) is absent. This reflects the fact that the central (and highly polemical) focus of this gospel is christological: Jesus is the *unique* Son who comes from the Father to reveal his glory to the world.

So believers are 'children of God'. This has numerous connotations. First, God is the source of their life (1:12-13; 3:3ff). Second, and conversely, believers belong no longer to the devil nor to those whose father he is (8:39-47; cf 1Jn 3:4-12). Third, salvation is universal, available to all who are born 'anew' or 'from above' (1:12-13; 3:14ff). Fourth, the believer's relationship with the Father is mediated by the Son and dependent upon obedience to the Son (14:6ff). Interestingly,

Jesus does not teach his disciples to pray 'Our Father...'. Instead, he says: 'Whatever you ask *in my name,* I will do it...' (14:13). Fifth, God's children are to love one another (13:33-35, noting *teknia* at v 33). So there is a 'horizontal' dimension to being a child of God which, though rather muted in John's Gospel, comes strongly to the fore in the distinctly ecclesiological concerns of the Johannine Epistles (eg 1Jn 2:1ff,12ff,18ff; 3:1ff).

CONCLUSION

Our findings for each of the four gospels confirm what we discovered in relation to Jesus. Their focus is not so much on children *per se,* but on *childlikeness:* on the metaphorical potential of the child and child-hood — as of kinship terms generally — for trying to express the kind of *attitudes* and *relationships* demanded now in the light of the breaking in of the kingdom of God with the coming of Jesus. Christian believers *can* affirm that Jesus is the 'friend of little children'. They can do so partly on the basis of what the gospels tell us about Jesus's dealings with children, and partly on the basis of the readiness of both Jesus and the evangelists to use the child as a metaphor of discipleship. Above all, however, they can do so on the firm theological grounds provided in the gospels (and in the New Testament as a whole) which root the salvation of the *whole created order* in the proclamation of the love of God revealed in Christ.

NOTES

1. An earlier version of this essay is due to appear as the entry on 'Child/Children' in Joel B. Green and Scot McNight (eds), *Dictionary of Jesus and the Gospels,* Downers Grove, Ill.: Inter Varsity Press, 1992.

2. See, in general, J. D. M. Derrett, *Jesus' Audience,* London: DLT, 1973, pp 31ff.

3. So too Jean Holm, 'What Shall we Tell the Children?', *Theology,* Vol. LXXVI, 1973, p 141.

4. Derrett, *Audience,* p 34.

5. For a classic expression of duty in the relation between father and son — and note that it is *father* and *son* who are talked about! — see Sirach 30:1-13. The following is typical: 'A horse that is untamed turns out to be stubborn, and a son unrestrained turns out to be wilful. Pamper a child, and he will frighten you; play with him and he will give you grief. Do not laugh with him, lest you have sorrow with him, and in the end you will gnash your teeth. Give him no authority in his youth, and do not ignore his errors. Bow down his neck in his youth, and beat his sides while he is young, lest he become stubborn and disobey you, and you have sorrow of soul from him' (vv 8-12).

6. See further, R. E. Brown, The *Birth of the Messiah,* London: Geoffrey Chapman, 1977, pp 471-496.

7. See further M. Hengel, *The Charismatic Leader and His Followers*, ET, Edinburgh: T. & T. Clark, 1981; and S. C. Barton, 'Discipleship and Family Ties According to Mark and Matthew', Ph.D. thesis, King's College, London, 1992.

8. Cf J. N. Sevenster, 'Education or Conversion: Epictetus and the Gospels', *Novum Testamentum*, Vol. VIII, 1966, pp 247-262.

9. See P. Ariès, *Centuries of Childhood*, ET, London: Jonathan Cape, 1962.

10. See H. R. Weber, *Jesus and the Children*, Geneva: WCC, 1979, and S. Légasse, *Jésus et L'Enfant*, Paris: Gabalda, 1969. Useful, too, are historical studies of the position of children in Judaism and in the Graeco-Roman world of the first century, amongst which the following should be mentioned: W. Barclay, *Educational Ideals in the Ancient World*, Grand Rapids: Baker, 1974; R. de Vaux, *Ancient Israel*, ET, London: DLT, 1961; B. Rawson, *The Family in Ancient Rome*, New York: Cornell UP, 1986; T. Wiedemann, *Adults and Children in the Roman Empire*, London: Routledge, 1989; and J. F. Gardner and T. Wiedemann, *The Roman Household: A Sourcebook*, London: Routledge, 1991.

11. Weber, *Jesus*, p 49.

12. Cf also S. Légasse, 'L'Enfant Dans L'Évangile', *La Vie Spirituelle*, Vol. 122, 1970, pp 407-421.

13. See further J. D. M. Derrett, 'Why Jesus Blessed the Children (Mk 10:13-16 PAR)', *Novum Testamentum*, Vol. XXV, 1983, pp 1-18.

14. Cf P. Billerbeck and H. L. Strack, *Kommentar zum Neuen Testament aus Talmud und Midrasch*, Munich, 1922-28, Vol. I, p 786.

15. Cf Josephus, *Jewish War* II. 120.

16. Cf E. Best, *Disciples and Discipleship*, Edinburgh: T. & T. Clark, 1986, pp 94-97.

17. E. Best, *Following Jesus*, Sheffield: JSOT Press, 1981, p 80.

18. For this preoccupation of some earlier New Testament scholarship, see O. Cullmann, *Baptism in the New Testament*, ET, London: SCM, 1950, and J. Jeremias, *Infant Baptism in the First Four Centuries*, ET, London: SCM, 1960.

19. Best, *Jesus*, pp 75ff.

20. Cf Légasse, *Jésus*, pp 189ff.

21. See further, B. E. Beck, *Christian Character in the Gospel of Luke*, London: Epworth, 1989.

22. Weber, *Jesus*, p 56.

23. A. Oepke, *Theological Dictionary of the New Testament*, Vol. V, 1967, p 653.

3

Tradition and Experience: Conservative and Liberal Models for Christian Education

JEFF ASTLEY

THE METAPHOR

Verbs of teaching, it is often said, govern two accusatives — one of the person taught and another of the subject taught. In education we teach someone (the learner) something (the subject-matter content). Educationalists frequently distinguish between two different educational approaches that may be broadly distinguished as the traditional and the experiential. Thus Lawton writes of the *Classical* and the *Romantic* ideologies of education, the former being *subject*-centred and didactic, aiming at the acquiring of knowledge and social conformity, whereas the latter is *learner*-centred and experiential, aiming primarily at changes in the learner's attitudes and values and the fostering of individual originality.[1] The Classical approach tends to be unifying and monolithic, assuming one agreed set of standards. The Romantic approach leads to diversity and pluralism, assuming a variety of views. Such an account clearly relates closely to debates within Christian education, understood here as the process by which people learn to be (more) Christian.

Within Christian education the role of the Christian tradition is crucial. Although it would be a mistake to conflate the rather different distinctions within Christian education that are usually designated as 'conservative'/'liberal' and 'traditional' (or 'didactic')/'experiential', in practice they share many similarities.[2] Liberal Christian education is usually described as an open-ended, risky affair. Through it the Christian tradition is 'passed on' in a much less restrictive and transmissive fashion than is envisaged by more conservative accounts of that process. The liberals' interpretation follows directly from their stress on the developing and self-critical nature of the Christian faith: 'there is no fixed and final form of Christian faith, and this is why there can be no fixed and final form of nurture into it'. This view has led to the adoption in Christian education discussion of an interesting metaphor about painting and paintboxes:

> when Christians seek to nurture their young into Christian faith, they literally do not fully know what they are nurturing them into. They only know what they are nurturing them out of, ie out of the Christian past. They know the resources but not the use which will be made of them. What we pass on to our children is not the painting but the paintbox.[3]

The purport of the metaphor is that Christian education does not pass on a ready-made Christian culture, belief-system or lifestyle, for that would be to pass on a second-hand, inherited Christianity that would not necessarily suit the needs of the next generation of Christians. Rather, elements within the past culture, belief and lifestyle ('re-sources') are to be handed over,[4] and it is from these that Christianity can be re-created for (and by) each generation in its new context.

IMPLICATIONS OF THE METAPHOR

Without evacuating the metaphor of all value by converting it wood-enly into an allegory, it might be useful to explore this particular example of figurative language more fully. In the metaphor the 'painting' represents incarnated Christianity: a Christian culture, worldview or lifestyle that is expressive of the Christian gospel in any given generation. 'What is handed on....is the life of a people.'[5] It represents a whole: it is a unified image. The 'paintbox', on the other hand, symbolizes the elements or resources that can be built up into such a Christian culture/life. It is a 'parts' image, and might represent the beliefs, attitudes/experiences and activities that together consti-tute an individual Christian life, and therefore the Christian culture of a group. Alternatively, the 'paintbox' may be taken as denoting the Christian symbols or stories that evoke and express these elements of Christian life and culture.

At this point a further element needs to be recognized as implicit in the metaphor: that is the 'painting skills' of using the resources of the Christian tradition, by integrating and synthesizing the pigments within the paintbox onto a completed canvas. (It is not clear whether the metaphor implies that these skills are 'passed on' with the tradition, or are part of the equipment already in the possession of each new generation.[6])

Most people would say that the variety of (painting) talents that people show is a function of in-built differences between people. These talents may be developed, exercised or blunted through teaching, but the skills of the 'natural artist' will often exceed those of other people however carefully and energetically these others may be taught. This recognition of inherent talents is an important qualification of over transmissive views of the teaching of painting or the teaching of religion. Creativity in religion, art and morality is not the responsibility of an unassisted will: 'when did mere will-power, decisiveness and determination ever make an artist, or indeed a real moral reformer. Talents are gifts... Not even God can invent himself from scratch.'[7]

Although the metaphor does not restrict Christianity to its cognitive dimension, we may appropriately relate each of the components of Christianity to that dimension by interpreting (a) the painting as systematically-integrated Christian belief ('The Faith') and (b) the paintbox as the elements within such a Christian belief-structure. In this example the painting skills would be the theological and hermeneutical skills needed to pull Christian belief together into a believable whole, ie the skills needed for synthesizing a new faith-for-today.

The liberal/conservative distinction in Christian education is expressed in the metaphor as a distinction between an education that passes on paintboxes rather than passing on paintings. Similarly what is often (somewhat confusingly) described as the experiential (or 'inductive': ie process-centred and learner-centred) style may be contrasted with the didactic ('instructional', teacher-centred and content-centred) style by means of the same metaphor. For some, the Christian 'art lesson' will consist of viewing the Old Masters and producing the best copies we can of them. For others the heart of the exercise will lie in creating a new work of art from the same pigments that were employed by artists of earlier generations who worked — however loosely — in 'the same tradition', and by means of similar techniques.

CRITICISM OF THE METAPHOR

If the metaphor will stand this sort of analysis, it can perhaps be made to yield something further, for it may be argued that the situations described so far have been contrasted too extremely. In particular, the original artist of today *also* needs to visit the art galleries that house her predecessor's work. Passing on pigments and training in painting skills are not enough on their own for the production of a contemporary Christian work of art. The claim may be made that only the Christian who views the products of other ages and learns from them will be able to paint her own picture.[8] Certainly such an artist will be better prepared for the lonely act of personal creation of a new Christian canvas in the studio. Several points may be relevant here.

(i) An experiential Christian education that focuses on life skills and the development of attitudes, emotions and behaviour may result in something that is properly (because 'characteristically') Christian, but which lacks the distinctive feature of what is Christian — an explicit, positive reference to Jesus Christ.[9] Only the final picture, in which the ('implicitly Christian') attitude/experience and activity pigments are combined with ('explicitly Christian') belief pigments, will make that reference explicit. Christian educators may differ as to the importance for Christian education of the creation of an explicitly Christian culture or life, in which the reference to Jesus is patent for all to see. If that feature is important to them, then so is the sense in which the new picture is identifiably part of a tradition that also includes the old ones. For them, all Christian pictures must contain somewhere within their frames a recognizable portrait of Jesus.

(ii) Artists need to see other people's paintings because they need before them a model of the sort of thing that the finished product looks like.[10] Perhaps it is too difficult a thing to organize, unify or use Christian resources for ourselves without seeing the ways in which such resources have been integrated in the lives of other people who have gone before us. *The production of a new painting* is the goal even of the liberal account of Christian education; the paintbox has only an instrumental point or purpose in fulfilling that goal. Some would argue that we can only get our ideas as to what that goal might be *for us* by seeing what it has meant *for others* to be Christian.

(iii) Many contemporary accounts of Christian education strive to combine the *traditional/didactic* element with what we have been willing to call the *experiential* element. Thus Thomas Groome's 'Shared Praxis Approach' to Christian religious education begins with the group's critical reflection on a particular aspect of its own activity: 'a reflection on "why we do what we do and what our hopes are in doing it" as related to the topic for attention'. This, Groome claims, is 'an affair of both the heart and the head' that engenders self-awareness of the learners' own 'stories' and 'visions' (biographies and hopes).[11] Many would describe it as a plumbing of their own experience. It is complemented by a more didactic process in which the Christian faith tradition and lived response/promise ('the Christian Community Story and Vision') is presented to the learners, so that an interpretative dialogue arises in which the Christian tradition confronts 'the human limit situation of our lives'.[12] This is the process that Groome calls 'present dialectical hermeneutics':

> In a dialectical hermeneutic of any 'text' there is an activity of discerning its truth and what is to be affirmed in it, an activity of discerning the limitations in our understanding of it that are to be refused, and an attempt to move beyond it, carrying forward the truth that was there while adding to it in the new understanding.[13]

In the fundamental movements of this Christian education process the Story that is the past tradition and the stories that undergird our present experience interact like conversational partners:

> In the dialectical hermeneutic between the present and past Story, the past Story is posed as a critique of the present... In this it will affirm some of our present, it will deny/condemn some of our present, and it will push us towards action that is more faithful to the Story. But then...the present must be posed as a critique of the past Story... In this there will be dimensions of the Story that we will affirm, dimensions that we must condemn (eg, the Church's record in regard to slavery), and a call to create upon but move beyond that past. Thus it is not merely asking 'what does the past Story say to our present?' but also posing the question 'what does the present say to the past Story?'.[14]

We may note the mutuality of this critique. It is not just that the tradition can and should change our present action and experience. Our present Christian experience may also, rightly and properly, amend the tradition. Liberals are far more willing to recognize this latter process than are conservatives, but all are subject to it. Even the most ardent scriptural or ecclesiastical-traditional fundamentalist interprets and selects from the past in the light of present needs and understandings. To take but one example, the liberal's lectionary may explicitly bracket or omit the imprecatory psalms. The conservative will just as surely pass over them as suitable material for feeding his worship and spirituality. The liberal may shout from the rooftops what the conservative does in secret. But both will be selecting and filtering the past tradition in the light of their present experience of what it is to be religious, moral and human. For both, current experience partly determines what is acceptable in the tradition, what is to be used and what is to be passed on. The tradition-experience junction has traffic that goes in both directions.

It is a junction that ceases to be effective if the roads diverge to such an extent that tradition and experience no longer properly 'connect'. Ninian Smart describes two ways in which a religion can lose 'living meaning'. One way results from a loss of interest in worship or other religious practices. 'Another way is the result of a gulf between a religion's practices and the existential concerns of men in a given milieu'.[15] Any religious tradition that is unconnected with the experience of real life soon dies.

(iv) The road junction image suggests a related metaphor. In many types of Christian education the Christian education vehicle is driven by an experiential engine. The starting point of the exercise, whether chronological, logical or psychological, is 'our experience', rather than the past tradition of the church. The tradition is brought in as and when it appears *relevant* to our experience. Christian education begins with the student's personal history, and only later moves on to link that with God's salvation-history.[16] The tradition aids our interpretation of the experience.[17]

James Michael Lee writes:

> If the religion teacher wishes to successfully facilitate desired instructional outcomes, he really has no choice other than to start with the learner where the learner is. To start with subject-matter content is not to start with the learner where he is. Subject-matter content should be fashioned according to the learner, and not vice-versa... In religion lessons the learner is at once the point of departure and the constant axis.

Elsewhere he comments on 'religious instruction' (the teaching of religion):

> Thus in religious instruction, religion is still recognizable; however it is recognizable as it exists in religious instruction and not as it exists in itself....

> In the religious instruction act, theology no longer exists as
> theology's theology but instead as religious instruction's
> theology.[18]

This is in contrast with more didactic (or, we might say, 'traditional')
approaches to Christian education that start with the Christian tradition and its theology and then go on to apply it to our contemporary
human experience. That would be Christian education 'as handmaid
of the message', with the emphasis on the content of the message:
ie 'primarily theological'.[19]

The strength of the first approach is clearly the educational one of
beginning where people are: with their own beliefs, concerns, experiences and practices. People are more likely to learn from the
Christian tradition if it is presented at its points of relevance to their
experience, if it 'scratches where they itch'. However such an approach
also has its weaknesses. All educational activities are selective, but this
one is notoriously highly selective in its use of the tradition.[20] Thus if
we seek not just to fashion, but also to *select* material *wholly* 'according
to the learner', we are in danger of omitting from the Christian
education curriculum ('learning experiences') whole emphases that
might include precisely those elements that a particular learner needs
in order to use, cope with or learn from her particular *future* experiences. There is much in Christianity that needs to be made available
to the learner even though it does not at the moment meet her needs,
or her 'eye'. The church, it has been said, is like a great junk-shop:

> It is as foolish to pass it by as to buy up its entire contents. There
> is a good chance that amongst the clutter there will be
> something useful or beautiful, something that, with a little
> adaptation or cleaning, we can make our own. That chance is
> missed by the people who insist that everything about them
> should be new and should have had as little previous history as
> possible before it became theirs. They do not only miss the
> opportunity of saving a little money. They also exclude
> themselves from the lively possibility of finding the great
> bargain. That stroke of luck usually comes only to the seasoned
> and dedicated hunters because they have given time and study
> to the matter.[21]

Of course the educational fact cannot be denied that 'meaningful-
ness is ultimately the decision of the learner'; nor can we deny the
educational imperative that 'the quality of learning will be much
greater if the students care about the subject and think it is valuable'.[22]

And Lee is certainly right in his claim that doctrine

> must be taught in such a way that it is inserted into the learner's experience, rather than in the traditional way of using the learner's experience as the first stage of a pedagogical rocket thrusted at the outer space of doctrine, a stage to be discarded as soon as the rocket penetrates into the rarefied regions of intellectual and spiritual activity.[23]

Yet it remains the case that, in the hands of less sophisticated Christian educators, an educational programme that is led *entirely* by the students' *current* educational needs may sell them short over the long term. And in 'modifying' theology to fit its perceived educational role (although, of course, it is not easy to say what an 'unmodified' theology would be), the inexperienced Christian educator may well unwittingly deprive her learners of some of theology's most important contributions to their Christian education. Is there not a danger in our adopting uncritically the principle of teaching only 'what these learners can now learn', and amending the content so that it can best be learned by them? It is the danger that only certain palatable drinks will be offered at the bar, while the real hard stuff is left in the cellar.

I am not trying here to depart from an objectives model of the curriculum of Christian education. I would argue that the tradition is 'taught' so as to produce desired learning outcomes (Christian beliefs, attitudes, values etc). We may regard these outcomes as good in themselves, and the tradition that 'contains' them as possessing intrinsic value. But the purpose of education is to change the learners — to pass on this tradition, in the sense of engendering in the learners the Christian beliefs, affections and dispositions to action that the tradition describes as being held by others before them. If any elements in the Christian tradition do not ever produce desirable learning outcomes in the learner (Christian beliefs, attitudes, values etc), then they should not be taught. My argument is only that we are often too hasty, and too 'contemporary', in our judgements about what parts of the tradition produce what desirable learning; and perhaps too limited in our perception of what comprises desirable Christian learning. Even the imprecatory psalms, if properly taught, will give rise to important learning: albeit learning that may itself not be 'useful' to the student for years to come. (Part of that learning is the recognition that even in the Bible religious people are still human, and that worship is an expression of what we currently feel in a context in which we are helped to feel differently.)

(v) A further danger of an experience-dominated Christian education process is that of the influence of its teachers. Didactic Christian education is clearly open to this criticism as well, but it is more openly open to it. The didactic teacher of the Christian tradition wears his theology much more on his sleeve. He certainly selects from the tradition what he is going to teach us, but his emphasis on the *whole* tradition should alert his learners to a recognition of the inevitably partial and partisan account of it that he is presenting. The teacher who majors on *relevance* rather than *application*, however, may find it easier to hide intentionally — or more difficult to achieve self-awareness about — the theological criteria of selection with which he is also working in his presentation of the tradition.[24] The more perceptive learner can become quite irritated by the unrevealed theology of the experiential teacher. It does not help when this irritation is put down to an unwillingness on the part of the learner to 'face her own experience'.

(vi) One strength of the approaches that stress the handing on of tradition is that they give us a respect for the whole: for 'incarnated', concrete — and therefore grubby and flawed — Christianity. Even if we argue that the essential feature of Christianity is the gracious demand expressed in the Christian gospel, rather than any particular incarnation of — or response to — that gospel, yet there needs to be *some* concrete response. Liberals point to a three-fold danger in over-exposing people to the Christian tradition:

(a) that in adopting someone else's response, learners will only have their Christianity at second hand, and therefore will not really own it for themselves;

(b) that they will take over a response that is inappropriate, unhelpful and perhaps unsustainable for their own day and life; and

(c) that they will think that Christianity is the sort of thing that can be expressed completely and without remainder in any particular individual or collective life.

Dangers (a) and (b) are certainly very real ones. To 'keep quiet' about the Christian tradition, however, except insofar as it seems relevant to contemporary and individual questions and concerns, is to run risk (c) even more acutely. A bits-and-pieces, pigments-only Christian education can delude Christian learners into thinking that perfect and complete responses to the gospel are possible. If the paintbox that is passed on includes only the ideals and principles of Christian living, without any indication of what actual lives that have responded to these things really look like, then pure (= 'true') Christianity becomes a possibility. But unfortunately *my* being truly Christian then becomes a patent impossibility. This is because the whole exercise has lost the realism brought home to the more traditional student of the Christian tradition by her study of the *flawed* wholes that constitute that tradition.

It has been said that the value of the saints is in the power of their example as 'a leaven of righteousness in the world':

> they are impregnators of the world, vivifiers and animaters of potentialities of goodness which but for them would lie forever dormant. It is not possible to be quite as mean as we naturally are, when they have passed before us. One fire kindles another...[25]

'Let us be saints, then if we can...', William James concludes. But he adds:

> each of us must discover for himself the kind of religion and the amount of saintship which best comports with what he believes to be his powers and feels to be his truest mission and vocation.[26]

The *variety* of the saints who are honoured in the Christian tradition is a liberating thing for the learner of Christianity. James reminds us that there are many different ways of being a saint. But their *humanness* is also positively instructive. The Christian gospel, in and of itself, is absolute and unconditional demand and promise. Yet the response to that gospel is inevitably relative and conditioned, human and tarnished by sin. The saints show us this. They show both that it is possible to be a saint, *and* that sinners may apply for the job. The biblical saints in particular are such spectacularly human sinners that we may all have hope. A highly selective, ideals-and-principles-only Christian education, which denies the learner access to the grubbier parts of the Christian tradition, can easily make it seem impossible that the learner could ever learn to be Christian.

(vii) Christian education must somehow balance past tradition and present experience so as to maximize respect for persons. The learner must be respected as a person and her insights, concerns and experiences given full acknowledgement. No one properly learns to be Christian until she can find relevance to her life in the old, old story. There must, however, also be a correlative respect for persons *in the tradition*. *Always* to begin and end with me is not to take (other) people seriously, and therefore — in the end — it is not to take me seriously. I need *also* to begin, though never to end, with others — including the hopes, fears and beliefs of the church down the ages — in order to allow myself to create my personal faith. These others are the subject-matter of Christian education not just as paintings to grind up so as to release pigments that I can then re-use, but as works of art that demand respect in and of themselves. To learn the Christian tradition seriously helps us to take Christianity seriously not as a set of abstract (and impersonal) universalizable elements, but as *people*: as lived lives and expressed lifestyles. Since Christianity is primarily a way of living, we need to respect other people's ways of walking the Christian way while we learn to do it our way.

CONCLUSION

The practical consequence of these reflections seems to be the, perhaps unsurprising, conclusion that a balanced Christian education needs two elements. It needs:

both (i) a set of Christian education experiences that begins with our reflections on, and explorations of, our own experience and viewpoint, and then *relates* these to an appropriate, selected element in the Christian tradition, so that our understanding of both is enlarged;

and (ii) a set of Christian education experiences that gives a more complete account of the whole range of past Christian tradition, articulated as far as possible from its own point of view (and therefore based on historical scholarship), and then *applies* it to appropriate, selected elements of our experience, to produce again a mutual learning.

Christian education needs, then, techniques that are *equivalent to* both a systematic, 'lectionary-based reading' of the Christian tradition *in extenso* with the exposition ('preaching') of its application to our lives;[27] and the more unsystematic or existential style of expository 'preaching' that begins where we are and brings the tradition alongside our contemporary experience so as to illuminate where we are. Christian education should be a both-and activity.

In the dialectic between tradition and experience that these two different techniques produce, tradition critiques experience and experience critiques tradition. The difference between the two approaches lies only in their starting-points and in the driving force of the educational exercise that produces the dialectic. They may both lead to identical journeys of Christian learning. But equally they may not; because the end of a journey is often determined by the place from which one starts, and on the motive power of one's vehicle.

NOTES

1. Denis Lawton, *Social Change, Educational Theory and Curriculum Planning*, London: Hodder & Stoughton/Open University Press, 1973, pp 22ff.

2. A perceptive analysis of these issues within education is to be found in Leon McKenzie, *Adult Education and Worldview Construction*, Malabar, Florida: Krieger, 1991, ch 2 and pp 112ff.

3. *The Child in the Church*, London: British Council of Churches, 1976, pp 23f. What follows in my unpacking of this metaphor may well depart from the intentions of its original authors.

4. 'Tradition' derives from the Latin *trans* (across, over) + *dare* (to give). A distinction may be made between the process of communication of the faith (*traditio*) and the contents ('traditions') that are passed on (*tradita*).

5. Maria Harris, 'Word, Sacrament, Prophecy', in Padraic O'Hare (ed), *Tradition and Transformation in Religious Education*, Birmingham, Ala.: Religious Education Press, 1979, p 53.

6. Robert Waddington has spoken in this context of the 'traditionally clustered grammar of skills that is the essential bridge between the past and the shaping of the future' ('The Unknown, Remembered Gate', Hockerill Lecture, London: Hockerill Educational Foundation, 1985). If this list of skills is extended to include 'critical' skills of enquiry (perhaps 'analysing' as well as 'mixing' pigments), then we may note James Gribble's comment, made about academic teaching, that both a body of knowledge and procedures of inquiry need to be passed on in order to teach such subjects. See his *Introduction to Philosophy of Education*, Boston: Allyn and Bacon, 1969, pp 63f.

7. Mary Midgley, *Heart and Mind: The Varieties of Moral Experience*, London: Methuen, 1983, p 9.

8. On the limits set on (artistic) innovation by a (painting) tradition or 'style' that includes a particular way of seeing, as well as a range of skills and techniques, see Ernest H. Gombrich, *Art and Illusion*, Oxford: Phaidon, 1959, *passim* and Glenn Langford, *Education, Persons and Society: A Philosophical Enquiry*, Basingstoke: Macmillan, 1985, ch 2.

9. In this context 'experience' may refer to experience of life previous to or 'outside' the educational process, experience deliberately arranged as part of education, or (for some) 'experience of being a student' — compare *Experience and Authority: Issues Underlying Doing Theology*, London: Advisory Council for the Church's Ministry, no date, p 17. On the 'explicit, positive reference' see Hans Küng, *On Being a Christian*, trans E. Quinn, London: Collins, 1977, pp 125f.

10. A similar point is made by V. Bailey Gillespie: 'We do not provide absolute freedom to reinvent the wheel. We look at the old wheels first, and then create our own' (*The Experience of Faith*, Birmingham, Ala.: Religious Education Press, 1988, p 137).

11. Thomas H. Groome, *Christian Religious Education*, San Francisco: Harper & Row, 1980, pp 211, 187. Others regard this as too cognitive an account: see James Michael Lee, 'The Blessings of Religious Pluralism', in Norma H. Thompson (ed), *Religious Pluralism and Religious Education*, Birmingham, Ala.: Religious Education Press, 1988, p 117.

12. Thomas H. Groome, 'Christian Education for Freedom', in Padraic O'Hare

(ed), *Foundations of Religious Education*, New York: Paulist Press, 1978, p 12.

13. Groome, *Christian Religious Education*, p 196.

14. Groome, 'Christian Education for Freedom', p 28.

15. Ninian Smart, *The Philosophy of Religion*, New York and Toronto: Random House, 1970; London: Sheldon Press, 1979, p 94.

16. Gabriel Moran, *Catechesis of Revelation*, New York: Herder & Herder, 1966 (= *God Still Speaks*, London: Burns and Oates, 1969), *passim.*

17. Compare D. S. Amalorpavadass, 'Catechesis as a Pastoral Task of the Church' (pp 357f) and Piet Schoonenberg, 'Revelation and Experience' (pp 304f, 310f), in Michael Warren (ed), *Sourcebook for Modern Catechetics*, Winona, Minnesota: St Mary's Press, 1983.

18. James Michael Lee, 'Toward a New Era: A Blueprint for Positive Action', in J. M. Lee (ed), *The Religious Education We Need*, Birmingham, Ala.: Religious Education Press, 1977, p 132; and Lee, 'The Authentic Source of Religious Instruction', in Norma H. Thompson (ed), *Religious Education and Theology*, Birmingham, Ala.: Religious Education Press, 1982, pp 169, 172. See also J. M. Lee, *The Content of Religious Instruction*, Birmingham, Ala.: Religious Education Press, 1985, pp 691ff.

19. Johannes Hofinger, *The Art of Teaching Christian Doctrine*, London: Sands & Company; Notre Dame, Ind.: University of Notre Dame Press, 1962, p 55, ch 8 *passim.* The full quotation on p 5 is 'a proper outline of the catechism,...should be primarily theological rather than didactic', but Hofinger seems to be using 'didactic' here to designate a particular type of teaching with an unsophisticated content.

20. Compare Iris V. Cully, 'Problems of Biblical Instruction in American Catechetical Literature', in Warren (ed), *op. cit.*, p 366.

21. John Drury, *Angels and Dirt*, London: Darton, Longman & Todd, 1972, pp 40f.

22. Jim Wilhoit, *Christian Education and the Search for Meaning*, Grand Rapids: Baker Book House, 1986, pp 114, 121.

23. James Michael Lee, *The Shape of Religious Instruction*, Birmingham, Ala.: Religious Education Press, 1971, p 18.

24. For a discussion of the same problem in a different context see Jeff Astley, 'Theology and Curriculum Selection', *British Journal of Religious Education*, Vol. 10, No. 2, 1988, reprinted in Leslie J. Francis and Adrian Thatcher (eds), *Christian Perspectives for Education*, Leominster: Fowler Wright, 1990.

25. William James, *The Varieties of Religious Experience*, London: Collins, 1960 (first edition 1902), pp 363, 348.

26. *ibid.*, p 364.

27. This appears to be what Gabriel Moran describes as 'a homiletic mode of teaching' in Christian education. See his *Religious Education as a Second Language*, Birmingham, Ala.: Religious Education Press, 1989, p 150. A particular type of preaching provides the best-known example of this style, as Moran argues, but the reference to 'preaching' in my text is merely as illustrative of the form of the two educational styles. I am *not* reducing Christian education to preaching alone, nor am I necessarily advocating a style of Christian education that is like preaching in other ways (eg in being a form of multiple communication with little or no learner contribution).

4

The Logical Geography of Catechesis

KEVIN NICHOLS

To attempt a logical analysis of the word 'catechesis' is not entirely a manifestation of clarity-neurosis. It is true that logical analysis, however successful, is unlikely to work any miracles. Groome rightly says that 'disagreement about terms must never be allowed to prevent dialogue about our common concern'.[1] Fine definitions butter no parsnips. Newman also warns of the danger of reasoning only with inferences. You 'starve each term down till it becomes a ghost of itself', a 'notion neatly turned out of the laboratory of the mind and sufficiently tame and subdued, because existing only in a definition'.[2] Still he allows that inference, notional assent and argument is the 'principle of the advancement of knowledge'.[3] Without it we may do well in our own line but will not be able to discuss, relate, demarcate and learn from one another. It is a condition of belonging to the commonwealth of learning, a matter not only of prestige but of practical importance.

Many writers have attempted to formulate a definition of catechesis that will encompass all its uses. These attempts fail not because of the difficulty of the material but because the endeavour is itself mistaken. The different uses of some words do not fall under a single logical definition such as we might offer for words like 'parallelogram' or 'pitchfork'. Rather, as Wittgenstein argued, they cohere in a family resemblance, a 'complicated network of similarities overlapping and criss-crossing; sometimes overall similarities, sometimes similarities of detail'.[4] This is especially true of general words and words having a long history. Frequently these have developed a varied and complex life of their own which no exact definition will comprehend. Instead we should look for logical and definitive criteria, and this is what the phrase 'logical geography' indicates.

'Catechesis' originated and lives its life in the relative privacy of the Christian community. This is why most of those who write accounts of it (apart from historical ones) usually borrow heavily from other disciplines, most often from the study of education or of socialization. Cuckoo-like, we want to lay our eggs in other people's nests. Warren is an honourable exception to this rule.[5] Of course it is a very understandable practice. Groome's reason for it is that to use the word catechesis 'severs the Christian educational enterprise from its commonality with education'. If this happens he asks, 'from what discipline does one draw to empower the activity'.[6] I am not absolutely clear what is meant here by the word 'empower' (not I think just the prestige of belonging to a 'proper' discipline). I think it means the desire to belong to a discipline whose coinage has universal currency. Well it is one thing to borrow concepts or methods from another discipline. It is quite another to say that catechesis is a case of education or is a case of socialization. It may be that the line which divides these two procedures is also the line which distinguishes being empowered from being enslaved. My argument here is that catechesis is not 'a case' of anything. But it is closely connected with both education and socialization and a consideration of these two concepts may lead us to its definitive criteria.

EDUCATION

Education is an ancient word with an ubiquitous life of its own and is common in natural language. This is what makes it so difficult to get a hold of; though not as difficult as words like 'justice' or 'knowledge'. Still some writers despair of making anything of it. So Groome thinks it means nothing very much. It is useless to argue whether definitions of education are true. They should be evaluated as 'more or less useful...whether they make evident essential aspects of the enterprise'; though since the author is writing a book entitled 'Christian Religious Education' it is a bit hard to see what that enterprise might be.[7] Lee on the other hand thinks that education includes everything:

> Whenever a person's behaviour undergoes change he is being educated. Consequently education can be said to be taking place during most waking (and possibly some sleeping) moments of a person's life.[8]

If this account were right then we should have to include under education, brainwashing, conditioning, behaviour therapy, bad example, casual encounters, eating hamburgers, getting electric shocks and having one's teeth out. This flies in the face both of usage and common sense. It also exemplifies a tendency common among writers on religion and education. This is the tendency to regard education as a non-normative word. It seems to me mistaken and I shall return to this point later. The self-denying ordinance of both the writers on education I have mentioned lands them in due course in a number of nasty logical tangles. I do not think that such conceptual despair is justified.

Wittgenstein also makes the point that not all words are like names which are connected with a typical referent. 'Justice' is not of this kind, nor 'conversion'. 'Education' surely makes a third. For 'education' does not pick out any particular activity as does the word 'bookbinding'. Rather it lays down criteria to which activities must conform if they are to be given this accolade. Although 'education' does not pick out specific activities, it does rule out some. Neither brainwashing nor muscle-training could be called education though for different reasons. Each fails to meet at least one of the criteria which are logically definitive of the concept of education.

We do not then pick out various activities as 'cases' of education as a general concept. Rather this concept consists of criteria against which various activities can be judged. It is therefore a normative word. Its central concerns involve the transmission of something which is worthwhile and the assurance that this is done in a morally acceptable way. It is the latter criterion which leads us to exclude from education such an activity as indoctrination, however excellent the doctrines which are transmitted through it.

Although it does not specify tasks, 'education' is connected with those words which are concerned with tasks and achievements, such as 'searching' and 'finding'. In these pairs, the latter word does not pick out an additional process. It indicates only the successful outcome of the task-word. Education, however, differs from these words in several ways. It is used for both trying and succeeding, both task and achievement. Moreover, unlike other task-words, education contains the implication of worthwhileness. We might search for a lost shirt-button or for the meaning of life. We would not speak of education if the object of an activity were essentially trivial; though trivial tasks might be called educational if they were done in certain ways. This criterion of worthwhileness then does not imply a judgement about a particular kind of content. Of course the content of education does always have to be judged true or worthwhile and the judgement justified. However the point here is that qua education there *need* not be any difference between philosophy and woodwork.

The normative character of education does not prevent us from speaking rightly about a 'good' or a 'poor' education. We may mean by this that, in our judgement, the content of a type of education is not particularly worthwhile. Or we might mean that other criteria of education are present but not prominent. It is true that it is difficult to draw the line of demarcation between saying, 'that is a bad education' and saying 'that is no education at all'. This is like deciding the point at which a man can be pronounced bald. But most concepts of this sort inevitably have border-line cases. It is only when we discover counter-cases that we must reconsider the concept itself.

The note of worthwhileness in education leads to a further point about its aims. It is common to extract the normative feature of education and treat it as a neutral process directed at an extrinsic goal, like an arrow shot at a target. This I think is a mistake. When we look to extrinsic and limited aims the word 'training' is more correct. To speak of 'educating more technologists' does not really envisage the educational process and misuses the word. This is not to say that the phrase 'vocational education' is meaningless. Training activities can be carried on in an educational way. But their educational character is found in the criteria by which the process is judged and not in the extrinsic aim. Newman, in his ideal university, contemplated the possibility of a department of brewing.

Among the aspects of the concept of education mentioned so far have been achievement, worthwhileness and a morally acceptable style. Much could be said about this last point concerning freedom, 'child-centredness', authority, responsibility and equality. However most of the ethical requirements of education seem to focus on respect for persons. This moral principle would need to be unpacked and justified. But the breach of it is usually what is meant when we speak of brainwashing, conditioning or indoctrination as morally unacceptable.

The same would not be true however of rote-learning which is often said not to meet the educational criteria. A different criterion is being invoked here and to get hold of it we should look again at the notes of achievement and worthwhileness. I hope to clarify these in offering the two criteria of initiation and cognitive perspective.[9]

The concept of 'initiation' differs from the concept of 'transmission'. The former requires some state of affairs into which entry can be arranged and in which active participation by the initiated can be promoted. Transmission lacks this note of entry. What is transmitted may be a body of inert facts. So we speak of initiation into a society or into a state of life such as adulthood with the implication of active membership. Once initiated the new member can make progress of his or her own accord. In education this initiation is into forms of knowledge or fields of activity, in Wittgenstein's phrase into 'forms of life'. This does not imply support for the 'moulding' theory of education as opposed to the 'leading out' one. On the contrary, initiation makes possible a new range of self-directed activity. For a form of life includes its own unique concepts and methodology and its own tests for truth. So initiation into differentiated forms of knowledge promotes autonomy and, since a form contains its own mechanism for self-criticism, critical autonomy also.

Such initiation is not restricted to the higher reaches of scholarship. For as soon as children develop a categorial apparatus even of a concrete kind it is possible for them to learn on their own, to grasp concepts and use them, to see the reason for things and to find out what is true and what is not. I suggest that this 'initiation into forms of life' is another criterion of education.

The phrase 'cognitive perspective' makes a similar point, though not necessarily in relation to differentiated forms of knowledge. Simply learning a trick or a knack would not count as education. Yet a child could learn to boil an egg in a way that advanced his knowledge and understanding of chemistry, biology and physics. To count someone as educated in a particular area, we require that he or she should understand the principles involved, know reasons and be able to make judgements and connect what is known with other pieces of knowledge and with experience.

The phrase 'cognitive perspective' suggests, wrongly I think, a narrow intellectualism in this concept of education. Human understanding is realized diversely in the various fields of knowledge and experience. Concepts, methodology and truth-tests are of one kind in the empirical sciences, of another in the mathematical, of yet another in the human sciences and again in the arts and in the fields of morality and religion. To have a cognitive perspective in any of these areas is to be able to understand in ways appropriate to it.

Some might say of this concept of education that it is a luxury for which there is no time when it is set against other urgent tasks — to train computer-technologists, to bring up Christians etc. There may be something in this argument. Even schools, whose central commitment is to education, find that they cannot avoid other tasks. They are involved in 'socializing' and 'training' activities also. However it remains true that much practical learning can be done in an educational way. Moreover, the case for this concept is a strong one. If, as a church, we are to 'go in' for education, I think we should recognize it and decide our priorities in accordance with it.

A more serious criticism of the concept is that its geography — initiation, critical thoughtfulness, understanding, moral sensitivity — really reflects the mental world of the liberal West. There is plainly some truth in this but it does not necessarily follow that the concept is false. If Marxists or Muslims or Christians work out a radical alternative view of education, we should have to see how well it stands up.

Thus the three criteria proposed are these:

(i) the transmission of something worthwhile in an initiatory way;
(ii) the development of a cognitive perspective;
(iii) the use of procedures which are morally acceptable in that they follow the principle of respect for persons.

It might be helpful to conclude by considering what we mean by 'an educated Norwegian' and 'an educated Christian'. In the first the adjective is a straightforward qualifier. If we speak of 'an educated, red haired, obese, left-handed, male Norwegian' then 'educated' describes the mental quality as the other adjectives describe his physical attributes. He is familiar with various forms of knowledge, he has a flexibility of mind, can bring concepts to bear on experience appropriately, does not take things at their face value etc. In 'educated Christian' the adjective could have the same force. But more naturally we should take it that this person is educated qua Christian. His profession of Christianity includes a thorough understanding of its structure and of the reasons for accepting it. He can locate it in relation to the religious 'form of life' and in relation to a wide range of human experiences. He is at home in the various idioms in which faith expresses itself. His religious life is characterized by flexibility and openness of mind etc. Is that what we mean by catechesis? Or should we say that this 'educated' character is not part of the central concerns of the phrase 'being a Christian'? Must we look elsewhere.

SOCIALIZATION

Unlike 'education', 'socialization' is a word of recent origin and one not frequently used in natural speech. So we shall have to rely, in analysing it, on those fields of scholarship which make use of it for their technical concerns. It is helpful to consider both its similarity to and its difference from education. Israel Scheffler expresses the difference in this way:

> Every culture we may say, normally gets newborn members to behave according to its norms, however these are specified, and many cultures have agencies devoted to this job. But not every way of getting people to behave according to some norm is teaching... To teach is at some points at least to submit oneself to the understanding and independent judgement of the pupil, to his demand for reasons.[10]

So it seems that it is in those educational criteria which have to do with understanding and autonomy that we shall find the difference.

The aspect of initiation is common to both words though in different ways. To socialize is to initiate into a culture or a way of life, embodied in a system of symbols and including beliefs, attitudes and patterns of relationship and behaviour. This differs from a form of [know]ledge or a form of life. It does not necessarily involve crucial nor a typical methodology. It is unlikely to include tests for any mechanism for self-criticism. Still socialization does into active participation. It is usually expected that those who are socialized will play a part in the common life, will advance it (though according to its own pattern), and will receive it in a way which is individual, within the limits which the culture sets. There seems no necessary logical connection between socialization and autonomy.

Socialization does not seem to require a cognitive perspective or any version of that. We would not necessarily expect someone who had been socialized to understand the workings of the culture, to be able to compare it with others or to receive its offerings selectively. Of course it might be done in such a way that the person socialized was able to do those things. But this we would regard as a bonus or perhaps even as a failure in socialization. The point is that we would not think such a person better *socialized* than a member of a primitive society who never looks beyond it. We would probably say he was an educated Trobriand islander or a freakishly reflective one.

Socialization is also not necessarily an intentional process. Most writers seem to agree that all people in all societies are socialized whether they like it or not, whether anyone intends it or not. The fact that some societies achieve a high degree of self-consciousness, are aware of the workings of socialization and set about it systematically, does not I think alter the logical requirements of the word. A primitive society which has none of these characteristics constitutes just as authentic a case. So we cannot necessarily connect socialization with task-achievement words. It is true that, like education, it does not pick out specific tasks. But this is because it is not a task word at all, but rather belongs with words describing processes such as 'growth' or 'recovery'.

The moral requirements implicit in the concept of education do not seem to apply to socialization, that is that it demands activities done in a morally acceptable manner. We should, I think, count as socialization any effective initiation into a culture, whether or not the doing of it showed any respect for persons. So the Spartan boys were genuinely socialized even though we think the manner of their upbringing barbaric.

Although one of the central concerns of the word socialization is the culture, the shared life of a group, it is not necessary that the group should be collectively engaged in the activity. An individual can socialize another so far as he/she adequately embodies the culture. Still it would be true to say that the culture, the collective, the community is definitive in the case of socialization, and that this is not true in the case of education.

CATECHESIS

Like education, catechesis is an ancient word. However, its use has been restricted to one religious tradition so that it has not developed the same ubiquitous life in natural language. Moreover it fell into disuse or — some would say — continued its life aside from its main track for many centuries. So in its recent revival it has a technical, academic air. It is minted by specialists, as socialization is produced by social scientists.

There are two lines of approach to the logic of catechesis. The more common relates it to education or to socialization. The other looks within church tradition for its logical landmarks — community of faith, pastoral ministry, evangelization etc. It is worth recalling the probable reason for choosing one line or the other: it is a question of being 'empowered' by a recognized discipline as against picking one's way across very uncertain logical terrain. It is also worth recalling the difference between borrowing concepts or methods, or even a 'model', and saying 'catechesis is a *case* of....'. Let us begin with the second approach and see where it leads.

Most accounts of catechesis agree that the development of faith towards maturity is its central concern. But there are many lines along which this development may occur and many activities through which it is attempted. Not all of these count as catechesis. So if a preacher comes to us afterwards and says, 'Well, I have done my catechesis for the day', we should say, 'Nonsense, you've been preaching a sermon'. But if a mother says, 'I've been teaching my little daughter to say the rosary', we would be less certain. We might ask how she had done this. Did she simply show the child how to move the beads and what prayer to say on each of them? If so we would call this instruction or training. But perhaps the mother spoke of the events of the life of Jesus, explained why we remember them in sequence. Perhaps she read and discussed some extracts from the gospels. In this case what she has done is certainly catechetical. This example suggests that 'catechesis' resembles 'education' in at least two ways:

(a) Neither picks out any specific tasks. Both examine the contexts in which various tasks are done, their relative flexibility and openness. Catechesis, like education, is not task-specific. We shall probably have more luck in looking for 'criteria' than in formulating a definition.

(b) Among the criteria for catechesis is something which looks suspiciously like the 'cognitive perspective' required in education. We ask: does the process encourage the connection of what is transmitted to other truths? Does it connect ideas and experience in an illuminating way? Does it transmit inert ideas or active ones?

The word 'cognitive' in this phrase raises many hackles. Again it suggests a 'narrow intellectualism'. It is a product of the 'epistemological shift' in Christian religious education of which Groome complains which lost hold of the 'relational, experiential and active' mode of knowing which the Scriptures evidence.[11] I do not doubt that as a matter of historical fact, something of the kind Groome speaks of did happen. Still I doubt if the objection is logically as damaging as is claimed. For the notion of 'cognition' required in the phrase is not modelled on mathematics or the empirical sciences. It is rather the type of cognition appropriate to the various forms of knowledge or realms of meaning. So there is a cognitive perspective appropriate to aesthetic forms. There is also a logic of the heart: a 'cognitive core' to the life of the emotions. It cannot rightly be objected that a cognitive perspective would tie catechesis narrowly to abstract concepts or to a discursive logical style.

However further objections to the importance of a cognitive perspective may be raised. It may be said that the central concern of catechesis is faith and that since faith is 'primal and preconceptual' its development may presumably follow a line which has no necessary connection with knowledge. The giftedness of faith precludes the direct generation of it. It is transmitted by the objects — doctrines, moral ideals, rituals, stories — in which a believing community corporately articulates its faith. By exposure to these, through participation in them, faith itself is communicated.

There is something odd about this argument. On the one hand, in order to assert the primacy of faith in catechesis it excludes from the concept of faith all the languages in which it is expressed. On the other hand, when it begins to speak of the development of faith these languages immediately appear as its only visible embodiment. However there does lurk in it an important truth. This is the assertion that no amount of knowledge about the languages of *faith*— however wide-ranging or unifying — can be counted as catechetical, unless it is precisely as languages of faith that they are learned. These expressions are communicative of faith in a privileged way. But their effectiveness depends on the believing community — or the individual catechist as its agent — expressing and enacting them as authentic expressions of its corporate faith, 'primal and pre-conceptual', and so drawing new members into that faith. A detached and enlightened learning of these expressions will make them coherent and reasonable, may make experience intelligible in their light. It may even initiate children effectively into religion as a form of life and so count as education. But immediately we have said that, we recognize where the chief logical difference between catechesis and education lies. It is that faith is a primary criterion, understanding a secondary one. It is also in this notion of participative initiation that the closest links between catechesis and socialization are to be found. For socialization views the objects of a culture primarily as communicating the central attitudes and beliefs of the culture. Wittingness, understanding, critical awareness are secondary considerations, if they are considerations at all.

This rather crucial point is similar to that made by the distinction between neutral and confessional styles of religious education. The confessional style constitutes, in my view, one of the catechetical activities. It is distinguished by the presence in the teacher of commitment, not to a professional task but to the tradition of faith with which she or he is concerned. By commitment here is meant an acceptance of the tradition for adequate reasons which includes an understanding of its crucial expressions and an acceptance of the moral consequences which the tradition entails. In our judgement of the case, for catechesis qua catechesis this commitment would be the primary criterion.

However once the primacy of faith itself has been established, the question arises whether we ought not to say that the understanding, the cognitive perspective, though secondary, is also definitive. For if cognition is taken in the broad, varied sense which it has here, we may ask: what other road towards maturity can faith take? Unlike socialization, catechesis seems to be essentially concerned with intent and understanding. The goal set by the *General Catechetical Directory*, 'adherence that is fully responsible', seems to be of a piece with the catechetical tradition (or setting it on its true track).[12] But free adherence, unlike acceptance, requires understanding of an appropriate kind. We do not commit ourselves to a truth without evidence, nor to a person without relevant reflection.

The criteria suggested for catechesis then are these:

(i) It characterizes tasks that have the goal of developing faith towards maturity. It is thus connected both with a theological and a psycho-social tradition.

(ii) It requires a commitment to the Christian tradition of faith; and so it is part of the church's pastoral ministry and engages at least indirectly the church community's corporate faith.

(iii) As a developmental process catechesis requires the presence of a cognitive perspective.

(iv) The understanding implied in this is that which initiates a person into the various crucial expressions of the Christian tradition.

(v) Such understandings are necessary for 'free adherence' of faith itself.

CATECHETICS AS A FIELD OF STUDY

I have remarked already how writers such as Groome and Lee seem to use words like 'education' or 'instruction' as definite commitments of catechesis to some other language-games (catechesis is a case of....). The reasons given are usually practical ones. These disciplines 'empower', they prevent isolation, they have a universal currency etc. I do not deny the practical advantage of these connections. However the line between a treaty and a colonial subjugation is an easy one to cross. My argument is that those who study catechesis should work out its own inner logic (with appropriate borrowings).

It is true that being restricted within the Christian tradition is rather different from just being a bit isolated. Still I do not think that restriction necessarily excludes catechetics from the commonwealth of learning. Its epistemological credentials are at least as good as those enjoyed by patristics or by church history.

What kind of study should catechetics be? It is useful to distinguish three ways in which knowledge is commonly organized:

(i) *Forms of knowledge.* Here the field is cognitively unified through key concepts, methods of working and tests for truth. Examples are mathematics, physics, music.

(ii) *Fields of knowledge*. Here the concepts and methods may be cognitively various (often borrowed). What holds the field together is a phenomenon which is the focus of study. A good example is geography.

(iii) *Practical theories*. Here again, concepts and methods are various. The focus of study is a practical activity. Examples are medicine and engineering.

Catechetics as a study belongs in the third category. The focal activity is the development of faith towards maturity. The components may be derived from theology, education, the social sciences, history etc. Or they may be original. This will give to the field of study (as in the case of medicine) a bi-focal character. The component elements will not cohere unless there is an effective shuttling between theory and practice. Theory without practice is sterile. Practice without theory is blind.

NOTES

1. T. H. Groome, *Christian Religious Education*, San Francisco: Harper & Row, 1980, p 28.

2. J. H. Newman, *Grammar of Assent*, London: Longman's Green, 1889, p 267.

3. Newman, *op. cit.*, p 34.

4. L. Wittgenstein, *Philosophical Investigations*, Oxford: Blackwell, 1953, p 32.

5. M. Warren, 'Catechesis and Religious Education', in M. Warren (ed), *Sourcebook for Modern Catechetics*, Winona, Minnesota: St. Mary's Press, 1984.

6. Groome, *op. cit.*, p 27.

7. Groome, *op. cit.*, p 20.

8. J. M. Lee, 'Key Issues in the Development of a Workable Foundation for Religious Instruction', in P. O'Hare (ed), *Foundations of Religious Education*, New York: Paulist Press, 1978, p 40.

9. In this section I have drawn largely on R. S. Peters, *Ethics and Education*, London: Allen & Unwin, 1966, Part I. Useful discussions are also to be found in R. F. Dearden, P. H. Hirst and R. S. Peters (eds), *Education and the Development of Reason*, London: Routledge & Kegan Paul, 1972 and G. Langford and D. J. O'Connor (eds), *New Essays in Philosophy of Education*, London: Routledge & Kegan Paul, 1973.

10. I. Scheffler, *The Language of Education*, Springfield, Illinois: Charles C. Thomas, 1972, p 57.

11. Groome, *op. cit.*, p 160.

12. *General Catechetical Directory*, London: Catholic Truth Society, 1972, para 12.

5

Christian Nurture, Indoctrination and Liberal Education

ELMER J. THIESSEN

Christian nurture is frequently subject to the charge of indoctrination. For many, such as Antony Flew,

> the outstanding paradigm case of indoctrination [is] the enormous and generally effective effort made [by the Christian church] to fix in the minds of children an unshakable conviction of the truth of its specific distinctive doctrines.[1]

Woods and Barrow, in their popular introductory text in the philosophy of education, introduce the topic of indoctrination with a description of a Catholic school as a paradigm case of indoctrination.[2] In an important recent sociological analysis of a fundamentalist Christian school in Illinois, Alan Peshkin concludes that 'as a total institution Bethany Baptist Academy logically indoctrinates its students'.[3] Discussions about religious indoctrination have recently also focused on the family, and writers such as Callan remind us that 'parents who rear their children within a particular religion incur a significant risk of indoctrinating them'.[4]

Religious instruction in state-maintained schools in Canada, the United States and Great Britain has undergone a major transformation in the last fifteen years. In the past, religious instruction was unashamedly Christian in orientation. But, as one writer has noted, public discussion about such an approach 'has continually been stalked by the ghost of "religious indoctrination"'.[5] And largely in response to this fear, religious instruction in state-maintained schools has shifted to teaching *about* religions or a phenomenological approach to religious education.

In Canada, for example, the recently adopted Canadian Charter of Rights (1982) has led to several landmark decisions with regard to religious instruction in public schools. On September 23, 1988 the Ontario Court of Appeal struck down a law which had compelled Ontario schools to hold daily religious exercises consisting of the reading of the Scriptures and the repeating of the Lord's Prayer. Then again on January 30, 1990 the Ontario Court of Appeal struck down a long-standing regulation requiring that religious education (ie Christian education) be included in Ontario public school curricula. The ruling specifically argued against the traditional approach to religious education on the grounds that the Canadian Charter of Rights and Freedoms does not 'permit the indoctrination of school children in the Christian faith'. The Court, however, hastened to add that it was not prohibiting 'education about religion'. In the same breath, however, the Court made this interesting observation:

> While this is an easy test to state, the line between indoctrination
> and education, in some instances, can be difficult to draw.[6]

Indeed, so! What is astounding is that a landmark court decision with far reaching implications for schools is based on a questionable distinction between indoctrination and education. Why is this distinction so difficult to draw?

INDOCTRINATION

In ordinary usage today the term 'indoctrination' carries with it strongly pejorative overtones. It was not always so. In tracing the evolution of the concept of indoctrination, Gatchel notes that, until a little over half a century ago, the term 'indoctrination' carried a positive connotation and was roughly equivalent to 'education'.[7] But meanings can change, some radically, and today 'indoctrination' is used largely in a derogatory sense, to refer to teaching that is somehow incompatible with true education. It is not my purpose here to explore why this shift in meaning has occurred, except to suggest that it is rooted in the acceptance of a very specific ideal of liberal education, which in turn is rooted in the overwhelming acceptance of some important liberal values such as individuality, freedom, autonomy, rationality, and tolerance.

Much has been written about indoctrination by educational philosophers over the past 30 years. Most of this writing has been within the analytic tradition which places much importance on defining concepts. Philosophers have therefore attempted to find the criteria that govern the use of the term 'indoctrination'.[8] Four criteria have been thought to be essential to defining the term.

Content

One of the central features most often associated with indoctrination has to do with its content. R. S. Peters, for example, argues that 'whatever else "indoctrination" means, it obviously has something to do with doctrines'.[9] Antony Flew bluntly states, 'No doctrines, no indoctrination'.[10] Flew goes on to define doctrines as beliefs that are 'either false or not known to be true'.[11] Doctrines are generally thought to be found primarily in such areas as religion, politics and perhaps also morality, and hence, 'The paradigm cases of indoctrination are to be found in religious communities and institutions'.[12] It is further generally assumed that science contains no doctrines and hence indoctrination is thought to be impossible in science.[13]

Methods

The content criterion of indoctrination is often closely associated with the methods criterion. Alan Peshkin, for example, links doctrine with methods when he argues that Bethany Baptist Academy indoctrinates its students, 'refusing to treat issues to which doctrine applies as matters for discussion'.[14] Kazipedes similarly links doctrines with questionable teaching methods:

> The indoctrinator, because he is inculcating doctrines, must resort to some educationally questionable methods such as failing to provide relevant evidence and argument or misapplying them, misusing his authority, etc.[15]

Generally it would seem that indoctrination is associated with the use of non-rational teaching methods.[16]

Intention

Others have tried to define indoctrination in terms of certain intentions. What is it that is suspect about the intentions of the parent or teacher as an indoctrinator? There are a variety of answers, though a common thread is apparent. Snook, who has defended the intention criterion, argues that a person indoctrinates if he teaches with the intention that the pupil or pupils believe what is taught regardless of the evidence.[17] More generally, indoctrination is frequently described in terms of the intentional inculcation of unshakable beliefs.[18]

Consequences

The intention criterion is closely connected to the final criterion often thought to be essential in defining indoctrination — namely consequences. Such consequences are frequently described in terms of 'a closed mind'. William Hare, for example, has written two books on the ideal of open-mindedness in liberal education.[19] Indoctrination, for Hare, 'involves coming to hold beliefs in a closed-minded fashion'.[20] Often the ideal of open-mindedness is associated with the ability to criticize one's beliefs, hence the frequent reference to 'critical openness'.[21] Indoctrination therefore is thought to involve the failure to produce minds that are open and critical.

CRITIQUE OF THE FOUR CRITERIA OF INDOCTRINATION

What then can be said by way of evaluating the four criteria that have often been proposed as essential to defining 'indoctrination'? Dunlop sums up rather nicely a general problem that seems to plague past philosophical work on this concept:

> Although indoctrination has perhaps attracted more attention from contemporary analytic philosophers of education than (almost) any other reasonably self-contained and isolated topic, there is still far from being general agreement about it. Method, content, states of mind, with or without teacher's intention — various combinations of these standard ingredients still emerge from philosophers' kitchens with astonishing regularity, but nobody has yet apparently managed to digest anyone else's concoction.[22]

Yet strangely, despite all this disagreement, most people go on making the charge of indoctrination as though they are perfectly clear as to what the term means. On the contrary, I would suggest that we are by no means clear as to what is really meant when the charge of indoctrination is made. I would further suggest that the continuing philosophical disagreement concerning the correct analysis of the concept of indoctrination reflects some deeper problems concerning both the assumptions that underlie the charge of indoctrination and the ideal of liberal education out of which this charge emerges.

I begin with an outline of some of the key problems associated with past treatments of the concept of indoctrination. Rather than deal with each of the criteria separately, I will focus on more general problems that are shared by all the criteria. As Ralph Page has noted,[23] there are some common threads that run through all four criteria and it is helpful to focus on these rather than on each criterion individually.

Shaping of Beliefs

One of the central problems of past treatments of indoctrination is that they tend to focus on the shaping of beliefs, where beliefs are construed in strictly propositional ways.[24] This leads philosophers to view indoctrination as essentially an epistemological issue. I would suggest that we need to shift our focus from beliefs to the believer, from propositions to persons. This will of course introduce a host of subjective considerations, but these get us to the heart of what indoctrination involves.

Epistemology

There is secondly a problem with the epistemology that underlies most discussions about indoctrination. There seems to be general agreement that indoctrination has to do with the rational justification of individual beliefs. Concern about rationality comes up in each of the four criteria traditionally associated with indoctrination. But what is missing in these accounts of rationality, according to Ralph Page, is 'just about every issue that has occupied epistemological debate for the last several decades'.[25] There is a general failure to take into account important discussions in the philosophy of science, the sociology of knowledge and Marxist critiques of liberal definitions of knowledge. Past accounts of indoctrination are generally based on a foundationalist approach to epistemology which assumes that knowledge must be grounded on 'basic facts' which we can know with complete certainty and which we can approach with complete objectivity. Foundationalism also assumes that there is a 'basic methodology' which allows us to draw conclusions in a formal manner and which will again yield complete certainty. Both of these assumptions are seen as problematic by many philosophers today.[26] It is also assumed that epistemology can be conceived of as essentially distinct from psychological and sociological conditions under which beliefs develop, an assumption which again is being challenged by many today.

Children and Indoctrination

The third problem that comes to the fore in past discussions of indoctrination is that they fail to address the question as to what is involved in educating young children. Dearden has well said that 'philosophers may have been too apt to overlook or ignore the fact that men have childhoods'.[27] Past definitions of indoctrination founder precisely when applied to children who necessarily learn via non-rational means. This leads some writers to admit that some indoctrination is inevitable and good. But if indoctrination involves non-rational teaching, and if indoctrination is immoral, then it is inconsistent to allow for some indoctrination via non-rational methods when dealing with children. Yet it seems we must do so, given past definitions of 'indoctrination'.

Autonomy

Fourth, past discussions of indoctrination are based on an idealized notion of personal autonomy which is philosophically indefensible. Children are simply not autonomous and it is an error to suggest that we should treat them so, as is so often done: for example when it is suggested that we need to let them decide for themselves with regard to religion. Growth towards autonomy always occurs within a certain context. We are necessarily shaped in part by our past and by our environment, and therefore we can only achieve limited autonomy. Human beings simply cannot achieve complete independence, perfect rationality, total objectivity, or complete openness. They cannot subject everything they believe to critical evaluation. Yet the charge of indoctrination often rests on the assumption that finite human beings can achieve this ideal of rational autonomy. What is needed is a more realistic ideal of *normal* rational autonomy, to use a term introduced by Haworth.[28] More will be said about this notion shortly.

Institutions

Finally, past treatments of indoctrination rest on an ideal of liberal education which is really an abstraction. 'You need institutions. How else can you make ideas real?', says a young journalist who is seeking revenge on a boss who has fired him, in a recent play entitled 'Pravda'.[29] Ideas do need institutions and are inevitably transmitted via institutions. Our thinking as human beings is necessarily shaped by institutions, as has been so ably demonstrated by Mary Douglas's book, *How Institutions Think*.[30] Thus any attempt to ignore the institutional context of liberal education is mistaken, and yet this is what is done in most discussions of the violations of the principles of liberal education, including that of indoctrination.

Given these problems inherent in past discussions of indoctrination, I would suggest that the charge of indoctrination as applied against Christian nurture is much weaker than is generally assumed, and that those making the charge should be much more cautious in making it. If one were to work out all the implications of the above mentioned problems it could be shown that there is no necessary connection between Christian nurture and indoctrination, and that the alleged probable connections are considerably weaker than they are often thought to be.

Science and Religion

Here I can only illustrate by working out some of these implications in one area. Earlier I pointed out that it is often assumed that indoctrination is probable or even inevitable in religious instruction, while science is thought to be immune to indoctrination. The exemption of science should not surprise us because the principles underlying the scientific ideal are very much at the root of the ideal of liberal education which is the context out of which the charge of indoctrination arises. The principles of empiricism, rationality, objectivity, autonomy, and open-mindedness are at the heart of the scientific ideal, together with concern about tradition, authority, and dogmatism. But as Ratzsch among others has argued, this traditional view of science has increasingly come under attack since the 1960s, largely as a result of the ground-breaking work of Thomas Kuhn.[31] Since Kuhn it is generally acknowledged that observation is theory-laden, that scientists are not as objective as is frequently assumed because they bring a host of assumptions, convictions and commitments to bear on their task, and that the process of science is not strictly rational or logical but rests on imaginative leaps, with several theories often being proposed to account for the same data. Further, as Polyani has shown, the scientific enterprise is not as autonomous as it is often portrayed, but is very much dependent on the existence of a scientific community, governed to a large extent by tradition and authority.[32] Indeed science is very much an institution in which pupils are apprenticed to masters, a 'modern version of the Apostolic Succession'.[33]

The 'new philosophy of science' therefore calls for a radical revision of the traditional ideal of science. If we apply the traditional concept of indoctrination (as defined by the four criteria considered earlier) to science itself, as traditionally understood, it will be found that indoctrination is common, indeed inevitable, in the teaching of science. This point will be, or at least should be, admitted by those familiar with the new understanding of science that seems to be emerging today. Thus we find Christians too sometimes making the claim that indoctrination is as common in science as it is in religion. This is what in effect has been suggested by Malcolm Muggeridge, for example:

> The dogmatism of science has become a new orthodoxy, disseminated by the Media and a State educational system with a thoroughness and subtlety far exceeding anything of the kind achieved by the Inquisition.[34]

While there is some truth in such a statement (ideas are always backed by institutions), Christians need to be careful not to rely on the 'you do it too!' argument which really involves a failure in logic as well as in faith. A better approach, I would suggest, is to draw on the fact that there is a general hesitancy to make the charge of indoctrination with regard to science. Yet the 'new philosophy of science' shows that the scientific enterprise is not as empirical, rational, objective, open-minded, and autonomous as is generally assumed. If therefore, despite these factors, we hesitate to make the charge of indoctrination in science, consistency demands that we should be much more cautious in making the charge of indoctrination in religion on the grounds that religion is not as empirical, rational, objective, and open-minded as many would like it to be. It can further be argued that with a more sophisticated epistemology, such as seems to be emerging in the philosophy of science, religion begins to look much more 'rational' than is often assumed. In summary, I would suggest that the contrasting divergence in the application of the charge of indoctrination in the areas of religion and science rests on an unrealistic idealization of science and a caricature of religion.

It should finally be noted that since the charge of indoctrination is based on the same principles that inform the ideal of science, the new philosophy of science calls for a radical revision of the concept of indoctrination itself. Defining indoctrination in terms of content or teaching methods that are not rational, or in terms of a lack of critical openness, simply will not do because scientific content and the teaching of science is not as rational as has been traditionally assumed; and because there are limits to the extent that everyone, even the scientist, can achieve critical openness.

All this is not to suggest that indoctrination cannot and does not occur in Christian nurture. But in order to determine if and when it occurs, we need to reconstruct the ideal of liberal education and then revise the notion of indoctrination accordingly.

RECONSTRUCTION OF THE IDEAL OF LIBERAL EDUCATION

R. S. Peters, who in many ways was the founder of the analytic approach to the philosophy of education, has in his later writings urged philosophers to move to a more constructive, integrative approach to thinking about education, more in line with the classical approach, such as Plato's, whose educational theory is 'exemplary in structure because he had a worked out theory of knowledge, an ethical theory and a theory of human nature'.[35] Other writers have suggested that a metaphysical theory is also needed for an educational theory.[36] I wish to highlight a few points in each of the above mentioned areas in my reconstruction of the ideal of liberal education. It should be noted that I am not rejecting the traditional ideal of liberal education in its entirety. I am merely attempting a reconstruction.

Metaphysics
There was a time when Christian nurture was not only compatible with liberal education, but viewed as an essential ingredient of it. The ideal of liberal education has undergone a process of secularization, and it is for this reason that initiation into a specific religious tradition is viewed with suspicion today. There are, however, some problems with the dogmatic empiricism that often underlies the scientific ideal and the secularist frame of mind. I would therefore suggest that there is a need to return to the older ideal of liberal education based on a more open-minded metaphysics.

Human Nature
Man is more than a rational animal. Peters has been rightly criticized for being:

> so concerned with the intellectual dimension of education that he virtually ignores those other physical, emotional, and spiritual activities which together make up a comprehensive definition of man.[37]

There is also a need for a more holistic view of human nature which recognizes that our rational nature is intimately bound up with the emotional, physical, moral and spiritual dimensions of our being. Thus we will not be able to define indoctrination in purely epistemological terms. Related to the above is the need to recognize human existence as 'necessarily situated in a contingent, historical, cultural and social context'.[38] We are also finite and dependent on others. All this will entail some revisions of the traditional liberal ideal of rational autonomy. At most, human beings should strive for *normal* rational autonomy.[39]

Epistemology

I have already drawn attention to the foundationalist epistemology that underlies past discussions of indoctrination and liberal education. A theory of liberal education needs to be based on an epistemology that recognizes that all observation is theory-laden, and that theorizing is an incredibly complex process, involving the justification of whole belief-systems, rather than individual claims. Theorizing also depends on a host of ingredients such as concepts, observations, presuppositions, past theorizing, present public agreement, etc. We simply cannot divorce epistemology from certain personal, social, historical, and material factors as the foundationalists tend to do.[40]

Values

I have no quarrel with Peters's description of the normative aspect of liberal education as implying 'that something worthwhile is being or has been intentionally transmitted in a morally acceptable manner'.[41] I would maintain, however, that Christian doctrine needs to be fully accepted as worthwhile content, at least for the people belonging to the Christian tradition, and I would remind liberals that it is rather presumptuous of them to judge this content otherwise, since the liberal tradition is after all just another tradition itself, as McIntyre has recently argued.[42] I further agree that the manner of education must also be morally acceptable, and that indoctrination is wrong. However my definition of indoctrination will differ somewhat from the traditional liberal definition, as will be shown shortly. More will be said about the compatibility of liberal with Christian values later.

Beyond the Present and the Particular

I need to mention one final ingredient in my reconstruction of the ideal of liberal education. Charles Bailey has described liberal education as an education which liberalizes a person and moves him/her 'beyond the present and the particular'.[43] But Bailey, along with many other philosophers of education, fails to address adequately the question as to how we get into the present and the particular in the first place. It should be rather obvious that children must first of all be initiated into a particular home, a particular language, a particular culture, a particular set of beliefs, etc, before they can begin to expand their horizons beyond the present and the particular. Liberal education, as traditionally understood, is therefore necessarily parasitic on something else, namely initiation into a present and a particular. The traditional ideal of liberal education is an abstraction from a larger whole. My reconstruction of the ideal of liberal education will therefore be more holistic in focus.

I therefore propose that liberal education be reconstructed so as to include both initiation and liberation. Hirst is therefore wrong in treating the traditionalist notion of education, with its emphasis on transmission (initiation) as entirely different from the concept of liberal education.[44] We have here not two different concepts of education, the one primitive and the other sophisticated, but two different and equally important phases of liberal education.[45] In my reconstruction, liberal education will be seen more in terms of a process of development, where due regard is given to the initiation phase of education, and where it will be especially important to adjust the 'liberating' phase of education to the psychological needs of the child. Ackerman has argued that children need a stable and coherent 'primary culture' and that this is a pre-condition of their subsequent growth towards rational autonomy.[46] To expose them to 'an endless and changing Babel of talk and behaviour' too soon will hurt them and prevent further development. As they mature the need for stability and coherence lessens, and thus the liberating phase of liberal education can be gradually introduced.

A New Definition of Indoctrination

This more holistic and developmental concept of liberal education will lead to a rather different definition of 'indoctrination'. I would suggest that the core idea of indoctrination be thought of in terms of *the curtailment of a person's growth towards normal rational autonomy.*[47] Several things should be noted about this definition. The focus here is not on propositions, but on persons, whole persons, whose growth towards normal rational autonomy can be curtailed in any number of ways. The developmental nature of my definition of indoctrination should also be noted. Indoctrination will mean different things at different stages of a person's development. It is especially important to note that initiation into the present and the particular is a necessary phase of a person's growth towards rational autonomy and therefore the charge of indoctrination is not applicable to this stage of development. It should finally be noted that indoctrination is understood as frustrating the growth towards *normal* rational autonomy, not complete independence, or perfect rationality. There are limits to the growth of any human being since we are all finite and situated within a contingent present and particular.

Christianity and Normal Rational Autonomy
There will no doubt be some, perhaps many Christians who will not be satisfied with my reconstruction of the ideal of liberal education, especially with my acceptance of the ideal of rational autonomy, even though I have qualified this ideal somewhat. In defence let me remind my readers that the ideal of liberal education has its Christian moorings as well. It is John Henry Cardinal Newman, former Protestant turned Catholic, who is generally acknowledged today as the classical exponent of the theory of liberal education. Ryken, in an important essay entitled 'Puritan Piety and the Liberated Mind', reminds us that it was Luther's opinion that 'you parents cannot prepare a more dependable treasure for your children than an education in the liberal arts'.[48] Similar observations could be made about liberalism generally. A biography of G. K. Chesterton illustrates this well. A. S. Dale describes, as one 'fascinatingly original aspect' of Chesterton's conversion, how he found that the roots of his liberalism were in fact orthodox credal Christianity. Chesterton found that the classic principles of liberalism 'were so intertwined in his thinking about Christianity that he himself seemed not to know where one began and the other ended'.[49]

Normal rationality is advocated in the Scriptures, notwithstanding Paul's comments about the foolishness of the gospel which, as Gooch has shown, are all too often badly misinterpreted.[50] Paul himself was a master at debate and was constantly defending the gospel, even in the presence of philosophers (Acts 17:2,17; 17:16-34; 18:4; 19:8). In the great commandment we are told to love God with all our mind (Matt 22:37). It is passages such as these — and many others could be supplied — which lead Os Guinness, among others, to suggest that:

> The Christian wholeheartedly supports genuine rationality...
> Christianity is second to none in the place it gives to reason,
> but it is also second to none in keeping reason in its place.[51]

The Scriptures similarly affirm the ideal of normal autonomy. The individual person is given value, dignity and worth (Genesis 1; Psalm 8; Psalm 139; Matt 6:25-34; John 10). Ultimately it is the individual who is called to respond to God and is held accountable by God (Ezekiel 3; Matt 16:24-8), and the individual's right of refusal is respected (Luke 9:5,55). This emphasis on the individual is of course balanced by an equal emphasis on the collective identity of Christians — the people of God, the church — but the emphasis on the individual still stands.

We are now finally in a position to consider some practical suggestions for Christian nurture: suggestions that grow out of my critique of past treatments of indoctrination and my reconstruction of the ideal of liberal education, as well as my revised notion of indoctrination. 'Ideas have consequences.' This ancient and profound truth, captured in the title R. M. Weaver gave to his brilliant and oft-reprinted book, also serves as a fitting introduction to the last section of this paper.[52] Philosophers especially need to be reminded of this when all too often we remain in our proverbial ivory towers absorbed in abstract and theoretical arguments, without ever bothering to show that our ideas do make important differences in real life. Not only do ideas have consequences, but they can also be tested by their consequences. The following suggestions can also be seen as providing a way to test whether my reconstruction of the ideal of liberal education and my revised notion of indoctrination are indeed better able to distinguish between what is acceptable and what is not acceptable in the all-important task of educating our children.

SOME PRACTICAL IMPLICATIONS

I wish to deal with two sets of practical implications. The first set concerns the initiation/transmission phase or component of liberal education. In this set the first practical implication I wish to highlight will no doubt startle some educators, but it needs to be stated, and stated openly.

Initiate Boldly
Christian parents should boldly initiate their children into the Christian faith. Here it needs to be stressed that this principle is dealing with the initial initiation phase of liberal education, ie the education of a child under the age of 5 or 6. I am further assuming that it is the parents who have the right to determine the nature of the primary

culture into which their children are first initiated.[53] My reason for encouraging Christian parents to initiate their children into the Christian faith boldly is that they are often made to feel guilty about doing so by liberal educationalists. The fear of indoctrination leads some parents to take a 'liberal' approach to child rearing in which they go to great lengths trying to avoid the imposition of their religion onto their children. The guilt and the fear that is imposed on Christian parents by so-called liberals is entirely unjustified. In fact I believe the charge of indoctrination is inapplicable to children at this stage of development. Therefore the advice: initiate boldly. Christian parents should not sell the Christian birth-right of their children for a mess of liberal pottage.

It should further be noted that Christian nurture will of necessity include an initiation/socialization/transmission component at *all* stages of a person's development, though in lessening degrees as a person matures. The Christian parent and teacher, as well as the Christian church and school, should therefore again boldly and openly initiate and socialize into the Christian tradition. Transmission of certain information unique to the Christian tradition and instruction in Christian doctrine are also viewed as essential to Christian nurture and growth towards normal rational autonomy, though obviously there are other components of Christian nurture at later stages of a person's development.

This advice grows out of the work of sociologists like Berger and Luckmann, who remind us that *some* degree of initiation/socialization/ transmission is essential for a person's mental development throughout his/her lifetime.[54] Liberal education, and more specifically Christian liberal education, must therefore accept this; and Christians must be careful not to allow the fear of indoctrination to stop them from ongoing initiation/socialization/transmission. The charge of indoctrination is inappropriate as long as other essential components of liberal education are present.

Christian Schools and Colleges
Finally, Christian nurture should occur within the context of a faith-supporting community and faith-supporting institutions, one of which is the Christian school. Here again I am building on the fact that the development of the mind never occurs in isolation from others. Without a social world, the individual will not only 'begin to lose his moral bearings, with disastrous psychological consequences, but he will become uncertain about his cognitive bearings as well'. 'The

world begins to shake in the very instant that its sustaining conversation begins to falter', Peter Berger has said.[55] All of us, liberals as well as Christians, need 'plausibility structures' in order to maintain mental sanity, according to Berger. Clearly the home and the church provide these plausibility structures, but they are not sufficient. We also need Christian schools and colleges where there is a systematic, serious and orderly initiation into and study of the Christian tradition. This suggestion is entirely in keeping with the recognition of other liberal educationalists like Oakeshott, who see schools as necessary to continue the process of initiation into the human inheritance, begun by parents.[56]

Most Christians will no doubt find the above set of implications quite palatable, while many liberal educators will no doubt have serious concerns about what has been said. I turn now to a second set of practical implications which I suspect will cause a reversal of reactions on the part of some Christians. This second set of implications concerns that phase or component of liberal education which has to do with nurturing towards normal rational autonomy. It should be noted that the principles outlined here are particularly, though not exclusively, applicable to post-secondary levels of Christian education.

Goals of Christian Education

As my first principle of this second set of implications I want to suggest that Christian parents and teachers should have as their goal for Christian nurture both Christian commitment and normal autonomy, where the latter goal is understood in terms of encouraging children or students eventually to make an 'independent' choice for or against Christian commitment.

Although it is inappropriate to talk of indoctrination at the initial initiation stage of a child's education, I believe it is still possible to talk of an indoctrinative intent. Christian parents must be careful not only to aim for Christian commitment. They must also aim for normal autonomy. It needs to be stressed that I am only talking about *normal* autonomy and hence the quotation marks around 'independent' in the previous paragraph. Complete independence is impossible. McLaughlin describes this dual requirement well when he states that Christian parents 'may well hope that their child's eventual autonomy will be exercised in favour of faith; but...this must remain a hope rather than a requirement'.[57] I believe that Christian parents and teachers sometimes fail to have this dual goal, and when they do they should be charged with indoctrination.

Growth Towards Normal Rational Autonomy

Not only should Christian parents and teachers have as their goal both Christian commitment and normal autonomy but they should actively be promoting growth towards both goals. Although their children and students are brought up within a context of Christian commitment, they will be taught and nurtured towards an eventual 'independent' choice for or against Christian commitment. How can this be done? Many liberals share a view recently stated by Callan, that in such areas as religion and politics parents should discourage their children from making any firm commitments until they are capable of doing so in an informed and mature manner.[58] While I am in partial agreement with Callan, this approach fails to satisfy the child's need for security within a primary culture. Further, children are by their very nature committed, although their commitment is obviously child-like. Instead, as McLaughlin has argued, 'the child should be encouraged to make — or brought up to have — an initial commitment'.[59] At the same time, the child should be reminded repeatedly that there will come a time when he or she will need to make an adult decision with regard to this early child-like commitment.

One application of this principle comes to mind here. I would suggest that this principle calls into question the continuing practice of infant baptism in many Christian churches. As Laura and Leahy point out, this practice fails to recognize that ultimately commitment is a matter of adult decision-making and that children need to mature towards normal rational autonomy before they make any *firm* commitments.[60] Parents who try to make decisions for their children and who do not actively encourage growth towards adult affirmation (or rejection) of child-like commitments are indoctrinating. Insofar as Callan is saying this, I agree with him.

Christian Nurture and Cognitive Growth

Here it also needs to be stressed that Christian parents and teachers should actively promote cognitive growth of the child within the Christian tradition. Such nurture within the Christian tradition is seen as an essential part of growing towards normal rationality. This suggestion is meant to counter the tendency on the part of many liberal educators to describe growth towards rational autonomy primarily in negative terms, in terms of independent questioning or critical thinking about the primary culture into which children have been nurtured. But surely there can also be positive cognitive growth with respect to children's understanding of the Christian tradition within which they have been raised. Such growth should also involve the development of higher level cognitive skills with regard to their Christian beliefs, skills such as analysis and synthesis. The failure to foster growth towards higher-level cognitive development should again be condemned as indoctrinatory.

Cognitive v Affective

Christian nurture should further seek a balance between the cognitive dimensions of religious development and the affective/dispositional dimensions of such development. Given a holistic view of human nature, it is important that religious development be seen as multi-dimensional. Unfortunately, all too often, Christian nurture is understood primarily in terms of affective/dispositional development, without due regard for the cognitive dimension. This principle needs to be stressed in light of the anti-intellectual forces that are often found within the Christian church.[61]

Doubt and Questioning

There is another principle which should govern Christian nurture. It should attempt both to foster growth in a rational grounding of Christian convictions, and to foster honest and serious grappling with doubt, questions and objections to Christian convictions. Unfortunately in evangelical circles doubt of any kind is all too often viewed with suspicion, and questioning is frequently discouraged. One specific example comes to mind. Various studies have shown that the Accelerated Christian Education (ACE) curriculum, which is used in many evangelical schools, is oriented towards information recall and discourages discussion and questioning.[62] I would suggest that ACE materials are weak in fostering growth towards normal rational autonomy and hence schools using these materials should be charged with a degree of indoctrination.

If we shift our focus from children to post-secondary Christian education, we find another occasional violation of the above principle. Christian parents sometimes criticize Christian colleges for allowing too much by way of honest grappling with doubts, questions, and objections to the Christian faith. Such criticism stems from an inadequate understanding of the nature of liberal education. Further, it is in conflict with biblical principles that stress the need for growth towards normal rational autonomy. Christian colleges should strenuously resist the 'hot-house' mentality which justly deserves to be labelled as indoctrinatory.

Broadening Horizons

Christian nurture, in addition to the ongoing nurture of the child within the Christian tradition, should also open a child's horizons to alternative religious/philosophical belief-systems in ways appropriate to the level of development of the child. Initially the child in a Christian home will be nurtured only into the Christian tradition. As the need for a stable and coherent primary culture diminishes, the child will gradually be exposed to other religious/philosophical traditions. This would entail that Christian schools should include the phenomenological approach to religious education as an essential part of their curriculum. This again becomes particularly important for post-secondary levels of Christian education.

Closely related to the above point is the imperative that Christian schools should offer a broad curriculum, initiating students into all the traditional forms of knowledge, thus satisfying the breadth requirement traditionally associated with the ideal of liberal education. One writer, in a recent essay attempting to show that the Puritans of the sixteenth and seventeenth centuries advocated general education, goes on to lament the narrowness of much Christian education today.[63] As examples he cites a graduate of a prestigious Bible College who recently maintained under cross-examination that he had never heard of John Milton. The writer further suggests that there are Christian schools where reading in English courses consists solely of missionary biographies. Such narrowness justly deserves to be condemned as indoctrination.

Here it should be noted that the imperative that the curriculum in Christian schools should include initiation into all the forms of knowledge should not be thought of as precluding the interpretation of these forms of knowledge as a revelation of God's truth.[64] For the Christian, all truth is God's truth and needs to be taught as such. Students should of course also be exposed to alternative interpretations of these forms of knowledge.

Security v Growth

Finally, Christian nurture should seek to maintain an appropriate balance between the individual's psychological need for stability and coherence, and the educational requirement for growth towards normal rational autonomy. This principle is well illustrated by Ursula King who reminds us of the example of Ghandi, 'who spoke of opening the windows of his own house to the winds from the outside world without being swept off his feet'. She continues:

Every individual needs to be deeply rooted in his or her own tradition but also has to learn to grow upwards and outwards like the many branches of a large tree.[65]

NOTES

1. Antony Flew, 'Indoctrination and Religion', in I. A. Snook (ed), *Concepts of Indoctrination*, London: Routledge & Kegan Paul, 1972, p 114.

2. R. G. Woods and R. St. C. Barrow, *An Introduction to Philosophy of Education*, London: Methuen, 1975, pp 65ff.

3. Alan Peshkin, *God's Choice: The Total World of a Fundamentalist Christian School*, Chicago and London: University of Chicago Press, 1986, p 284.

4. Eamonn Callan, 'McLaughlin on Parental Rights', *Journal of Philosophy of Education*, Vol. 19, No. 1, 1985, p 117.

5. Harry Fernhout, 'Education versus Indoctrination: Religious Education in Ontario's Public Schools', in T. Malcolm and H. Fernhout, *Education and the Public Purpose*, Toronto: Curriculum Development Centre, 1979, p 20.

6. Canadian Civil Liberties Association *et al.* v Ontario (Minister of Education) and Board of Education of Elgin County, Ontario Court of Appeal, 1990. No. 18, 70.

7. R. H. Gatchel, 'The Evolution of the Concept', in I. A. Snook (ed), *Concepts of Indoctrination*, London: Routledge & Kegan Paul, 1972, p 9.

8. For two important works on indoctrination within the analytic tradition, see I. A. Snook (ed), *Concepts of Indoctrination* and I. A. Snook, *Indoctrination and Education*, London: Routledge & Kegan Paul, 1972.

9. R. S. Peters, *Ethics and Education*, London: George Allen & Unwin, 1966, p 41.

10. Flew, in Snook (ed), *op. cit.*, p 114.

11. Antony Flew, 'Indoctrination and Doctrines', in Snook (ed), *op. cit.*, pp 70f; cf his 'Indoctrination and Religion', in *ibid.*, pp 112f.

12. Tasos Kazepides, 'Indoctrination, Doctrines and the Foundations of Rationality', in Barbara Arnstine and Donald Arnstine (eds), *Philosophy of Education 1987: Proceedings of the Forty-Third Annual Meeting of the Philosophy of Education Society*, Normal, Illinois: Philosophy of Education Society, 1987, pp 234, 230; cf Flew, 'Indoctrination and Religion', pp 106-116.

13. Kazipedes, *op. cit.*, p 229. Woods and Barrow also make a similar claim: 'The very nature of scientific activity precludes the possibility of indoctrination in science' (*op. cit.*, p 72).

14. Peshkin, *op. cit.*, p 284.

15. Kazipedes, *op. cit.*, p 233.

16. Snook, *Indoctrination and Education*, p 22.

17. Snook, *Indoctrination and Education*, p 47.

18. T. H. McLaughlin, 'Parental Rights and the Religious Upbringing of Children', *Journal of Philosophy of Education*, Vol. 18, No. 1, 1984, pp 75-83; J. P. White, 'Indoctrination without Doctrines', in Snook (ed), *op. cit.*, pp 119f.

19. William Hare, *Open-Mindedness and Education*, Kingston and Montreal: McGill-Queen's University Press, 1979; *In Defense of Open-Mindedness*, Kingston and Montreal: McGill-Queen's University Press, 1985.

20. Hare, *Open-Mindedness and Education*, pp x, 8; *In Defense of Open-Mindedness*, p 21.

21. See, eg, J. M. Halstead, *The Case for Muslim Voluntary Aided Schools: Some Philosophical Reflections*, Cambridge: The Islamic Academy, 1986, ch 5; John Hull, *Studies in Religion and Education*, Lewes: Falmer Press, 1984, ch 18.

22. Francis Dunlop, 'Indoctrination as Morally Undesirable Teaching', *Education for Teaching*, Vol. 100, 1976, p 39.

23. Ralph C. Page, 'Some Requirements for a Theory of Indoctrination', unpublished dissertation, University of Illinois at Urbana-Champaign, 1980.

24. Page, *op. cit.*, p 35.

25. *ibid.*, p 37.

26. See, eg, N. Wolterstorff, *Reason Within the Bounds of Religion*, Grand Rapids: Eerdmans, 1976.

27. R. F. Dearden, 'Autonomy as an Educational Ideal', in S. C. Brown (ed), *Philosophers Discuss Education*, London: Macmillan, 1975, p 6.

28. Lawrence Haworth, *Autonomy: An Essay in Philosophical Psychology and Ethics*, New Haven and London: Yale University Press, 1986.

29. H. Brenton and D. Hare, *Pravda: A Fleet Street Comedy*, London and New York: Methuen, 1985.

30. Mary Douglas, *How Institutions Think*, Syracuse, New York: Syracuse University Press, 1986.

31. Del Ratzsch, *Philosophy of Science: The Natural Sciences in Christian Perspective*, Downers Grove, Illinois: InterVarsity Press, 1986.

32. Michael Polyani, *Science, Faith and Society*, Chicago and London: University of Chicago Press, 1946/64.

33. Polyani, *op. cit.*, p 47.

34. Malcolm Muggeridge, *Jesus: The Man Who Lives*, London: Fontana/Collins, 1975, p 25.

35. R. S. Peters, *Education and the Education of Teachers*, London: Routledge & Kegan Paul, 1977, p 120.

36. John White, *The Aims of Education Restated*, London: Routledge & Kegan Paul, 1982, ch 2; R. T. Allen, 'Metaphysics in the Philosophy of Education', *Journal of Philosophy of Education*, Vol. 23, No. 2, 1989, pp 171-183.

37. B. A. Cooper, 'Peters' Concept of Education', *Educational Philosophy and Theory*, Vol. 5, 1973, p 61.

38. R. T. Allen, 'Rational Autonomy: The Destruction of Freedom', *Journal of Philosophy of Education*, Vol. 16, No. 2, 1982, p 205.

39. Haworth, *op. cit.*, ch 2.

40. Page, *op. cit.*, pp 37, 141.

41. Peters, *Ethics and Education*, p 25.

42. Alasdair McIntyre, *Whose Justice? Which Rationality?*, Notre Dame, Ind.: University of Notre Dame Press, 1988.

43. C. Bailey, *Beyond the Present and the Particular: A Theory of Liberal Education*, London: Routledge & Kegan Paul, 1984.

44. Paul Hirst, *Moral Education in a Secular Society*, London: Hodder & Stoughton, 1974, ch 5.

45. See Elmer J. Thiessen, 'Two Concepts or Two Phases of Liberal Education', *Journal of Philosophy of Education*, Vol. 21, No. 2, 1987, pp 223-234; 'R. S. Peters on Liberal Education', *Interchange*, Vol. 20, No. 4, 1985, pp 1-8.

46. Bruce Ackerman, *Social Justice in the Liberal State*, New Haven: Yale University Press, 1980, ch 5.

47. Interestingly this kind of description of indoctrination was introduced very early in the discussions about the concept of indoctrination by analytic philosophers of education. See R. M. Hare, 'Adolescents into Adults', in T. H. B. Hollins (ed), *Aims in Education: The Philosophic Approach*, Manchester: Manchester University Press, 1964, pp 47-70.

48. Leland Ryken, 'Puritan Piety and the Liberated Mind', *Christianity Today*, No. 7, 1980, pp 26-29.

49. A. S. Dale, *The Outline of Sanity: A Life of G. K. Chesterton*, Grand Rapids, Michigan: Eerdmans, 1982, p 103.

50. P. W. Gooch, *Partial Knowledge: Philosophical Studies in Paul*, Notre Dame, Ind.: University of Notre Dame Press, 1987.

51. O. Guinness, *In Two Minds: The Dilemma of Doubt and How to Resolve It*, Downers

Grove, Illinois: InterVarsity Press, 1976, p 253; see also John R. W. Stott, *Your Mind Matters: The Place of the Mind in the Christian Life*, Downers Grove, Illinois: InterVarsity Press, 1972.

52. R. M. Weaver, *Ideas Have Consequences*, Chicago: University of Chicago Press, 1948/71.

53. For a bold and unique defence of parental rights in education, based on the child's need for a stable and coherent primary culture, see McLaughlin, *op. cit.*.

54. Peter L. Berger and T. Luckmann, *The Social Construction of Reality: A Treatise on the Sociology of Knowledge*, New York: Doubleday, 1966/67, p 23.

55. Peter Berger, *A Rumour of Angels: Modern Society and the Rediscovery of the Supernatural*, Harmondsworth: Penguin, 1969, p 22.

56. M. Oakeshott, 'Education: The Engagement and its Frustration', in R. F. Dearden, P. H. Hirst and R. S. Peters (eds), *Education and the Development of Reason*, London: Routledge & Kegan Paul, 1972, pp 19-49.

57. McLaughlin, *op. cit.*, p 79.

58. Callan, *op. cit.*, p 111.

59. T. H. McLaughlin, 'Religion, Upbringing and Liberal Values: a rejoinder to Eamonn Callan', *Journal of Philosophy of Education*, Vol. 19, No. 1, 1985, p 120.

60. R. S. Laura and M. Leahy, 'Religious Upbringing and Rational Autonomy', *Journal of Philosophy of Education*, Vol. 23, No. 2, 1989, p 259.

61. See Richard Hofstadter, *Anti-Intellectualism in American Life*, New York: Knopf, 1963, chs 3-5.

62. Susan D. Rose, *Keeping Them Out of the Hands of Satan: Evangelical Schooling in America*, New York and London: Routledge, 1988; Harro Van Brummelen, *Curriculum Implementation in Three Christian Schools*, Grand Rapids, Michigan: A Calvin College Monograph, 1989; Alberta Education, *An Audit of Selected Private School Programs*, Edmonton: Alberta Education, 1985.

63. Ryken, *op. cit.*, p 29.

64. See Elmer J. Thiessen, 'A Defence of a Distinctively Christian Curriculum', *Religious Education*, Vol. 80, No. 1, 1985, pp 37-50.

65. Ursula King, 'A Response to Howard W. Marratt', in M. C. Felderhof (ed), *Religious Education in a Pluralistic Society*, London: Hodder & Stoughton, 1985, p 97.

6

Can Christianity Avoid Enculturation?

W. S. F. PICKERING

INTRODUCTION

I was struck a little while ago by a bland statement made by Reginald Bibby, a Canadian sociologist. Writing about religion at the present time in his country, he stated: 'culture leads: religion follows' (1987, p 233). Whether this is a true statement of the situation in Canada is not an issue for the moment. What is important is that he contrasts the two entities, religion and culture and offers a very simple, perhaps too simple, relationship between the two. Another example occurs in a recent book by Adrian Hastings. He wrote: 'It is, quite obviously, necessary for Christian thinking to change in response to cultural change' (1990, p 234). Other writers sometimes speak of the failure of modern Christianity insofar as it represents an outmoded culture.[1]

The point I wish to make, from these and other examples, is that both academically-inclined thinkers and those concerned with pastoral and evangelistic affairs do in fact differentiate culture from religion. And the differentiation is easy to make today in a pluralistic society and where a bare tenth of the adult population can be found in church on a Sunday. But the assumption about separating religion from culture raises a number of questions. For example, can a rigid line of demarcation be made between them? Is there only a one-way relationship, and does not religion influence culture? Can culture affect the basic tenets of a religion? Is culture a unitary concept? What sub-cultures dominate society and does one modify religion more than another? How should a religion come to terms with a culture? Does preaching the gospel fail because it is presented in the wrong cultural vehicle? Can there be a cultureless Christianity?

The questions are endless and because they are particularly important at any time, but above all today, it is necessary to try to start at the beginning and to wrestle with fundamental issues. Unless they are tackled the more practical questions are valueless. One such basic approach is the theme of this paper — an approach some may well think naive. But a start has to be made somewhere. The search for some kind of model is called for.

THE NATURE OF RELIGION AND CULTURE

Not necessarily all religions, but the vast majority of them, contain a component which relates to an order of existence beyond the present: beyond the here-and-now, the ordinary, the material. Such an order is associated with a god, gods, spirits, life after death, and so on. This component can be called the transcendental element of religion. But it could just as readily be referred to as the unchangeable content of a religion or its core-structure.[2] Whatever the unchangeable element is, it is protected and non-negotiable.

Every religion also has within itself a non-transcendental, 'material' component, for the simple reason that a religion uses objects and may involve people as vehicles of the transcendental component. There is no religion which is purely transcendental or without a material association with, or expression of the transcendental. Ritual, as a cultural element, is one of the more obvious ways in which the transcendental is seen to be at work in the action of human beings. And language is an even more fundamental vehicle of religious communication: without it religion could not exist.

The cultural element of a religion is seen clearly in the symbolism a religion uses, not only in its ritual but in the architecture of the buildings with which it is associated, in the dress of the religious leaders, in the music used in worship, in the way people assemble, are organized, and so on. These components of an institutional religion have through the course of history been influenced by local cultures of many kinds.

Religion is part of culture and, as in the case of a preliterate society, very frequently the dominant part. Culture is defined here in the way that Malinowski defined it as 'the body of material appliances, types of social grouping, customs, beliefs and moral values' of a given society (1936, p 482). What is of immediate concern is the place and nature of the cultural element within a religion. In a preliterate society the material and transcendental elements can be labelled as cultural, that is they are both part of the culture and may be unique to that culture.

Those elements within a religion which involve objects, learned behaviour, and the agency of people are of the culture of the society. There is thus a close association, if not identity, between the culture of the society and its religion. Furthermore, the transcendental element is very much bound up with the society and remains identified with it. One clear example of this is Hinduism, rooted as it is in the Indian subcontinent. The transcendental element of Hinduism is irrevocably rooted in Hindu society. For anthropologists the transcendental element is part of culture since it is man-made. The separation of the transcendental or non-cultural from the cultural is of value only for analytical purposes for the theologian or missionary.

The problem of the relation between the transcendental and the cultural elements within specific religions becomes complex in those religions which claim to transcend culture. Such religions are Christianity and Islam (and to a lesser extent Buddhism). Their ideology is based on notions of universalism. The transcendental component, including of course concepts of God and salvation, is usually held by leaders and adherents to be without cultural mediation. It is for all times and for all people, for all societies and all cultures. But the same problem over the dichotomy of the cultural and the non-cultural can occur in a religion without universal aspirations, for example that which confronts Jews or Hindus living in European countries.

Christianity — and we concentrate entirely on that — has been established in most countries around the world and in innumerable local cultures. Wherever it is located there will be found within it what we have called the transcendental element and a cultural element. As Shorter says 'the Christian faith cannot exist except in a cultural form' (1988, p 12). But this raises a number of logical problems. On the one hand it assumes that somewhere there exists a transcendental or unchangeable element — 'the Christian faith' — which is devoid of all cultural variation, that is it is a-cultural or supra-cultural. This is in accord with what we have just suggested, but at the same time it is assumed that the core-structure *cannot* appear in society without some form of cultural manifestation. How then can the transcendental, universal be known in itself, a-culturally? For the moment we do not wish to pursue this ambiguity, other than to say that at least theoretically there exists some unchangeable idea of what Christianity is — some concept of transcultural truth which is expressed in verbal statements which can be rationally communicated, although the relation of the statements may not be unambiguous.

Some argue, for example certain theologians and church historians, that such an analysis pertains only in an ideal situation, based on
such assumptions as have been mentioned here. In practice the two
components, one fixed and one variable, have never operated in this
way. The transcendental element has not been the same in every
society and the same over time, even within one church. In empirical
terms the transcendental element may in the process of time become
subject to modification from the influence of a surrounding culture.
But it must be recognized that whilst both elements change, the
transcendental component changes extremely slowly at an irregular
snail's pace compared with the theologically less important cultural
element, which can be subject to an almost jet-pace change, as in the
case of reforms proposed by Vatican II (see below).

The idea that the unchangeable is said to change can be viewed
from another angle. In differentiating the transcendental from the
cultural, disagreement can be found amongst theologians about the
precise contents of the transcendental. This gives rise to contested or
grey areas over which theologians are divided. Some put them within
the transcendental; others in the cultural. Such areas relate to the
ordination of women, to the necessity of using bread and wine in the
eucharist, to belief in the physical resurrection of Christ, and so on.

In order to clear up any confusion we use the notion of culture in
two dimensions. First, the culture of a local society seen in its entirety;
and secondly, the cultural element of any concrete social form of
Christianity (or any religion) where it is differentiated from the
transcendental element and where it is a reflection of the culture of
the society from which it has come.

THE TRANSCENDENTAL ELEMENT: IS IT ALTERABLE?

We need to explore in more detail the problems surrounding the
transcendental component of a world religion such as Christianity.
We have referred to it as the transcendental element because it relates
to an order of reality not of this world. It is transcendental insofar as
it transcends culture or claims to transcend it. It exists within culture
and in a sense it cannot be independent of it. It is therefore both
immanent within, and transcendent beyond, culture.

In Christianity the transcendental element can be expressed more
specifically. According to various traditions, as we have said, it is
referred to as 'The Faith', 'The Gospel', 'The Word of God', 'The

Truth', 'The Creed', 'The Deposit of Faith', 'The hierarchy of truths' (this, now to be held by all Catholics, appeared at Vatican II), and so on. Whatever name it is given it has a prior, objective existence outside the individual. It is invested with an authority — that of the whole church (if such a universal institution exists), or of a particular church; or it relates to the *ipsissima verba* of Christ. All these concepts have associated with them a sense of divine authority. No matter the term, it denotes something which is permanent, something which is not subject to change and which is eternal. This characteristic is strengthened by the fact that the transcendental element is protected by the notion of heresy, which means holding doctrines contrary to that element. Further, in a society where Christianity is allied to the state, the element is often protected by laws against blasphemy and heresy.

These preliminary observations about the transcendental may be seen to be either an ideal approach or a simplistic one. Either way, it inevitably gives rise to a number of problems.

The first is whether in practice the unchanging element is as static as it has been made out to be, or whether it is open to development. The notion of a developing doctrine, even a developing or progressive understanding of the faith, is rejected by fundamentalists of various kinds, who point to the unchanging gospel or the Deposit of Faith which does not change. It does not change because it cannot, by definition. Any 'apparent' historical changes are held to be due to false interpretation.

The notion of development was common amongst liberal Protestant theologians of the nineteenth century. In a more or less radical form it has also found its way into the Roman Catholic Church. Newman was one such exponent: other Catholics were more radical and of a slightly later time, people such as Tyrell and Loisy. But many developmentalists and fundamentalists agree at least on one point, namely, that there does exist a knowable transcendental core which is eternal. Both Protestant and Catholic fundamentalists stop there; developmentalists go a stage further, not that they necessarily claim to add to or alter the core, but they offer further interpretations and reformulations of it. The reformulation, however, may with the passage of time become part of the core itself. As we have just noted, such a danger is often seen by fundamentalists who are wary of any attempt at reformulation or reinterpretation of the core. For them it may mean a watering down of the transcendental element, or the emergence of an unwarrantable addition to it. The problem with a developmental theology is to differentiate clearly the permanent element from that which can be developed or reformulated. In the end the decision to reformulate or develop, or to accept reformulations and developments, must rest with some authoritative body. The doctrine of Papal Infallibility has been held to be a legitimate development of Catholic doctrine. To the more conservative minded it was not so much a development as a denial or unwarrantable accretion of the universal and eternal core.

The other question relates not so much to that which divides theologians, but to that which is concerned with sociological issues. The transcendental element is itself not free from cultural encapsulation and, moreover, may be subject to cultural modification. The gospel, a church's doctrine, doctrine enshrined in the creeds, all these are derived from situations rooted in specific cultures. The alleged eternal truths were formulated at a particular time and in a particular society: they were not given to Christians cultureless. The culture may have been national or ethnic. The gospel proclaimed by Jesus was based on particular religious ideas which were essentially Jewish, and belonged to a given period of time. Similarly the creeds were not a product of one nation or ethnic group but were formulated within a wider cultural base — a Romano-Greek culture of a particular period. So what is handed down is not something that is timeless and cultureless, be it the gospel or the creeds, but is itself the product of a culture, raised in the case of the gospel to the level of the eternal. Expressed in theological terms reminiscent of Kierkegaard this is the scandal of Christianity which can be seen to be in part a reflection of the scandal of the Incarnation — that a person was born at a particular time and in a particular culture and becomes a universal and eternalized saviour. The status of the creeds is somewhat more complex, and is not considered here other than to say that many church leaders would hold them to be 'well nigh eternal'.

Some theologians would deny the existence of an 'eternal' or unchangeable core, certainly of an essence, within Christianity or a particular church (see the controversy on this point in Dummett, 1987 and subsequent issues of *New Blackfriars*). Our position is not to accept or reject the opinions of particular theologians concerning the true nature of Christianity but to take a position of how the majority within Christianity or a church sees the issue of the changing and unchanging elements of their religion — as it has been viewed down the centuries. Within any given church there exists a constitution, a creed, a statement of fundamental beliefs, the Bible, the *magisterium*. It is true that these can be reinterpreted and have been at different times, but at least all interpretation acknowledges something prior to it — some starting-point, which remains constant over a given period of time. If all is flux there can be no stable component. For it to exist there must be a constant thread and for Christians that thread is seen to be unchangeable.

One might, however, concede a point. To those who hold that there is no unchangeable element, we would suggest that there are two levels of change: one which is extremely slow — what we have called the transcendental, and another which is seen to be less important and which can change relatively easily and over shorter periods of time — the cultural. It must be admitted that the first element is protected in a way which the second is not. A church at the official level often is of the opinion that certain elements can be changed, liturgies for example, but they would not dream of changing particular sentences of the creed, which the church has held to for centuries. Vatican II changed a great deal, but its architects held that the *magisterium* was not changed.

SYMBOLISM

A crucial issue within the transcendental-cultural tension is that of the place of symbols in a religious system. Symbols stand at the centre of religion: they are necessary in order to express the transcendental or spiritual. Some anthropologists see religion *simply* as a system of symbols. The question to which we should address ourselves is whether the symbol, which is basically a cultural element, is also part of the transcendental element.

A symbol or symbolic system is embedded in or stems from a culture. It involves objects, representations, art forms, and so on. As such, symbols are related to a particular culture or family of cultures. They are socially created. What is interesting about symbols is that although they have been created at a particular period of time, they are often 'semi-timeless' insofar as they have been employed over long periods of time and their historical origin is frequently unknown. The cross, which is so much at the heart of Christianity, is as powerful a symbol for Christians today as it was 2,000 years ago. As a religious symbol it emerged shortly after Christianity came into existence. Such a symbol, along with others, has become sacred. To violate it is to threaten the very heart of a believer's faith.

Some symbols are contained within the universal component of religion and to negate or to alter them would of necessity bring about changes in the universal element. The cross cannot be eliminated, for it is part of the gospel. To substitute a circle for a cross would be an act of blasphemy in the symbolic system of Christianity. Of course it might be argued that the cross was an historical fact and that the fact cannot be abrogated. Symbols of the cross are not the reality but indicators of the reality. Symbols can be disregarded or forgotten and in a logical sense the cross can be replaced by the circle, provided the circle is held to symbolize the cross. But this involves complications within the logic of symbolism.

There are, however, certain symbols which are not contained within the transcendental, which are often held to represent Christianity or some vital part of it. Take, for example, the fish. This is clearly a man-concocted symbol which is a convenient means of communication, indicating Christianity or some aspect of Christianity. But there is nothing 'eternal' about the symbol and it can be conveniently forgotten. Some alternative can replace it to signify the same thing, though of necessity with subtle differences. All symbols are unique in their ramifications.

This would imply that there are two categories of symbol. The first is one where the symbols are held to be intrinsic to the gospel. The second contains symbols which are not as sacred as those in the first category and which are not eternal. But can the line between the two categories be readily drawn so as to produce universal agreement? Hardly so. A symbol which has been open to considerable debate is that of the bread and wine in the eucharist. Can these symbolic substances be changed? Clearly under extreme circumstances other substances can be and have been used, as in the case of Christians celebrating the eucharist in prison-camps. But what if the Christian society is one where bread and wine are not derived from the natural habitat or are not part of a common diet? In such circumstances do these substances have to be imported for Christians to celebrate the eucharist? If they have to be imported, then clearly here is a case of cultural captivity of the rite and an affirmation of the fact that the symbols are a part of the transcendental element. Such symbols are alien to the local culture and their meanings have to be learned in the context of the incoming religion. Another example that has become crucial for the future of Anglicanism is that of the ordination of women. Here the issue is whether priesthood for men only is to be seen as part of the transcendental component, or whether it is nothing more than a reflection of the geneal patterns of social thinking at the time when the priesthood was initiated. If it is of the former, traditionalists are quite right in rejecting the ordination of women. If it is of the latter, then those who advocate such ordinations correctly see that new social attitudes towards women should be incorporated into the 'official' ministry.[3]

CULTURE CHANGE ENGINEERED OR ACCIDENTAL?
THE CASE OF MISSIONARIES

The way in which the cultural element of religion is formed is highly complex. Sometimes cultural change is deliberately engineered by church leaders. Sometimes it is forced on a population by a military invasion. Sometimes it just grows like Topsy; it infiltrates a church by subtle means, by the growth of science, by changes in philosophical ideas, by values conveyed by the mass media. It is almost impossible to make generalizations. Every case has to be examined on its own merits (many examples are worked out in Dillistone, 1973).

Often the ways by which the churches absorb and deal with culture is more clearly seen in 'simpler', recent situations, as in the development of Christianity in colonial Africa and other (similar) areas, than in societies which have been Christianized a long time. Thus those who have seen the contrast between Christianity and culture the clearest have been missionaries. Facing them, by way of an almost insurmountable obstacle, has been an alien culture. For them there is initially no difficulty in making the differentiation between the gospel which they have come to preach and the man-made culture they encounter which is seemingly so distant from it. To make the gospel penetrate into the culture is their, at times impossible, task. They are forced to analyse and appraise the culture, and frequently include parts of it within the missionizing church.

In examining missionary work, as well as studying the missionary 'conscience', interest is centred on the missionary situation which is the province of the historian and anthropologist, whose prime concerns are far from those of the missionary or local church leader. One example may help. What the missionary often does not realize is that he carries within himself not one but at least two cultures. The first, more obvious one, is the culture with which he is identified — the culture he has learnt in the society in which his socialization occurred, and is usually bound up with a nation. The second culture is that of the message — the gospel — which the missionary is proclaiming. We assume it is based on the New Testament. But the Bible and the written gospels are culturally skewed, for they come out of a Jewish culture and can only be understood in terms of that culture. Further, it can be argued that the interpretation of the gospel which the preacher himself uses is itself derived from a particular, modern hermeneutic of the old Jewish culture. Thus the local listener is bombarded with ideas from not just one, but several alien cultures.

SOME BRIEF AND UNEXPLORED QUESTIONS

(1) If all Christianity is culturally encapsulated, then:
   (a) There is no such thing as an a-cultural Christianity which exists in some pure form.
   (b) If not, then there is no transcultural transcendental element.
   (c) All forms of Christianity are relative, since all are culturally skewed. To overcome relativity a particular church selects one culture, one period of time and assumes that this is the relatively 'pure', 'cultureless' form, eg the early church.
   (d) The universalism (or transcultural form) claimed by the Roman Catholic Church is false because of its western cultural encapsulation.
(2) Culture indeed 'leads' Christianity in the West where in most countries it has assumed sectarian status and no longer 'leads' in a secular society.
(3) In the United States, where Christianity is more strongly held by individuals, an overall material/technological culture pervades.
(4) There is no such thing as a 'Christian culture', though there is a Christian morality.
(5) Are Orthodox churches amongst the most inculturated of churches, embedded in national, ethnic and local cultures?
(6) Do churches follow, consciously or unconsciously, a particular sub-culture?
(7) The first missionaries who went overseas took their European culture with them. They could not do otherwise.

NOTES

1. Recently there were these words in the *Tablet* (28 October 1989, p 1251): 'Catholics [and we might say Christians] all over the world, including western countries, feel strangers in their own Church because its ideology, pastoral structure,

mode of worship and model of life no longer match the cultural identities of the people.... No one who visits Catholic Africa can fail to notice the shrill, glaring, scandalous absence of cultural identity. Lethargic congregations in Italian-style buildings sing to English tunes, listen to sermons laced with western notions and worship God through symbols imported from Europe.' 'The mismatch between belief and culture in the West', the writer continues, 'may be less apparent to us' but it is clearly there. There is the same imbalance between what is found in our churches culturally and the culture found outside them. The basis of the argument that the churches of all denominations today are ineffectual, rests on the acknowledgement of the mismatch. Is it really the case that the mismatch is inevitable? That the churches from their very nature contain a cultural element which can never be of the contemporary age? That even if the cultural element in the churches did approximate to that outside them, the churches would not be any more effective?

2. We have referred briefly to that element of religion which in the eyes of its adherents is unchangeable, everlasting, and which in a direct or indirect way relates to an order of reality beyond the present. This order of reality cannot be modified by human beings, since it stands above and beyond them. The problem is to find a satisfactory term to conceptualize the phenomenon.

One might be tempted to call it the 'sacred' element of religion, but the content of the sacred undergoes change in the course of time and some religious believers might hold that the sacred is created by humans and is an amalgam of the unchangeable and the cultural. This is distinct from the unchangeable element itself. Not only is the term sacred too broad for our purposes, though clearly it has possibilities, but the academic treatment of the term may confuse the intention of finding a simple, neutral word.

The adjectives 'everlasting' or 'eternal' in conjunction with the substantive component might be acceptable, and in many ways they are. They denote the idea of unchangeability but they also have strong theological connotations within particular religious traditions and on those grounds alone are to be rejected.

Also to be rejected is the term 'essence', with the corollary that the cultural element constitutes its accidents. This has a particular philosophical connotation especially within a Christian context of scholastic philosophy. The intention here is to avoid metaphysical connotations and find a neutral, non-contentious term.

The word 'transcendental' clearly has its dangers in connection with that element of religion which is held to be unchangeable. The chief danger is that in the eyes of many Christian theologians and philosophers the word can only be applied to God. We could accept the fact that this is a common implication of the word. The word transcendental has many meanings and it seems wrong to suggest that it can have relevance only with regard to God. Overall, transcendental seems to fit best the phenomenon which we are describing. One meaning of the word is clearly that which is beyond the grasp of reason and cannot be changed by humans. The term, of course, is man-made but it is used to cover the status of that which is totally other and which is very close to the idea of the divine. Indeed the word 'divine' can be taken in this context as an equivalent of transcendental, and may be used for it. What is important is to see how adherents of a religion treat that element which is beyond modification by human beings. Within Christianity, the Truth, the gospel, salvation, the magisterium, the creeds are, as we have suggested, transcendentally viewed. They contain ideas that extend beyond human existence, and are basically unmodifiable by human processes. The contents so conceptualized are inviolable. For to violate or change them is by definition an impossibility. If in fact they are even slightly changed some kind of backtracking or double-think is required. That does not alter the fact that they can be interpreted in different ways at different times in history and indeed that is what has happened.

3. See *New Blackfriars*, May 1989, pp 210-1. For a study of symbolism in Christianity see Dillistone, 1955 and 1973.

REFERENCES

Bibby, R. W. (1987), *Fragmented Gods: The Poverty and Potential of Religion in Canada,* Toronto: Irwin.

Dillistone, F. W. (1955), *Christianity and Symbolism,* London: Collins.

Dillistone, F. W. (1973), *Traditional Symbols and the Contemporary World,* London: Epworth.

Dummett, M. (1987), 'A remarkable consensus', *New Blackfriars,* October 1987, pp 424-436.

Malinowski, B. (1936), 'Native education and culture contact', *International Review of Missions,* Vol. 25, pp 480-515.

Shorter, A. (1988), *Toward a Theology of Inculturation,* London: Chapman.

7

Theology or Social Science?
The Theoretical Basis for
Christian Education

DAVID HEYWOOD

Christian education is in the throes of a crisis of identity. One collection of articles on the discipline and methods of Christian education is entitled, *Who are We?*.[1] Seymour and Miller's book, *Contemporary Approaches to Christian Education*, lists five separate approaches, each with contrasting understandings of scope, aims and methods.[2] Underlying these differences of approach is a single basic question. Christian education is a religious undertaking, and as such needs to be informed by theology. Christian education is a form of education, which has its own body of theory, in which the social sciences play a major role. In Christian education, the practices of education and theology meet. Yet what is to be the relationship between them? Is Christian education simply a particular variety of education, or is it a branch of practical or pastoral theology? Which is to be the dominant or foundational 'macrotheory' for Christian education, theology or the social sciences?

Not all writers, of course, accept the issue in these terms, as a question of dominance. For Thomas Groome, for example, the relationship between theology and his praxis methodology is one of dialogue, a 'two-way street' which 'holds *theoria* and praxis in a dialectical unity'.[3] James Fowler takes the concept of faith, giving it a particular theological significance as a 'human universal', and then attempts to understand it from a social and psychological point of view.[4] The one unites the two disciplines in the context of a particular method, the other through a particular concept of religious education's aim. Others, however, accept the issue as an either/or and come down on one side or the other. It is to a resolution of this dichotomy that this paper is addressed.

On one side of the debate are those for whom Christian education is primarily a theological discipline, those for whom it is theology which, in the words of Randolph Crump Miller, provides the 'clue' to Christian education. In the book of that title, published in 1950, he wrote:

> the centre of the curriculum is a two-fold relationship between God and the learner. The curriculum is both God centred and experience-centred. Theology must be prior to the curriculum! Theology is 'truth-about-God-in-relation-to-man'.[5]

Thirty years later, concluding a chapter on educational philosophy, Miller wrote that since 'Christian education deals with the data of common experience':

> the problem is to work out some coherent unity for our belief system. Thus, Christian education comes back to theology for its primary content and its organising principle.[6]

Miller maintains the priority of theology even for an experience-centred approach because, in his view, it is theology which interprets experience. Theology supplies the 'primary content' of Christian education, a unified belief-system. Theology supplies an understanding of the learner, as a person in a particular relationship with God. That relationship is the presupposition for Christian education.[7] Theology provides a definitive understanding of the context for Christian education, as part of the church's pastoral ministry. And finally, theology judges the methods of Christian education. In the words of John Westerhoff, 'our theological presuppositions provide the screen for understanding both theory and practice'.[8]

On the other hand a number of writers look to educational theory for their basic models in Christian education, and criticize this theological approach. Leon McKenzie, for example, begins *The Religious Education of Adults* with an attack on the 'conventional wisdom' of the 'theological' school.[9] Perhaps the most outspoken of these authors is James Michael Lee, whose trilogy outlining his 'macrotheory' of 'Religious Instruction' has the sub-title *A Social Science Approach*.[10] Against the theological approach, Lee and McKenzie bring a number of substantial criticisms. First, in Lee's words, 'Religion is learned according to the way the learner learns and not after the manner of its own existence'.[11] In other words the religious teacher must start where the learner is: must take full account of the learner's past experience and existing understanding of religion or the religious life before attempting to add to that understanding. This entails choosing areas of content not according to the way they cohere in a given theology, or by the way they occur in the biblical narrative, but according to the needs and capacity of the learner. The neglect of this principle leads to a concept of Christian education as the transmission of authoritative content, and the characterization of the learner as an empty vessel for whom Christian education will consist of the passive reception of a theologically defined belief-system. 'In too many places', writes McKenzie,

> teaching is apprised as authoritative telling; learning is equated with listening and accepting. The faith-process becomes the receiving of a cultural hand-me-down and not the wrestling with Jacob's angel that leads to authentic commitment.[12]

On the other hand acceptance of the principle that learning involves the active participation of the learner commits the teacher to the attempt to understand the way the learner learns. This is an area of investigation which lies outside the field of theology and within the purview of the social sciences. There is no theological theory of educational method, just as there is no theological theory of farming or child-care. These are areas of common human understanding in which the means of prediction and evaluation are empirical.

The second substantial criticism of the theological approach and foundation of the alternative, social science, approach is related to the first. This is the view that it is religion and not theology which is the authentic content of Christian education. As an active participant in the learning process, the learner encounters the content of the religious education lesson at the point of his or her lived experience, and the result is to be seen as a change in orientation or behaviour, a change in his or her way of life. The outcome is not simply a new understanding but a new attitude. The content, then, must be more than a theory. It must be, in Lee's word, a 'lifestyle'. Religion, he maintains, differs from theology in that while theology relates only to the cognitive sphere, religion embraces a person's whole life. The authentic aim of 'religious instruction' (the facilitation of religious learning) is the production of a lifestyle. The content of religious instruction is therefore not theology, but religion.

Lee goes further than this. He maintains that there is an 'ontic difference' between theology and religion. Theology is a way of knowing rather than a way of living. As a way of knowing, it is tentative and liable to error. Christianity, however, consists not in theology but in a way of living. It is, therefore, religion and not theology which is the norm for Christianity. 'Religion lived in good conscience is never tentative and never in personal error.'[13] Lee proposes that religious instruction acts as a 'mediator'. This is a 'new ontic reality' which subsumes two components previously existing separately and autonomously, incorporating and retaining the essential features of these original components. Religious instruction is a mediator of religion and instruction. Religion is its substantive content, instruction its structural content; the religious instruction act fuses these existentially in such a way that they become united in a new reality.[14] Theology's role is, therefore, largely external to the religious instruction act. It forms part of the cognitive aspect of substantive content. It proposes norms which religious instruction is free to take up and to utilize 'in whatever way is helpful'.[15] Theology enters religious instruction only 'insofar as theology is logically related to and existentially bonded to religion according to religion's manner of existence in the religious instruction act itself'.[16]

These, then, are the extreme positions on the relation of theology and Christian education over against social science in Christian education. But even the literature of the respective positions indicates that neither is satisfactory. Take, for example, the way the theological side deals with educational techniques. In one of the essays collected in *The Theory of Christian Education Practice*, Miller asserts: 'The techniques will pretty much take care of themselves once we grasp the fundamental theological significance of what we are doing'. But in the following chapter he gives a sympathetic account of educational philosophy, and concludes: 'Christian education in most ways is like secular education'.[17] In the discussion which follows on the role of the Bible in Christian education, Miller is heavily dependent on the psychology of development in deciding whether and how the Bible can be taught to young children.[18] Westerhoff, despite his assertion that theology is the theoretical basis for Christian education, builds his own strategy around the concept of enculturation, which is drawn from the social sciences.[19] Despite his disapproval of 'schooling' on account of its secularity, examples of educational techniques abound in Westerhoff's work.[20] On the other side, the 'social science approach' itself requires a theological underpinning. In particular it requires a theology of immanence, a vigorous assertion that God works in and through his creation and not simply in a supernatural way, by what Lee calls 'proximate zaps' of the Holy Spirit.[21] Both positions are inadequate. Thus in writings on both sides of the debate, genuine insights and valid criticisms jostle together with oversimplification and inaccuracy. Some resolution of the dichotomy is clearly required.

THE STRUCTURE OF SCIENCE

Up to now the argument for the relative merits of the 'theological' approach and the 'social science' approach has centred around a contrast between the relation of theology to education on the one hand and the relation between social science and education on the other, with the question at issue being which discipline has the most valid claim to dictate the norms for education in a religious context. It is intended in what follows to leave the practice of education out of account for the time being, and to enquire directly into the relationship between theology and the social sciences. This is something not often attempted, but it will become clear that this approach holds the key to the resolution of the problem in Christian education. The point of re-entry to the educational debate will be that over which the two approaches divide, the understanding of the learner.

The progress of science has two complementary aspects. These are the discovery of new facts and the clarification of concepts. In the course of scientific progress these two aspects go hand in hand. The discovery of a set of new facts calls forth an explanation of these facts by means of concepts. The elaboration of new ideas stimulates the search for new facts. There remains, however, a danger that the scientist, and indeed the casual observer of science, may fall into one of two opposing errors. The philosopher of science Stephen Toulmin calls these the Baconian error and the Cartesian error, after the seventeenth century scientist Francis Bacon and the philosopher René Descartes.[22] The first proceeds from the obvious fact that there can be no science without phenomena, to the conclusion that the 'proper' way of doing science — the essence of research — is continual discovery, the collection of new facts. The opposite error begins with the premise that science requires concepts to explain its discoveries, and concludes that what the scientist is really doing is working out the implications of a few basic logical principles — or what Descartes called 'clear and distinct ideas' — a process more akin to philosophy than to science. An interesting example of this error was the physicist Eddington's claim that the theory of relativity was, in fact, independent of observation, and could have been deduced from first principles — a claim which was only made *after* relativity had been discovered.

Behind both these oversimplifications lies a single basic error, the error of positivism. This is the belief that we have access to the facts simply by observation. Of course, this theory concedes, our powers of observation are greatly enhanced by various technological aids. Astronomical telescopes, microscopes, X-rays and so on, all help us to see better. In the social sciences, techniques of research and experiment design make us more accurate in our observation, but the assumption is that all that is needed in order to do science is first to observe the facts and then to explain them. This assumption, however, is a grave error. We do not see first and then think; first observe and then explain. What we see is conditioned by what we think. We need concepts *before* we can observe. Like the infant, the scientist is an initiate into a new world. Much of his or her training consists in learning to see what other scientists see. This requires taking for granted not only the technology behind the various aids to observation, but also the conceptual frameworks within which observations are to be interpreted. A doctor looking at an X-ray, a physicist looking into a cloud chamber, or a social scientist analysing the data from a set of questionnaires, all 'see' more than the lay observer because of the conceptual frameworks of explanation which they have learned as a result of their training.

All data is thus, in the words of N. R. Hanson, 'theory-laden'.[23] There are no neutral, independently observable facts waiting for a theory to explain them. It is the theory which decides how experimental observations are to be interpreted and what significance is to be granted to apparent 'anomalies', observations that are difficult to interpret within the given theoretical framework. It is the theory which suggests which of the possible research problems is likely to be most fruitful, the theory which influences the design of the research and the theory which tends to control the way the results are interpreted.[24] There is no neutral standpoint from which all the facts appear, 'value-free', no privileged level of observation 'uncontaminated' by a given theoretical framework. To accept a given fact as *significant* involves the acceptance of a whole framework within which its significance is explained and by which it is related to all the other relevant facts.[25]

Yet science is not generally thought of as a field in which anything goes, in which one person's interpretation is as good as any others. One of the most impressive features about the scientific community is its unity: not only its unity of purpose, but the unity of its interpretation. Scientific data is public, its observations replicable, quantifiable, empirical, 'objective' and, supposedly, 'value-free'. One scientist can request the results of another's experiment for independent analysis. One scientist can build on the other's results; science progresses by taking as certain the results of previous series of experiments, by establishing reliably-tested laws and axioms. Is the philosophers' view of science outlined above to be discounted then, treated either as an error or as having little practical relevance? If our object is to understand the relationship between science (social science in particular) and theology, we cannot afford to ignore the philosophy of the scientific endeavour. Nor is it necessary to do so. The 'objectivity' of science can be readily integrated with the 'value' or 'theory-laden' nature of its observations. This objectivity is achieved within the scientific community by the acceptance by its members of a shared conceptual framework. It is not the case that the dependence of fact upon theory means that one person's theory is as good as any other. Science is essentially the enterprise of a community, which defines itself by the acceptance of a 'paradigm' or common theoretical framework.

The term 'paradigm' is taken from the work of Thomas S. Kuhn. His major work, *The Structure of Scientific Revolutions*, first published in 1962, caused considerable controversy, but its implications not only for science but for philosophy in general have been far-reaching. Kuhn's initial statement, including his definition of 'paradigm', has been modified and developed in the course of discussion. A volume of collected papers, *The Essential Tension*, published in 1977, gives a more subtle and considered version of his theory than the earlier statement. In this modified form, it has been increasingly accepted by scientists and philosophers of science. One of the features of Kuhn's theory is that it is an attempt to describe what scientists *actually* do, rather than what they *should* do. This means that, like Wittgenstein's philosophy, it 'leaves everything as it is'. In practice, Kuhn points out, the conceptual framework of a given branch of science is simply taken for granted. Scientists get on with their work without actually reflecting philosophically on its paradigm.[26]

It is the shared paradigm that specifies the precise meaning of all the terms which fall within it. For scientists who share the paradigm, then, every term and every observation has a definable public, quantifiable, 'objective' meaning. When Einstein proposed his theory of relativity, part of what he was proposing was that many of the most important terms in physics, such as force, mass and velocity, should be understood in a different way. For this theory to be accepted, it had to cease to be simply Einstein's theory and become the generally accepted 'language' of physicists. Acceptance of a scientific paradigm is a more thoroughgoing and methodologically demanding example of what we all do all the time in order to communicate with one another. No one can be a Humpty Dumpty, for whom words mean whatever he wants them to mean. We all share a common framework of agreement about meaning, a framework within which we understand one another.

The effect of this understanding of science is to rule out the old style positivist or inductivist understanding of the relation between fact and theory. There is no pure observation, no value-free facts from which theories are built up simply by a process of induction. Something must always be taken for granted, usually a considerable amount. Agreement within a scientific paradigm is agreement about what can be taken for granted. The investigation of a scientific theory, according to Sir Karl Popper, always terminates at a collective decision to accept some basic statement as a valid description of reality. These basic statements, which depend on scientific consensus, are like 'piles driven into a swamp'. They do not reach the solid bottom of indisputable fact, but are sufficient for the time being to support the structure.[27] The paradigm, or shared conceptual framework, must be 'bracketed' or taken for granted so that the work of empirical investigation can proceed. But if the work of empirical observation is dependent on theoretical frameworks, the work of conceptual analysis is similarly dependent on empirical observations. Science does not proceed by deduction from first principles. Its 'first principle' cannot any more than an empirical observation be taken as an indisputable definition of reality. There is no axiom which can be taken with confidence as the 'rock bottom' from which deduction may begin. Rather, what can be proposed is a 'model': a fundamental statement to be taken as closely analogous to reality, a best possible approximation. The task for the scientist is then to discover, by experiment and analysis, how far the particular model is applicable, and what are its limitations. Such a model or fundamental analogy is what Imre Lakatos calls a 'research programme'. We shall meet some examples of these in the section on social science to follow. Lakatos's idea is that the research programme is capable of suggesting new avenues of research, new problems requiring solution and new potential applications; but that as these avenues are followed up and the theory developed, gradually the programme runs out of steam due to its inherent limitations. Anomalies arise from the empirical research which the programme generates, and eventually the model is replaced by a new and more powerful analogy.[28]

We are now in a position to attempt a preliminary conclusion about the relationship between science and philosophy, as a first step in the attempt to gain an understanding of social science and theology. Science and philosophy are to be understood as interdependent. Science is primarily the work of empirical investigation. It is what takes place *within* a given paradigm or conceptual framework. Philosophy is primarily the work of conceptual analysis. It is what takes place when the theoretical framework is in a process of *revision*. Science and philosophy are not two separate and independent spheres. Their work is related. The scientist works within a conceptual framework, the analysis of which for coherence and logical implication is the work of the philosopher. On the other hand, the logical systems and conceptual frameworks which are the subject of philosophy cannot be isolated from reality. So long as philosophy is an attempt to describe the conditions which govern our understanding of the world we live in, philosophers must make empirical statements, statements which are open to scientific investigation and possible refutation. Science and philosophy are two complementary and necessarily inter-related aspects of the attempt to understand.

SOCIAL SCIENCE

To turn from the analysis of the natural sciences to that of the social sciences is to introduce additional levels of complication. In the first place, the social scientist is attempting to explain the behaviour not of the natural world, but of people. Unlike the phenomena of the natural world, from electrons right through to animals, people are not simply the passive objects of observation. People can answer back! They have their own frameworks of explanation, their own ways of understanding their own behaviour. There are some extremely influential schools of social science in which people's own explanations for their actions are treated as unimportant. A truly scientific explanation of behaviour, it is thought, requires that we take a detached point of view. In behaviourism, for example, it is axiomatic that any statement about the mind, such as one which includes a concept such as 'thinking', 'expecting', 'desiring' or 'hoping', must be treated as unscientific, since these are explanations which people give for their own actions which are not open to scientific observation. All such statements are to be translated into a 'neutral', 'objective' observation-language.

Assumptions such as these, however, can be shown to depend on the inductivist or positivist ideal of science, which we have already found to be mistaken.[29] They depend on the assumption that it is possible to discover a level of observations, and a language with which to describe such observations, which is 'neutral' or 'value-free' — one which describes the facts and nothing but the facts, and that theory arises simply as a summary statement of those facts without any additional content by way of explanation. A term such as 'thinking' or 'believing' is an explanation which goes beyond the observed facts of behaviour to a supposed underlying cause, which is unobservable. This account of scientific method we have already shown to be untenable. In practice, persons' everyday explanations for what they do cannot be ignored. The explanation of human behaviour is a hermeneutical exercise. It consists not simply of the attempt to test one given framework of explanation, that of the scientist, against observed events; but involves interaction between the scientists' explanation and the various common sense, everyday explanations of the people under observation.

Nor do the complications end here. People's explanations and understandings of their own behaviour typically arise in a given cultural context. They depend on shared frameworks of understanding, which may be implicit in the institutions of a given society. What people actually say and believe about their own individual actions is, therefore, only part of the story. What people are able to say they believe rests on a deeper level: that of what they, in common with most others in their society, simply assume to be true. This basic level of intersubjective agreement, without which society itself could not exist, includes the social scientist. The social scientist is also a member of a society, and the assumptions he or she brings to the study of society themselves arise from the experience of being a member of society.

It is becoming increasingly recognized, among both practitioners and philosophers of social science, that implicit in the theoretical frameworks of social scientists are certain 'images of man'. The 'image of man' is the fundamental analogy or 'research programme' behind any particular school of social science.[30] The 'image' in behaviourism has been called 'man as the sophisticated rat'.[31] In the new and growing field of cognitive science the model is that of man the 'information processor'.[32] In social psychology it is the 'actor'. Like all paradigms these 'images' are models or analogies, which are limited in the extent of their applicability. When pushed too far, they tend to become inappropriate and break down. In cognitive science, for example, the attempt to extend the information processing model to the study of attitudes suffers from the drawback that this model is incapable of dealing with the affective domain. The account of attitudes that it produces tends to be rather one-sidedly cognitive.

Social science, then, differs from the natural sciences in that the social scientist is not simply an external observer. He or she is a member of society, whose assumptions are in dialogue with those of the people under observation. The social scientist brings forward a certain 'image of man' as a framework for interpreting a given society or portion of society. But within that society is an implicit foundation of intersubjective understanding, and this too consists of an 'image of man': in the words of Charles Taylor, a particular definition of 'man, human motivation, the human condition', a particular 'vision of the agent and his society'.[33] Social science, then, differs from natural science in that while in the natural sciences the theoretical framework can be 'bracketed' or taken for granted for the purposes of empirical investigation, in the social sciences certain implicit understandings of the human condition are internal to the investigation, and cannot be ignored without a distortion of the nature of the object. In the social sciences empirical investigation and conceptual analysis cannot be separated. The social scientist is required to do both science and philosophy at the same time, a combination which lies at the heart of a genuine hermeneutical method.

The conclusion of this discussion is that we cannot accept the claim which lies at the heart of the 'social science' approach as advocated by Lee, that social science is 'value-free'. The 'public' nature of the social sciences and the 'objectivity' of its results is dependent upon the acceptance of a given paradigm, and on the relevance of the particular image of human being implicit in the research from which its data result. This paradigm includes a set of beliefs and values — beliefs about the nature of the scientific task, but more important about the nature of the people who are the object of the study. In educational research it is a particular image of the teacher and the learner which implicitly governs the research. This image does not arise simply from the facts. It is part of the paradigm shared by the researcher. If the theologian is to reject a certain school of social science, behaviourism for example, this will not be because it is deemed ethically wrong to treat people as programmable automata or animals. It will be for the more fundamental reason that behaviourism's 'image of man' is incompatible with almost any theologically acceptable belief about the nature and status of human beings. It is not being suggested here that Lee is a behaviourist, or that he is a positivist. The attention to behaviour which he stresses is proper to all branches of social science, and is, in Lee's case, heavily dependent on theological premises, his interpretation of the nature of religion. The inductivist or 'bottom-up' picture of science is one he has learned from the very many social scientists whose writings he has studied. It is a widely shared but unfortunately inadequate account of science.

Far from being 'value-free', social science is conceptually open. Its very nature requires a continuous interaction between empirical research and conceptual analysis. Peter Winch has even suggested that social science is in essence little different from philosophy, and this claim is balanced by that of Berger and Luckman to the effect that philosophy is in fact sociology.[34] Social science, however, must include a large amount of empirical research and observation, for the purpose of which the conceptual framework will be taken for granted. But its conceptual or philosophical side extends much further than the interpretation of results. In the social sciences the adequacy of a number of competing frameworks of investigation must be continually under review.

THE IMAGE OF THE LEARNER

However, if the social science approach is inaccurate in its portrayal of social science and its relation to theology, the same can be said of the theological approach. The same naive inductivism which is a feature of the social science approach can be found in the writings of the theologically-orientated Christian educationalists wherever they turn to the subject of social science. The idea seems to persist that however factual, however empirically grounded the studies of social scientists might be, they are somehow irrelevant to theology; that once the learner is designated a sinner, or a 'person-in-relation-to-God', knowledge of the learner as a member of the human race becomes unimportant. The result is a complete inability to specify the relationship between learning, which is a feature of all human beings, and revelation, which lies at the heart of religious learning. Thus religious learning is separated from everyday learning, and becomes a separate process altogether — in Westerhoff's terms a process of 'conversion' which is unpredictable, not open to investigation.[35] 'Faith', declares Westerhoff, 'cannot be taught'.[36] Miller speaks for a large body of opinion when he writes:

> the process [of Christian growth] cannot be guaranteed by the processes of either education or evangelism or by the relevance of theological concepts. The response...is in the last analysis a personal decision that rests in the mystery of God.[37]

The dogmatic assumption that knowledge of effective methods is powerless in the field of religious learning leads to a denigration of the value of social science, and a lack of concern for its relation to theology.

CONCLUSION

What I have sought to demonstrate in this paper, however, is that every field of study is conceptually linked to each of the others. The natural sciences and philosophy are, by their nature, in dialogue. Empirical research is carried on within a framework of concepts, whose analysis is the province of philosophy. Social science, on the other hand, embraces both sides of the dialogue. It partakes of the nature of both science and philosophy. Its empirical work must be carried on against a background of continuous conceptual analysis and reappraisal, of ongoing dialogue between the scientists' explanations and those of the society in which the research is being carried out. Theology enters the situation as a partner in this continuous dialogue. In relation to social science, its point of entry is anthropology. The fundamental models of the social sciences are certain 'images of man', whose applicability is a subject of both empirical investigation and philosophical discussion. Theology criticizes these images, and brings its own into the conversation, models such as 'man in revolt' or 'man-in-relation-to-God'. Theology contends that these images offer potentially greater explanatory power over a wider range of experience than do those proposed by the social scientist. But theology does not deny the applicability of the images of social science. The idea of people as 'actors' or 'information processors' may be valid within a given sphere, whether social relationships or cognitive functioning. Theology, however, predicts that these images will ultimately fail, reveal their intrinsic limitations, and perhaps be replaced. Behind the images of human life proposed by theology are further areas of understanding dependent on revelation, the nature of God, his actions in history and in Christ. The source for theological anthropology is the wider area of theology as a whole. But the task of applying theological statements about mankind to experience, of selecting and appraising the evidence by which such statements are to be validated, is the task of the social scientist — albeit a theologically-aware social scientist. Perhaps it is because this task has not been recognized that the justification of theological understandings of the human condition tends to be overwhelmingly anecdotal and prescriptive.

If theology and social science meet in a dialogue over their respective images of human life, it is with respect to the image of the learner that the theological and social science approaches come together. The basic difference between the two approaches is that one tends to see the position of the learner from the point of view of theology, the other from the point of view of social science. For Miller, for example, it is the fact that the learner is in relationship with God which guarantees the legitimacy of the theological approach. Theology provides the learner's authentic self-understanding, a sinner in need of reconciliation. Theology defines the dynamic of the 'I-Thou' situation in which the learner is involved. Theology specifies the need for teaching techniques to be relationship-centred.[38] For Lee, on the other hand, it is the learner as learner which is the relevant anthropology for religious instruction, and an understanding of how the learner learns is not to be found within the province of theology. Just because, for a theologian, learning has certain theological presuppositions, this does not make the study of learning a branch of theology any more than farming or child-care, which also have theological presuppositions.[39]

The statement which lies at the heart of the argument, then, is the one quoted earlier, which sums up the justification of the social science approach. 'Religion is learned according to the way the learner learns and not after the manner of its own existence.'[40] But this statement requires more than simply empirical validation if it is to become operative in Christian education. It requires incorporation in a theological understanding of the learner. And this, in fact, is what Lee does. His justification for it does not rest simply on the observation that there is no empirical evidence for the contrary. It rests also on a certain theological understanding of the teaching-learning situation. The statement that religion is learned naturally, the way the learner learns, is dependent on the belief that natural ways of learning are not supernaturally overridden. The requirement that the work of the Holy Spirit and the influence of the faith community become a specifiable environmental influence is based on the belief that the Holy Spirit works within and not outside of the laws of nature. The insistence that religion and not theology is the proper content of religious instruction is a theological statement, and Lee's understanding of theology itself and its relation to religion is an implicit part of an overall theological viewpoint.[41] The 'social science approach' is not independent of theology. On the contrary, it is a particular type of theological approach, based on a theology of immanence.

In this respect, moreover, the social science approach is clearly a more adequate theological statement than much of what lies behind the theological approach. It is more adequate because it includes a well developed conception of God's work in and through the conditions of creation. There is clearly a close relation between the social science criticism of the appeal to the Holy Spirit as variable or 'primary proximate cause' in the process of Christian learning, and Horace Bushnell's protest against the supernaturalism of nineteenth century revivalism which allowed no place for 'the organic powers God has constituted as vehicles of grace'.[42] A theology which ignores creation, which *begins* with the image of people as sinners in need of grace rather than as created human beings sharing a common human nature, is clearly inadequate not simply for Christian education, but as theology. It is a theology which has gone beyond its province in proposing solutions in areas beyond its capacity, proposing them moreover with an ill-grounded authoritarianism — a theology guilty of 'imperialism'.

However, once it is realized that science, and in particular social science, is not isolated but in dialogue with theology, the way is open for the incorporation of both the methods and the insights of social science into an overall theological perspective. The images of human life thrown up by theology become the starting point for empirical research and enter dialogue with the interpretations of secular social scientists. In Christian education the way is opened for the understanding of the learner *as a learner* as well as as a sinner, person-in-relationship, and so on.

The nature of human self-understanding is such that there is no fixed point of certainty from which theorizing can begin. Consequently the relationship between theology and social science can never be finally fixed. It will remain an item of theological and scientific examination. The relationship between theology and education, concludes Sara Little, 'is possible only when theology and education are both viewed as dynamic, not static, processes'.[43] In a similar way D. Campbell Wyckoff, in an article first published in 1967, claims from within the theological approach that 'Christian education as a discipline is an enquiry into teaching and learning as modes and means of response to revelation'. But Wyckoff does not thereby dismiss the various contributory disciplines in the field of education as irrelevant. He recognizes the interdisciplinary nature, not only of education, but of Christian education. 'Religious education', he writes, 'belongs in the context of a total education'.[44] His proposal for a discipline of Christian education involves the practitioner becoming conversant with a number of fields, each with its own sphere of relevance to the task of Christian education.

Whether in the end we espouse the theological approach or the social science approach is not the most important question. The issue of primary importance is whether we have a consistent and workable understanding of the relationship between the two areas. It is not a question of whether theology or social science provides 'the clue' to Christian education. But if theology is to be 'in the background', it is important that questions of method and effectiveness figure in the foreground.

NOTES

1. J. H. Westerhoff (ed), *Who are We?: The Quest for a Religious Education*, Birmingham, Ala.: Religious Education Press, 1978.
2. J. L. Seymour and D. E. Miller (eds), *Contemporary Approaches to Christian Education*, Nashville: Abingdon, 1982.
3. Thomas H. Groome, *Christian Religious Education*, San Francisco: Harper & Row, 1980, p 228.
4. James Fowler, *Stages of Faith*, San Francisco: Harper & Row, 1981.
5. Randolph C. Miller, *The Clue to Christian Education*, New York: Charles Scribner & Sons, 1950, p 5.
6. Randolph C. Miller, *The Theory of Christian Education Practice*, Birmingham, Ala.: Religious Education Press, 1980, p 180.
7. Miller, *Theory*, pp 156-160; Westerhoff, 'Risking an Answer', in *Who are We?*, pp 269f.
8. John H. Westerhoff, 'Christian Education as a Theological Discipline', *SLJT*, Vol. 21, 1978, p 285.
9. L. McKenzie, *The Religious Education of Adults*, Birmingham, Ala.: Religious Education Press, 1982.
10. James Michael Lee, *The Shape of Religious Instruction*, Birmingham, Ala.: Religious Education Press, 1971; *The Flow of Religious Instruction*, Birmingham, Ala.: Religious Education Press, 1973; *The Content of Religious Instruction*, Birmingham, Ala.:

Religious Education Press, 1985.

11. Lee, *The Flow of Religious Instruction*, p 58.

12. McKenzie, *The Religious Education of Adults*, p 11.

13. Lee, *The Content of Religious Instruction*, p 637; see also his 'The Authentic Source of Religious Instruction', in Norma H. Thompson (ed), *Religious Education and Theology*, Birmingham, Ala.: Religious Education Press, 1982, pp 108-110.

14. Lee, 'Authentic Source', pp 166-172; *Flow*, pp 17-18.

15. Lee, 'Authentic Source', p 182.

16. Lee, *Content*, pp 42-43.

17. Miller, *Theory*, pp 160-179.

18. *op. cit.*, pp 202-205.

19. See especially the reading list for chapter 2 in John Westerhoff and Gwen Kennedy Neville, *Generation to Generation*, New York: Pilgrim, 1979.

20. See especially J. H. Westerhoff, *Inner Growth/Outer Change*, New York: Seabury, 1979.

21. Lee, *The Shape of Religious Instruction*, pp 258-297; Lee, 'Authentic Source', pp 192-197. See also Ian P. Knox, *Above or Within?: The Supernatural in Religious Education*, Birmingham, Ala.: Religious Education Press, 1976, pp 80-114.

22. Stephen Toulmin, 'The Concept of "Stages" in Psychological Development', in T. Mischel (ed), *Cognitive Development and Epistemology*, New York: Academic Press, 1971, pp 25f.

23. N. R. Hanson, *Patterns of Discovery*, Cambridge: Cambridge University Press, 1958, pp 1-30.

24. J. Phillips, 'Theory, Practice and Basic Beliefs in Adult Education', *Adult Education*, Vol. 31, 1981, pp 93-106.

25. Ian Barbour, *Issues in Science and Religion*, London: SCM, 1966, pp 139, 146-148; *Myths, Models and Paradigms*, London: SCM, 1974, pp 94-98.

26. T. S. Kuhn, *The Structure of Scientific Revolutions*, Chicago: University of Chicago Press, 1962, second edition 1969; *The Essential Tension*, Chicago: University of Chicago Press, 1977. The use of the term 'paradigm' in this paper, to mean 'shared conceptual framework', is deliberately simplified. For a better account see Kuhn, 'Second Thoughts on Paradigms', in *The Essential Tension*, pp 293-319 and also in F. Suppe, *The Structure of Scientific Theories*, Urbana: University of Illinois Press, 1974.

27. Karl Popper, *The Logic of Scientific Discovery*, London: Hutchinson, 1959, sections 29 and 30, especially pp 110-111.

28. I. Lakatos, 'Falsification and the Methodology of Scientific Research Programmes', in I. Lakatos and A. Musgrave (eds), *Criticism and the Growth of Knowledge*, Cambridge: Cambridge University Press, 1970, pp 116-165; M. Masterman, 'The Nature of a Paradigm', *ibid.*, pp 76-85.

29. C. Taylor, *The Explanation of Behaviour*, London: Routledge and Kegan Paul, 1964.

30. See, for example, A. Bandura, 'Behaviour Theory and the Models of Man', *American Psychologist*, Vol. 29, 1974, pp 859-869; E. Sampson, 'Scientific Paradigms and Social Values', *Journal of Personality and Social Psychology*, Vol. 36, 1978, pp 1332-1343 and 'Cognitive Psychology as Ideology', *American Psychologist*, Vol. 36, 1981, pp 730-743; G. A. Miller: 'Psychology as a Means of Promoting Human Welfare', *American Psychologist*, Vol. 24, 1969, pp 1063-1075; J. Shotter, *Images of Man in Psychological Research*, London: Methuen, 1975.

31. B. Schlenker, *Impression Management*, Monterey, Calif.: Brooks/Cole, 1980, p 9.

32. P. Barber and D. Legge, *Perception and Information*, London: Methuen, 1976.

33. C. Taylor, 'Interpretation and the Sciences of Man', *Review of Metaphysics*, Vol. 25, 1971, reprinted in R. Bechler and A. R. Drengson (eds), *Philosophy of Society*, 1978, pp 182, 193.

34. P. Winch, *The Idea of a Social Science and its Relation to Philosophy*, London: Routledge

& Kegan Paul, 1958; P. Berger and T. Luckmann, *The Social Construction of Reality*, New York: Doubleday, 1966.

35. Westerhoff, *Inner Growth/Outer Change*, pp 20-23.

36. J. H. Westerhoff, *Will Our Children Have Faith?*, New York: Seabury, 1976.

37. Miller, *Theory*, p 162.

38. Miller, *Theory*, pp 156-164.

39. Lee, 'Authentic Source', pp 124-125, in criticism of Miller.

40. Lee, *Flow*, p 58.

41. Lee, 'Authentic Source', pp 128-142.

42. Horace Bushnell, *Christian Nurture*, Grand Rapids, Mich.: Baker Book House, 1979 edition, p 187.

43. S. Little, 'Theology and Religious Education', in M. J. Taylor (ed), *Foundations for Christian Education in an Era of Change*, Nashville: Abingdon, 1976, p 38.

44. D. C. Wyckoff, 'Religious Education as a Discipline', in Westerhoff (ed), *Who are We?*, pp 173, 177.

PART TWO

'At Eye Level':
The Contextualization of
Christian Education

SECTION ONE

The Congregation and Parish

INTRODUCTION

Elizabeth Varley develops the concept of 'shared ministry' in 'Ministry, Mission and the People of God', arguing that models of ministry which emphasize status or suggest a monopoly of ministerial responsibility by the clergy or reflect the hierarchies of the business world are fundamentally flawed. Experiments in lay ministry are desirable on both pragmatic and theological grounds. Nevertheless, such developments raise urgent questions about the relationship between lay and ordained. The second half of the paper identifies some of the practical problems that may arise when shared ministry is taken seriously, while continuing to maintain the rich possibilities inherent in the vision of a whole ministering laity.

In 'Feeling and Form in Worship' Kevin Nichols expounds a view of the liturgy which gives it a central role in ordering the life of feeling. Traditionally the church has been ambivalent about emotions and has seen raw, unstructured feelings as dangerous, even demonic. But while 'eros depends on logos for its regulation' it is equally true that 'logos depends on eros for its life'. In the liturgy, as with the arts in general, private emotions are drawn into a 'strong framework of meaning'. In the subtle interrelatedness of sign, symbol, music and gesture, the mysteries of faith are made present, and feelings are set in a new context and given new bearings. The liturgy thus has the power to draw the flow of our vital feelings into the realities which it celebrates.

Jeff Astley's paper, 'Christian Worship and the Hidden Curriculum of Christian Learning', explores the claim that there exists a set of tacit and informal learning experiences which underlie those educational processes that are more clearly labelled as such. This 'hidden curriculum' has been variously assessed by philosophers of education. Astley reviews some of this discussion and relates his conclusions to the role of the hidden curriculum in Christian education and the life of the churches. Its significance in Christian worship — which is described here as a most potent medium of Christian learning — is then discussed. The importance of empirical study for liturgical reform is stressed.

In 'Human Communion and Christian Communication' Edward Bailey, after beginning with a personal anecdote, works outward into a series of reflections on the position of children in modern society and their role in the 'implicit religion' of a community, outlining *en passant* 'seven ages of childhood'. The archetypal nature of childhood is illustrated in a variety of ways, not least in its capacity to embody power through powerlessness and to evoke, through weakness, what is distinctively personal in others. In a concluding section these insights are directly related to the issues of communion and communication.

In 'Apples of Gold' David Day investigates a neglected area of Christian education, that of proverbial wisdom or aphoristic teaching. He reconsiders the role of the proverb, cliché, slogan or stock formula and by drawing on biblical and contemporary examples attempts to identify their value and function. He concludes that an approach with such interpretive, affiliative and inspirational power ought not to be prematurely dismissed but that aphoristic teaching needs to be balanced by strategies that encourage questioning and testing of the tradition.

In 'How to Win Congregations and Influence Them' Martyn Percy casts a critical eye over the principles upon which the Church Growth Movement is based. Using James Hopewell's narrative genres (Canonic, Empiric, Gnostic, Charismatic) he subjects the language of the movement to a detailed analysis which exposes the essentially manipulative nature of Church Growth rhetoric. Percy argues that the emphasis on mechanistic methods and programmed effectiveness, coupled with a view of the church as a 'sick' body, ultimately distorts the gospel and leads to a flawed and restricted conception of God's relationship with the world.

8

Ministry, Mission and the People of God

ELIZABETH VARLEY

Rabbi Lionel Blue tells a story about the Jewish Day of Atonement, the most solemn and serious fast in the Jewish Year. Waiting for the service to begin, the congregation watched as their venerable rabbi, tears standing in his eyes, went to prostrate himself before the Holy Ark. 'Lord', he begged, 'have mercy on me, for I am only dust and ashes'.

The rabbi rose and took his place to begin the service. Then the cantor, reverently following his rabbi's example, in his turn went to the Holy Ark. Lying prostrate, he made confession: 'Lord, I too seek mercy, for I too am just dust and ashes'.

Rising and returning to his place, the cantor signed that the service could begin. But as the rabbi opened his mouth, the insignificant beadle, head bowed and tears in his eyes, left the synagogue door. Under the moved and astonished gaze of the congregation, he too went to the Holy Ark, prostrated himself and quietly prayed, 'Lord, have mercy on me, a sinner, who am but dust and ashes'.

The rabbi breathed deeply and turned to the cantor. 'Look', he said, 'who presumes to think he is only dust and ashes'.[1]

SERVICE AND STATUS

It is one of the paradoxes of life in the Church Militant that questions of ministry should be so intimately bound up with questions of status. Jesus told his disciples:

> You know that among the pagans their so-called rulers lord it over them, and their great men make their authority felt. This is not to happen among you. No; anyone who wants to become great among you must be your servant, and anyone who wants to be first among you must be slave to all. For the Son of Man

himself did not come to be served but to serve, and to give his
life as a ransom for many.[2]

Within the Christian community all forms of ministry, leadership
included, derive from the same model of self-emptying servanthood.
Yet issues of power and precedence refuse to be excluded.

The tradition of choosing, consecrating and training certain
members of the community to be ministers in a special sense goes back
to the beginnings of Christianity, tracing its pedigree to Jesus's own
calling of the Twelve. It has an honourable root. The service of the
Holy, Almighty and Eternal God is a solemn and serious matter,
deserving of the best God's people can offer. The setting apart of
carefully selected and trained people to devote themselves to ministry
is a sacramental realization of first-fruits: a token and earnest of the
total self-offering of the Christian community to the work of the Holy
Trinity. Care in the selection of those who are to minister is at this level
an appropriate jealousy for the honour of God, and concern that our
sharing in God's work be done as well as is humanly possible.

It is a misunderstanding of the nature of a sacrament, however, to
view it as a substitute for the realities it consummates. Participation in
the eucharist does not excuse us from striving to make our whole life
a sharing in the risen life and continuing work of Christ. The ordained
are not scapegoats, through whom the laity can discharge their whole
ministerial responsibility at no further cost to themselves. Rather, the
ministry of bishops, priests and deacons focuses the whole participation
of God's people in God's mission here on earth. Ordained ministry
therefore partakes of, but does not monopolize the various callings of
the church: to challenge to repentance, to guide and build up the life
of the faithful, to make the good news real to each generation, to heal
and renew; in and over all, to offer worship to the God who creates,
redeems and comes to us.

CHURCH AND BUSINESS

In a paper entitled 'A Church is not a Business', Gillian Stamp drew
attention to the infiltration of Christian understandings of ministry
and authority by a model drawn from business practice, named 'the
executive hierarchy'.[3] In this model: 'The clergy are seen as employ-
ees, bishops become chief executives, and rural deans middle managers, whilst the only role left to the laity is that of customers or clients'.

Stamp characterized this infiltration as one particular manifestation of 'a kind of organisational heresy' whereby a prior holistic conception of the Church of England came to be fragmented into 'separate parts, each of which can be mistaken for the whole'. She argued that this was itself part of a profound re-orientation of institutional self-understanding as the Church of England 'moves from its historic position as a full partner with the State into a new — and as yet ill-defined — role as a national church'.

Traditional understandings of hierarchy, Stamp argued, include an element of subordination: priests are under the authority of the bishop, the clergy have authority over the laity. This element is however qualified by the important parallel principle that each part of the hierarchy is God-given as an expression of the presence of God in the midst of his people, and is thus of equal value as a witness to the beliefs of the whole. On this principle, the worshipping and missioning laity stand as a sign of the presence of God with the whole human population of the parish, not as consumers of a religion handed down from Central Office. The business model demotes the parish priest to a minor functionary, and the parish to a branch office.

Stamp pleaded for 'a firm rejection of the business model' in favour of a model which stressed integration rather than control, seeing the work of the hierarchy within a total context of 'sustaining the life of the whole and...disciplining members for the sake of that life'. Her conception placed the church emphatically in and for the whole human community, rejecting any members-only approach.

SHARED MINISTRY

At a recent Deanery Synod meeting a woman explained how she had come to be involved in making a special effort to fall into friendly conversation with people at the church of which she is a member: 'The vicar does his best, but while he talked to one person the rest were getting away'. The penalty for concentrating all ministry into the hands of a numerically small group of the ordained is simple: a catastrophic loss of potential scope for Christian mission.

Much of the current debate about the place of 'shared ministry' in the life of the Church of England starts from this point. It is argued that the parochial system faces imminent collapse (some would argue that there are areas where it has already collapsed) unless ways can be found of harnessing lay people for the work of ministry. This bringing of lay people into spheres of work traditionally regarded as clergy preserves is an important component of the strategy set out in the Tiller Report.

The first of the two basic ideas on which Tiller bases his strategy is that 'the local Church, as the Body of Christ in a particular place, should be responsible for undertaking the ministry of the Gospel in its own area', and he elaborates numerous possible lines of development for 'shared' and lay ministry.[4] Tiller's preferred strategy, as expounded to the General Synod in February 1984 by the Bishop of Newcastle, calls for a conception of shared ministry which 'will find expression in a style which is collaborative, not competitive; collaborative at every stage — congregation, parish, deanery, diocese — and it will be expressed in the sharing of resources in leadership, in mission, and on an ecumenical basis', emphasizing 'the contribution of every member, lay and ordained'.[5]

The General Synod on the same occasion passed a motion asking dioceses and deaneries to 'consider whether a development of "shared ministry"...involving both corporate leadership in the Church at every level and the recognition of the gifts for ministry of every baptised member of the Church, is the right basis for future strategy'.[6]

Practical experiments in lay ministry going forward at the present time in the Church of England cover a wide spectrum, from small informal local projects using lay people as pastoral visitors to large and complex diocesan training/accreditation schemes. Three very different parochial schemes in the see of York are described by Ronald Metcalfe in *Sharing Christian Ministry*.[7] This flowering of ministries has enormous potential for enriching the life and work of the Church of England, but it is not without problems and risks. In particular, it poses urgent questions about the relationship between lay and ordained ministry.

It would be possible to employ a model of ministry which posited ordination as the implicit goal of all believers. Any Christian wishing to explore a vocation to minister would be encouraged to do so, subject to the limitations of his or her commitment and ability. Those sufficiently able and committed would go forward to ordination; those whose commitment or ability fell short would evolve a less complete ministry suited to their personal position on the scale. I would wish to argue that this model is open to theological criticism; that the vocation to ordained ministry and the vocation to minister as a lay person are different and equally valid, and that to use vocation to the ordained ministry as an index of Christian commitment rests on a misunderstanding of the place of sacramental ordination in the life of the Christian community.

Lay ministry is the enactment of the ministerial responsibility accepted by the Christian at baptism. (It may be remarked in passing that one consequence of this connection of ministry with baptism, if it should become influential in the life of the churches, would be to require serious consideration of the place of the believing child in ministry.) Lay ministry would be characterized by diversity and flexibility. The ministry of each individual would develop from his or her individual capabilities and opportunities interacting with the mission needs encountered; shaped also by the discipline, integrity and sustaining presence of the church. An individual might minister in widely differing ways at differing times in his or her life cycle, would indeed be likely to engage in a range of ministerial activities concurrently. Some branches of lay ministry would be exercised in a formal context of special training and accreditation, others 'soul by soul and silently'. Some would be done purely for the joy of doing the Father's will, others would also be paid in money. There would be lay ministries liturgical, evangelistic, pastoral; also, maybe, lay ministries of administration and oversight. Some would be based closely on the Christian community and the church building; others would be concerned with outreach into the wider world, and 'detached work' with those who might shun any formal contact with the institutional church.

Ordained ministry has much in common with this model of lay ministry. This is hardly surprising, if it be accepted that deacons, priests and bishops remain members of the *laos*, the people of God. The crux of the distinction between clergy and laity is simply the fact of ordination. The ordained have accepted a calling apart, a public identification on the (powerful) level of symbol with the life of the church. They have received whatever of testing, training and preparation the church deems appropriate to their ministry. They have made a lifelong commitment to this ministry, and have received the grace of Holy Orders. They are thus uniquely equipped to embody the nurturing, disciplining and unifying functions of the whole church. This will involve ordained ministers in some special functions, exercised for, with and on behalf of the ministering laity: notably, those actions in which the sacramental authority of the church is expressed. It will also have more general implications, placing the ordained in a relationship of enabling and training, guiding and restraining, and building up the common life of those committed to their care. Clergy who have experienced good sharings of ministry may find that their workload shifts in some respects; but their personal and professional abilities become, if anything, more valued and more fully used.

A model which envisages ministry as the responsibility of the whole people of God has far-reaching implications. It may not look so very different from what already happens, at least under ideal conditions; but it contains a challenge to assumptions deeply embedded in the institutional self-understanding of the churches, especially the Church of England. The axiom that ministry is for the clergy to exercise and the laity to receive is held to, in practice if not in theory, by many clergy and by even more lay people. From this perspective, 'shared ministry' can look like a dastardly plot by the vicar to inveigle others into doing the work he is being paid to do, or a fiendish conspiracy by the diocese to prove that the parish can manage without a vicar. Lay people offering to minister in some capacity without 'going all the way' and seeking ordination can be seen as thrusting themselves forward: 'Look who presumes to think (s)he is only dust and ashes!'.

If the 'passive laity' stereotype is to be overturned, serious questions are posed for all levels of the hierarchy. There are real anxieties to be engaged. If accredited ministries proliferate unchecked and unco-ordinated, there is a risk of confusing the church's basic structural unity. There are ways of understanding accreditation which undermine and de-skill less formal ministries. If training and commissioning a team of lay pastors means that other members of the congregation feel inadequate or unauthorized to continue the informal outreach in which they were already engaged, the total ministry of the local church may in practice be impoverished rather than enriched. 'Lay ministry' could be interpreted as pulling lay people out of Christian engagement with their own piece of the world to concentrate on doing things of an isolatedly churchy nature. Where pioneering projects run ahead of the mind of the whole church, lay people who have undergone demanding courses of training and preparation can find themselves denied the opportunity to minister by a geographical move, or indeed by a change of incumbent.

In considering how to take the concept of shared ministry into the life of the Church of England, serious attention needs to be given to these anxieties. Doubts about the wisdom of involving lay people in ministry are by no means restricted to authoritarian clergy jealous for their own rights. Indeed, an authority/dependency relationship between a priest and his parishioners may owe more to the expectations and wishes of the laity than to those of the priest, and is contributed to if the church hierarchy insists on channelling all relationships with the parish through the incumbent. Challenging the church to new forms of life and growth in obedience to the summons of the Holy Spirit is essential, but needs to be done prayerfully, recognizing the proper respect due to apostolic tradition, and listening very carefully to what the protesters are really saying. Even the bristly 'who do they think they are' response needs hearing. In the best designed of lay ministry schemes there will remain Joe, who is perfectly convinced that he would make an ideal lay elder, and is the only person (with the possible exception of his mother) who thinks so. While it is true that ecclesiastical high horses are beasts to be dreaded and shunned, there remains a proper demand for testing the acceptability to the church, both locally and at large, not only of individuals claiming a personal ministerial vocation but also of proposed new forms of authorized ministry.

The ultimate objective of 'shared ministry' is not to produce a fuzzy penumbra of quasi-clerical minor orders which leaves some lay people accredited and others untouched, but to develop habits of thought and practice which make the mission and worship of the people of God in each place naturally the responsibility of the whole people, both lay and ordained.

PROBLEMS AND POSSIBILITIES

Ways need to be found of ensuring that training, support and acknowledgement for particular forms of lay ministry strengthen and encourage other ministries within the local church, rather than devaluing and discouraging them. It is thus important that new patterns of lay ministry, where these are found appropriate, should be designed with respect for existing lay involvement in the life of the church, whether the formal offices of readers, churchwardens and PCCs, or unaccredited personal forms of Christian service.

There is also an imperative, balancing the responsibility of the hierarchy to exercise proper authority over the life of the whole, for lay ministries to develop in a manner responsive to local needs, local sensitivities and local cultural patterns. The historic ordained ministry of bishops, priests and deacons may be seen as primarily the ministry of the Church Catholic, the sign in each place of the presence of the Triune God and the One Body. Lay ministry is primarily the ministry of the Church Indigenous, the Missioning Church, those charged in each place with finding the right way in word and action to be truly bringers of the good news into that place. To say this is not to deny the role of the clergy in mission, nor the place of the laity in the Body of Christ. It *is*, however, to argue strongly that the degree of centralization and standardization which characterizes contemporary selection and training for ordained ministry would be inappropriate for lay ministry. If ordained ministry may legitimately be seen as a 'called-out' ministry, a setting apart, lay ministry is of its essence ministry in, among, for and by the local people of God, and training and selection for such ministries should reflect this.

A theological understanding which emphasizes the role of the local church as people of God in each place gives a distinctive perspective and urgency to ecumenism. A 'church in and for the place' fragmented into competing denominations is an embarrassment to mission on theological and practical levels; a church characterized by a diversity of tastes, outlooks and strengths which was nevertheless able to find unity in being the one Body of the one Risen Lord would be a priceless asset. We need to find again the means of living as a Great Church; we need our unity back without losing the treasures of the Spirit imparted to the various traditions of Christianity; we need it badly. The quest may be a difficult one, involving the reconciling of different understandings of authority and the healing of long histories of division, but that does not mitigate its urgency.

Shared ministry also has implications of an 'internally ecumenical' kind. It is vital that the calling to minister should extend to the whole people — not just a particular tradition or traditions within the Church of England, and not just the 'educated', the articulate, the confident. Lay ministry schemes need to be designed and operated in ways which make them attractive to Christians who have never previously been encouraged to develop their personal talents and abilities. If in practice they turn out to draw only 'professional people' then they will have fallen short of the vision of a whole ministering laity, and huge areas of potential expertise in mission will remain untapped.

Finally, the development of lay ministry is essentially a matter for prayer. All of our service to God is a participation in the self-offering of our Master, whether liturgically, in the service of worship, or diaconally, in the service of practical love of neighbour. It needs to be constantly nourished, informed, corrected and reinforced by prayer. Some lay ministries might indeed develop as ministries of prayer, particularly when exercised by people who are housebound, hospitalized or otherwise restricted in their opportunities for more physically active forms of service.

Jesus, travelling with his disciples, opened their eyes to the needs of the world and taught them: 'The harvest is rich but the labourers are few, so ask the Lord of the harvest to send labourers to his harvest'.[8] In our own time we feel the force and urgency of our Lord's demand. Shared ministry offers a means of greatly increasing the church's ability to respond.

NOTES

1. Lionel Blue, *Bright Blue*, London: BBC Publications, 1985, pp 52-53.
2. Mk 10:42-45.
3. G. Stamp, 'A Church is not a Business', *Crucible*, journal of the General Synod Board for Social Responsibility, October-December 1983.
4. John Tiller, *A Strategy for the Church's Ministry*, London: CIO, 1983, *passim*.
5. *Report of Proceedings*, General Synod, February Group of Sessions 1984, p 129.
6. *ibid.*, pp 156-157.
7. Ronald Metcalfe, *Sharing Christian Ministry*, London: Mowbrays, 1981, pp 93ff.
8. Mk 9:36-37.

9

Feeling and Form in Worship

KEVIN NICHOLS

The life of feeling has been much scrutinized by philosophers. Their accounts undermine our simple reports 'I am anxious', 'I feel sad' with analyses of great variety. The passions of the soul known immediately and invulnerably through introspection? Mental states known only by behaviour and learnt through belonging to a language community? In medicine too the emotions are a matter of concern. 'Psychosomatic', a word taken with increasing seriousness, bears witness to this. For some the emotions are a reservoir of primitive energy, bubbling blindly into consciousness, channelled only with difficulty by the structures of personal and social life. Others see the emotions as a vapour of the mind, given off by the activity of nerves and muscles. Drugs, not talk, can reach them and set them in order. Yet others think that at the heart of the emotions lie the deepest patterns of human meaning. They are in touch with the consciousness of the race.

Artists deal with the emotions unselfconsciously; not holding them at arm's length but using them as the stock-in-trade of life and work. The Romantics thought that a poet should be like an Aeolian harp, set in a tree, timed to resound when the great winds of feeling blow. The business of the artist, Susanne Langer argues, is to make out of semblance, air or image, a significant form which is an analogue of emotional life. In the mirror of art we recognize our inner selves. The rough particularity of image or story is so set in a form as to speak of, and to, 'not this or that particular man but mankind'.

Emotion plays an important part in religious life though religious believers — especially theologians — are not always ready to admit this fact. Feelings — often caricatured as 'enthusiasm' — feature largely in the pathology of religion but cut a poor figure in the cool orthodoxy of conventional belief and practice. Shakers, Barkers, Holy Rollers,

Hot Gospellers are made to seem the archetypes of religious emotion. The exuberance of their religious practice — heartfelt no doubt, yet anarchic — seemed a poor guide to the complex world of doctrine and practice. 'What must I believe?'; 'How must I act?'. The sweeping away of these questions in a tide of feeling subverted religious order and menaced its social respectability. Yet precisely in undermining the subtle structures of religious tradition, the revivalist meeting created a nostalgia for the simple and the passionate which came to seem a more authentic mode of faith; a certain envy for those who:

> ...sang their Amens
> fiercely, narrow but saved
> in a way that men are not now.[1]

The Protestant Reformation, Nietzsche wrote, was a revolt of the simple against the complex. In the Catholic world a couple of generations ago reason and will were definitive, doctrine and law their instruments. Emotion was suspect — product of raw force, concupiscence, which it was the business of mind and will to subdue. In the seminary the arts were discouraged unless they could be disciplined into safe forms such as church music. They were banished for the same reason that led Plato to drive away the poets — although crowned with bays — from the ideal republic. Their incarnations of power must come from the regions where the dark gods dwell. They could have no place in the city of God, would threaten its battlemented doctrine, undermine its serried laws. There were of course popular devotions of a dramatically emotional kind. But these were conceded rather as the Grand Inquisitor gave bread to those from whose shoulders he had lifted the burdens of thought and freedom. There were of course Catholics who took the arts more seriously. But even they shared the prevailing opinion that the function of the arts was a decorative not a substantive one; as Sydney argued that the honeyed words of poetry served to make palatable the bitter rhubarb of morality. Enthusiasm for the arts, or trust, as Keats put it, in the truth of the imagination, was viewed as the early Cistercians saw the Cluniacs. It exuded a faint but unmistakable aura of corruption. It was an uncomfortable reminder of the courts of Renaissance popes and Josephist emperors.

Over the last twenty years emotion in religion has regained respectability, indeed has exploded into church worship, into pastoral relationships and into spiritual counselling. There are many reasons for this, but also some deep current of change behind it. Leonardo Boff, in his book on St Francis, argues that we are at the end of the age of logos: the instrumental-analytic reason which gave the concept power over the symbol, and the problem dominance over the mystery, and whose familiar daimon is power. We sense the beginning of the age of eros and pathos, of affection and sympathy. He argues (with Pascal) that it is the heart which determines the premises of all possible knowledge and that 'the ultimate structure of life is feeling not only as a movement of the psyche but as an "existential quality", the ontic structuring of the human being'.[2] Words that move in such a cosmic sweep cannot easily be brought to ground by close analysis or argument. For myself I sense a deep truth in them: as one recognizes in the weatherman's prediction, what the farmer sniffs and the sailor feels in his bones.

The rehabilitation of feeling is not without its problems. Its results are not always happy ones. Eros looks to logos for its regulation. Loose feeling without forms or targets is indeed a demonic force. Plato and the church were right to be nervous about it. It is often said of bad poems that 'the plangency is all on the surface'. It is not embodied in the muscles and sinews of imagery and form. So in Christian worship and other aspects of the life of faith, an enthusiasm for spontaneity and openness sometimes releases a lot of emotion which is raw and formless; and this is usually hard to handle and sometimes downright dangerous. My general interest in this essay is to reflect on the place of feeling in the life of Christian faith.

LITURGY

I begin with the liturgy of the church. Like many others in the aftermath of the Second Vatican Council, I had high hopes that the liturgy of the church would be the summit and the fountain of renewal. These hopes have not been altogether realized and I suspect that one reason may be that the relation between structure and feeling in the liturgy is not well understood. Susanne Langer speaks of music as 'a tonal analogue of emotional life'.[3] I would like to see what can be made of the notion of the liturgy as a structure of feeling.

Some might object to this way of approaching the liturgy that it is too analytic. It murders to dissect. Rather than speaking of thought and feeling, better speak of 'experience' as an indivisible fact. 'Experience' — like 'need', another popular word in discussions such as this

— is an ambiguous word, sometimes a mischievous one. It is often a way of avoiding questions, especially epistemological questions, by presenting a self-authenticating *fait accompli*. Its Protean being is often contrasted with the 'bookish' or the 'academic' greatly to the discredit of the latter. The academic shuts himself up in an airless library stuffing his head with Shakespeare or Wittgenstein until his veins silt up and he gets weevils in his brain. The aficionado of experience lives in the fresh air and knows what's what along the pulses and in the guts.

Although I am a little wary of arguments to which the concept of experience is central, I recognize that there are more subtle understandings of the word. Henry James writes of it as:

> an immense sensibility, a kind of huge spider web of the finest silken threads suspended in the chamber of consciousness and catching every airborne particle in its tissue. It is the very atmosphere of the mind.[4]

The relation of feeling and form in the compounding and the vitality of that atmosphere is precisely what I intend to discuss here. Eros depends on logos for its regulation, logos on eros for its life. Neither thought nor feeling is absolute monarch. Each fulfils its proper function in relation to the other.

In this discussion, I have three questions in the forefront of my mind. The first is: in liturgical worship, what is it to mean what we say? The second: what is the relation of feeling to liturgical words and acts? The third: how, if at all, is feeling altered through participation in liturgical rites? Although I do not treat these questions systematically, they provide focal points for the whole discussion and summary of its conclusions.

Let us begin with a funeral. Funerals are said to ritualize grief and present the clearest case in which liturgy is recognized to be psychologically beneficial as well as religiously important. Grief, pain, lostness, and the way in which we deal with these feelings lie at the heart of the liturgy of death. Recently a custom has grown up which, far from ritualizing grief, ignores it to concentrate on other matters. White vestments are worn, cheerful hymns are sung, the liturgy is centred on the resurrection of Christ. This seems to me a mistake, an instance of the deductive fallacy. This is the tendency to allow liturgical renewal to be overwhelmed by theological principles or even fashions, so that its main lines of force derive from religious ideas rather than from the existential reality of faith in the world. Newman complained of the philosopher Locke that he 'consults his own ideas of how the mind should act instead of interrogating human nature as an existing thing as it is found in the world'. Of course there must be a dialogue between theology and liturgy. But we ought to beware of the imperialism of the concept.

Such didacticism has been a particular danger for Roman Catholics since the introduction of the celebration of liturgy in the vernacular. The transition from a dead language to a living one opened up new areas of liturgical communication. It was easy in the early days to slip into identifying this new form of communication with notional understanding. The meaning of the words must be clear, the significance of symbols made plain, metaphors transposed into ideas. In some extreme cases there occurred a gross distortion of the very nature of liturgy; its transformation into a didactic lesson. There is certainly a time and place for the exposition of Christian beliefs about death, judgement and eternal life. A funeral is not such a time, nor such a place. The way in which the rites embody these beliefs is enough.

Ritualizing grief involves three things. First, it makes private grief a public fact, since the liturgy is celebrated by the whole community. Secondly, it sets it in a tradition; liturgy carries the church's tradition — not a baton in a relay but a living, organic growth — steadily and more powerfully than any other idiom. Thirdly, it places grief in a different context of meaning not through didactic expressions or 'words of comfort' but by drawing grief into the more powerful net of symbol and sacrament. And so grief is altered. It is drawn into a new place where it has not lost its sharp edge but has changed its bearings. When we look at it in this way, 'ritualizing' throws some light on the question, 'In liturgy, what is it to mean what we say?'. Private feeling finds a public context. All of us are saddened and sobered by death. The liturgy expresses our common feeling in a faith-filled way. The private grief of the bereaved differs from this common feeling. It is personal and raw. Yet it is connected with the common fund and is drawn into it.

Often we feel hypocritical when we proclaim ourselves filled with joy at the memory of Christ's resurrection or the conviction of our redemption, when in fact we are feeling liverish, worried about money or irritated with the bishop. Such discordant feelings do not invalidate common worship. It is enough to be there, participate, enter into the ritual words and acts. The faithful feelings which motivate us to do that establish us in the common reservoir of felt faith belonging to the church, and our ruffled emotions are reset in a different context and so altered. This is one reason behind Vatican II's requirement of intelligent participation in the liturgy. It is from liturgical worship that the faithful 'derive the true Christian spirit' and this requires that 'their minds be attuned to their voices'. The sense of 'mind' here is not the abstract intellect but the sentient being, eros as well as logos.

THE TARGET OF EMOTION

We can speak then of feelings being re-directed through liturgical acts and so altered in themselves; rather as a different context can change the meaning of an event and so alter the way in which it is experienced or even perceived. The uniformed figure glimpsed through the glass door ceases to inspire nervous anxiety when it is recognized that he is here to read the meter. So by setting feelings in a new context of meaning, by drawing them into a common fund of meaning, liturgical rites are able to alter their bearings. This may become clearer if we consider the connection between feelings and external events or states. Changes in such events or their disappearance or even their reinterpretation can alter feelings in several ways, causing them to evaporate, lessening them, even reversing them. Sometimes this is because the external event which changes is the cause of the feeling. I discover that the buff envelope with a window contains not a tax demand but the butcher's receipt. But the objects of emotions and their causes are not always the same. We might say, 'I was irritated with the children because it was my fiftieth birthday'. Here the children are the unfortunate object but the cause is the sadness of ageing. Rather vague, ill-defined emotions are often focused on an object which is not their cause. Sometimes — as in the above example — this connection is irrational and disordered. But not always. My fear of death may project itself to salt or saturated fats and here there is a real connection.

The word used by Wittgenstein for the object of emotion is 'target'. Sometimes they find the wrong targets, simply by some kind of emotional mistake: 'I was angry with my wife so I kicked the dog'. But sometimes they find targets which are really connected with their cause, and this may be reasonable and beneficial. One function of liturgical acts is to provide targets for feelings which are connected with their cause. The grief of the bereaved is caused by the loss of someone loved. The rites are also about that event. They provide a secondary target for grief but one which is really connected with it; setting it in a context of common faith and in this different perspective, changing its bearings. It is also, I shall argue later, a function of liturgy to move feelings from targets that are genuinely mistaken to those which are true and appropriate.

We sometimes use language which suggests that feeling is a kind of perception. 'I feel the truth of your remark.' But clearly this is loose talk, for feelings do not give us new information about the real world. On the other hand feelings most often do entail some belief. If I am fearful at meeting a lion it is because I hold certain beliefs about the habits of lions. These are probably correct but the beliefs entailed in my fear of mice or spiders or heights are probably mistaken. Yet as we all know, it is sometimes not possible to alter people's feelings by showing that the beliefs involved in them are mistaken. A neurosis is such a feeling, attached to an irrational target and not to be dislodged by concepts or logic.

The emotions central to the life of faith are also sometimes based on mistaken beliefs. We may be in awe of the wrong things such as statues or the music of Tallis or church authorities. We may feel guilty about the wrong things, say the accidental breaking of rules. The power of these mistaken beliefs is not to be broken by reading the Catechism or by a good talking-to or even by the study of theology. For these remedies deal only with notional assents which have no power to move us. Notional assents lead to repose rather than action or struggle; which is why, writes Newman, intellectuals who deal in them are rarely devout. Liturgy, however, has the power to lead our feelings towards different targets.

I have suggested that emotions are sometimes diffused from their cause to other targets which have a real connection with them. Such transfers we call reasonable, or, better, appropriate. A liturgical act, say a sacrament or a funeral, does not have the same organic connection with death or forgiveness that salt or unexploded bombs have with the prospect of death. It is an artificial or constructed target, more like the horrific warning signs we see near army firing ranges. The purpose of these is to translate our feelings into motives for action — we are to avoid this area. Liturgy sometimes does this. It may lead us to conversion, to a different way of life. But its first effect in serving as a target for our feelings is what I have described as giving them new bearings or a new context of meaning. Liturgy does this because of its mediating or transparent quality. It does not gather feelings to itself as to a final end. It works according to Aquinas's principle: the terminus of faith is not the expressible but the real. Sign, symbol, music and gesture make present, in a uniquely powerful way, the mysteries of faith. In this, liturgy is similar to the arts which do not focus our feeling finally on an object, but lead them through it to a participation in experience or the recognition of our own. So the Christian funeral does not ritualize grief as the Lord Mayor's Show ritualizes his status. It actualizes a Christian tradition of faith and feeling into which personal grief is gathered.

PRESENTATIONAL FORM

I have spoken of liturgy ？ ... ... adage, *lex orandi, lex credendi* implies the s? ... ...des of expression, though the prayer' ... ...m that which is composed of conc... ... ... 'diom, I do not mean that liturgy has ... ... language It combines, rather like opera, sever... ... ... each strand ' retains its own characteristic modes ... ... symbol etc. Still, liturgy has its own ... ... 'ch the several strands are subsumed i.. ... ...

To characterize liturgy as a mo... ... ...se of Susanne Langer's distinction betw... ... ... forms. The discursive form is propositi... ... It mo... ... ... of logically linked stages from a premiss o... ... ... solution. Each stage in this movement is ina... ... ... its logical force is established. Once that is don... ... ... oblivion for attention is focused only on the ... ... solution or the conclusion. So, discursive thought n... ... ... as a whole, nor can it do so, for in its movement throug... ... ...ne conclusive movement is significant.

Presentational forms on the other hand do not move in the same way through logical space burning bridges behind them. They are compounded not of concepts and logical links but of semblance, space, symbol and metaphor. The elements are linked in such a way that their interrelatedness in one glance is what constitutes significant form, what makes the form expressive and communicative. This is true even in the case of music where duration in time, the disappearance and reappearance of themes, is of the essence. For musical time is not chronological time. The form is not present to us until the last note is struck.

Liturgy is the presentational form of faith. Its presentational characteristic makes it an effective target for feeling, though an

unsuitable one for analytic thought. It is characterized — as
D. H. Lawrence wrote of the novel — by 'subtle interrelatedness'
rather than logical structure. Lawrence went on:

> Communication can only happen when a whole novel
> communicates itself to me. The Bible — but *all* the Bible —
> and Homer and Shakespeare are the supreme old novels. These
> are all things to all men. Which means that in their wholeness
> they affect the whole man, which is the man himself, beyond
> any part of him. They set the whole tree trembling with a new
> access of life, they do not just stimulate growth in one direction.[5]

Notice that the whole man alive includes intelligence — eros requires
logos for its regulation. But the real source of life is the flow of the vital
feelings, and the liturgy has the power to draw these away from things
which are mistaken or dead towards things which have in them vitality
and truth.

A CONCRETE EXAMPLE

These high-flown ideas seem a long way from yesterday's evensong or
from next Sunday's mass. Let me try to bring them some way to earth
with another example. This is the Rite of Reconciliation. This sacrament is the most individual and private of all. Its substance has
become, over the centuries, the totally secret and detailed acknowledgement of sins guarded by the seal of confession; with a cursory and
rather legalistic absolution. It has thus become totally detached from
liturgical tradition and connected rather with church authority ('the
power of the keys'), problems of conscience and spiritual direction.
     Apart from the oddness of a sacrament being wrenched from its
liturgical setting, there were other causes for unease in this situation.
One was that the classification of sins (mortal and venial, kinds and
categories) led to rather an external, behaviouristic moral outlook
and consequently attached guilt to the wrong targets. The renewal of
this sacrament set out first of all to restore it to its place in the public
worship of the church. Sin is social as well as personal. It occurs in the
Body of Christ. Reconciliation too should occur within the church
community and should be a public act. Also this sacrament is an object
(target) for feelings of guilt.
     Guilt, although it has had a bad press in the literature of religious

psychology, is not in itself a morbid or unhealthy feeling. It is harmful when it is loose in the psyche or attached to irrational or mistaken targets. We feel guilty about our sins; quite rightly so. But, as I have suggested, guilt is often misdirected or short-circuited. Concentration on external acts and their classification leads guilt sometimes to focus on these and to disregard intention and the heart. We feel guilty because we have broken a moral rule, and the rule, the focus of our guilt, becomes a kind of idol, occupying the place which in Christian moral life should belong to God alone. So there grows up a narrow, legalistic moral outlook which fails to break through into the truly religious sphere. The public liturgy of reconciliation — readings, prayers, music, gesture — sets out to lead the flow of our feelings away from a blinkered and legalistic morality into the church's common fund of feeling; and beyond that into the mystery of God's reconciling love and the assurance of forgiveness.

Another way of describing this process is to say that the liturgy leads us to conversion. The word raises hackles; the archetype is what occurs as a result of an evangelistic sermon which is often said to be 'too emotional', or even 'mere emotion'. I think what is implied here is that such a stimulus looses emotions — which may be fear, joy or even self-disgust — without providing targets clear enough or strong enough to channel their force. Edwin Muir in his *Autobiography* describes his two youthful conversions, to evangelical Christianity and to Marxism. Both provided an immediate resolution of emotional tension, but neither lasted long. The liturgy deals with feelings in a gentler, more oblique way. Its subtle interrelatedness, its multi-faceted unity, its doctrinal and institutional strength, enables it to draw and contain feeling in a way which is more sure-footed and offers greater steadiness and permanence. Of course what the liturgy does is deep and complex and so gradual.

Bernard Lonergan writes of conversion that it:

is a change of direction and, indeed, a change for the better. One frees oneself from the unauthentic. One grows in authenticity. Harmful, dangerous, misleading satisfactions are dropped. Fears of discomfort, pain, privation have less power to deflect one from one's course. Values are apprehended where before they were overlooked. Scales of preference shift. Errors, rationalizations, ideologies fall and shatter to leave one open to things as they are and to man as he should be.[6]

Although Lonergan is interested primarily in a comprehensive theory of knowledge, his idea of conversion as invariant in structure though occurring at different levels, illuminates the argument here. Knowledge certainly is involved as 'errors, rationalizations, ideologies fall'. But values are also apprehended, preferences shift, one is liberated from fears, inauthentic life is unmasked. The invariant structure yet the varieties of embodiment offers an image of the multi-faceted unity of the liturgy and of its power. The presentational form of Christian faith, it embodies that faith in many ways. Its 'immense spider web' is subtle and powerful enough to bring the different levels of conversion together.

    This sacrament is an example of how liturgy arises when particular events in our lives are touched by the mystery of grace; the beginning of life, marriage, ministry, the inner collapse of sinfulness, the *tempi forti*, times of power. There is another way in which in the whole stretch of our lives our feelings are drawn and directed by the liturgy. A first case of this is the annual liturgical cycle. In the course of this, it is often said, we live through the Paschal mystery. The word 'mystery' — a truth of such range and scope that it lies beyond exhaustive expression — fits most naturally into liturgy of all the idioms of faith. The liturgy, as Paschal, is not an exposition of the doctrines of Incarnation, Redemption, Sanctification. As a presentational form, renouncing didacticism, liturgy is able to leave aside problems and concepts and has a power to express the mystery itself. Its meaning goes beyond following prayerfully the events of the Lord's historical life. Rather, we can say, it embodies the mystery of God's redeeming grace as this is enfleshed in his life, death and resurrection. Its power lies in the 'subtle interrelatedness' of word, symbol and action which draws us into its movement. We identify. Through following in the footsteps of Christ's earthly life, we are able to work our way into the reality which that life embodies; into the rhythms of incarnate grace moving in history. When we watch *King Lear* we identify with character and action, are attracted, appalled, saddened, puzzled. We also go beyond that, to enter into the truths and values which are there embodied, clash, fail, triumph. 'All truth', wrote Coleridge, 'is a species of Revelation'.[7] In the liturgy, this identification is with the words, actions, failure and triumph of God's Word made flesh, of which indeed all human truth and value is a fragmentary reflection. So the flow of our vital feelings is drawn into the pattern, rhythms and meaning of death and resurrection. As a pedagogy, the task of liturgy is to people the world of imagination and feeling. This I take to be the deepest meaning of the Council's teaching that it is from the liturgy primarily that we derive 'the true Christian spirit'.

CONCLUSION

Each year is a year of grace. God's power made flesh in Jesus, moves through it drawing the ebb and flow of our deep feelings into its own redemptive pattern. Liturgy also has its long cycle. It serves as a target for the whole arc of life, shaping it into that same redemptive pattern. In the liberal West we have grown used to a life with a very low degree of patterning. This is because of our liberal and permissive ideals which lead us to minimize the structuring of life in order to allow the maximum elbow-room for personal choice. In earlier folk societies, structures and demarcations were numerous and clear. The stages of life — birth, adolescence, adulthood, marriage — were clearly marked out; vital social functions such as war and fertility were also solemnized by ceremonies and rules. So everyone knew where they stood even if, 'narrow but saved', no one saw very far. The danger of our way of life — the point has often been made — is the danger of meaninglessness, lostness, anomie. The blurred and crumbling concept of 'lifestyle' cannot bear the weight of our deep feelings. This is why we find that many people — especially the young — are drawn towards authoritarian total systems.

The liturgy is neither authoritarian nor total. It is a strong framework of meaning which encompasses the principal passages and stages of our life and how we move through them. So the beginning, establishment and active independence of life is the existential ground of the sacraments of initiation. Crucial areas of marriage and ministry are sacramentally solemnized. Human decline — failure, suffering, death — is encompassed by sacraments of wide pastoral range and scope. This is especially true in western Catholicism. Here — in opposition to the 'sudden life', initiatory sacraments in Eastern orthodoxy, and the 'adult ideal' of Baptists — sacramental life is marked by stages and gradualness. The sacramental principle encompasses a faith journey, marked, as life is, by different stages and levels. The sacramental pattern contains and engenders a strong sense of purpose, but one which can be renewed and re-created at different levels and in diverse life-situations. Its meaning is not fully revealed until the arc of life is complete; as a symphony is not grasped until the last note is struck.

140   Kevin Nichols

NOTES

1. R. S. Thomas, *Laboratories of the Spirit*, London: Macmillan, 1975, p 31.
2. L. Boff, *St Francis: A Model for Human Liberation*, London: SCM, 1985, p 10.
3. S. K. Langer, *Feeling and Form*, London: Routledge & Kegan Paul, 1953.
4. Henry James, 'The Art of Fiction' (1884), in *Henry James: Selected Literary Criticism*, ed Morris Shapira, Harmondsworth: Penguin, 1968, p 85.
5. D. H. Lawrence, *Phoenix*, London: Heinemann, 1936, p 536.
6. B. Lonergan, *Method in Theology*, London: DLT, 1972, p 52.
7. S. T. Coleridge, 'Letter to Poole', in *The Portable Coleridge*, ed I. A. Richards, New York: Viking Press, p 293.

10

Christian Worship and the Hidden Curriculum of Christian Learning

JEFF ASTLEY

THE HIDDEN CURRICULUM

In educational literature the word 'curriculum' is used to denote a set of experiences from which people learn. The most familiar use of the term is with reference to the learning experiences provided in different subject areas by books, teachers or test-tubes, ie courses of study. This standard use thus refers to a *manifest curriculum*: learning experiences that come explicitly labelled as such, and planned to be such. But many have argued that there also exists, in association with each of these manifest curricula, a *hidden curriculum*. This is a set of learning experiences that are tacit, implicit, informal and (usually) unstructured. The hidden curriculum underlies the manifest curriculum, like that part of an iceberg that is hidden below the waves. We also learn from this set of experiences; but we do not usually recognize their role as learning experiences, for they do not come with any accompanying educational label. It is tempting to call this learning 'unconscious learning', but we must do so warily since many definitions of learning specify that it occurs as a result of conscious experience. By referring to such learning as unconscious we mean only (a) that we are not conscious that we are learning through these experiences, and (b) possibly that those who provide the experiences are unconscious of their effects. This is to be contrasted with the explicit recognition by both learner and teacher of the learning effects of attending a lecture, reading a textbook, or experiencing other examples of the manifest curriculum.

An analogy may be useful here, although it should be stressed that it is only an analogy. I communicate with people in an explicit way through my verbal behaviour. I talk, and so reveal myself in my words.

But as I do so I am also communicating through my non-verbal behaviour of facial expression, posture, gesture, tone of voice, choice of clothes etc. A great deal is revealed about me (note that the verb is in the passive voice) through this non-verbal communication. It is often a revelation of myself 'despite myself'. There is much interesting research that shows that people attend more to these non-verbal messages than they do to the explicit verbal message of a communication. Thus 'superior' messages delivered in an 'inferior' style (tone of voice, accompanying gestures etc) are received as 'inferior' by the listeners, and vice versa.[1] Similarly our body language, for example of nervousness or boredom, can be a more effective communicator than our carefully planned verbal messages, for example of confidence or interest.

The situation is similar with regard to the hidden curriculum. It can often wreck the learning intended by the manifest curriculum. Certainly it is frequently more effective than the intentional, and openly-acknowledged, learning experiences that it accompanies. So there is always a danger that it will work against, rather than reinforce, our explicit educational activities.

John Westerhoff writes of the implications of this situation in Christian education:

> So much of our most significant learning is unconscious. For example, a church whose customs for years have dictated silence in the church prior to its service of worship, the avoidance of personal contact with others in the pews or the sharing of emotion during the service will have difficulty getting its members to engage in a contemporary community celebration. We learn all the time. My conviction is that this hidden curriculum, this unconscious learning, is so important we cannot afford to let it remain unconscious. We need to look at the total learning experience of people and bring as many aspects of it as possible into our conscious, deliberate, systematic, and sustained efforts. That is what it means to make learning education.[2]

CURRICULUM UNMASKED?

Westerhoff is recommending here that we don our wet suits and plunge under the water to examine the hidden curriculum of the Christian learning iceberg. One of the tasks of the educationalist is to make people conscious of the effects of this hidden curriculum, so that the learning can be recognized as such and its sources properly handled. We may, after such an examination, judge it to be good Christian learning. In that case, it may be argued, we should seek to control it better and to plan it as explicit Christian (teacher-facilitated) *education*. But if it is discovered that the hidden curriculum results in learning that is different from, and opposed to, that which is being encouraged in the intentional, manifest Christian curriculum, then the church should surely seek to remedy the situation. We can all think of examples of such negative effects of a hidden curriculum. I can remember being kept in at school to write out the Sermon on the Mount as a punishment for 'ragging' the Scripture teacher: the verse about turning the other cheek did not flow off the pen too well on that occasion. Many readers will be familiar with something similar to this little scene:

'We welcome you to church' proclaims the half-illegible notice on the church notice board which is badly in need of repainting. (The time of the morning service is incorrect anyway.) The sidesman thrusts a prayer book into the hands of the newcomer without further comment. He leaves her to find her own way through the service, as does the minister and her neighbours in the pew — despite her obvious inability to find any text corresponding to the words being spoken.

In this context it just will not do to say that the newcomer has been 'welcomed into the family of the church'. Rather, she has learned the true message of this congregation: 'they do not really care about me'.

Clearly Christian educators need to reflect on the hidden curriculum that underlies *their* more obvious attempts to facilitate Christian learning. Unfortunately it is often as hidden from the teachers as it is from the learners. And, to make matters worse, there is 'a lot of it about'. All the aspects of the church's life provide such learning experiences, and many of them need to be more openly acknowledged and evaluated. All Christians, and all Christian activities, operate as sources of Christian learning whether they intend (or are intentionally designed) to teach us Christianity or not.

Of course this is not just a problem in the church. Every institution and context gives rise to a hidden curriculum from which we learn its implicit values. Educationalists argue that many of our deepest attitudes and values are formed through the hidden curricula of school, home, peer group, work place and club. In the 'de-schooling' debate many have criticized the hidden curriculum of schools as being perniciously sexist, racist, capitalistic, nationalistic and materialistic, often in ways that work against and undercut the intended (or at least trumpeted) values of those schools. Some go further and argue that the existence of compulsory schooling *as such* inevitably produces a hidden curriculum through which children learn conformity, competition (rather than cooperation), consumerism, how to cheat, and — for most children — how to fail. This is the hidden curriculum of schooling:

> Inevitably, this hidden curriculum of schooling adds prejudice and guilt to the discrimination which a society practises against some of its members and compounds the privilege of others with a new title to condescend to the majority. Just as inevitably, this hidden curriculum serves as a ritual of initiation into a growth-oriented consumer society for rich and poor alike.[3]

Much of this is doubtless extreme talk. But it is needed to counterbalance, and perhaps help to erode, the illusion that schools are neutral with regard to such moral, political and social values. They are not, nor could they be, for there is no such thing as a neutral educational process.[4] The answer, however, is not to get rid of the schools. Because all groupings and institutions have their hidden curricula, axing a particular institution does not necessarily get rid of a particular unsavoury tacit learning experience. The answer is rather to bring the hidden curriculum up into our consciousness: to make ourselves aware of it and then, if necessary, to change it.

It is proper to ask first, however, what makes the hidden curriculum 'hidden'? There are three ways of answering such a question:[5]

(a) The phrase 'hidden curriculum' is usually taken to imply that this curriculum is *hidden from the learners*. They are the ones who do not know what is going on: for it has not been openly acknowledged to them that they are being taught to believe a, b, and c, or to be x, y and z. This is learning unrecognized as such by the learners.

(b) But the hidden curriculum may also be *hidden from the teachers* (and the rest of the school/church/institution's administrators and leaders): *they* know not what they do. This may result in 'unintended learning' — the unintended consequences of human actions that are designed to produce learning that *is* intended.[6] An example would be the learning that took place when a clergyman in my hearing once castigated a teenager for attending church with dirty hands, during an introductory session of a confirmation course that waxed eloquent about God's willingness to accept people as they are, and the church as a place for everyone.

(c) There is a third, 'conspiracy theory' of hiddenness. This claims that the hidden curriculum is hidden from the learners because it is *hidden by the teachers* (or the school, or the church, or — generally — 'them'). Here the effects of the hidden curriculum are intended, but the experiences that produce those effects have been deliberately placed below the water-line so that they go unnoticed by the learners. Although analysis (c) may be true of some advertisers and politicians, and is certainly true of subliminal advertising and political brainwashing techniques, it is not very likely as an analysis of most educators in schools or churches. No one has hidden the hidden curriculum. It is just that we cannot see it, unless and until we hunt for it. It is not only hidden from those who receive it, but very frequently also from those who have unintentionally created it: ie both (a) and (b) are usually true.

WHY BOTHER?

But why should we try to search it out? What is wrong with a curriculum being hidden? Such questions will attract both a specific and a general answer. The nature of the specific answer must depend on the specific nature of any given hidden curriculum, and also on our assessment of it from our own (particular) moral, social, political — and religious — standpoint. The questions also require a general answer, however, first with reference to the teachers of the manifest curriculum whose unintended consequences it comprises (the hidden curriculum being often part of the setting or context of the manifest curriculum), and secondly with regard to those who learn from the hidden curriculum.

Teachers and institutions first: it is wrong that this curriculum should be hidden from their eyes because they have a responsibility to know what they are doing. If the hidden curriculum represents unintended consequences of their educational activity, then surely they are morally obliged to search for, and to make themselves aware of, those consequences. This is, in any case, mere prudence; for we know that the hidden curriculum so often works against what its manifest counterpart is striving to achieve. Nicholas Burbules writes:

> By making the latent functions of actions apparent to the agents
> — by revealing the hidden curriculum to educators, for
> example — we enlarge the domain of their responsibility by
> adding to the store of *expectable* consequences of their actions,
> despite the fact that such consequences may still be
> unintended.[7]

But what about the workers? Do the *learners* have a right to know about the existence and nature of these secret educational forces that are influencing them? So far we have uncritically accepted this proposition. It is often argued that it is 'the task of the school to raise the hidden curriculum to the consciousness of the pupils, in order to protect them from its influence'.[8] Such a claim seems to be based on the principle of the autonomy of the learner. It is usually considered right, at a certain stage in the intellectual and moral development of the students, to let learners in school and church take 'responsibility for their own learning', at least in the minimal sense that they become aware of what they are being taught to believe and to be, and can reject such teaching if they wish. Those who prize freedom in education will speak of the need for such awareness; and those who value religious freedom — the freedom to embrace a religious position — often claim that this implies a correlative freedom to reject religion.

A CAUTIONARY NOTE

I would argue, however, that the situation is not as clear-cut as some liberal educationalists would have us believe. One problem revolves around the extent to which we may ever be said to be 'free' with regard to the beliefs and values that we adopt. This is a theme touched on briefly in my 'Growing into Christ' paper in this volume   (see p 310 below). Other points, however, may be raised here.

On the one hand, as young children we are nurtured and moulded for a considerable period of time in ways that lead to our accepting certain values and developing certain attitudes. This happens long before we are able intellectually to reflect on what, or whether, we are learning. On the other hand, there may be certain learning situations where an insistence on an explicit articulation of all learning can only disable it. Examples that might be mentioned here include the learning of the sort of 'tacit knowledge' that Michael Polanyi regarded as so crucial and so widespread. In tacit knowledge we attend from certain things to others, for there are things of which we are focally aware only through our subsidiary awareness of other things. Thus we recognize a natural history specimen or another person's face through a whole host of implicit clues which we cannot name and do not explicitly notice. If we attempt to shift our attention to these proximal terms (the clues) we often find ourselves unable any longer to recognize the distal term (the object). The same thing may be true of our tacit knowledge of motor skills which, if articulated or attended to, will only make us unable to learn how to ride our bikes. Polanyi writes of how an unbridled lucidity:

> can destroy our understanding of complex matters... By concentrating attention on his fingers, a pianist can temporarily paralyse his movement. We can make ourselves lose sight of a pattern or physiognomy by examining its several parts under sufficient magnification.[9]

At another level 'we know more than we can tell' in that it may be the case that the learning of attitudes like affection and trust is not well served by an explicit, focused consciousness of the role of certain experiences in that learning. Here we need, as elsewhere, to balance the value of possessing rational autonomy against the value of possessing other skills and attitudes. Those who stand firmly in the liberal educational tradition often come down too quickly and too decisively in favour of autonomy, arguing that this will not compromise other worthwhile learning outcomes. Liberals in Christian education frequently adopt the same position, referring perhaps to Jesus's *logion* about the need for people to exercise their own judgement.[10] Others, however, are more cautious — and rightly so. They contend that rational autonomy is only one among many elements in the life of the properly educated, and particularly the properly religiously educated, person. 'Unbridled lucidity' is not an unqualified educational virtue, at least not in Christian education.

As is the case with the problem of indoctrination, it is perhaps all a matter of degree. At one end of the degree spectrum we find a situation that most would regard as 'A Bad Thing': where the hidden curriculum remains forever immersed in impenetrably dark water, and children (and sometimes adults) never come to know what is teaching them what. This is the sort of situation that often results in problems in later life, when a person blames herself for certain attitudes that she has unconsciously learned at her parent's — or minister's — knee. Retrospective consciousness of the hidden curriculum of this past learning may then be necessary to remedy the situation. Yet at the opposite end of the spectrum we sometimes come across people who never learn certain skills or attitudes that they wish to learn and need to learn, because they will insist *ad nauseam* on 'knowing what is going on'. They are *too much in control* of their own learning: their control has become a veto, and they are forever uprooting the plants of their own learning to see in which direction their roots are growing. Unfortunately many species cannot stand that much light. A point in the mid-range of this spectrum would seem to be more healthy, and educationally more realistic, than either of the extreme positions.

Before we leave the discussion of the hidden curriculum, we may ask the rather technical question as to whether consciousness of the hidden curriculum does not in fact destroy it. After all that which is made manifest is no longer 'hidden'. This is surely correct. The hidden curriculum, once revealed, remains a part of the curriculum, but it is no longer a hidden part. But this is only true for those who have come to recognize the learning power of these experiences. For the rest we may talk as before of a 'hidden curriculum', distinguishing it from its manifest counterpart. The iceberg remains with its bulk under the water hidden from most of those aboard the ship. It is for their sake that the sailors (at least) have to learn to see what lies below the water-line, for the alternative could be disastrous. Possibly we do not need to make everything equally clear to everybody. I have hinted that there are some who will not be helped by such lucidity. The church as a whole, however, *does* need to know what is going on. And those who are particularly responsible for Christian education within the church particularly need to ensure that they are aware of what is going on. That is their educational duty. It is the duty to do research into the Christian learning of Christian learners. Anything less is irresponsible Christian education.

THE ROLE OF WORSHIP

I shall now attempt to illustrate and earth this account of the role of the hidden curriculum in Christian learning by reference to the activity of Christian worship. Worship is patently a significant element in Christian formation. It has been argued that Christian education, understood broadly, connects in a number of different ways with the worship of the Christian church:

First, catechesis provides the community with a means for initiating persons into its ritual life and for reflecting on the meaning of participation for the life of faithful stewardship. Second, catechesis takes place explicitly within the Service of the Word or the Rite of the Catechumens, that part of the liturgy in which we proclaim and respond to the Word. Third, catechesis takes place implicitly throughout the totality of the liturgy insofar as our symbolic actions in the ritual shape our understandings and ways of life. Because this is true, we must take seriously what we know about learning as we plan the Service of the Word and be more intentional about our ritual actions so that they aid in our formation as stewards of God. Fourth, catechesis aids the community to integrate its cultic life and its daily life.[11]

It is with the third of these relationships between Christian education and worship that we should be particularly concerned in any discussion of the hidden curriculum. In and through the acts — and also, very significantly, the words — of the church's worship, Christians learn ('implicitly') to be Christian. Worship is arguably the most important medium of implicit Christian learning.

I would argue that worship should be viewed as an activity that both *expresses* certain religious attitudes, affections and experiences and also tends to *evoke* them. In their worship Christians express their Christianity. Such expressions serve to reinforce these attitudes and emotions in the worshippers and to evoke them in others, as well as supplying other people with (second- hand) expressions of what it means to be Christian. Both the language and the actions of worship have this sort of effect. In situations of worship, speech-acts and ceremonial are of course focused on God, and one's theology may allow one to think of God as being affected by them in one way or another (being 'pleased' or 'persuaded', 'entering a covenant with us', etc). As Christian educators, however, we may leave the discussion of such 'vertical' effects to the theologians; restricting our discussion rather to the more tangible, 'horizontal' effect of worship on fellow worshippers (and — in a reinforcing way — back onto the worshipper herself).

We should note that the study of these liturgical/catechetical effects requires the investigative exploration of an empirical psychology of religion. We cannot simply rely on an armchair theological or liturgical account of 'the nature of worship'. It seems to the present writer that the difficulty with much liturgical reform is that this empirical work is hardly ever done. Changes are made to the ritual and ceremonial of worship on the basis of *a priori* theological or historical insights into its proper form and content. But worship has an effect, and a very profound effect, on the worshipper. It is through worship that many people primarily learn their Christianity. It is therefore incumbent upon those with a responsibility for the worship of the churches to discover how the liturgy 'works'. By this I mean what the actual effect is — in terms of Christian formation — of these particular words, and of the other components of the hidden curriculum of worship, especially music, actions, symbols and setting. We must recognize that the 'effect' of sacraments and other liturgical symbols is not limited to the non-empirical realm of a metaphysical relationship between God and the worshipper. Sacraments have their more mundane, but perhaps no less significant, psychological effects as well; or they should.

The sociologist David Martin has criticized the symbolic limitations of some examples of modern liturgical reform in ways that are relevant to this discussion:

> Suppose that your reformer wants the people of God to stand in a circle facing each other rather than in rows facing the altar. He intends in this way to show that God is in the centre of human concerns and that we are all joined one to another. He sees the circle as communitarian and democratic whereas a line of worshippers facing east implies authority and externality. But the line facing east may just as well signify open-endedness. A priest with his back to the congregation may signify that both he and they are subject to the divine transcendence and judgement. Equally the circle has symbolic disadvantages: the people of God are all turned inward with their backs to the world. If they are a circle, how can they be *en marche, en route?* They have lost their orientation and the external point of reference to which they may move and to which all things tend. A person pulled into a circle is exposed to the immediate and continuous inquisition of other eyes. His defensible space is overwhelmed... Yet the circle, so widely insisted upon in God's house, is a very deliberate attempt to cut down the space within which an individual may protect himself.[12]

The strengths or weaknesses of criticisms like this can only be assessed on the basis of an empirical study of what, and how, Christians learn in worship. We need to know what is actually being communicated through the hidden curriculum of symbol and ritual.[13] Again, we need some serious research.

Lest I be accused of adopting too subjective and psychological an account of worship, it is necessary to add finally that one should not fear that a proper psychological study of worship would somehow undercut more objective theological claims about that which transcends the worshipper's psychology. Those who wish to claim that the primary purpose of worship is to evoke religious experience need not be alarmed. Their point would be that worship serves to prepare for, allow and evoke experiences of God. It puts people in the place, psychologically and epistemologically, where God can be 'seen' and 'heard'. That would be learning-through-experience with a vengeance. Nothing that is said here should be seen as forbidding such an account of how worship leads to learning. Yet even on this more objective analysis, God is known *through* his symbolic representation in the language of worship. Experience of God is only recognizable as such when it comes mediated through some images of God.[14] So some account still needs to be given of the psychological effect of those images in Christian learning, even if that effect is construed as merely part of a divine-human encounter that transcends it. God indeed moves in mysterious ways, but unless he affects our psychology we shall have no knowledge of his movements — or of his existence.

I have argued in this essay that we learn to be Christian primarily through the psychological effects of worship, and that such learning is properly to be described as mediated through the 'hidden curriculum' of the liturgy. If this argument is accepted, it follows that the worshipping community carries a great responsibility for influencing, for good or ill, the learning of the Christian gospel.[15]

NOTES

1. See M. Argyle, *The Psychology of Interpersonal Behaviour*, Harmondsworth: Penguin, 1983, ch 2.

2. J. H. Westerhoff (ed), *A Colloquy on Christian Education*, Philadelphia: Pilgrim Press, 1972, pp 64f; compare also his *Will our Children have Faith?*, New York: Seabury Press, 1976, pp 16ff and J.W. Berryman, *Godly Play*, New York: HarperCollins, 1991, pp 80ff.

3. I. Illich, *Deschooling Society*, Harmondsworth: Penguin, 1973; San Francisco: Harper & Row, 1971, p 39. See also E. Reimer, *School is Dead*, Harmondsworth: Penguin, 1971, p 15 and *passim*; and the passages from John Holt and others in I. Lister (ed), *Deschooling: A Reader*, Cambridge: Cambridge University Press, 1974.

4. See R. Shaull, 'Foreword' to P. Freire, *Pedagogy of the Oppressed*, Harmondsworth:

Penguin, 1972, pp 13ff.

5. See J. R. Martin, 'What Should we do with a Hidden Curriculum when we find one?', *Curriculum Inquiry*, Vol. 6, No. 2, 1976.

6. Compare D. C. Phillips, 'Why the Hidden Curriculum is Hidden', in C. J. B. Macmillan (ed), *Philosophy of Education 1980*, Normal, Illinois: Philosophy of Education Society, 1981, p 279.

7. N. C. Burbules, 'Who Hides the Hidden Curriculum?', in Macmillan (ed), *op. cit.*, pp 286f.

8. D. Gordon, 'The Immorality of the Hidden Curriculum', *Journal of Moral Education*, Vol. 10, No. 1, 1980, p 3.

9. M. Polanyi, *The Tacit Dimension*, New York: Doubleday, 1967, p 18. On 'tacit knowledge' see also Polanyi's 'The Logic of Tacit Inference', *Philosophy*, Vol. XLI, No. 155, 1966; 'Faith and Reason', *Journal of Religion*, Vol. XLI, No. 4, 1961; 'Knowing and Being', *Mind*, Vol. LXX, No. 280, 1961; and *Personal Knowledge*, London: Routledge & Kegan Paul, 1962, *passim*.

10. Luke 12:57, compare John 7:24. See *Understanding Christian Nurture*, London: British Council of Churches, 1981, 'Introduction'.

11. J. H. Westerhoff, *Building God's People in a Materialistic Society*, New York: Seabury Press, 1983, p 75. See also his *Living the Faith Community*, San Francisco: Harper & Row, 1985, p 96, and J. Astley, 'The Role of Worship in Christian Learning', *Religious Education*, Vol. 79, No. 2, 1984.

12. D. Martin, *The Breaking of the Image*, Oxford: Blackwell, 1980, p 98.

13. Compare M. Douglas, *Natural Symbols*, London: Barrie & Jenkins, 1973, chs 1 and 2.

14. See G. D. Kaufman, *God the Problem*, Cambridge, Mass.: Harvard University Press, 1972, chs 3 and 5; H. P. Owen, *The Christian Knowledge of God*, London: Athlone Press, 1969, ch 8. Cf also J. Astley, 'The Idea of God, the Reality of God, and Religious Education', *Theology*, Vol LXXXIV, No. 698, 1981.

15. For some further discussion of the role of Christian worship in the formation of Christian understanding, values and lifestyle, see also D. W. Hardy and D. F. Ford, *Jubilate: Theology in Praise*, London: Darton Longman & Todd, 1984, p 10; D. M. Martin, 'Learning to Become a Christian', *Religious Education*, Vol. 82, No. 1, 1987, p 103; C. Dykstra, 'The Formative Power of the Congregation', *Religious Education*, Vol. 82, No. 4, 1987, pp 540ff; W. H. Willimon, *Worship as Pastoral Care*, Nashville, Tennessee: Abingdon Press, 1979, pp 122f. For more general accounts, see M. Warren, 'Catechesis: An Enriching Category for Religious Education', in M. Warren (ed), *Sourcebook for Modern Catechetics*, Winona, Minnesota: St Mary's Press, 1983; R. L. Browning and R. A. Reed, *The Sacraments in Religious Education and Liturgy*, Birmingham, Ala.: Religious Education Press, 1985; G. K. Neville and J. H. Westerhoff, *Learning Through Liturgy*, New York: Seabury Press, 1978.

11

Human Communion and Christian Communication: Religion Implicit and Explicit

EDWARD BAILEY

BABY-POWER

In a volume marking the anniversary of an institution (NEICE) it is appropriate to think of births.[1] The first of our three children was born twenty years ago, soon after I became rector of the parish where I am still.[2] She came home at nine days old on a Tuesday in Lent when the parish branch of the Mothers' Union was holding a service in our sitting-room. Afterwards I took the baby into the room and placed the carry-cot in the middle of the floor. With one accord the ladies, most of whom were of grandmotherly age, rose up from their easy chairs around the edges of the room and crowded round the object in the centre. There was virtually nothing to see of the baby because of all the wrappings (the house was exceptionally cold, as the electricity was off, due to a miners' strike), but the spontaneous 'O-o-h' was so loud that those members who had gone to prepare the tea came running from the kitchen, two rooms away. The 'Oohs' were simple (positive) expletives of the 'Joy' and 'Bliss' that carols speak of at Christmas: the 'gift of tongues' in one of its most 'elementary forms'.

There was, of course, nothing particularly exceptional about the incident. Babies constantly have this effect upon people. It was just that as a newcomer to this area of human experience, I suppose my perceptions were sharpened. Subsequently I noticed how many people wanted to peer into the pram, when this baby or any baby went on trips to the local shops. Mothers especially, but other females also, expressed envy when I took holy communion to new parents: envy of my opportunity to see day-old babies. (Day-old chicks or kittens have a similar appeal.) Again, the desire of a certain well-known bishop's wife to get her arms round this baby became comprehensible as one experienced a new relationship with the babies one was given to baptize. The desire to steal a baby was no longer completely incomprehensible, simply immoral.

Once upon a time (say from about 1860 to 1960, when men seemed to rule, and the only justifiable *rationales* seemed to be the rational, conceptually conceived) this strand in human experience might have been ignored, as merely transitory or sentimental in character, or biological in origin. Such a dismissive attitude was itself irrational and, in the best sense, unscientific. It was reminiscent of the attempt to dismiss (say) dreams — or the whole congeries of phenomena lumped together under such labels as 'alternative', or 'para-psychology', or 'superstition'. In this case salvation from the prejudice (pre-judgement) that blinds was probably due to the advice of a prominent activist in the local community. Discussing how to establish a branch of the United Nations Association she said, from experience: 'You've got to get the children involved, and then the parents have to come'.

The observation is a statement of the obvious. Advertisers are so familiar with it that their exploitation of the principle, on television before Christmas for example, has had to be curbed. Stated so pithily, however, like some proverb from the accumulated wisdom of community organizing, it impressed a novice in the field. The anthropologist in him saw it not only as a device by means of which to gather individuals, but also as an indicator of the springs of human voluntarism. 'People will do anything for children', or 'People will do anything for their children', may not always be true, but such sayings certainly point to important strands in the total picture of human motivation.

All the world seems to know (and professes to believe) that 'statistics can prove anything'. Anecdotes (statistics of a single instance) are equally open to exploitation, as the arts, journalism and politics can demonstrate. Yet small-scale societies ('communities' in the more subjective sense) especially apprehend truth in the particular, whether it takes the form of a story or an instance, a myth or a parable, a sacrament or a proverb. Mass societies ('cultures' might be more accurate), in their 'secular' aspect, apprehend greater truth in the general, and ideally therefore in the universal and unexceptionable. So to bestow the mystique of abstraction, upon the combination of incident and advice (act and word) just described, we might say that the spontaneous response to the baby mattered because it revealed a functional principle in community organizing: that identification is a power in the land.

The suggestion that this phenomenon of human attraction could be described in terms of power can be paralleled by reports of comparable observations elsewhere. Thus convicts may not be typical (in the sense of 'average') of the societies that incarcerate them; but prison may reveal, in starker simplicity, archetypal elements within human being. So it is noteworthy that convicts are said to share two (if only two) universal ethical criteria: hostility towards any fellow-convict who 'grasses' to the prison authorities, and hostility to anyone who has harmed children. So deep is the latter, fundamentally altruistic, value, that child-molesters may need isolation from their fellow-inmates for decades, throughout indeed literally life sentences.

Nor are comparable reports limited to similar societies. The cult of the child may seem to be a recent development in the West but the child in India has long been compared to 'a king', until the age of seven. Among the Baganda, the *Kabaka* (king) was traditionally (and to some extent is still) seen as also child-like: autocratic to the point of petulance, he is nevertheless to be honoured to the point of indulgence.

British experience similarly includes a period when the king could 'do no wrong'. Indeed the Crown is still supposed to be 'above' (not beneath, or without, or outside) politics. At the same time grand-mothers especially still say of the Queen, 'I wouldn't have her job for anything, poor dear'. The simultaneous reciprocity of power and powerlessness can be predicated as a universally human, rather than culturally specific, characteristic.

While the power of the new-born baby and the growing child is felt to possess an underlying, continuing identity (like that of the developing person, himself or herself), the character of its influence changes. Another form, of a similar power, is apparent in the case of the elderly. Locally this was very apparent about the time of the two observations already noted. Subsequently it was found that the elderly had so many outings provided that they were unable to fit in any more; and they began to speak as those with rights, rather than willing victims for lionizing. But in the early 1970s, both locally and nationally, any criticism of them would have come as a blasphemy; a crime against one of them, when it took place, as a sacrilege. So they enjoyed (or they could enjoy, at least in their relationships with others) a position akin to a 'second childishness'.

THE SEVEN AGES

Indeed seven 'ages' of 'childhood' can be traced. The Baby is a means of blessing. The 'blessing' is 'pronounced' when it smiles. If this blessing is bestowed in the course of eye-to-eye contact, the recipients feel blessed in themselves, and feel life as a whole is a blessed phenomenon. The baby gives a human face to the natural laws of the universe, and enables it to enter into a personal relationship with its individual parts. The creature takes on something of the significance of the Creator: adult creators respond as creatures.

In the second stage the Toddler is a stimulus to a widening unity. The mother who spoke, on a one-to-one basis, with two or three other mothers about the intimate *minutiae* of babycraft, now comes out of the home again, meets other mothers at Mother-and-Toddler groups, and talks with them while delivering or collecting from playgroup. She becomes a member of a neighbourhood in a way she may not have been since she was old enough to become mobile independently of the family and to leave school. She may try to see her child as a particular instance of a general category, and pretend to consider him or her 'objectively'. Yet the ultimate impossibility of the task is demonstrated by the fact that the only commonality among the mothers present, apart from their propinquity, is the fact of their individual motherhood.

The Primary or Junior School-aged Child (five, or seven, to eleven years, in most of the United Kingdom) spurs his or her parents or quasi-parents into sociability. Indeed at this stage the father, who until the late 1980s (at least in this community) rarely took the child to such gatherings as playgroups, may now also be introduced, or re-introduced, into a locality, to an extent he has not known since his mid-teens. Gradually the children's own interests and friendships decide to which formal and informal groups they belong, but in each case transportation will sometimes be necessary. Peer contacts therefore develop among the adults. This may lead to membership of a committee, or else alternation of responsibility for transport, all of which encourage a parallel process of *parental* socialization.

The Adolescent, it must be said, is predominantly a cause of anxiety. For whatever reasons, in this society at least, it seems that ability in numerous directions outstrips discretion; experimentation now has to precede wisdom. In some ways earlier stages are re-lived, for the parent as for the child. Thus there is a determined effort to 'let them go'; and yet examinations, for instance, can be almost as much of a strain upon the older generation as upon the younger.

The Adult inevitably passes a judgement upon his or her parents. At least in this community (it seems to me) they stand aside with remarkable restraint. So much so that if and when things go wrong, they may well place the chief responsibility upon their own children, rather than upon his or her partner or place of work or other circumstances. Nevertheless their grown-up child's life, marriage, family, career, and relationships are felt to represent a judgement ultimately upon their own lives and efforts.

The 'elderly child', or Grandparent, then becomes a source of tradition. They often help out with child-minding or house improvements, while both parents go out to work. They are around, have time, appreciate the growing child's unfolding character, are free of final responsibility, and also stand in a similarly subordinate role to the middle generation. Through anecdote, reminiscence, comparison, they bring history to life in both senses: they make history come alive, and they provide the historical background for life today.

The Senile Baby, however, is an occasion of crisis. He or she has to be looked after, but by whom? If by relations, then in whose home? If professionally, then in which 'home' — and will the re-dependent, 'second' child, agree? Behind all the practical questions, the moral ones: how far do we put ourselves, or my spouse, or my children (or even, today, grandchildren) in second place, and how far should the aged have first place? And, as they lose their mental faculties, how far is anything of a symbolic, rather than purely physical, nature worthwhile anyway?

The possibility of transposing the 'seven ages of man' into 'seven ages of childhood' demonstrates, if nothing else, the archetypal nature of childhood in this society. Of course the culture is 'personalistic'; but of equal importance is the ever-changing meaning of 'person', not least in a post-modern world. The incident with the baby suggests that it is akin to the *'wilful divinities'* of those who live in green, rather than in concrete, jungles. Divinity being found in tandem with individual will, it is potentially comprehensible following the other's self-expression, but never mechanistically predictable in advance. Thus the gods can only be revealed in history, for they are always gods of surprises.

THE POWER AND THE GLORY

Such comments may spark off a number of reflections from the point of view of religion. In the first place to 'see the baby' meant primarily to see its face, even when so little of the baby's face, or head, was visible. On the one hand to 'show one's face' is to appear, reveal oneself, bestow one's self, prove one's presence, give oneself as present (in both senses). So the Lord God in the Old Testament makes 'his face to shine upon' his own people; and the Emperor of India gave *darshan*, that the people might do him homage. On the other hand the sight of a face 'blesses' insofar (as Alan Morehead explained, with reference to Livingstone, in *The White Nile*) as it makes people feel better, bigger, happier, luckier, more fully alive, greater selves.

To put it quasi-arithmetically, one and one may make two, but one-to-one makes three. This would appear to be a vital consideration in all communication; what is the nature of the relationship involved?

Secondly, the power of the powerless can be *abused* by enlisting public sympathy for the 'powerless'. Yet the need to allow for changes in the balance of power only confirms its efficacy. In the same way that the baby's power depends on its size (smallness), a sight of the face is only necessary to complete the bliss of blessedness. As a principle this power would seem to have been recognized both by St Paul and by Jesus. The former considered his weaknesses were at least as fruitful as his strengths for demonstrating the power of the gospel, over himself as well as in winning public acclaim. The latter (according to the Fourth Gospel) foresaw and predicted that if he were 'lifted up' — apparently on the cross — then he would 'draw all men' to himself. More generally, he seems to have concluded at the time of the temptations that the way of the cross was itself the way of his Father.

The power-less may attract by being seen but, conversely, the power-*full* can only fully attract if it is self-effacing. Compelled to operate symbolically, it requires revelations — of its hiddenness. As 'the greatest art is to conceal art', so it discloses its omnipotence most completely in self-mastery. The Collect for the Eleventh Sunday after Trinity in *The Book of Common Prayer* makes the same point: 'O God, who declarest thy almighty power most chiefly in showing mercy and pity...'. So inter-personal communication, which allows each party to be personal because the communication itself is personal, bestows personal significance upon its impersonal media.

Thirdly, weakness seems to have power not simply to bring together, but to bring out all that is distinctively personal, and to glue it together in a personal manner. Two years before the birth of NEICE, our third child had a major operation when she was one day old. It was illuminating to observe the influence she had in a big hospital. The weakness concomitant upon her 'age' (ie her lack of it), and on the seriousness of her condition, seemed to overcome all the very considerable differences of culture and nationality, and the equally rigid distinctions of specialism and hierarchy.

The fragility of her existence as a person evoked the most deeply personal in individuals who were used to operating in accordance with their role within a highly organized, rational bureaucracy. If the individual subjectivity of personal being is the *imago Dei* in contemporary society, then the weakness of the baby enabled others to reveal themselves as children of precisely such a divinity (compare Romans 8:18-21). So teams should demonstrate finitude, as well as enhance competence.

A further reflection may be put in the form of an anecdote, and a question. Ninian Smart tells a story about a (then unknown) American academic who was in Saigon visiting two friends from the State Department. Apologetically they explained they would be out that evening, as they were eating with some Buddhist monks. His reaction showed that he could see no point in spending time in that way. Henry Kissinger became better known later — and discovered that no weight of bombs could win a single heart.

So the question is: Is not this why, in contemporary culture, the concept of love (whether romantic, or agapeistic) enjoys universal approbation? It signifies the one and only 'irresistible force' which has the power to motivate the otherwise 'immovable object' of human free will. In this respect at least, do not all remain adolescent, if not childishly so?

COMMUNICATION AND COMMUNION

However, an editorial invitation to expound the incident of the baby, in a context such as this, requires that it be related to the 'problems' (or pleasures!) of Christian communication. This raises the question of the relationship, firstly, between communication and communion (between explicit religion and implicit religion, for the former is simply the explication of those *commitments* which constitute the latter); and secondly between those phenomena and Christianity.

The connection between communication and communion is

phenomenal, rather than merely semantic or coincidental. Those who are morally committed to the virtue of communion may be inclined to plead, 'No communion without communication'; thus raising ethical questions regarding (for instance) the number of Christmas cards we send, and the length of the messages we add, and the desirability (or otherwise) of 'circular' letters. Similarly, those who are committed to the value of communicating may argue that successful or valid communication is dependent upon communion (which they may see as identity of immediate or vicarious experience). Each appears to be an over-statement of a point that is important.

For the relationship between them is a chicken-and-egg situation, except that neither occurs purely mechanically. Communication is both assisted by, and productive of, communion; but need not be either. Communion is both fostered by, and facilitates, communication; but can occur independently. Indeed, Thomist sacramental doctrine would appear relevant to the relationship between them (which may hardly be surprising): communication both expresses, and effects, communion. It is sacramental by nature, simultaneously revealing and obscuring the self.

The relationship between each of these phenomena and Christianity is likewise close, but ambiguous. On the one hand the ultimate goal must be a communion which is partly ineffable, because personal; and yet one in which communication plays the vital double role of allowing the participants simultaneously to distance themselves from each other and to unite themselves with each other. On the other hand that goal must be a communion that is not only with the holy, but with the human. Can indeed the holy be found outside the human, when the human is seen as coinherent? Must not *human communion* (in which all three elements are personal) be inevitably holy?

But what, it might be asked, does this mean in practice? What are the local particulars behind such cosmopolitan generalizations?

Three stand out. First that Christians, because of their proper insistence upon their common peculiarity, look to their ecclesial life primarily for communion. They thus regard the content and phenomenon of communication, ultimately, from a symbolic point of view. So, for instance, the church is constituted by the Spirit, and includes Christ — and not just Jesus — within its membership, although not knowing quite what the title (or the name) might mean.

Secondly, members of the church — not least when 'teaching the Christian faith' — will ideally encourage all the participants to contribute their own, existing insights. Thus a confirmation class can offer valuable, original reflections as to why we use water in baptism, at the same time as having its suggestions compared with the tradition. (Today even the youngest artist *interprets* the score. Education has pioneered in spirituality, as well as in liturgy.) A politically active lay group will demand evidence of charity, in the sense of 1 Corinthians 13; given 'their' head, if they meet in his Name, they will demonstrate their Head.

Thirdly, the church is, ideally, a body of people who *disagree* together, in the name of Christ; for only when we recognize the depth of our differences can we disciples 'be one, [in the same way] as we [Persons of the Trinity] are one'. Indeed Trinitarian doctrine seems to provide a — if not the — model of persons in *personal* community. It is the Spirit of communion that gives communication its potential. At all levels, faith speaks to faith.

NOTES

1. Brief summaries of the empirical data (gathered from interviews from working in a public house and from living in a parish) behind these reflections may be found in: Edward Bailey, 'The Implicit Religion of Contemporary Society: an Orientation and Plea for its Study', *Religion: Journal of Religion and Religions*, Vol. XIII, 1983; 'Implicit Religion: a bibliographical introduction', *Social Compass*, Vol. XXXVII, No. 4, December 1990.

2. Experience in the parish is particularly reflected in: Edward Bailey, 'The Sacred Faith of the People', in Tony Moss (ed), *In Search of Christianity*, London: Firethorn, 1986; 'The Folk Religion of the English People', in Paul Badham (ed), *Religion, State and Society in Modern Britain*, Lampeter: Edwin Mellen Press, 1990; 'Civil Religion in Britain', in H. Kleger and A. Muller-Herold (HRSG), *Religion des Burgers: Zivilreligion in Amerika und Europ*, München: Kaiser Verlag, 1986; 'Implicit Religion as a Tool for Ministry', *Focus*, Vol. XXIII, No. 3, August 1990.

12

Apples of Gold:
The Role of Proverbial Wisdom in
Christian Education

DAVID DAY

THE PROVERBIAL SAYING

'Like apples of gold in settings of silver is a word fitly spoken'.[1] The purpose of this essay is to examine the role and value, if any, of proverbial teaching in Christian education. Such teaching may consist of maxims, aphorisms, clichés, epigrams, mottoes, slogans, rules of thumb, proverbs or stock formulas. It can be found at every level from the pre-schoolers to the confirmation class, from the Sunday school to the adult study group.

It would seem sensible at the outset to try to delineate the characteristics of these sayings. But the attempt to find features which all share in common has proved surprisingly difficult. As a rough working definition we can follow Zeller's guidelines.[2] According to his analysis the most significant feature of the proverbial saying is its generalizing character. The proverb describes a law or spiritual principle; it deals with situations which can be repeated, broad classifications of experience which are to a large extent independent of a specific context. Individuals can fit their name into the blank provided by the proverb — 'whoever', 'everyone who...', 'the wise...'.

A second characteristic of the proverb proper consists of its linguistic form. The typical proverb is couched in pithy, succinct language. It may employ alliteration, parallelism or exaggeration. It may draw sharp contrasts or use vivid metaphor or paradox. It is, in other words, a literary artifice, a saying carefully constructed in order to make an impact; it must be memorable even at the risk of over-simplifying.

Not all proverbs evince these characteristics in their purest form, of course. The definition will need to be applied generously. In particular I wish to include in the discussion doctrinal formulas, since they often demonstrate the requisite tightness of structure; and clichés, in that they are clearly related to folk wisdom.

This kind of didactic material is to be found within the biblical corpus. In the Old Testament it is associated primarily with the Wisdom literature. The book of Proverbs in particular contains hundreds of examples: 'Train a child in the way that he should go and when he is old he will not depart from it'.[3] 'The Lord tears down the proud man's house, but he keeps the widow's boundaries intact.'[4] Wisdom in Israel proceeds from 'father' to 'son'; from 'old' to 'young'; from 'sage' to 'novice'. It is the language of the home, the classroom and the pulpit. There is no mistaking its didactic setting. It is a form of speech characteristic of the teacher, the elder and the parent.

When we move to the New Testament we find a suggestive parallel in the epistles. It is a commonplace of biblical scholarship that various kinds of catechetical material may be found embedded in these documents. Many years ago Selwyn's commentary on 1 Peter isolated this material and set it out in a tabular form. Once again there seems little doubt that the setting of these sayings was an educational one; the first exponents of Christian education were content to employ proverbial wisdom in their programmes of baptismal instruction.[5] Broadly speaking, the material addresses two needs. First there are pithy statements telling the new Christians how to interpret what has happened to them and how they are to see themselves in the post-conversion phase: 'You are children of light'; 'a new creation'; 'you have been reborn'; 'you have passed into the New Age'; 'put off the old man and put on the new'. Second, alongside this kind of material lie exhortations to practical Christian living. 'Abstain from...'; 'Put off...'; 'Put on...'; 'Be subject...'; 'Watch...'; 'Stand...'; 'Resist...'.

All this bears many of the marks of proverbial or aphoristic teaching, though one would have to concede that they lack something of the generalizing quality specified above. Nevertheless, the sayings are short, sharp and to the point; they are easily remembered and authoritative by reason of their form; they claim to have access to 'what is the case'; they represent the wisdom of the community — a shared wisdom into which the neophyte is invited to enter.

PROVERBIAL WISDOM IN ADOLESCENT CHRISTIANS

My attention was drawn to this teaching material when I was in the process of gathering data for a study of adolescent understanding.[6] Reading accounts of interviews with young Christians aged 15-18, I could not help noticing the wealth of proverbial wisdom which appeared in the transcripts. This was particularly true of two interviewees, who appeared to speak naturally in terms of generalizing spiritual principles or laws.

Further investigation showed that they were both young, working class and non-academic. They had come to faith through the efforts of a man with considerable skills in youth work, who had been almost entirely responsible for teaching them the elements of the Christian faith. He appears in their accounts as something of a hero, friendly, open, straight-talking, giving the impression of having his faith and life well sorted out and integrated. ('He's got nae worries' was one comment.) This leader was a person of some influence, perceived as a guru by the two young disciples ('He was, well, he still is, my spiritual father'). In such a situation many of the conditions presupposed in the book of Proverbs and in the catechetical tradition obtained and clearly a good deal of teaching about life and faith was transmitted. 'Listen, my sons, to a father's instruction; pay attention and gain understanding.'[7]

Unfortunately most of what the leader had said was not directly reported in the transcripts. One interviewee did tantalizingly refer to a technique which the leader was in the habit of using when encouraging someone 'to take the big step' of faith.

> He had a habit, like. He'd try to put them off. He'd say, 'Soon as you become one, it'll be really hard. It'll be a hard life – but the Lord'll be with you.'

Apart from this one reminiscence we do not have access to the instruction which was given. Nevertheless it is possible to do a little judicious reading between the lines and catch echoes of its style from the recorded comments of the two young men.

The most notable feature of the transcripts was the greater than expected number of comments which might be characterized as spiritual laws or principles. These sayings do very often possess the generalizing tendency which is the primary mark of proverbial wisdom. One group consisted of perspectives on the nature of God and his relationship with the world. Taken as a whole they constitute a whole worldview, a cosmology, expressed as irrefragable truths:

> The Lord's always with you;
> No guilt from God;
> Jesus picks the naebodies;
> Satan can deceive you, y'know;
> That's the way the Devil's brought it out –
>   to make it natural (on sex before marriage);
> You shall burn, y'know;
> Prayer is powerful;
> To have the peace you've got to be right with him;
> However daft it may seem to be there's a purpose for it,
>   y'know;
> Daily he puts some sort of test like;
> Fear is Satan's biggest weapon;
> His work is his will.

The effect of these phrases is to order the world, to make sense of it in Christian terms. They open up an invisible realm which interacts with the visible in an intelligible fashion once the secret has been communicated.

A second group concerned the practical conduct of the Christian life. Again they often took the form of a principle or law, which would bring an element of consistency or predictability into experience. With the help of such principles one might obtain an understanding of how the life of faith worked and be led to shape behaviour appropriately:

> When you're blessed in the Lord, the next day you get pounded
>   by the Devil;
> The longer you're away from the Lord the harder it is to get
>   back;
> When you come back, you come back stronger, y'know;
> Anything good can be done through the Lord – without the
>   Lord it just can't be done;
> [The Lord says] If I can't trust you with the tiny jobs, how can
>   I with the big one?;
> (On the Bible) It's not how much you read, it's how much you
>   take in;
> If I haven't read it I get hungry;
> (On prayer) Expect a specific answer. Don't need half and
>   half;

Only pray for the things that you've got faith to believe will
   happen;
If you pray for nowt, nowt will be done;
He doesn't put me through anything I can't take;
He lets you go through hard times to make you stronger;
It's always fear that holds you back.

These young Christians had a very clear understanding of their faith, which demonstrated how efficiently they had been socialized into it. Their personal accounts also exposed the importance of a different use of language. Embedded in their ordinary conversation were a very large number of Christian clichés. They had learned a whole new vocabulary which at times sat uneasily with the first language of home, school and teenage culture. This parallel linguistic code was 'the language of Zion' and they knew how to use it:

I don't want to mix with darkness;
He's fell away from the Lord;
The thing that comforts me and warms my heart;
Satan used him to deceive me;
I was going on with the Lord;
I was really blessed with the confidence in it;
I feel the power and presence of the Spirit;
He put it on my heart;
I took it to the Lord;
A sort of burden;
I feel blessed and happy;
I wasn't getting fellowship.

These are not phrases that one associates with seventeen-year-olds living in the inner city. For most of the interview their language was that of the surrounding culture. But embedded within one linguistic code was the other. Both codes could be drawn upon, unselfconsciously, appropriately and easily. Both revealed the socializing process that had gone on.

PROVERBS AND THE EVERYDAY WORLD

Here are two young men who have been 'well-taught'. They appear to have internalized a Christian worldview mediated to them largely by means of aphoristic instruction. Such a method of teaching seems to have been remarkably effective. It is slightly surprising, therefore, to find relatively little discussion of the method in the literature on Christian education. If the setting of the aphorism lies firmly within the educational enterprise, if at least a prima facie case can be made out for its value then one might have expected some analysis of its nature and function and some evaluation of its power and limitations. That this is not generally the case may well be because it belongs to a thoroughly transmissive kind of education, reminiscent of a bygone age, to catechetics of the old style when the passive reception of timeless truths was all that was required of a pupil. The proverb appears to sit uneasily with active, experientially-based inquiry, with discussion and argument, with learning and discovery.

And yet aphoristic teaching is to be found in many settings which have nothing to do with religious nurture. It is illuminating to observe its use in a variety of different contexts. 'Feel the burn' and 'no pain no gain' come from the world of keep fit; 'measure twice, cut once' is a tip passed on by the DIY enthusiast who has made enough mistakes to make him cautious; 'one for each person and one for the pot' defined the principles of teamaking before the advent of tea-bags; 'mirror-signal-manoeuvre' has been part of the learner driver's catechism for years. Examples multiply, 'Troubles always come in threes'; you've got to eat a peck before you die'; 'three times wet, three times dry' (traditional advice to those mixing cement by hand); 'look right, look left and if the road is clear, walk, don't run'; 'if you can't stand the heat keep out of the kitchen'; 'if you're not part of the answer you're part of the problem'; 'business is business'; 'boys will be boys'; 'big boys don't cry'. The slogan, maxim or proverb may be a very humble player in the linguistic game but it clearly has its uses.

JESUS AND PROVERBIAL TEACHING

This conclusion is corroborated by the model of teaching afforded by Jesus in the synoptic gospels. He was apparently prepared to make extensive use of aphoristic teaching.

At first sight it may seem difficult to sustain this assertion against those who fasten upon the parables as Jesus's characteristic mode of instruction. In some cases this assessment has almost turned him into a nineteen-sixties progressive. It is said that parables are by their nature open-ended. The answer is never given to the listeners on a plate. 'He that hath ears to hear, let him hear' may be loosely translated as 'work it out for yourselves'. Jesus was as keen on discovery learning as any child-centred teacher.

There is clearly some truth in identifying the parabolic method as one of Jesus's favourite techniques, at least according to the synoptic portrait of him. But Jesus also appears to have presented his hearers with pre-packaged aphoristic statements of the truth. Ever since Bultmann identified Jesus as 'a teacher of wisdom', New Testament scholarship has been more prepared to find elements of proverbial wisdom in his words.[8] A few illustrations will serve to make this point clear:

> Where your treasure is there will your heart be also;
> Do not worry about tomorrow, for tomorrow will worry about
>   itself;
> All who draw the sword will die by the sword;
> If a house is divided against itself, that house cannot stand;
> No one sews a patch of unshrunk cloth on an old garment;
> Whoever is not against us is for us;
> He who is not with me is against me;
> A city set on a hill cannot be hid;
> The spirit is willing but the flesh is weak;
> The harvest is plentiful but the workers are few;
> No one can serve two masters.[9]

It is not entirely unfair to characterize this material as pre-packaged. Jesus presents his hearers with pithy, succinct and memorable statements about what is the case. Far from allowing his listeners to work things out for themselves this kind of teaching offers an interpretation of experience which comes ready made. 'You must see things this way' is implied by the aphoristic form.

We may draw parallels with the material in Proverbs, the epistles and in the interviews by pointing out that once again such teaching depends for its effectiveness on a particular construction of the situation. It finds its home in a didactic setting where the teacher is acknowledged to be an authority. It is true that the proverb appeals to the observable world but it does so in a tone of voice which implies that there is very little room for disagreement. The teacher is guru or sage rather than discussion group leader or facilitator. The disciple pays attention and shapes his or her view of experience according to the determinative interpretation which the proverb affords. One would be surprised to read of a disciple faced with the saying, 'No one can serve two masters' who responded, 'Well, I agree it's very difficult but

I think what you've just said is a bit of a generalization'. One would be equally surprised to read the proverb in the form, 'In my opinion, for what it's worth, no one can serve two masters'.

It is not difficult, therefore, to present Jesus as an instructor of the faithful, a guru to his disciples, using generalizing statements and pre-packaged interpretations of experience. In this way he corresponds to the teacher of folk wisdom. But in two important ways his methods go beyond those already outlined. In the first place his teaching is vibrant with life. He does not trade in clichés and often one gets the impression of being present at the coining of a phrase which will later in the course of transmission become a piece of proverbial wisdom. There is thus a freshness and a shock value to much of what Jesus says. Secondly, Jesus employs a great many sayings which are paradoxical and disturbing. 'Blessed are you when men hate you' is a generalizing proverb-type statement but the effect is to call into question the settled understanding of the world. Perrin observes that such sayings 'are so radical that they shatter the form of proverbial saying altogether and become something quite different'.[10] They jolt the hearer into a re-assessment of the situation.

THE FUNCTIONS OF APHORISTIC TEACHING

This may be an appropriate point at which to pull some of these observations together. What are the functions of aphoristic teaching and what seem to be its strengths and value for Christian education?

(i) Aphoristic teaching has an interpretive function. In the typical case a segment of experience is presented as a window into the way things are. The apothegm offers a cosmic perspective. The proverb or maxim presents the listener with a truth which is inevitable. It may be taken for granted because the speaker and the unseen cloud of witnesses behind him take it for granted. This is an important teaching function, since interpretation is one of the most basic of human activities. Seymour and Wehrheim write of it as a 'calling into existence', a process which continues throughout life.[11]

The objection is often made that this kind of teaching is altogether too dogmatic, that it forces the pupil's experience into a straitjacket. Surely interpretation should emerge out of reflection on experience?

A more persuasive position is that which argues that no experience can exist for long without an interpretation attached to it. The framework through which it is viewed determines the meaning of the experience, sometimes instantaneously, but at least as soon as it is reflected upon. Because frameworks are the instruments by which we locate experience within a network of concepts, values, hierarchies, causalities, there can be no meaning without the framework. The point is well illustrated by Donald Hudson who speculates on the answer St Paul would have received if he had asked, 'What's gone wrong with my eyes and ears?'.[12] A different frame of reference generates a different set of questions and gives a different interpretation of the raw empirical data. Reductionist accounts of religion operate in precisely that way, explaining, and therefore 'explaining away', religious faith as 'obsessional neuroses' or 'wish-fulfilment' or 'father fixations'. As Seymour and Wehrheim observe, 'It is impossible for one to look value-free at an experience. The lens one uses is focused by one's physical and logical possibilities, by one's personal history, by one's language, and by one's motivation or need to understand.'[13] For the Christian the faith-story is one of the most powerful factors in the creation of that lens.

If this is so then aphoristic teaching is one of the ways in which interpretation is applied to experiences which would otherwise be explained according to different, even rival, frames of reference. This makes the mode of teaching enormously significant within the process of education. The learners are confronted with succinct, memorable, authoritative, easily portable pigeon-holings of their experience.

This point remains valid even in those cases where the personal appropriation of the interpretation is delayed. A girl in her late teens speaks of suddenly discovering that an interpretation had been queueing up, as it were, until the right moment came for it to be attached to the experience. The formula had been in the memory banks for some time but had remained inert. Suddenly it became a powerful and personal way of making sense of experience.

> For years people had told me, 'Jesus died for you so you can be forgiven now'. But I'd never really understood the magnificence of his death, if you see what I mean – the strength of it. And I saw it on this film and it just hit me like a brick – you know, actually seeing him die. It was awful. And I wept for hours that night.

The authoritative quality of the actual form is worth examining a little further. Proverbs and apothegms lay implicit claim to universalizability. They sound less like personal opinions than plain statements of fact. The speaker's own authority is considerably strengthened because it is couched in a form which makes it seem blindingly obvious. This is especially the case with significant tautologies which appear to say very little but carry great weight; 'boys will be boys' after all.

(ii) The aphorism also fulfils an affective and affiliative function. Clichés and banalities are not without their uses. They may yield little by way of illumination but be rich in the production of solidarity and a sense of corporate unity. Thus, the phrase 'nowt so queer as folk' is not an invitation to explore idiosyncrasy but a comment with which to close an exchange and bind the group together in a warm sense that they at least are 'all right'.

The function of such clichés has been explored by Richard Hoggart with particular reference to the culture of the working class. In his study he remarked on the use of proverbial sayings, 'not in a racy or lively but in a formal manner: the phrases are used like counters, "click-click-click"'. He argues that although they are no longer part of a vibrant tradition they do represent a harking back to a body of truth constituting a 'still largely trustworthy reference in a world now difficult to understand'. However, the aphorisms are not integrated into a coherent system or worldview. Contradictory proverbs are accepted without demur, people do not look for consistency. Their function is less to be part of an intellectual construction as to provide a kind of comfort.[14]

From quite different data – a study of a curriculum project – Shipman observed how the members increasingly showed their affective commitment to the enterprise by recourse to crude central propositions uttered with varying degrees of emotional intensity.[15] This is the value for any movement of the slogan. 'Black is beautiful'; 'Four legs good, two legs bad'; 'Every baby a wanted baby.' In some Christian circles the phrase 'Bible-believing Christians' will generate the same sort of group loyalty.

Aphorisms, slogans, mottoes have this effect because they exude certainty and function as stop cards to discussion. They refer to things woven into the fabric of the cosmos. They also suggest the tradition of the forefathers. The listener can take comfort in the fact that these things have been believed 'since the beginning'. Moreover, their frequent use makes them familiar and therefore reassuring. One can take refuge in the word without necessarily having to defend it or articulate its meaning.

It may be relevant at this point to introduce the idea of doctrinal formulas. A large number of the adolescents in the research already cited responded to the question, 'In what way do you think Jesus is special?' with a comment about Christ's atoning death. Many of these revealed what can only be described as stock responses, apparently drawing on a common store of phrases and images. I should add that the respondents came from many different parts of the United Kingdom. There is no suggestion that we were tapping just the language of one congregation or a particularly influential youth leader.

We may ask what the function of this conventional phraseology is. Certainly it contributes to the process of world-construction and world-maintenance which has already been noted. But part of the point of a cliché is that many people use it. It represents common currency or a kind of *lingua franca*. It carries overtones of acceptability, of belonging, or group affiliation. Its value as a signal of group loyalty should not be underestimated. It is a shibboleth, a peculiarly appropriate term in that it recalls the language test imposed in the Old Testament story on the out-group by the in-group.[16] Use of such language is one of the ways in which young Christians signal that they are insiders and have their message received and understood.

(iii) The third function of the aphorism concerns its capacity to inspire to action. Sometimes it is couched in the form of an imperative or an exhortation. 'Never doubt in the dark what you saw in the light'; 'Keep the faith, baby'; 'Witness by lip and by life'; 'Trust and obey, for there's no other way'; 'Earn all you can, save all you can, give all you can'; 'Read the Bible and it will scare the Hell out of you'; 'Do the thing that lies to hand.' Form contributes to function.

Sometimes the call to action is concealed within the aphorism, which takes the form of a statement about what is the case. But in Beardslee's words:

> There is an implied imperative in the declarative in the sense
> that there is an implied challenge to see it this way.[17]

Obviously, if such and such is really the case one would be ill-advised not to work with it, seek its implementation or obey its implicit command.

Some examples will illustrate this point. 'You are either a living Bible or a living libel'; 'Satan finds some mischief yet for idle hands to do'; 'Some people are so heavenly minded that they are no earthly use'; 'Nothing that's done in love can ever be lost.' In each case the course of action which is commended is embedded within the generalizing statement.

PROVERBIAL WISDOM IN CHRISTIAN EDUCATION

We are now in a position to survey the use of proverbial and conventional wisdom in Christian education and estimate its value:

(i) Insofar as it is couched in a sharp and pithy form it makes an impact on the hearer and is therefore easier to remember than a more discursive statement.

(ii) It avoids complexity and smooths out the untidiness of real life. The succinct maxim bypasses the need for overmuch reflection. It does not ask for academic intellectualizing.

(iii) It provides a shorthand and easily accessible handle on reality. Its ordering function offers a way of grasping a reality which otherwise will seem elusive, complex and resistant to systematization.

(iv) It emerges from the specific situation, from life as it is lived. It is thus grounded in personal lived experience; there is always a real situation to turn back to for reference.

(v) But since the specific situation is what immediately produces it, proverbs and aphorisms which contradict each other are less important than they would be in a comprehensive system.

(vi) It resonates with feelings of group loyalty and thus contributes to cohesiveness and boundary maintenance.

(vii) Its generalizing form carries with it a claim to authority.

A mode of education which is able to achieve so much is not to be despised. Perhaps one ought not to dismiss too easily a method which produces two young men who have such a clear grasp of their faith and are able to interpret experience in terms of well-defined categories, which are at least recognizably Christian. Nevertheless, despite its effectiveness as a way of nurturing the Christian disciple, we may still be uneasy. The method may smack too much of instruction, of indoctrination even. The learner is presented with a pre-packaged understanding of experience, with doctrines cast in formulas which are impermeable. Banalities may have an affective value but are they really the way to produce thoughtful Christians? Clichés have their uses, perhaps, but they may inhibit thought. Worse still, by lumping together under one utterance things which are actually unlike one another, their use may distort reality and preclude any movement towards greater refinement and complexity. Surely, no one wants young Christians to have to leave their brains behind at the church door?

The whole tone of these sayings may be reminiscent of the 'plonk-ing' mode humorously defined by Stephen Potter in his books on Gamesmanship and Lifemanship:

> If you have nothing to say, or, rather, something extremely stupid and obvious, say it, but in a 'plonking' tone of voice, ie roundly, but hollowly and dogmatically.[18]

This is the tone of the 'man in the pub', the 'man who knows what's what', who begins every other statement with the confident assertion, 'you will find'. It is the language of father to son: 'You will find, my lad, when you're a bit older...'

THE WISDOM OF DISORDER

It must be granted that the objections have some force. In responding to them I want to turn again to the Wisdom tradition in Israel and in the synoptic gospels. An important feature of Israelite Wisdom was what might be called 'anti-wisdom'. Within the accepted traditional teaching, dogmatic, assured and reassuring, offering unquestioned ancient truths, there can be heard dissentient voices, challenging and undermining. In different ways both Job and Ecclesiastes call the time-honoured formulas into question. They dis-order what was laid out in a tidy fashion. The point has been well made by David Hubbard:

> Proverbs seems to say, 'These are the rules for life; try them and find that they will work'. Job and Ecclesiastes say, 'We did, and they don't'.[19]

There is no New Testament equivalent to these books. Nothing matches Job or Ecclesiastes for critical comment on the received wisdom. We may, however, return once more to the portrait of Jesus the teacher. Perhaps the radical, scandalous, dis-ordering sayings legitimate an educational strategy which disturbs conventional pieties and traditional understandings. Such a conclusion needs to be subject to one important qualification, however. J. G. Williams makes the point that, unlike the negative scepticism of Ecclesiastes, Jesus's paradoxes are overwhelmingly positive. They point the disciple towards new life and the kingdom of God; they reverse expectations but always in the direction of hope.[20]

The interviews with teenagers did produce a modest amount of evidence to illustrate the questioning process at work. Significantly, the examples I shall cite are adolescents who were themselves cradle-Christians. They had been well-socialized into the Christian sub-culture and knew how to speak the appropriate language. They had heard proverbial wisdom from childhood. It is interesting to hear them testing the tradition:

> I've got to be honest with you. You have to believe it happened but not really the way you wanted it to. 'The Lord works in a mysterious way.' It's a good quote, isn't it? That time when prayer is not answered and you pass it off ...yeah, yeah... You pass it off.

This young woman is not happy with the standard response to 'unanswered prayer'. A seventeen-year-old Roman Catholic is similarly beginning to react against too naive an understanding of God's love and care for the world:

> People turn round to you and say, 'If your God's so good why does he let disasters occur, why does he kill off people who are innocent and haven't done nothing?'... You haven't got an answer for that. Because there's no way you can justify what God's done... It just doesn't seem right. And it does just not seem right.

It is not possible at this stage to explore further this questioning of the received wisdom. I have been unable to find anything in the style of Ecclesiastes which will use the aphoristic form itself to provoke questioning. Certainly there has been nothing to match the Jewish saying, 'If God were a man people would break his windows'. Christians do not seem to create such anti-wisdom apothegms. However, the two examples quoted will serve as a reminder that passing on the tradition is not the only way of fostering Christian growth. Allowing and even encouraging the testing of that tradition is also a significant part of assisting a young person's spiritual development. Each individual needs both to receive *and* to reflect; to be nourished by conventional wisdom *and also* question its validity and comprehensiveness.

This brief discussion of the role of proverbial type instruction may have usefully drawn attention to a mode of teaching which has become a little unfashionable. Perhaps Christian educators should look again and with sympathy at some neglected emphases — the concept of the teacher as the transmitter of truths and spokesperson for a community; the value of the generalizing word which orders reality and creates a mould by which experience may be shaped and given meaning; the importance of the simplifying word, which even while it distorts, by its directness provokes to practical action; the edifying function of conventional pieties and clichés; the idea of the learner as one who is socialized by learning to fit experience into a given frame of reference. Who knows? Within this setting even traditional catechizing and memorization may have their humble part to play.

NOTES

1. Proverbs 25:11.
2. D. Zeller, *Die weisheitlichen Mahnspruche bei den Synoptikern,* Wurzburg: Echter Verlag, 1977.
3. Proverbs 22:6.
4. Proverbs 15:25.
5. For details see E. G. Selwyn, *The First Epistle of St Peter,* London: Macmillan, 1947, pp 363-466.
6. The full account of this research has been published in D. V. Day and P. R. May, *Teenage Beliefs,* Oxford: Lion, 1991.
7. Proverbs 4:1.
8. Rudolph Bultmann, *History of the Synoptic Tradition,* Oxford: Blackwell and New York: Harper & Row, 1968.
9. Matt 6:21; Matt 6:34; Matt 26:52; Mark 3:25; Mark 2:21; Mark 9:40;Luke 11:23; Matt 5:14; Mark 14:38; Luke 10:2; Matt 6:34.
10. Norman Perrin, *Jesus and the Language of the Kingdom,* London: SCM, 1976, p 51.
11. J. L. Seymour and C. A. Wehrheim, 'Faith seeking Understanding: interpretation as a task of Christian education', in J. L. Seymour and D. E. Miller (eds), *Contemporary Approaches to Christian Education,* Nashville: Abingdon Press, 1982, pp 123-143.
12. W. Donald Hudson, *A Philosophical Approach to Religion,* London and Basingstoke: Macmillan, 1974, p 22.
13. *op. cit.,* p 127.
14. R. Hoggart, *The Uses of Literacy,* Harmondsworth: Penguin, 1957, p 29.
15. M. D. Shipman, *Inside a Curriculum Project,* London: Methuen, 1974.
16. Judges 12:6.
17. W. A. Beardslee, *Literary Criticism and the New Testament,* Philadelphia: Fortress Press, 1970, p 31.
18. Stephen Potter, *Some Notes on Lifemanship,* London: Hart-Davis, 1950, p 43.
19. D. A. Hubbard, 'The Wisdom Movement and Israel's Covenant Faith', *Tyndale Bulletin,* 17, 1966, pp 3-34, quoted in J. Goldingay, *Theological Diversity and the Authority of the Old Testament,* Grand Rapids, Michigan: Eerdmans, 1987.
20. J. G. Williams, *Those Who Ponder Proverbs,* Sheffield: The Almond Press, 1981, p 61.

13

How to Win Congregations and Influence Them: The Anatomy of the Church Growth Movement

MARTYN PERCY

INTRODUCTION

> Nine outstanding alumni pastors join Dr Robert Schuller for a power packed Institute for successful church leadership... You will learn...how they made their churches grow, what makes success, how obstacles are overcome, ministry principles that work, how to build a great church...[1]

> I used to be a little church on the beach of life; small and insignificant. No one paid any attention to me. People would come by and kick sand in my face, laugh, and remind me of my declining congregation. Then one day I read about Dr McGavran's Church Growth Principles for building a better 'body', and I enrolled in his course. Now I am a big, full, healthy church, the envy of the beach.[2]

The adaptation of the title for this paper from Dale Carnegie's *How to Win Friends and Influence People* is no accident.[3] Since publication in 1936, it has proved to be an enduring envoy for the power of positive thinking, and an ardent champion of 'persuasion': how to win people to your way of thinking, how to change people, how to increase your popularity and prestige, get out of a rut, and so on. This paper is an anatomical investigation into the Church Growth Movement (hereafter called the CGM), and its peculiar form of rhetorical persuasion, which, like Carnegie's work, centres on 'winning' (growing churches in both numerical size and number) and 'influence' (what the CGM brings to bear on its adherents).

At present the CGM enjoys considerable popularity. Its principles were first devised by Donald McGavran, who examined churches and their numerical growth in the Third World and later founded the Institute for Church Growth in Eugene, Oregon, subsequently relocating it to Fuller Theological Seminary, California.[4] Stemming from there, the movement now touches thinking from the hedonic ecclesiology of Robert Schuller, to the austere revisionist Calvinism of Arthur Glasser, to the restrained dispensationalism of George Peters, to the pentecostalism of John Wimber. Since the 1970s there has been prodigious literary production in support of the CGM, from personal testimonies to the 'How to' type of handbook. Yet there are still very few studies critical of CGM principles, and the consecrated pragmatism of the movement has usually meant that criticism has often been answered in a rather *ad hoc* fashion.[5] Unfortunately this paper will only really serve as a general introduction to the CGM, so it is therefore necessarily broad, seeking to highlight the main areas of concern that need further study.

There is, of course, nothing new about church growth principles. Early church leaders like Marcion knew only too well that the promulgation of selected essentials from within Christianity led to popularity and growth. Cults, schisms and heresies have often grown by affirming an apparently 'lost' doctrine or revelation, denying others, or oversimplifying certain beliefs in order to appeal to a new or wider audience. However, the principles presented by the CGM are not quite like this. On one level anyone can use church growth principles; they are said to be 'neutral tools' for growth, and can be used by Christians, but also by people of different religious persuasions. Yet on another level what the CGM offers is a new pathology for the twentieth century church; it assumes it to be a sick 'body', in decline, whereas God intended the church to grow.[6] Therefore a complex array of curatives that will bring healing and restoration has been devised. New converts and disciples are God's revealed priority, and the church must be the means for harvesting them. The 'formulas' the CGM offers, if applied correctly, will bring salvation to others, along with growth, success and prosperity for the ailing church.[7] C. Peter Wagner is now perhaps McGavran's most famous disciple, and a chief spokesperson for the CGM. His own description of the CGM supports some of the views I have outlined:

> Church Growth is that science which investigates the nature,
> function and health of the Christian church as it relates
> specifically to the effective implementation of God's
> commission to 'make disciples of all nations'. Church Growth
> is simultaneously a theological conviction, and an applied
> science which strives to combine the eternal principles of God's
> Word with the best insights of social and behavioural sciences,
> employing as its initial frame of reference the foundational work
> done by Dr Donald McGavran.[8]

The first thing to note in the quotation above is the use of the word
'science'. What in fact is being suggested here is that an axiom of
correspondence exists between an ideal or desired reality, and the
current state of the church. The 'reality' is contained within 'the
eternal principles of God's Word', and the church should match up
to this reality. The rhetoric of the CGM is an attempt to argue for this
axiom, and what does not fit into this axiom is necessarily defined out
of existence. The central questions for us to consider, therefore, are
two-fold. First, what realities are people being pointed to by the CGM?
And secondly, how are people being pointed to these realities? The
second question will be dealt with first since the brevity of this paper
means that only a small amount of space can be devoted to the
(distorted) theological realities present in the CGM. The arena for
analysis here is potentially vast, covering as it does many types of
theology, ecclesiology and missiology. Therefore in order to move
towards providing an anatomy of the pathology, what I propose to do
is to deal with the works of the CGM as 'rhetoric'. The CGM is
essentially a selective form of realism, which is emphasized by rhetorical means. Rhetoric is the examination of the way in which discourses
are constructed to achieve certain effects. Its focus is the power and
concrete performance of discourse, viewing it as a means of pleading,
persuading, inciting, and so on, and on the response of the audience
to the linguistic structures and the material situations in which they
function.[9]

RHETORIC AND THE CHURCH GROWTH MOVEMENT

Rhetoric, classically, is part of the Trivium of grammar, rhetoric and
logic. Grammar is the specific art of the ordering of words (like
narrative), and logic is the art of producing meaning, although logic
and meaning can be the same thing. In the past suspicion with

rhetoric both as a creative and as a critical activity has sometimes meant that assertive, descriptive or factual writing has been viewed as a direct union between grammar and logic. Yet it is probably true that the only road between grammar and logic 'runs through the intermediate territory of rhetoric'.[10] Northrop Frye has divided rhetoric into two types or stages: Ornamental and Persuasive speech or writing. 'Ornamental rhetoric' attempts skilfully and admirably to state the case for its audience. 'Persuasive rhetoric' tries to lead the audience kinetically towards a course of action. In other words, one articulates the state of play, the other manipulates or directs it.

In view of this, it is important to recognize that the CGM — with all its books, courses, exponents and other forms of apologia — is a presentation of or an argument for a particular type of Christianity, supported by 'evidence'. This 'evidence' might be an increase in numerical growth in the congregation, more people 'equipped' with spiritual gifts, or just a more 'powerful' church. Therefore the starting point for the arguments and the subsequent ways they are developed must be examined first. This division is essential, and should not be misunderstood. The unfolding as well as the starting point of argument presupposes the agreement of the audience. When a speaker or writer selects and puts forward an argument, reliance upon the basic adherence of the audience to the underlying premises is crucial, before propositions or arguments can be developed. Thus, acceptance of CGM principles is usually dependent on the audience agreeing in the first place about the present nature of the church (eg weak, powerless), of God (eg strong, powerful) and of creation. In this way, it is common to encounter church growth literature introducing itself by pointing to slow or no growth in church life, or 'nominal' church attendance in the western world, in contrast to the booming growth in some Third World countries. Thus, the establishment or selection of a proper 'context' is a necessarily rhetorical device; it sets the stage for the CGM presentation of Christianity.

Examples of this sort of contextual rhetoric abound in the CGM, as the functional use of statistics in the church growth courses illustrates. If Pentecostal 'converts' in Latin America can rise from 20,000 in 1900 to 20 million by 1980, 'why can't God do something similar in your neighbourhood?'.[11] Testimony to growth in one area, compared with no testimony of (measurable) growth in the audience's area, begs a contextual rhetorical question. In a similar way, it is quite common to find CGM practitioners drawing a distinction between 'dead' and 'alive' churches. There can actually be no such thing as a 'dead' church; logically, the phrase is an oxymoron. Yet terms like 'dead' and 'alive' are used to denote those with 'the right attitude' to evangelism, worship, spiritual gifts, and so on. And because no one actually wants to be part of a 'dead' church, audiences are often persuaded to select the life-giving formulas and principles that will ensure that their church is saved from obscurity. Even the style of worship employed can establish premises and contextual boundaries that are 'hidden persuaders'. Words set to militant marching music encourage activity rather than reflection, and 'crusading' songs against obstacles to growth ('powers, principalities, witchcraft', etc) are all usual in the CGM. Other worship often exalts the majesty of God in an almost monarchian way (obsessions with the power and fatherhood of God), or reflect a romantic worldview, in which power, glory, fulfilment and desire are intrinsically bound up in intimate relationship with God.

Persuasive discourse is effective because of its insertion as a whole into a situation which is itself usually rather complicated. Since the various elements of the discourse interact with one another, both the scope of argumentation and the order of arguments need to be looked at with care. Having established context, it is important that the next stage of rhetorical argument is exegesis or eisegesis: appealing to sources or authorities, seemingly beyond the realm of the specific argument or possible self-interest of the rhetorician. In the CGM statistics can again be functionally applied here, or perhaps the nature of God appealed to, given the context already set by the type of worship employed. The Bible is often used too, since it apparently contains — according to the CGM — formulas and strategies for church growth, and reveals that CGM principles are 'on the heart of God'.[12]

There are numerous examples of selective exegesis or eisegesis. For instance, one might expect Matthew 22:36-38 to form the heart of a mission strategy for a church under any normal circumstances; love of God and neighbour was what Jesus himself described as the only 'great' command. But in CGM thinking Matthew 28:18-20 is the key text for mission; it is the 'great' commission. This is partly because it permits a mechanistic view of conversion and discipleship, but also because it can be specifically interpreted from the axiom of correspondence to suit existing CGM principles. Much of McGavran's *Understanding Church Growth* is devoted to establishing the centrality of Matthew 28:18-20 and thereafter drawing CGM principles from the text.[13] Similarly, the work of James Engel serves the CGM cause by grading responses to God using a scale. Beginning with no personal knowledge of God (minus ten), the scale ascends to the Matthaean text, which is the pivotal point (zero) at which a new disciple is born. A new convert can then go on in the faith, passing 'stages' evaluated and numbered from one to ten.[14]

The development of this mechanistic approach in CGM discourse can be seen in the final stage of the rhetorical argument, which is usually the identification of principles (from the previous stage of argument) culminating in 'application'. Like rhetoric, mechanistic approaches to Christianity focus on the effectiveness of a proposal, and therefore usually operate according to rational principles. This final phase of the rhetorical argument is crucial to the CGM, since these are the directives or principles that the audience is being led to, and being persuaded to adopt. These are the governing formulas of successful church growth, and are the result of applying the exegesis or eisegesis that came out of the context. Of course these applications, isolated here for study, form part of the whole rhetorical discourse and are in constant interaction at more than one level: interaction between various arguments and presuppositions that are put forward, interaction between the arguments and the overall drive of the rhetoric, between the arguments and their conclusions, and, finally, between the arguments occurring in the discourse and those that are about the discourse. Yet it must be noted that directives and principles are not the same as 'logic'; logic aims at articulating truth, whereas the goal of rhetoric is the adherence of the audience or judge.

So, the applications or conclusions of church growth rhetoric are designed to be effective in action (mechanistic) and thus convincing to the audience. But that effectiveness includes supporting the supporting rhetoric and the choices of context. Peter Wagner again provides an excellent illustration of this as he describes on several occasions the 'Seven Vital Signs' of a 'healthy church':

> 1. A pastor who is a possibility thinker and whose dynamic leadership has been used to catalyse the entire church into action for growth.
> 2. A well-mobilized laity which has discovered, has developed and is using all the spiritual gifts for growth.
> 3. A church big enough to provide the range of services that meet the needs of and expectations of all its members.
> 4. A proper balance of the dynamic relationship between celebration, congregation and cell.
> 5. A membership drawn primarily from one homogeneous unit.

6. Evangelistic methods that have proved to make disciples.
7. Priorities arranged in biblical order.[15]

Wagner's vital signs are, of course, packed with persuasive power. Indeed he uses numerous images of power or mechanism to induce his audience: dynamics, catalysis, mobilization, size, range, balance, unit, priority, and order. A 'healthy church' is clearly going to be one in which there is a lot of 'energy'. The CGM then argues for and presents us with this view of Christianity: the successful church is a 'power-packed' one, and God himself, the supreme power-packed being, is just waiting to energize his people.

My distinctions about the phases of CGM rhetoric may or may not be convincing, but before I continue space is needed here to reflect on what has taken place. First, rhetoric cannot be avoided in argument, and so to leave an argument at this stage would inevitably invite criticism about being caught in a hermeneutical circle. Secondly, I ought to make it clear that I am not actually complaining about the use of rhetoric, but its abuse. CGM rhetoric is rhetoric of a bad type. Good (or Classical) rhetoric should be constructed around a debate, in which the audience can decide between one argument or another; this construction ensures that the audience has a measure of freedom. CGM rhetoric, though, is a subtle form of manipulation; anything that does not promote 'growth' is relegated or excluded, with no alternative. The implicit CGM doctrines of God, church, redemption and creation all close down the options of the audience, inducing them to accept the 'life' offered, rather than the (certain) death they face if they do not.

Rhetoric has attracted suspicion in the past for its corruptibility for precisely these reasons: manipulation, lack of proper debate and subsequent loss of true freedom for the adherents. In addition, bad rhetoric is usually a sign that what is actually being witnessed to in the discourse is of itself corrupt. As I have already said, I believe the CGM to be a complex pathology. It is a 'problem-centred' activity or curative that is obsessed with power in God and in the church: simplistic, dismissive and pragmatic in orientation, yet complex; mechanistic in composition, yet dualistic and romantic in its theology and worldview. Seeing the discourses of the CGM as rhetoric though, as well as how the rhetoric is structured, only partly supports this proposition. To provide a more accurate anatomy of this particular pathology will require deeper work.

In order more precisely to ascertain the trends that are at work within the overall rhetoric, some deeper linguistic analysis is needed that will provide a taxonomy of forms suitable for further analysis. Deconstruction, as a way forward, has been rejected here, since if pushed too far everything can be reduced to a stale and immobile form of relativity (although pure deconstruction — perhaps best represented by the work of Jacques Derrida — is arguably exempt from this criticism).[16] It is true that the CGM uses a common discourse and language that is identifiably 'conservative' in theological terms. It is also true that the CGM is severely realistic and fundamentalist in its methodologies, giving its audiences a systematic distortion of some, or a selection of, fundamental realities. What is required is a system of analysis that will illustrate that the CGM rhetoric is rhetoric in the service of distorted realities and indicates in part the nature of those realities. There are a number of ways forward at this point but I have chosen to use a developed synthesis of Northrop Frye's work, in conjunction with the adaptations of James Hopewell.[17] In assessing the CGM, the total sum of rhetoric has to be broken down into genres, and temporarily isolated before further analysis can take place. An applied set of existing genres or categories that work for narrative, rhetoric and logic will be used, and then it will be seen which type of genre the CGM rhetoric mostly employs, and how. Frye and Hopewell use four, which I have adapted in the following way.

The first genre is *Canonic (or Tragic)*: reliance upon an authoritative interpretation of a world pattern, often considered God's revealed word or will, by which one identifies one's essential life. The wholeness or soundness of the pattern requires that the followers reject any knowledge of union with the pattern but instead subordinate their selfhood to it. The second is *Empiric (or Ironic)*: a high degree of realism is required about the way things work, and the supernatural is often excluded. The third is *Gnostic (or Comic)*: generally it relies upon a process in the world that guarantees a development from dissipation towards unity. Fulfilment and agreement are the ultimate expectation, as in all good comedy, with alienating genres rejected as impediments to unity. The fourth genre is *Charismatic (or Romantic)*, and is dependent upon a transcendent spirit, personally encountered, that will disregard empirical presumptions. In place of normal order, supernatural irregularities will instead be witnessed. Given this set of genres for analysis, which offers a square or grid rather than a simple bipolar scale, the next task is to see what truths or forces the CGM rhetoric protects and witnesses to.

THE ANATOMY OF THE PATHOLOGY

There are many different types of CGM discourse that need attention: assorted forms of worship that give an indication of the kind of God being invoked for church growth, types of biblical interpretation, the use of statistics and the use of personal testimony, to name but a few. However, brevity requires that only a few may be analysed, and my aim here is to provide a rather sweeping survey that will offer a broad picture of what major forces and truths are operating in the CGM.

Let us consider a simple testimony of church growth, taken from a newly established and growing church:

> I wanted to speak God's creative word into the situation to bring about change, not to dwell on general principles...it was necessary for the way ahead to be clearly charted and declared without debate. This was the way we were going. This was what God wanted. And if this sounds arrogant, I can only confess that I do believe God gave me no option....[18]

The author goes on to cite how many people left his church as a result of the changes made, and although this was painful, he maintains that it was God's overall desire that the church should grow. There was an initial drop in congregational numbers but they rose later, as more people joined who were attracted by the very specific ministry being offered there. Thus, the justification for offending some existing members was that they were obstacles to growth, and therefore had to 'join in or opt out'. This stance can be criticized on a number of different levels; it is not far from saying the end justifies the means, and it is also an inversion of the New Testament doctrine of the church which struggled with difference to maintain unity constantly, and did not ever advocate a pre-millenial weeding process. But it is the choice of words that is of most interest.

First, there is a strong Charismatic (or Romantic) tint to the testimony; general principles are to be disregarded in favour of seeing direction and action. The change that will come is unstoppable, because it is 'God's creative word' that will do the work; debate is pointless, because God has already decided what is going to happen. Secondly, the Gnostic (or Comic) genre is also much in evidence; the way ahead is agreement, clarity and fulfilment. Those who do not see now what God is doing will come to understand in the fullness of time, which is why the writer is so sure about the direction, yet slightly concerned about the criticism of 'arrogance'. Naturally, the writer would not see himself as arrogant, but simply rather more visionary than his congregation. Thirdly, the Canonic (or Tragic) genre is also present, simply by virtue of the stress laid on 'without debate' and 'no option'; the writer is working to a pattern which he partly glimpses through the Charismatic genre, is working towards in the Gnostic genre, yet does not fully see. Fourthly, the Empiric (or Ironic) genre manifests itself in the rampant pragmatism of the testimony as a whole. The writer is a realist, possibly a ruthless realist; the changes that come to his church are guaranteed to bring growth, as any person with knowledge of marketing skills could tell him. This testimony illustrates the full range of genres present in CGM rhetoric, yet it is vital that we begin to see which ones are more usually favoured in discourses that present the CGM to its audiences.

The Homogeneous Unit Principle, for example, demonstrates the Empiric pragmatism of the CGM at its peak:

> Dr McGavran has said, '[People] like to become Christians without ever crossing racial, linguistic or class barriers'... It has been found that where cultural obstacles are recognized and new converts nurtured in churches of their own culture, the evangelistic efforts are far more effective...[19]

Again, note the stress of the word 'effective'. The fact that Homogeneous Units are little more than a developed form of apartheid is not considered crucially important, as 'effectiveness' is the guiding reality. Nor is how this 'type' of evangelism relates to the New Testament really considered; attempts to justify it from Scripture have been made, but only with the aim of justifying what is currently the apparently most fruitful way to spread the gospel. The Homogeneous Unit Principle shows that an Empiric genre is certainly forcibly at work within the CGM, and that this empiricism is witnessed to in the overall rhetoric. Furthermore, the force or truth behind this rhetoric is twofold: mechanism in faith and works, with a relentless drive towards simplicity in the interests of effectiveness. That is not to say that the CGM is not complex. It is. But it is complexity of discourse, belief and organization that is determined towards simplifying a Christianity which is in the service of effectiveness and growth. That is why there is 'no option', or change is made 'without debate'; discussion of wider options would complicate matters, upset mechanisms, and possibly decrease the overall effectiveness of strategy and discourse.

The Canonic genre most clearly manifests itself in some of the theology that underpins the CGM. It will be no surprise to learn that the overwhelming majority of churches that adopt CGM principles are 'conservative' in their approach to Scripture and other forms of Christian tradition. Indeed, McGavran and others have at times taunted non-conservative churches for their lack of growth, thereby implying that a Canonic genre is an essential force within the CGM.[20] So it is perhaps opportune here to briefly reflect on one way in which the Bible is used to justify church growth.

> Those who enter the Kingdom should give the King and the Kingdom their first priority of loyalty and service (Matt 6:33) and should pray for the Kingdom to come (Matt 6:10)...Jesus taught his disciples to expect this growth of the Kingdom... He taught that their obedient service would spread the good news of the Kingdom... The agricultural motif of so many parables illustrates the expected growth of the Kingdom.[21]

The CGM uses the Bible in a way that suggests that the pattern for church growth has already been established by God in Scripture. Jesus taught that growth would come, so it will. All that is required on behalf of the adherents to CGM teaching is that they give their obedience and service to this mandate. Subjugation to this authoritative interpretation of mission and the world is essential if growth is to be achieved. For those who do not subordinate themselves, the outcome is therefore equally obvious: 'Those who refuse to submit to his reign over their lives or who are insincere in their professed allegiance do not enter the Kingdom, even though they may appear to (Matt 7:21)'.[22] More time could be spent considering the strength of the Canonic genre within CGM discourse, and the rhetorical and real threat it holds over its audience. However, two more genres need to be covered briefly.

The Charismatic (or Romantic) genre is perhaps the most detectable genre in the 'new wave' of church growth teaching, and has laid heavy stress on spiritual gifts and the importance of charismatic renewal. Yet, due to the pragmatism of CGM, we must again note that spiritual gifts are seen as being in the service of effectiveness and growth; Peter Wagner describes them as just one more 'powerful spiritual instrument' to be incorporated into the tool-kit of the church growth specialist. Despite this, the extreme romanticism of the CGM reveals itself in the ordinary expressions it uses to describe God and the world: Jesus is Lord over demons; the Bible is a programme or guide book (almost as though it was being used by an adventurous tourist); the gospel is 'power' and the church a 'harvest'; authority, although partly derived from Scripture, is mostly found in personally manifested evidence of God's immanence. Thus 'Signs, Wonders and Church Growth' is a perfectly natural development of the CGM; the supernatural will be witnessed, which will in turn lead to growth.

An additional factor related to the Romantic genre is worth mentioning here, namely the implicit sexual language present in CGM rhetoric. For example, a European Church Growth Conference was entitled: 'Explore, Expand, Explode!'. This is not so much the language of populating (churches) as of copulating. Much of the worship employed in charismatic CGM churches implicitly carries these sexual or orgasmic overtones:

> Lord you are more precious than silver,
> Lord, you are more costly than gold,
> Lord, you are more beautiful than diamonds,
> And nothing I desire compares with you...[23]

> Lord, I'll seek after you,
> Because you're the only one that satisfies,
> Turn towards to kiss your face,
> And as I draw near to you,
> I will give you all my love,
> Bow down to seek your face...[24]

This is the language of submission yet power, of fulfilment yet longing, of desire yet gratification. This sort of Romantic worship exercises a powerful influence over the context in which much of the CGM rhetoric sets itself. Anxiety about powerlessness, impotence and decline in the church is being relieved by worshipping a God who is intimate and all-powerful. The audience have nothing to fear, because God is so close to them, assuring them of his presence in this deep time of worship. In the Romantic genre, the Christian life is an adventure, and God the source of power and love.

The last genre for consideration is the Gnostic (or Comic). The simplest way to deal with this is to focus on the strong interest CGM adherents have in healing either the church or individuals. In the case of churches, I have already suggested that the CGM is a pathology; it believes the church to be a sick body, in need of healing, renewal and restoration. This is 'the dissipation towards unity' of the Gnostic genre; one day, all believers will be like-minded, and will not be divided by doctrine, schism or other barriers. Growth, healing and harmony will be universal. Similarly, in the case of individuals, there has been a prodigious production of books on healing in recent years, concentrating on technique, testimony or teaching. There is not space here to examine the vast range of approaches, and in any case this would not be entirely relevant. What is interesting to note is the underlying assumption of many books, which can be encapsulated thus: 'You may not see things quite this way now, but in the fullness of time, all will come to understand'. Some may feel this to be an overstatement, but the following example will illustrate my point.

In the much publicized case of David Watson's death from cancer, and the attempts of CGM practitioner John Wimber to heal him, two points have emerged. First, some Vineyard members (Wimber's network of churches) now say that if David were alive today, they could heal him, as their methods of prayer have improved. Again the axiom of correspondence is worth noting: correct prayer means the ideal reality will be realized. Nothing can ultimately interfere with the Romantic conclusion: individuals and churches will all experience growth, fulfilment and redemption, and those who resist will be (lovingly) conquered. In the ideal Comic world, all live to the end to come to new understandings and insights about themselves and the world; they are spared the alienating Empiric or Canonic structures that might spoil the conclusion (like death or failure). Consequently and secondly, Wimber's only explanation for Watson's death was that 'Satan murdered him';[25] the only way the Gnostic genre has of dealing with ordinary tragedy is to make it a random act of absurdity, yet an act that could be redeemed if there were a chance to repeat the scenario. Thus, in this particular case, the ending has been spoilt, yet one is left with the impression that a day will come when such disappointments need not happen.

More could be said of the Gnostic genre, but space is limited. Attention, for example, needs to be paid to the area of 'intuition' in Charismatic CGM churches. Equally, the stress on harmony and its relationship to Canonic and Empiric structures (like Homogeneous Units) is worth noting. What is clear though, from this brief survey of genres, is that there are some extremely powerful truths and forces that CGM rhetoric is either implicitly or explicitly witnessing to. In turn, these forces are influencing those that are adherents of the CGM; their expectations about God, the church and the world are all being quietly moulded and manipulated. In the conclusion to this paper, I want to briefly mention three of the important forces I believe to be behind the CGM rhetoric, and the consequent implications.

CONCLUSION: ROMANCE, MECHANISM AND POWER

As has already been suggested, the four genres used for analysis provide us with a grid for mapping the bias of language in the CGM, rather than a simple bipolar scale. What is clear from my survey of CGM rhetoric so far is that in negotiation between the four sides of this grid, the discourses of the CGM are primarily gravitating towards a Canonic and Charismatic corner. True enough, there are strong pulses of Gnostic and Empiric discourse, but in the case of Gnostic language much of it is justified or couched in phrases more akin to Charismatic genres. Similarly, anything Empiric is often relocated in Canonic spheres, as the justification for most pragmatism, such as Homogeneous Units (Empiric) from Scripture (Canonic), clearly illustrates. In addition, we must note that the heteronomy of the movement, its heavy emphasis on healing and pathology, dualism, miracles, intimate worship, growth, success and power, also point to a drift towards a Charismatic and Canonic corner. This drift in turn gives a historical insight into some of the directions the CGM is taking at present. Due to the popularity, power and effectiveness of Wimber's peculiar brand of pentecostalism, the CGM has found its pull almost irresistible, and much of church growth teaching has now become synonymous with teaching on spiritual gifts, new styles of worship, and other pentecostal phenomena such as speaking in tongues.

A conspicuous Romantic tendency, noticeable in the CGM, counters rationalism, the decorum of the Enlightenment and fear of church decline, by reverting to the stark drama and suprarational mysteries of the Christian story and doctrines. Violent conflicts and abrupt reversals of the Christian inner life, turning on the extremes of destruction and creation, heaven and hell and so on, provide a context packed with adventure and drama that ultimately saves human history and destiny, religious values and experiential paradigms by reconstituting them in a way that is not only intellectually acceptable, but also emotionally pertinent. The Romantic genre in the CGM is an enterprise that aims at sustaining the inherited spiritual order against what seems like the imminence of chaos, decline and disaster. Inevitably though, Romanticism 'is split religion'.[26] Its interest in sustaining order and promoting growth leads it into a dual search for power and mechanism, which initially seems at odds with Romance. Yet neither pursuit is surprising, since both act as guarantors of the Romantic outcome. In the case of power, transcendence and immanence are appealed to; in the case of mechanism, structures and paradigms are set up to protect, monitor and foster the power and romance. Yet the Romanticism of the CGM is ultimately a technique that is in the service of realism. It is not the reality itself. Romanticism is an inducement for audiences to commit themselves to the realities being pointed to by the CGM, and offers a worldview in which their realities become real possibilities.

This in turn leads us to the question of the power of God in CGM rhetoric. The usual picture portrayed of God's power is one that sets it up in competition with creation's freedom, thereby reducing it to a rather coercive and persuasive force. Power is also usually linked to activity or effectiveness, concluding in achievement that will provide undeniable evidence or certainty. It is for this reason that 'power healing' and 'power evangelism', two phrases coined by Wimber, are seen as 'signs' of God's activity.[27] Indeed, the presence of God, it is said, can almost be measured by the amount of power 'felt' or 'discerned' in individuals or congregations. Thus power for the CGM is a sign of God's activity that manifests itself in phenomena that lead to effectiveness and growth; the goal of the church and individuals should be to become as it is said God, Jesus and the Holy Spirit are like, namely reservoirs of power that will change people and the world. Consequently scant attention is paid to the freedom God has given to and in creation, or to the peculiar way in which God makes himself powerless and vulnerable. Here again we see the selectivity of premises in CGM reality, which in turn are compounded by selectivity of rhetoric, which leads to overall distortion.

Mechanism is intrinsically linked to the forces of romance and power at work within the CGM; its whole focus is on programmed effectiveness. The church, people, pastoral problems, God and his activity, all are treated with an eye to efficiency, as though a machine was being dealt with. Basic structures and beliefs within Christianity and the local church have to be sound and dynamic, if goals are to be achieved. The efficiency of these mechanisms is now in turn checked by results, such as greater numbers in church, increased giving, or more people 'equipped' for service.[28] If the results are inadequate, the mechanisms are checked: for example, 'Has the right sort of prayer and worship taken place? If so, we wouldn't still have this problem; if not, we need to change things in order to reach our goal'. It is perhaps here in mechanism that the pathological approach of the CGM to Christianity is at its most obvious. The church as a body is deemed to be sick, asleep or dead; the 'sickness' is then articulated and diagnosed, and the cures applied. Mechanists, though, are not opposed to activity that is not directly related to efficiency; fellowship, reflection and introspection can be welcomed in context. However, the primary goal of the CGM is the 'rationalisation of congregational process and the animation of social will to achieve results'.[29] Because the CGM sees salvation as occurring somewhat mechanistically in individual souls, reliable formulas will always be sought for gathering large numbers of persons into congregations.

The CGM is ultimately a window into a type of flawed missiology, expressed in 'bad' rhetoric, that protects and addresses forces that 'win' and 'influence' adherents in a manipulative way to a Christianity that is flawed. The realities the CGM witnesses to are twofold: 'power' (in God, church and individuals) and 'mechanism' which both communicates and searches for power. Like a classic heresy, it is right in some things it affirms but corrupt in what it denies. The CGM represents a selective form of theological realism, which is emphasized by rhetorical means, but by its axiomatic approach denies other equally important fundamental realities. But to leave the criticism at this point might just imply that the CGM is a perversion of something that is basically sound. Yet the very vehicle and content of Christian communication is under scrutiny here.[30] The CGM presents its brand of Christianity rhetorically, in functional terms; it is useful for meeting individuals or groups in need, averting anxieties or crises, overcoming limitations, or other problems. It is a pathological Christianity that heals and repairs what has gone wrong. The seductiveness of this approach is that it is partly correct. There is indeed good news for every painful, needy and problematic situation or person. The flaw lies in the fact that it ties God into an axiomatic relationship with the world in which his communication and being centre on personal or corporate problem-solving activity, and fails to acknowledge his freedom inside and outside creation, inside and outside the church, as well as inside and outside invented or perceived axioms. In short, it fails to acknowledge his total abundance and dynamism, and the centricity of the missiological approach shifts quickly and imperceptibly from being dynamically theocentric to being problem-centred; that is to say, the identity of God becomes too linked to limitations or problems, and therefore limited. What needs to be appreciated is that God is already ahead of all evangelism, mission and church growth, his abundance poured out way beyond all mechanisms, romantic frameworks or any reservoirs of power there might be. The task for the church is to discern this abundance and grace, indeed the very movement of God; to accept it and to share it.

NOTES

1. This is a real advertisement for a Church Growth Conference, taken from *Christianity Today Magazine*, July 1987.
2. This is an advertisement for church growth I have written myself, with apologies to Charles Atlas.
3. Dale Carnegie, *How to Win Friends and Influence People*, Tadworth: Cedar Books, 1953 (originally published 1936).
4. Donald McGavran, *Bridges of God*, New York: Friendship Press, 1955; *How Churches Grow*, New York: Friendship Press, 1959.
5. See for example C. Peter Wagner, *Church Growth and the Whole Gospel*, San Francisco: Harper & Row, 1981, chs 4ff.
6. See The Bible Society, *Church Growth 1*, Swindon, 1980, pp9ff.
7. *ibid.*, pp 25ff.
8. Wagner's definition is quoted in *Churchman*, Vol. 95, 1981, p 227.
9. See *A Dictionary of Literary Terms*, ed J. A. Cuddon, London: Penguin, 1976.
10. Northrop Frye, *The Anatomy of Criticism*, Princeton: Princeton University Press, 1957, p 331. See also Brian Vickers, *In Defence of Rhetoric*, Oxford: Blackwell, 1988, and C. Perelman and L. Olbrechts-Tyteca, *The New Rhetoric: A Treatise on Argumentation*, Notre Dame, Ind.: Notre Dame University Press, 1969.
11. *Church Growth 1*, p 17.
12. *ibid.*, pp 17ff.
13. Donald McGavran, *Understanding Church Growth*, Grand Rapids: Eerdmans, 1970.
14. *Church Growth 1*, pp 49ff.
15. C. Peter Wagner, *Your Church Can Grow*, Glendale, California: Regal Books, 1976, p 159.
16. See for example J. Derrida, *Writing and Difference*, ET, Chicago: University of Chicago Press, 1978, pp 279ff.
17. James Hopewell, *Congregation: Stories and Structures*, ed Barbara G. Wheeler, London: SCM, 1988, p 69.
18. Roger Forster (ed), *Ten New Churches*, London: MARC Europe, 1986, p 153.
19. Roy Pointer, *Why Do Churches Grow?*, London: MARC Europe, 1984, p 53.
20. Dean Kelley, *Why Conservative Churches are Growing*, New York: Harper & Row, 1972. See also *Understanding Church Growth*, pp 354ff.
21. *Why Do Churches Grow?*, p 65.
22. *ibid.*, p 64.
23. Lyrics from *Lord, you are more precious*, Anaheim, California: Mercy Publishing.
24. Lyrics from *Lord, I'll seek after you*, Anaheim, California: Mercy Publishing.
25. I have heard Wimber himself say this. It is clear from correspondence with people associated with Wimber and Watson's death that a good systematic theodicy is absent from Wimber's teaching.
26. M. H. Abrams, *Natural Supernaturalism*, New York: Harper & Row, 1971, p 68.
27. See John Wimber's *Power Evangelism*, London: Hodder & Stoughton, 1985, and *Power Healing*, London: Hodder & Stoughton, 1986.
28. This is the aim behind *Equipping the Saints*, a quarterly magazine from the Vineyard Fellowship examining how spiritual gifts can 'equip' churches for growth and effectiveness.
29. *Congregation*, p 26.
30. See Daniel Hardy and David Ford, *Jubilate*, London: Darton, Longman & Todd, 1984, pp 137ff.

PART TWO
'At Eye Level':
The Contextualization of
Christian Education

SECTION TWO
The School

INTRODUCTION

John Hull approaches the question of 'The Bible in the Secular Classroom' through the universal human experience of loss. This enquiry suggests that there are alternative ways of unlocking the meaning of the Bible and that the church may have domesticated it by laying down approved principles of interpretation. This ecclesiastical prerogative is challenged in the name of an alternative yet complementary hermeneutic, based on the standpoint of unbelief, secularity and anthropological ecumenicity. Such a secular approach provides a legitimate perspective from which to interpret the Bible and a rationale for handling it which is appropriate to the secular context of education. Pupils in school may thus learn *from* the Bible in a way that is educationally defensible and makes it equally accessible to believers and unbelievers alike.

Robin Minney's study of 'Otto's Contribution to Religious Education' demonstrates the relevance of Rudolf Otto's thought to the current debate about 'multi-faith RE'. He argues that Otto's emphasis on the numinous as a depth dimension within all religions can prevent the subject from degenerating into a 'sterile cavalcade of outlandish phenomena'. Equally, the stress on experience encourages a pupil-centred curriculum and the role given to rational analysis provides the teacher with a tool with which to help pupils make sense of their experiences and integrate their lives. In these and other ways, Otto points the way forward for contemporary religious education. In a final section Minney shows how Otto can also assist teachers in their approach to the complex area of spirituality in the classroom.

Drawing on evidence gathered from interviews with adolescent Christians, David Day challenges traditional views about the ways in which schools contribute to spiritual development. His 'Godliness and Good Learning' suggests that modern secondary schools are less schools for saints than training grounds for martyrs. Nevertheless it is possible to argue that the sharp separation between adolescent Christians and their peers which is engendered by school life may have some beneficial effects. The consequent development of a 'character' and a distinctive identity is far from irrelevant to spiritual growth.

Peter Sedgwick's paper on 'The Sectarian Future of the Church and Ecumenical Church Schools' is an exercise in practical theology which relates the institution of the church school to the debate about the nature of the Christian church, particularly as this is interpreted in an ecumenical context. The paper includes a discussion both of the problems of the Christian church in today's world and of modern society in general, and attempts to relate these to the debate about the role of church schools today. Sedgwick argues for 'a way of seeing church schools based on a theology of baptism'. He concludes: 'What matters is that in religious nurture, ecumenical relations and involvement in community the church school should unify nature and grace'.

14

The Bible in the Secular Classroom: An Approach through the Experience of Loss

JOHN M. HULL

THE BIBLE AS A BOOK ABOUT LOSS

The story of the Garden of Eden is the story of the loss which humanity has suffered. With the loss of the garden went the loss of innocence and the loss of home. This basic and universal loss is re-enacted in the history of Israel. This is the story of a people who won a land and then lost it, who established a kingdom and then lost it, who centred all their hopes upon a city which they lost and on a temple which they lost. The New Testament is a story of people who found someone who seemed to be the bearer of a fulfilment for the destiny of the nation, which had been lost, and a revival of the royal line of kings, which had also been lost, but they lost him. Just as the Old Testament centres around the loss of the city, so the New Testament centres around the loss of that person. Jesus is the culmination of the experience of loss not only because he was experienced as lost but also because of his own experience of loss. 'They all forsook him and fled.' 'My God, why hast thou forsaken me?'[1] Jesus is the summary of our loss of friends, of life, and of God.

But how can a book, which deals so thoroughly with our experience of sheer loss stimulate us to creative thinking? On a minor scale, loss can stimulate activity because it can be an insult to pride. There is a loss which stimulates, which irritates, which challenges. But there are losses so deep that they numb the mind. There is that loss so awful that one becomes paralysed. This is particularly so in the case of those experiences of loss in which what is lost is identity, the self itself. The infant who bursts into tears when his or her mother disappears from sight is not merely complaining of feeling lonely. If it is true that the face of the mother is the mirror of the self, then loss of the mother is experienced as loss of the self. To lose oneself, to become lost is not a matter of *finding* oneself in unfamiliar surroundings. It is to become detached from that supreme centre of value from which one derives all sense of worth. Alienated from this, one is worthless. Cut off from this, one is not merely diminished, one is divided, dissolved.[2] That is why in these deep experiences of loss, one cannot summon up action to redeem the loss. The will, the hope, the vision from which that activity should come are themselves lost. So also, in the Bible, we find an account not merely of the losses that people have experienced, but of humanity experiencing loss of itself. They are 'not my people'. 'But I am a worm, and no man.'[3] What Adam lost was not so much the Garden of Eden but Adam.

GOD'S LOSS

In the Bible, men and women are not only described as experiencing loss; they are experienced as lost. It is God who has lost his people. God is impoverished in the loss of humanity. God is bereaved. The Bible is the story of God's long search to retrieve his totally unacceptable loss, his loss of humanity.[4] In Jeremiah 2:13 God is seen crying out, 'They have forsaken me'. The Bible is the dramatic story of the struggle, the interchange, we might almost say the competition between these two unbearable losses: the loss of humanity and the loss of God.

It is often as if the human loss must become more severe before the divine loss can be mitigated. The threat that God has lost the inner devotion and the sincere service of Job cannot be assuaged until Job has lost more and more.

This brings us to the mystery in the biblical account of how to deal with loss. There is no such thing as 'cutting one's losses'. Rather, once you have lost something, you can only redeem that loss by going on and losing everything. The paradox of loss is that loss is redeemed by becoming complete. 'Whoever would save his life will lose it; and whoever loses his life...will save it.'[5] When God meets a person in his or her loss, God goes on stripping that person until he or she stands absolutely naked. This is the story of Adam. 'You are dust, and to dust you shall return.'[6] It is the story of Joseph. He began by losing his coat of many colours and finished up in Egypt, having lost his family, his country, his honour, his liberty, and being daily in fear of losing life itself. It is the story of Job, who began rich and prosperous, and was finally seated on the town rubbish heap scratching his sores. It is the story of Jesus, who 'though he was rich, yet for your sake he became poor', who 'became obedient unto death, even death on a cross'.[7] The cross represents God's abandonment of humanity and humanity's abandonment of God. It is at this point, and not at any earlier point of the process of loss, that creative thinking emerges from the Bible.

CREATIVITY OUT OF NOTHING

Just as creation is out of nothing, so creative thinking is also out of nothing. We should distinguish between manipulative and calculative thinking, where thinking has *something* to manipulate, something about which to calculate, something which is not yet lost, and, on the other hand, creative thinking, which is out of nothing. Those of us who live in industrialized societies are all prone to the 'tinkering' approach to problems. We are used to the thought that some modification of the production line will solve the problem. The process is re-routed, or if the machinery has stopped, somebody goes inside with a spanner.[8] The 'do it yourself' mentality with its calculating, bit by bit, patching up approach to life may show ingenuity. But ingenuity is not creativity. Creative thinking in the Bible does not start on this side of the loss of the city, where one is still bargaining, still scheming, but on the far side, when the city has been lost. It is indeed that loss which makes the mouth mute. 'How shall we sing the Lord's song in a foreign land?'[9] There is, however, a place beyond despair. Creative thinking does not begin on this side of the Red Sea when it is still a matter of working out whether the Egyptians will catch us. It begins on the other side of the realization that they *will* catch us. Creative thinking does not begin on this side of the flood, when every store has sold out of rain gauges and you can't get a do-it-yourself book on boat-building for love or money. It begins on the far side of the flood, when there is nothing but an empty earth, a dove with a twig in its beak, and a rainbow. It does not appear on the earlier side of Calvary. When Peter took Jesus and rebuked him for his determination to go to Jerusalem and die, his thinking was not creative but calculative. Calculative thinking is always full of bright ideas, clever suggestions. When, on an earlier occasion, Peter cried out, 'Master,...let us make three booths...', it was a bright idea, but it was not creative thinking.[10] Creative thinking emerges out of the way of the cross. 'Unless a grain of wheat falls into the earth and dies, it remains alone; but if it dies, it bears much fruit.'[11] Creative thinking arises not out of plenty but out of poverty, not out of wealth but out of want, not out of freedom but out of fetters:

> When you were young, you girded yourself and walked where you would; but when you are old, you will stretch out your hands, and another will gird you and carry you where you do not wish to go. (This he said to show by what death he was to glorify God.)[12]

In this strange passage, youth, vitality, independence and strength are contrasted with old age, impotence, frustration and constriction, but it is out of the latter that God is glorified. Creative thinking does not arise out of the confidence of strength nor out of the pain and fear of loss but out of that strange place beyond all loss. Loss is the gateway to creativity. Loss creates the possibilities for it. Loss is the loss of something, which makes possible the emergence of creativity out of nothing.

In speaking of this strange place beyond loss, one is speaking of that which is eery and uncanny. Because it is *beyond* our experience of life, there is a sense in which creative thinking is not a 'life-theme', not experiential. When, in order to overcome God's loss, the loss which humanity has endured is pushed to the ultimate, a new God and a new humanity discover each other. The source of this new humanity is not the old humanity but the creative ground of life itself. It is experienced, but it cannot be calculated or manipulated from experience, and in that sense creative thinking must be described as being transcendent rather than experiential. It is experienced as the creative thinking of God about humanity.

The stories of the resurrection appearances of Jesus are the outstanding symbols of this strangely creative place beyond despair. The empty tomb is precisely an encounter with emptiness. 'See the place where they laid him.'[13] There was nothing. Neither faith nor disbelief but amazement is the experienced characteristic of the life which is created in that strange place.[14] In that state of amazement, men and women became the recipients of peace, of Holy Spirit, of vocation. The experience of amazed receptivity which came out of nothingness when everything had been lost became the source of the immensely creative rebirth of language, relationships and culture which came to be known as Christianity.

THE RELIGIOUS IMPRISONMENT OF THE BIBLE

It would not have occurred to the people of the Bible that the Bible was a religious book. That epithet, with its implied distinction between the religious and the secular, was unknown to them. From their point of view, the Bible was the record of their experiences of life and of that recreation of life which goes beyond experience. For us, however, the Bible has become a sacred book; it is now the Holy Bible. It has now become the divinely inspired literature of a particular religion, just as other divinely inspired books are the sacred norms for other religions. The Bible, in other words, has become the property of the church. The church has become its custodian and its interpreter. Instead of being perceived as the book which drives humanity towards nothing, and on beyond nothing, it is now received as a very important Something: something to be learned, something to be obeyed, a book of instructions, of doctrines, of morals. The Bible itself now becomes the object of religious reverence. It is revered as offering divine truths external to the growing personality, truths which together form a doctrinal structure which then itself becomes an object of belief, so that acceptance of that belief-structure is held to be the gateway into an understanding of the Bible and so to salvation. The Bible as being in itself an object of belief is not mentioned in the Apostles' creed nor in the Nicene creed but today one comes across many interpretations of Christianity in which the first article of faith is acceptance of the supreme authority of the Bible in all matters of faith, doctrine and conduct. So the Bible, God's book about all humanity, is now the book of Christians. The Bible, which is the book pointing to the Kingdom of God, has become the book of the church. Only by identifying the Kingdom of God with the church can this domestication of the Bible be justified.[15] Christian and Jewish people are now regarded by Muslims as being people of the book. All three religions forget that all humanity is a people of the book. It is as if squatters have taken up residence in this vast mansion, which is really public property, and refuse to let anyone in, unless they become like the people who have already squatted there. The first responsibility of a religious education concerned with faithfulness to the Bible is to deny that any religion or race or nation or creed or generation or period in time can establish a squatter's right to the Bible.

This may mean that religious education in our day must sometimes attack the squatter's Bible. For the squatter, this may well be experienced as loss. Loss of the Bible as the religious book of a particular section of humanity, a book which gives meaning and identity to that section of humanity at the cost of excluding others, may often be the first curriculum objective for the religious education teacher dealing with the Bible today. This process of losing the orthodox, Christian Bible can be seen in the birth of the new religious movements in primal societies today. These new movements, of which one is born everyday in Africa alone, are almost entirely due to the impact of Christianity upon such societies, and one of the major factors in this is the translation of the Bible into local languages.[16] What orthodox Christians have often failed to observe is that this translation of the Bible has not only meant the availability of the Bible, it has also meant the loss of the Bible. Possessing the Bible as a nothing (ie without reading it through the doctrinal structures of Christendom), emerging peoples in primal societies have entered into creative encounter with it quite apart from the ecclesiastical traditions which have interpreted the Bible. There is thus a sense in which modern European Christianity, which is developing from the encounter between the industrial societies and the Bible, has no particular primacy or guarantee of authenticity over and above that which the new religious movements may be able to establish, since they also are biblical traditions. Any number of religions could emerge on a biblical basis, and this is exactly what is happening today. This does not mean that all of these biblical religions will not possess certain common features, but these common features will be common to humanity, and not merely distinctive of a particular ecclesiastical tradition. The Bible is thus becoming an ecumenical book, a book for the whole inhabited world.

This loss of the Bible at a corporate or inter-religious level will often be paralleled by a loss of the Bible at the level of individual piety. Whenever continuity with the people of the Bible has been lost because the Bible has itself become a sacred object, then a critical educational task must be begun. In some cases, this may involve an enquiry into the nature of the authority or the inspiration of the Bible. When the Bible is approached under the direction of some exalted theory of authority or special inspiration, it is already being interpreted within a set of doctrinal expectations. To some extent, the structure of religious assumptions and expectations through which one approaches the Bible introduces distortion, and acts as a pre-selector conditioning the response of the reader or listener and, to that extent, preventing her or him from approaching the Bible with a willingness to listen to it in its own terms, rather than in terms of the doctrinal structures created by later ages and now used as a filter for the Bible.

We cannot be thrust into creative thinking in an encounter with that which is conceived of as telling us what we should think. These doctrines of inspiration and authority domesticate the Bible into our religious worldview. The Bible is then pressed into the mould of our religious readiness. It then becomes a sacred possession, part of our religious heritage, part of our devotional life.

If the Bible has no special inspiration, then it has no special invulnerability to criticism, and is free to join in a relationship of mutual criticism with us, its readers and interpreters. But if the Bible is specially inspired in some way which protects it from the vulnerability of our human condition, and is beyond questioning, then our relationship to it will be one-sided. We will be internally related to the Bible, in that we will be affected by the Bible, but the Bible will be externally related to us, in that it will remain unaffected by its relation with us. In that sense, the relation between ourselves and the Bible would be similar to the relationship between people and God, as construed by the medieval theology, where God remained unaffected and only humanity was changed. The Bible must be removed from this position of absolute autonomy if it is again to enter into the dynamics of human life out of which it first arose. The Bible is changed by our study of it, just as we are changed by its message to us. In our relationship to the Bible we are sons and daughters, not slaves, and it is the nature of the Bible, free from special revelation and instructional, doctrinal and ethical authority, which demands that in our relationships with it we act as responsible human beings, not as obedient containers of its message.

If, on the other hand, the Bible *is* regarded as being the product of some sort of special inspiration, then we must ask whether that inspiration lies in the original manuscripts, or in the documents which are actually in our possession. If the answer is the former, then the actual Bible available to us is not inspired in any special sense and the situation is just as described in the last paragraph. If, on the other hand, the inspiration does lie in the actual documents in our possession, then the problems become extremely difficult. If every variant in every document is equally inspired, there seems little point in trying to establish the best text, since the whole idea of a 'best' text would be rendered superfluous. If, however, a best text is to be established, the criterion for inclusion and exclusion cannot simply be that the documents are in our possession. Discrimination must be attempted between the various documents and readings using the normal critical methods. We see then that although the logical and psychological consequences of a doctrine of special inspiration might be such as to render the Bible immune to criticism, this could not arise as long as we hold firmly to the implications of the fact that the Bible is available to us in the way in which history has presented it to us. The Bible itself offers no obstacle to our learning and to our creative thinking. Many obstacles are created by the ideologies and theologies of unlearning with which we protect ourselves from the challenge of the real Bible.

INTERPRETING THE BIBLE

The implications of the preceding discussion are that in the interpretation of the Bible a set of principles might be drawn up which would be compatible with the nature of the Bible and with the nature of education and with Christian faith, although rather different from the conventional hermeneutical assumptions. It is often argued and assumed that the Bible will only reveal its meaning to faith, ie faith acting as a hermeneutical principle. It is also often taken for granted that the Bible must be interpreted religiously, and that this interpretation shall be carried out under the watchful eye of the religious group which regards itself as the trustee of the Bible (the Christian church). These then are three of the traditional principles of interpretation: faith, religion, and the religious community.

Our previous discussions suggest that to these principles we might be able to add their opposites, namely, disbelief, secularity, and ecumenicity. It is not being suggested that faith, religion and the church have no suitability as principles for interpreting the Bible, but that these principles are too restrictive unless they are complemented by their opposites. While not denying that faith can be a principle for interpreting the Bible, it is necessary to affirm that unbelief can also be a standpoint for the interpretation of the Bible. The Bible may be interpreted from a religious perspective, but it may also be interpreted from a secular perspective. The church as the religious community which has been most consciously and deeply influenced by the Bible has a natural part to play in interpreting it, but the Bible is for all humanity, and it is in the name of all people everywhere, in the name of what we might call anthropological ecumenicity, that any exclusive prerogative of the Christian church to interpret the Bible must be challenged.

(i) Unbelief

The Bible not only speaks to people who have passed into the uncanny world on the far side of despair, the world where absolute loss has been sustained, accepted and overcome; it also speaks to everybody who has suffered loss, whether great or small, whether partial or complete. It is as much directed to those men and women who are symbolically with Jesus at Caesarea Philippi as to those who walk the Emmaus road with him. Perhaps it might be said that although the Bible is addressed to sinful people (and who would deny that?), this does not mean that sin can be used as a principle for interpreting the Bible. But what are the implications of claiming that the Bible is addressed to this particular group of creatures? The Bible is precisely *not* addressed to angels in their purity but to people in their sin. That fact affects the entire form and content of the Bible. The Bible deals with Adam and Eve *after their fall* and *in their fall.* It would have no relevance to them before the fall, any more than it has for angels, or would have for perfect people who had never suffered loss. That which provides context, relevance and meaning for a text is surely a principle for the interpretation of that text. Just as the Bible takes humanity seriously in its sinfulness, so it is only initially in its sinfulness that humanity can take the Bible seriously. To deny one's sinfulness, ie to fail to recognize one's loss, is to put oneself in a position where one is unable to understand the Bible, because one is unable to grasp the nature and intention of the Bible; one is unable to hear it speaking because one has not appreciated the fundamental anthropological principle for its interpretation, of which the experience of human loss is one aspect.

(ii) Secularity

The Bible does not deal only with spiritual or religious loss, but also with material loss and political loss. It deals with loss of health, loss of friends, loss of prestige and power. It is not only a book about the temple but a book about the city, the nation, and the world. It is just as important in interpreting the Bible to take the affairs of this world, this age and these societies seriously as it is to take seriously the coming age, the divine society. This pair of perspectives, like the previous pair, is complementary. The Bible cannot be interpreted exclusively from the point of view of the priests. The experience of the prophets is also relevant, and it must never be forgotten that the prophets were sometimes attacked because they were not all religious. The experience of women and of children is increasingly recognized in the Bible literature as offering a guide to the interpretation of life's meaning.

This meaning speaks to us through nature, human love and war and peace (as well as through the experience of loss), just as it speaks to us through the sabbath and the sacrificial rituals. All of this is implied in saying that secularity is a principle for the interpretation of the Bible.

(iii) Ecumenicity

Implied in everything that has been said is the thought that the Bible is not for some people but for all. There is no people that is not a 'people of the book'. Whether this may also be true of other sacred literature is a point which need not be discussed here. The Bible has this universal status whether other books have it or not. It is because we have taken a fundamental theme of universal humanity (the experience of loss) as a key to the understanding of the Bible that we feel bound to emphasize that the anthropological principle for the interpretation of the Bible must be equally universal, and, to reverse the situation and so to complete the picture, it is because we have begun with the assumption that universal humanity must be a hermeneutical principle for biblical meaning that we have been led to select one such theme of universal experience (the experience of loss) as a key to the integration of the Bible. Both poles (ie universal humanity and specific religious revelation) of this hermeneutical ellipse may be grounded in the person of Jesus Christ, the universal person and the 'true man'. Although it is through the Christian community that we have the faith which centres on Jesus, his person is not wholly under the patronage of this religious community, nor is he to be interpreted as being a religious person rather than a secular person (his death certainly profaned and secularized him),[17] nor even his humanity to be interpreted entirely and exclusively from the perspective of faith.[18] In his baptism he identified himself with sinners, doing that which might well appear to the religious mind (eg John the Baptist)[19] to be inappropriate, and in his death he identified himself with doubt.[20] There is thus a sense in which our hermeneutical principles are also christological principles, and the complementarity of the opposites found in each of the pairs we have been considering (faith/belief, religion/secularity, the religious community/ ecumenicity) is also indicated in the person of Jesus Christ.

This does not mean, however, that we are suggesting an approach to the Bible which is only accessible to Christians or that we still insist on interpreting the Bible through the framework of Christian doctrine. The search for a lost humanity is a theme common in both Testaments. We need to find an approach which does not exclude the New

Testament, but is at the same time faithful to the Torah, the Prophets and the Writings. If our hermeneutical principles are mirrored in Jesus Christ, as well as in Adam, Joseph, Job and Jeremiah then the claim that the theme of loss integrates the Bible is strengthened without impairing the dignity of scriptures older than the New Testament.

A RATIONALE FOR THE BIBLE IN SECULAR RELIGIOUS EDUCATION

The understanding of the Bible which we have been discussing provides us with a rationale for its use in our schools. These schools exhibit the pairs of complementary characteristics which are our hermeneutical principles. The schools are multi-faith yet unbelieving, they are secularized yet remain partly religious, and they are situated in a community where the Bible is acknowledged to be a book peculiar to Christians and to the church and yet at the same time having a meaning which is universal and being open to all sorts and conditions of people. In the sense in which the Bible is the book of the church, it is the source of a Christian nurture, but in the sense in which it is a universal book for all people everywhere, it is a book appropriate in the educational context of modern societies. Once, religious education was conceived of as a faith fostering activity. It sprang from faith and it spoke to faith, it took place in schools which were regarded as being Christian communities, and the Bible was its text book. If the principles which we have been discussing are acceptable, then the Bible may be seen as having an important place in a secularized religious education which aims to educate understanding, and not to deepen faith. There is a sense in which the Bible is not only a confessional or a neo-confessional book which has its place within a confessional religious education, the Bible is not only a convergent book suitable for convergent teaching, but is also a divergent book suitable for divergent teaching.[21] The Bible describes how convergent personalities such as Jonah and Peter were challenged by a divergency more complex and universal than they had dreamed of. 'God has shown me that I should not call any man common or unclean.'[22]

But, it might be objected, is not the intention of the Bible to move its readers towards faith? Is it not true that although it speaks to all who have experienced loss, its message to them is that they should no longer remain in a state of loss? It is true that this is the intention of the Bible, and that this cannot be the intention of the religious education teacher in the secular classroom. To that extent there remains a challenging, inner tension between religious education and the Bible. But if we have succeeded in showing that the Bible speaks to all people, and that universal humanity in its experience of loss and unbelief does provide a legitimate perspective from which to interpret the Bible, then what we have shown is sufficient for the requirements of modern, professional religious education. The fact that more may be gathered from the Bible in other contexts, such as the context of faith, does not mean that the approach suggested here for the secular religious education classroom is invalid. Although less than the whole, it is faithful to the Bible *as far as it goes*, and it goes far enough to be educationally adequate. The Bible presents itself as God's interpretation of human loss. This interpretation can be considered by any human being who has suffered loss, whether he or she accepts it as *true* or not. The possibility that pupils will understand that the Bible presents itself as God's search for lost humanity is not negated by disbelief in God. That the Bible so presents itself is true phenomenologically, and can be accepted by the pupil who brackets out her or his personal faith or unbelief, and that the Bible can throw the light of this amazing possibility upon the lives of those who then go on to *include* their faith or their unbelief as legitimate perspectives from which to interpret its message is true existentially. The phenomenological and the existential aspects of religious education are thus adequately met in this understanding of the role of the Bible in the classroom. It is no good encouraging your pupils to search for a meaning in life unless they are prepared to consider the possibility that there is a meaning in life searching for them.[23] Encounter with the Bible enables them to encounter this possibility. A possibility which could never be actualized would not even be a possibility, and if it is the case that there are some pupils for whom the Bible is not only an account of a possible meaning in search of human beings, but is also that which conveys the actual meaning which has found humanity, that merely illustrates the complementarity of the hermeneutical opposites. Religious education teachers cannot intend that that possibility should be actualized, but they cannot exclude it as a further possibility either. This statement of professional limits and of professional and personal tolerance is a sufficient rationale for the use of this dynamic religious literature by religious education teachers today.

Perhaps the relationship between the secular use of the Bible in religious education and the use of the Bible within the context of faith can be expressed in an analogy. Those who have visited Coventry Cathedral will know that there are two main perspectives on the nave of this famous modern building. When visitors are entering the cathedral and are walking down the nave towards the altar, they are challenged by the 'Words of Witness' which speak to them from both sides of the nave. Reaching the altar, and turning around facing the west, the 'Words of Witness' have now disappeared and the panels of stained glass in the walls of the nave are seen. So also there is a view into the Bible from the street. When entering you are challenged by the questions which the Bible asks. There is another view when you stand inside the faith of the Bible. Now, as you look out into the world from the position of faith, the Bible is transformed with light. Each perspective on the nave of the cathedral is legitimate; indeed, the cathedral was designed to be seen in these two different ways. Your total perspective is certainly richer if you have both viewpoints, but that does not mean that the visitor who only noticed the view from the street would not have seen something worthwhile. In the same way, a secular insight into the Bible based upon our common humanity is a worthwhile understanding of the Bible; indeed, the Bible was made to encourage this viewpoint as well as the perspective from faith. It is not necessary to deny the glories of the Bible when seen in faith in order to maintain the worthwhileness of the view 'from the street'.

METHODS OF TEACHING THE BIBLE IN BRITISH RELIGIOUS EDUCATION

We can conclude our enquiry by considering the situation from the perspective of the various ways in which the Bible has been taught in British religious education. Our previous discussion was conducted in the light of theology, with special reference to anthropology and hermeneutics. At this point of our discussion, we enter religious education as a discipline, considering its history and pedagogy insofar as these offer a complementary comment on the first, theological section of our discussion.

Learning about the Bible
The oldest and the most persistent style of teaching the Bible in British classrooms could be described as 'learning about the Bible'. Much of this is background information to the Bible, and consists of details about the daily life and customs of the Bible people. We may also place under this heading materials which deal with the external history of

the Bible: its text, translations, transmission, influence and spread throughout the world. Another type of 'learning about the Bible' is the study of the influence which the Bible has had upon history, literature, music and art.

Learning about the Bible continues to be popular because it enables the teacher to avoid difficult and perhaps controversial questions. Moreover, such teaching and learning can be thought of as being academic in an objective and factual sense, especially if studies such as archaeology and language are included. Such teaching is suitable for examination work and the material is not without interest for many young people.

In this approach, however, the Bible is treated as an historical book, a cultural book, a moral book and even as an exciting and romantic book, but not necessarily as a religious book. So there is a sense in which this first approach should be regarded as preliminary to the genuine religious education of the pupil.

Learning the Bible
Another way of dealing with the Bible in British schools, far from being indirect or dealing with the Bible in an external way, introduces the pupil immediately to the text and message of the Bible. Indeed, in some of its forms, particularly in the nineteenth century, this way of teaching the Bible involved nothing but the actual text. Many non-conformists did not want the Bible taught in schools at all because they thought that the church and the home were the places for such teaching, and they were afraid of the Anglican influence in the schools. So they insisted that if the Bible were to be taught in the Board Schools at all, it should be without note or comment.[24]

This approach did have a certain externality, in that no attempt could be made to relate the Bible to the lives of the pupils, and the text stood alone without being mediated through the experience of either teacher or pupil. The so-called 'simple Bible teaching' of the late 19th and early 20th centuries was a development of this approach. The basic doctrines of the Bible were taught, or so it was claimed. Opponents of this approach were quick to point out that the result was often as denominational as any other approach to the Bible, hence what was taught under the guise of 'simple Bible teaching' was evangelical Protestantism.[25]

From those early beginnings, the movement to learn the Bible itself became the major concern of British religious education, and from well before the First World War until the 1950s, the major concern was to interpret the Bible to young people with the aid of biblical scholarship. The movement gained force during the period between the two wars, sometimes under the influence of the neo-orthodox movement, and was further strengthened by the 'biblical theology' movement of the 1940s and 1950s.[26] Although there was considerable interest throughout the whole of this fifty year period in the psychological problems raised by trying to relate biblical material appropriately to the age and development of the pupil, and a similar interest in the methodological problems of communicating a lively interest and a sense of personal involvement on the part of the pupils in the biblical text, particularly in the emerging secondary schools, it remained the case that the Bible itself and not the pupil was the major focus of attention. It was taken for granted that a knowledge and an understanding of the Bible would contribute to the personal development of pupils, and that the direction of this development would be towards Christian discipleship.[27] The Bible continued to function as 'the Word of God' in a way which was often only implicit in the 'learning about the Bible' approach. When one learned the Bible, in the way we are now discussing, such teaching and learning was from faith to faith. This comment is not made in criticism of that approach in its own day, but in order to clarify the position of the Bible in British religious education at the present time.

Learning from the Bible
Two major factors affect the place of the Bible in the classroom today. First, the Bible may no longer address the pupil 'from faith'. The Bible will be taught by a teacher in whose religious education syllabus a variety of sacred literature will appear. Other sacred literatures can no longer be relegated to a sixth form course on 'non-Christian religions'.[28] The Bible continues to have great cultural and personal relevance in Britain but its position is seriously affected by the fact that it must be considered as a member of a class, ie it may be thought of as one sacred book among others. It is not for the school or the teacher to discriminate between the books of this sacred literature, presenting one as the Word of God while others are merely described as being the Holy Book of a particular group. In this sense, the Bible can no longer be taught from a position of faith, although this is not to deny that the teachers of religion *may* have faith and that their faith may help them in achieving an educational understanding of the place of the Bible. So although the teaching of the Bible cannot be from faith in any simple and direct way, it may be perfectly consistent with faith, and

faith may generate this approach to teaching.[29] The approach out-lined in this article is not only consistent with Christian faith, but may actually be generated by it. Nevertheless, the approach proceeds upon the principle that faith and unbelief are complementary prin-ciples for the interpretation of the Bible, and that unbelief is a particularly important principle in the county school. In this sense, the Bible may be thought of as being taught from unbelief to unbelief. It may be taught and learned by anyone who is open to the questions which the Bible asks about men and women in their fundamental humanity including their experience of loss, even if the teacher and the pupil have not yet begun to ask the questions that arise from faith in God.

The second factor is that the teaching of the Bible can no longer be directed *towards* faith. It would no longer be right to assume, let alone to intend, that the teaching of the Bible should promote Christian discipleship amongst pupils in county schools. The contri-bution of the Bible towards the religious education process must be differently construed. It is at this point that the expression 'learning from the Bible' may be useful.[30] To learn 'from' the Bible includes both learning about the Bible and learning the Bible itself, but the focus is different. Here we shall be mainly concerned with the personal development of our students. They are to learn as persons, to deepen their humanity through learning, to learn their way towards values, commitments, beliefs and aspirations, and this learning is to be carried on in dialogue with the Bible, it is to be stimulated by the Bible, the Bible is to be one of the agents of this learning. It is primarily themselves that pupils are learning about, and the Bible is conceived of as being that book which offers them a possible account of themselves. It offers a powerful scenario for criticizing ideas of identity and destiny in human living. Pupils may or may not come to accept that view of human life, for the Bible will not be presented as being normative, nor as having any intrinsic authority or any right to prescribe what they shall be, for the authority to declare the truth is conferred upon the Bible by faith. At this point, learning from the Bible will differ from the experiential Christian education of the later 1960s. In that approach, passages from the Bible were laid alongside experiences from the lives of pupils so that a sort of mutual illumina-tion or convergence took place, the Bible being presented as the normative interpreter of life-experiences, in the hope that some pupils would participate in the biblical point of view. Learning from the Bible makes none of these assumptions. What the pupils shall conclude about themselves and about people in general goes beyond the scope of education, if education is to remain faithful to itself, and is not to become indoctrination. It is the duty of the educator, however, to ensure that the pupils' processes of self-discovery should take place in contact with the arts and sciences, and in the case of the religious educator this means that the pupils' self-discovery and their understandings of people must take place by way of an encounter with the sacred literature and the religious communities of humanity, and, in particular, with the Bible.

Learning from the Bible, understood in this way, is faithful to the requirements of education since it does not propose to control learning but only to promote it. The secularity of the Bible relates it to education as a secular and autonomous profession. A distinct role for religious education teachers is suggested by this approach. Unlike priests or ministers, they would not be custodians or representatives of the biblical tradition, but would be more like door-keepers, enabling pupils to have access to it. They would be the promoters of the learning, not transmitters of the religion. The ecumenicity and universality of the Bible set it free to be a resource for the development of human potential and not an agent for the proselytizing intentions of one particular religious group. This approach is also faithful to the nature and meaning of the Bible itself, for the Bible is the record of how generation after generation of people learned how to learn.[31] In learning from the Bible, our pupils may become continuous with the people of the Bible, entering into that world of wonder, mystery and discovery, not in the sense that they will necessarily become members of the community of faith but in the sense that they will be confronted by the questions of faithfulness and destiny, responsibility and community, identity and service, questions which challenged the people of the Bible.

Central to this conception of the place of the Bible in modern religious education is the idea that the Bible is not to be considered as being primarily a human book about God but is to be approached as if it were God's book about humans. It is not so much a book in which religious answers are offered through the questions which life promotes, God being thought of as one such answer, but it is a book which presents itself as a record of revelation, of religious experience, a record of God dealing with people and God's concern for humanity. Thus it is a book about the nature and meaning of human life as determined by creation and covenant.

This approach to the Bible is not only phenomenologically adequate, in that this is indeed just how the Bible does seem to present itself to us, but it is an approach which is also adequate to faith, since this is also how faith perceives the Bible, and it is adequate to the requirements of education, since it provides a rationale for human development in relation to this particular sacred record of the education of humanity.

CONCLUSION

This article has suggested that one basic and universal theme of our human experience could be used as the key to the meaning and interpretation of the Bible. This is the experience of loss. The apparent success of this idea has led us to suggest that the features of our common humanity such as unbelief, secularity and ecumenicity may well be thought of as being complementary to the faith, religion and the insights of a particular religious community in forming principles for the interpretation of the Bible. This in turn has led to the provision of a rationale for the teaching of the Bible in religious education today which will be available equally to believers and unbelievers, which will be appropriate within the secular context of education as well as within the religious context of Christian nurture, and which will seek to humanize not to proselytize.

NOTES

1. Mk 14:50; 15:34.
2. Ana-Maria Rizzuto, *The Birth of the Living God*, Chicago: University of Chicago Press, 1979, p 186.
3. Hosea 2:23; Ps 22:6.
4. Abraham Joshua Heschel, *God in Search of Man: A Philosophy of Judaism*, New York: Harper & Row, 1955.
5. Mk 8:35.
6. Gen 3:19.
7. 2 Cor 8:9; Phil 2:8.
8. Peter Berger *et al.*, *The Homeless Mind: Modernization and Consciousness*, New York: Random House, 1973, ch 1.
9. Ps 137:5.
10. Mk 9:5.
11. Jn 12:24.
12. Jn 21:18f.
13. Mk 16:6.
14. Matt 28:8; Mk 16:8; Lk 24:41.

15. Thomas H. Groome, *Christian Religious Education*, San Francisco: Harper & Row, 1980, n 49, p 55.

16. These points were made to me in a conversation with Dr Harold Turner, the Director of the Centre for the Study of New Religious Movements in the Selly Oak Colleges in Birmingham.

17. Gal 3:13; Heb 13:11f.

18. Mk 1:24,34.

19. Matt 3:14f.

20. Mk 15:34.

21. See 'Open Minds and Empty Hearts? Convergent and Divergent Teaching of Religion', in my *Studies in Religion and Education*, Lewes, Sussex: Falmer Press, 1984, pp 175-187.

22. Acts 10:28.

23. 'The pursuit of meaning is meaningless, unless there is a meaning in pursuit of man.' Abraham Joshua Heschel, *Between God and Man: An Interpretation of Judaism*, New York: The Free Press, 1959, p 238.

24. R. W. Dale, *Religious Worship and Bible Teaching in Board Schools: a Letter to the 'Two-Thousand'*, 1885.

25. Henry W. Crosskey, *Sectarianism in National Education, being the substance of a speech delivered at the annual meeting of the British and Foreign Unitarian Association*, London: BFUA, 1884; J. A. Picton, *The Bible in School*, London: Watts & Co, 1901.

26. E. F. Braley, *The Teaching of Religion*, London: Longmans, Green & Co, 1938; G. L. Heawood, *Religion in School*, London: SCM, 1939; M. Vivian Hughes, *Scripture Teaching Today*, London: SCM, 1939; B. L. Kennett, *The Teaching of Scripture to Elder Pupils in Secondary Schools*, Cambridge: W. Heffer, 1932; N. P. Wood (ed), *Scripture Teaching in Secondary Schools: Papers Read at a Conference held in Cambridge*, 1912.

27. Charles Raven, *Christ and Modern Education*, London: Hodder & Stoughton, 1928.

28. D. J. Bates, 'The Nature and Place of Religion in English State Education, 1900-1944, with Special Reference to the Conceptions of the Relation of Religion to Education etc', unpublished Ph.D. thesis, University of Lancaster, 1976, Appendix, 'Religious Education and the Study of Religions other than Christianity circa 1920 — circa 1944', pp 281ff.

29. See 'Divergence as a Theological Problem', in my *Studies, op. cit.*, pp 183f.

30. I am adapting the expressions 'learning about' and 'learning from' from the use made of them by Michael Grimmitt in 'When is Commitment a Problem in RE?', *British Journal of Educational Studies*, Vol. 29, No. 1, 1981, pp 42-53.

31. J. L. Segundo, *The Liberation of Theology*, New York: Orbis Books, 1976, pp 118f.

15

Otto's Contribution to Religious Education

ROBIN MINNEY

INTRODUCTION AND SUMMARY

Rudolf Otto's book *The Idea of the Holy*[1] has deeply influenced a few religious educationists, and is known by report to many more. Although Otto died fifty years ago, his thought is suggestive for RE in Britain today for a number of reasons.[2]

Among state-run education systems that require religious education in schools, the place of RE in modern Britain is unlike that in other countries. For instance in this country a non-confessional stance is required in maintained schools, and also a range of world religions is taught, always within a neutral framework. In this situation Otto's work can suggest developments in the following four areas:

(i) World religions
Otto went to the heart of religion in his analysis of 'the holy'. He drew on the phenomena of all the major world religions to illustrate his points in detail, because he held that all particular religions contain genuine expressions of the holy. This approach recognizes the worth of all religions and is the very opposite of trying to judge other world religions by the standard of one of them. On this basis Otto provides a charter for world religions teaching.

(ii) The value beyond the phenomena
But the world's religions are more than 'phenomena'. What makes them *religious* is their relationship to the holy, which is Otto's name for the basic category in religion. Thus religious education has a point of reference which is beyond any particular religion. This position is in

strongest contrast to the practice of deluging pupils with a range of religious phenomena, whose meanings, if they are discussed at all, appear subjective or even arbitrary. As RE teachers well know, world religions considered only as phenomena can be fun for a time but this approach leads in the end to indifference and boredom.

(iii) Human experience
Otto found the ultimate relationship with the holy in religious experience as human experience. This area holds a number of well-known problems, but it also provides some basis for current discussions of spirituality, whether 'spirituality' is seen as subsisting inside or outside recognized religions. The validity of spirituality for post-1988 education in England and Wales lies in its *human* quality.

(iv) The use of reason
Yet at the same time Otto realized that reason must not be thrown aside. Although he saw the foundation of the holy in the 'numinous', which is his name for the non-rational, Otto knew that it was necessary for human reason to come to terms with it and to interpret it. Thus he gave his approval for the English translation of his book *Das Heilige* (The Holy) being rendered as *The Idea of the Holy*. The word 'idea' is significant.

Rudolf Otto was a professor of theology at Göttingen, Breslau, and finally Marburg. His approach to religion by means of different religions and his stress on the value of religious experience anticipate changes in British RE. Perhaps more interesting still, his ideas for communicating and clarifying things that impress people most at the level of feeling, suggest ways forward for religious education in the next ten years.

The plan of this essay, drawing on the work of Rudolf Otto, is to explore these themes in turn, and from them to draw out the implications for teaching religion using Otto's 'Means of Communicating the Numinous'. This is to suggest a new development for RE, both by drawing on human experience and by applying human reason. The idea is to explore traditional expressions of religion, explicit religion, as a reasoned means for refining the deeper feelings which form personal experience. This should facilitate clearer expression at a personal level.

WORLD RELIGIONS

Otto drew on the widely different religions he encountered on his travels in Europe and North Africa, India, China and Japan. To these traditional faiths he put the questions of personal commitment and religious experience. This aspect may be missing from religious education in our schools today, if pupils study phenomena from a range of world religions, but are unable to connect them with their own experience, commitment or potential commitment.

Otto's use and acceptance of non-Christian religions as genuine examples of religion offended some of his critics. Some traditionalists in Britain have reacted against world religions teaching in schools, and this came to the surface afresh in the controversies over the 1988 Education Act.

It is clear that pupils are interested, especially when studying the religious and social practices that are part of their local life in Britain's multi-cultural society. But rarely are specific religions explored for their value and significance as *religions*. This is an important point. No one teaches swimming exclusively in a classroom, and just as teaching history requires pupils to enter into the process of being historians, learning to weigh evidence and evaluate primary sources, so in the teaching of Buddhism, for example, pupils need to practise medita- tion, or in studying Islam to experience at least a few hours of the Ramadan fast, and to take some part in the processions and selected rituals of other religions. This should be for sound educational reasons and must not be held to be a statement of commitment.

It is as if by restricting us to standing on the outside looking in, world religions teaching in schools has made us simply into observers. It is as if swimming lessons were confined to reading texts and watching videos of swimmers, and history in schools stuck on 'facts' and never let pupils sift and assess the evidence, or imagine themselves into another place and period. Otto finds the religious centre of religion, the holy, within the world's religions. Yet much of our RE in schools uses world religions exclusively for their social and cultural importance, denying them their roots in the holy. For Otto the importance of the phenomena lay in their religious meaning and origin.

THE VALUE BEYOND THE PHENOMENA

The world's rich variety of religious expressions and forms are not just for our entertainment. By ascribing value to the basic experience in all religions, Otto denied the exclusive right of any one religious tradition to discredit all the others. Yet one of the risks of world religions teaching, as many have recently found, is that pupils fail to see the importance of any of them: they are just the strange things that funny people do. There is all the more need to relate the phenomena of religion to the basic religious experience, through symbols, music and other forms of expression. In this process it becomes possible to engage with the learner's own religious or pre-religious stirrings.

This does not mean that Otto thought all religions equally valid. Nor need the RE teacher. We need to be quite honest about this. All religions have both religious and human validity, based in the last resort upon their dependence on the holy. On this basis too we see practical steps towards interreligious co-operation on world problems such as human disasters, hunger, threat of war and to the environment.[3] But there is a need to search for some criteria of value in religion, and the move within the world religions and multi-faith teaching to focus more especially on one faith tradition to be taken in depth and others in relation to it is possibly a sign of this, but one which should be explored with great care.

HUMAN EXPERIENCE

Experience is primary
The basis of Otto's book is the assumption, based on the appeal to the reader's personal experience, that experience is primary and that without religious experience the phenomena of all religions can arouse or convey no meaning which is genuinely religious. Otto drew on William James's book, *The Varieties of Religious Experience*,[4] and added much material from the liturgies and practices, art and artefacts of religions round the world, as his now well-known *Religionskundliche Sammlung* in Marburg shows.

Otto finds the heart of religion not in the authoritative doctrines and rituals of the learned and the experts, important though these are, but in the inmost self of the ordinary follower. Otto's stress on the primacy of experience is quite clear, and it is a basic kind of haunting awareness which according to Otto underlies all religion. It is to this kind of experience that all forms of religion, art, rituals, scriptures, etc give shape and expression. This means that without experience, all forms of religious expression known to human-kind are something other than religion itself. They may exemplify aesthetic sense, express or support social and political structures, reinforce moral norms, relate to society's need for order, but without a fundamental experience of the holy, religious forms are peripheral to religion itself.

This requires the understanding that all humans have the innate capacity, however underdeveloped in some, for religious experience. Otto sometimes made a comparison with a musical sense. Even the tone-deaf have a feel for rhythm. Unless RE teachers accept this premiss, there can be no justification for teaching religion in our schools.

For Otto, genuine expressions of religion are expressions either directly or indirectly of a particular kind of happening. He argues that our complex idea of 'the holy' includes rational and non-rational aspects, and that the heart of it lies in the non-rational, for which he invented a new term, 'the numinous'. So the heart of religious experience is an encounter with an overpowering force which outstrips all the descriptions which are used of the supreme power in all religions. Human awareness of this is therefore not due to teachings and concepts, but to a sense of feeling, which Otto calls the *sensus numinis* or sense of the numinous.

This is something of a key term, because the *sensus numinis* actually has a double reference: it both refers to the supreme power itself which lies beyond description, and at the same time to the experience of meeting within the human mind and soul which can be described, yet is a kind of a shadow or reflection of the numinous itself.

Otto's descriptive analysis is now well known. The subject is aware of an encounter with a presence which is 'really real', an experience summed up by the statement: 'I felt I was if anything the less real of the two'. Otto calls this the 'creature-feeling'. With this goes a feeling of awe, a feeling that there is great, supreme power in this presence, which has a kind of compulsive aspect to it, and with it a sensation of energy. The characteristics which Otto draws out are summed up by his famous formula, *mysterium tremendum et fascinans*. This he elaborates as the feeling of awe or dread, a kind of uncanny fear. This is the *tremendum*. The presence is further felt as something real and present, but ultimately mysterious, something in the last analysis beyond human research and human reason. And finally there is a strong element of attraction which is indicated by the word *fascinans*. This refers to all those religious experiences of grace, relief and love.[5]

Experience puts emphasis on the child
Once the basis of religion is seen in the personal experience of individuals,[6] the authoritative tradition of revelation is moved into second place. Otto freely recognizes this as the democratizing of religion and sees it as one of the fruits of the Reformation. No priestly or doctrinal barrier is placed between the believer and God, or between the student and the religion under study.

This has implications for the curriculum too. Just as the teaching authority of the church or established religious tradition no longer prescribes the content of basic religious instruction, so within the school the curriculum need no longer be exclusively or mainly based either on content (content-based), nor with a view to a particular result (objectives-led). There is scope now for a teaching approach in RE which is worthwhile for its own sake, that is the process curriculum, and other approaches which are pupil-centred. This would seem to be the logical result of a field of study whose centre was in the consciousness of the pupil.

Spirituality — religious and non-religious
It is clear from this that what Otto makes central for religion is a kind of experience which many others have also described, but with a variety of frames of reference. This is Maslow's 'peak experience' and Laski's 'ecstasy'; for Wordsworth these are 'intimations of immortality', loaded with mystic longing. William James is quoted by Otto. For explicit links with childhood we have evidence collected by The Sir Alister Hardy Foundation,[7] and the researches of David Hay which have led to experimental work in RE.[8]

Otto rarely used the word 'spirituality' which has become something of a growth industry in modern British RE. Attempts at sharp definitions seem artificial as the idea seeps into several general areas without much in the way of a break-off point. We shall suggest later ways in which the spirituality of particular religions could help refine our understanding of non-religious spirituality or the spirituality of nature.

Spiritual is not the same as religious, as a simple exercise with pencil and paper will demonstrate. People describe awe and wonder as spiritual experience and many other human happenings which are not obviously connected with recognized religions. Laski's ecstasy and Maslow's peak experiences have already been mentioned. So we could write a list of words or phrases which are examples of spirituality and which would include much that is not connected to a specific religion.

A second list of words and phrases could be written down which relate to religion. The ideas here would no doubt include some things which seem to be spiritual, but there would be much else, including history, doctrine, architecture, morality and social structures, which can obviously be religious but would not figure on our first list of spiritual things. Our two lists could then be put side by side, and points of overlap or common ground picked out. There are certainly some. The whole could be represented by a Venn diagram of two intersecting circles, and where they overlap would be the area of things which are both religious and spiritual. The idea which derives from Otto is to use the better known and more easily accessible aspects of the explicitly religious as a means of clarifying and refining the fuzzy-edged feelings which often lie hidden in the emotions.

Empirical evidence for children's religious experience includes the many case histories collected by The Sir Alister Hardy Foundation. What mainly distinguishes these from those collected by William James is their innocence of the formulations of Christian (or any other) tradition. They thus represent children's spirituality as openness to religious emotion at an early age.

Otto published some similar examples in a brief article,[9] and many more are given in a book by August Miehle.[10] Miehle's book is particularly interesting because he uses Otto's descriptive analysis of response to the numinous (from *The Idea of the Holy*) to classify the experiences of children. Miehle also notes the problems inherent in collecting such experiences from children who lack the words and the concepts to express them, a fact which makes it necessary to rely on the recollections of adults some decades later.[11] One result of this is that only things which made a really deep impression survive the attrition of growing up and the processes of formal education.

Within the general area of children's spirituality it is open to question how much of it may be defined as explicitly 'religious'. It is also easy to see that programmes of formal education, both in schools under the heading of RE, and even in catechism classes, Sunday schools and confirmation classes, have failed to make much of this kind of experience which, it now seems, large numbers of individuals must have had. Some of the cases collected by The Sir Alister Hardy Research Foundation stress that at the time of such a happening adults were far from encouraging or supportive, and that young children in most cases were simply not taken seriously.

THE USE OF REASON

We have suggested that current practice in RE teaching can make the phenomena of the world's great religions seem little more than entertainment or optional leisure activities unless attention is paid to their specifically religious value. There is an equal risk that exclusive concentration on the non-rational aspects of religion may lead students to dismiss it in the last resort as an emotional adventure with no meaning for the serious affairs of life.

In his preface to *The Idea of the Holy* (English edition) Otto stressed that he had only come to write about the non-rational after a thorough study of the philosophical or rational aspects of religion. His previous books bear this out.

Kant had worked out a distinction between Pure Reason which is approximately intellectual (thought), and Practical Reason which is ethics (action). He wrote further about a third possibility in the field of aesthetics (feeling and attitude). Otto drew also on Schleiermacher's reworking of this into three aspects of the human psyche: intellect, ethics, and feeling. Otto further followed Fries and Apelt in a systematic analysis of three modes of *knowing*: reasoned knowledge, knowledge directly derived from experience, and intimation or presentiment, what we could call knowledge by intuition.

Otto's work here raises problems which are not relevant to RE and have been discussed elsewhere. What is relevant, however, is that feeling or intuition also appeals to reason in a not strictly logical mode. Reason is the only tool we have with which to make sense of human experience. This is important if we are not either to consign religion to the emotional and sentimental, or else give it its own logic quite separate from 'normal' life. This can lead to the kind of schizophrenia sometimes seen in intensely religious people. Education should encourage pupils to integrate their lives, and reason forms the unifying factor in making sense of human experience.

Religious educators sometimes contrast concepts and attitudes, classing concepts as clear and rational, and attitudes as emotional. The distinction is useful but not absolute. An example may help to make this clearer. In the Durham Agreed Syllabus for RE the first item to be listed is 'Awe and Wonder'.[12] The syllabus was constructed on the basis of concepts, skills and attitudes, and Awe and Wonder comes first as concept number 1, in Group A. Yet the 'Approach to the Syllabus' on the previous page explains that 'Awe and Wonder' is a 'fundamental idea' and adds:

> In religion the comprehension of a concept comes not only through the intellect but also through the emotions, the imagination and through experience — it is an 'empathetic awareness'.

Obviously the word 'concept' for those who drew up this syllabus was a less precise term than for Otto. The area is further widened by grouping separately A Concepts and B Concepts, and it is seen that B Concepts apply explicitly to religion and religions, while A Concepts are implicit. This was given practical application in several pieces of research done in a comprehensive school in County Durham in 1981-82 whereby children's capacity for this emotion and ability to express it in human terms were explored.[13] The attempt was made to draw parallels with Otto's scheme in *The Idea of the Holy*.

FURTHER DEVELOPMENTS AND WAYS FORWARD

(i) Can spirituality be taught?
This poses a considerable problem for religious education. If religious experience is non-rational, and cannot even be conceptualized, how can a teacher communicate it? If, as Otto asserts, it is spontaneous as well, how could it be contrived, and what use are the explorations and exercises which have been tried under the influence of the Nottingham Project?[14] But the fact that these experiments have had some encouraging results should stimulate us to take the enquiry further.

There is spirituality within religion, as when one speaks of Christian spirituality, Islamic or Sufic spirituality and so on. This is seen at least by those who practise it as the depth dimension of religion, as opposed to outward forms in ethics and doctrines. Books on Sufism usually begin with *tariqa*, the inward path. If the Venn diagram suggested earlier is to be applied, then it will be useful to look at certain aspects of religious spirituality too which may help to organize and refine some of the ideas already considered.

If the essence of religion which Otto designates by the word 'holy' is a complex of rational and non-rational, then a way forward is at least suggested. The technique would involve using the rational and the visible to help organize and refine the non-rational. The rational has long been the basis of learning. Much in religion is in any case conceptual and can be taught like any other subject area. This is true whether the learning context is the home, the home community (of mosque, temple, parish church), or the maintained school. To take

GCSE as an example, the basic approach is intentionally through pupils' own experience, but there is in every subject area an amount of necessary content which has simply got to be put across and learned. RE is no exception, and Otto recognizes this when he writes about means of expressing and transmitting the numinous.[15] The rational can be communicated by 'direct means' of expression.

Otto has many pages on 'Means of Communicating the Numinous'. He states that there are certainly aspects which can be passed on conceptually and taught directly in the traditional ways. Indirect means take up a far larger section of Otto's book. The most that can be done is to evoke, indicate, remind, and this means that this sort of experience cannot be communicated, but only refined and developed *provided that* it has occurred spontaneously already. But the development of an awesome experience of any kind requires the careful refining away of cruder phases and the encouragement of reflection. Patanjali gives a picture of the farmer who has to water his land: all the irrigation channels are in place, the water is already there, and only the channels need to be cleared of debris.[16] In terms of pedagogy, this problem is not confined to religion. Religious discussion has for centuries used two teaching methods: analogy, 'What is it like?', and negation, 'It is not this, not that'. In fact many subject areas use both these methods.

(ii) 'Schematization'

Since aspects of religious experience can only be referred to by particular words, questions must be answered about the relationship between a particular figure and that aspect of the numinous which it either evokes or refines. Otto is insistent that this relationship cannot be arbitrary, and he appeals to personal religious experience to prove it. This centres on his discussion of the *ideogram*, of which one of his examples is the figure of divine *Wrath*. A chapter which is only two and a quarter pages long (XIII) deals first with the process by which primitive religious consciousness in the form of demonic dread is refined to 'the fear of God' and so to worship, and secondly with the development of rational and moral aspects of the holy which accompany the refining of the cruder phases. This second process, the way in which rational aspects of the holy serve to bring out the non-rational with which they are interwoven, Otto discusses in several places, and borrows the expression 'schematizing' for this.

The word 'schematization' comes from Kant (*Schematisierung, Schema*) but Otto uses it in a different way. For Kant, schematization is the way we use empirical experience to bring to our consciousness the clear but otherwise inaccessible ideas and categories of pure reason. Otto wants to apply the language and forms of actual and particular religions to schematize the unclear feelings induced by encounter with the *mysterium tremendum et fascinans*.

Otto's use of schematization was widely discussed by his critics, who tended to focus on whether he was justified in borrowing the *word* rather than on the *process* he was bringing to analysis.[17] But the application is more important than argument over the origin of the term.

First steps in applying this method can already be seen in experiential teaching methods where, for example, traditional techniques for meditation are adapted from actual religions, perhaps Buddhist, Hindu or Christian meditation techniques, and used to help the spiritual development of children in contexts which are not themselves explicitly Buddhist, Hindu or Christian.[18] To use this method for religious education, it need not be assumed that the teacher has a greater understanding of spirituality and of religious experience than the pupils, although the teacher needs to plan out the forms of specifically religious spirituality that will be used to refine and define spiritual experiences, awe and so on, which the class is to work on, or in some way express. Where a process model of the curriculum is in use, the group can decide together, and this process will obviously help them to refine and clarify their own understanding.

(iii) Scripture and liturgy mediate human experience
Since the publication in 1972 of Schools Council Working Paper 36 on *Religious Education in Secondary Schools*, it has been usual to speak of *explicit RE* meaning teaching particular religious systems such as Islam, Buddhism, Christianity or whatever,[19] and to speak of *implicit RE* when discussing possible feelings, questions and responses that are thought to be of religious significance but arise from ordinary, ie nonexplicit, human experience. From this brief description it is easy to see that explicit religion is recognizable as such, but that there can be some doubt about the religious relevance or otherwise of what may be claimed as implicit.

Otto writes of crude forms of religious experience which need to be purified or refined in order to be brought to recognizably religious expression. He gives many examples from a variety of recognized religions which show that the presentation, experiencing and study of these relatively pure forms of religious expression have a central role to play in this clarification process. This is made more definite by the way Otto has arranged his examples under aspects of his description of the numinous experience, the *mysterium tremendum et fascinans*. Although no actual example within a religion may express just one aspect of the numinous to the exclusion of all others, he suggests that the examples he has chosen at least represent one or other aspect emphatically and mainly. It is of course central to his thesis that the experience of the numinous is prior (in both temporal and logical senses) to any actual forms of religious expression. Therefore with the important proviso that they must be appropriately chosen, explicit religious forms may provide means for refining the cruder emotions.

The first stage in refining is the process of clarification. This requires thinking, reason and developing the power of expression. Although the numinous is independent of the empirical, one becomes aware of it, even in its most indistinct presence, only by means of sensory experience. Otto writes:

> Sensory data and the empirical material of the natural world are the incitement, the stimulus, and the 'occasion' for the numinous experience to become astir, and, in so doing, to begin — at first with a naive immediacy of reaction — to be interfused and interwoven with the present world of sensuous experience, until, becoming gradually purer, it disengages itself from this and takes its stand in absolute contrast to it.[20]

In a chapter devoted to 'The Numinous in Luther', Otto shows how Luther and Tauler had to use 'figures' and 'images' to try and bring out the numinous.[21] While in this context verbal images are meant, like those of Scripture quoted in various parts of the book, it is clear that in many religious contexts literal images, statues of the Buddha for instance, perform this same function. These religious 'figures' are able to inspire numinous feelings as well as refining them.

CONCLUSIONS: THE FOUR ASPECTS AND FURTHER DEVELOPMENT

RE today has greatly benefited from contacts with the world's religions. There have been many advances. But if some of it has failed to engage the pupils in any depth, this is because 'phenomenology' so-called has in fact been a sterile cavalcade of outlandish phenomena. Otto, however, showed years ago how to see the depth dimension in all religions, and his examples develop and enhance our understanding (intellectual) and engagement (emotional). Obviously this depends on his analysis of the effects of the *sensus numinis*.

So the emphasis on human experience which some modern RE shows makes this connection. At the same time reason has an important part to play in the educational process.

Spirituality is seen to be much broader than religion, with a small but essential overlap. It is here that Otto's method of using what is rational, clear and conceptual to refine what is shadowy though deeply felt, can take us forward. Examples we have given do not directly derive from Otto. But Otto, like a sensitive compass needle, points the direction and suggests a method for education in this field also. By reference to *The Idea of the Holy* we can clarify and plan for spiritual development not only in the religious, but also in the educational context as envisaged by the 1988 Act.

NOTES

1. *Das Heilige*, first published Breslau, 1917, and many subsequent editions, ET John Harvey, *The Idea of the Holy*, Oxford, 1923, and subsequent editions, including Oxford paperback to which page references are made. Both books are still in print.

2. This paper develops two contributions to recent NEICE seminars, both of which have already been published: 'Rudolf Otto and Pupil-Centred Religious Education' appeared in *Curriculum*, Vol. 10, No. 3, Winter 1989; and 'What is Spirituality in an Educational Context?' appeared in *British Journal of Educational Studies*, Vol. 39, No. 4, November 1991.

3. Otto wanted people of all religious traditions to work together in the 'Religiöser Menschheitsbund' which he founded at the end of the First World War. Otto saw its influence in dialogical and ideological rather than aid terms, not unlike the League of Nations set up by the Allies at about the same time.

4. Originally the Gifford Lectures for 1901-2, now available in Fontana paperback; translated into German by G. Wobbermin, 1907.

5. Otto's thesis that human experience is primary has been the focus for much criticism. A trenchant and early example is that of J. Geyser, *Intellekt oder Gemüt?*, Freiburg, 1922, who maintains that religious experience is impossible without prior knowledge of doctrine and liturgy, both of which are specific to a particular religion. Geyser was Roman Catholic. This dispute cannot be settled by empirical tests.

6. Emphasis on individual experience, which Otto derived from William James, has also been a focus for adverse criticism. But Otto's thesis does not depend on this; it is personal rather than individual, and can be experienced also in community.

7. Edward Robinson, *The Original Vision*, Oxford: The Religious Experience Research Unit, 1977, and other publications of the Foundation.

8. David Hay, *Exploring Inner Space*, Harmondsworth: Penguin, 1982.

9. 'Religiöse Kindheitserfahrungen', in *Religionspsychologie*, Vol. 1, 1926. Otto does not give the source of his accounts.

10. Miehle's book, *Die kindliche Religiosität*, Erfurt, 1928, is explicitly modelled on the schema which Otto set out in *Das Heilige*. Some of his examples are from classic childhood autobiographical writing, for instance Gottfried Keller's *Der Grüne Heinrich*.

11. This is clear also from Robinson, *The Original Vision*.

12. *Growing in Understanding*, Durham County Council, 1982.

13. R. Minney and M. Potter, *Awe and Wonder in the Classroom*, Durham: Durham University School of Education, 1984.

14. The Nottingham Project was led by David Hay. The most accessible result of its work can be found in J. Hammond *et al.*, *New Methods in RE Teaching*, Harlow: Oliver & Boyd, 1990.

15. See *The Idea of the Holy*, ch IX, especially p 60.

16. Patanjali's date is variously reckoned between 200BC and 500AD.

17. F. K. Feigel, *Das Heilige — kritische Abhandlung über Rudolf Ottos gleichnamiges Buch*, Tübingen, 1948.

18. eg J. Hammond *et al.,.op. cit.*

19. G. Read, J. Rudge and R. Howarth, *How Do I Teach RE?*, London: Mary Glasgow, 1988, call the explicit in RE the 'systems approach'. M. Grimmitt in *What Can I do in RE?*, Great Wakering: Mayhew-McCrimmon, 1973, calls this 'dimensional RE' after Smart's 'six dimensions' of religion (see N. Smart, *The Religious Experience of Mankind*, London: Collins, 1971, and his contribution to Schools Council Working Paper 36).

20. *The Idea of the Holy*, p 113.

21. *ibid.*, p 104.

16

'Godliness and Good Learning': The Role of the Secondary School in the Spiritual Development of Adolescent Christians

DAVID DAY

The Education Reform Act 1988 laid on schools the responsibility of furthering the spiritual development of pupils. It envisaged that religious education, collective worship and the ethos of the school would all contribute to this aim in a substantial way. Research for the book *Teenage Beliefs* focused on a group of sixty-seven, 15- to 18-year-olds for whom spiritual development was a matter of serious concern.[1] They were by definition, 'young people, who were prepared to consider themselves committed to the church'. Of all adolescents this particular group might be expected to have interesting and relevant comments to make about the school and spiritual development. It is clearly a matter of importance to discover how they, at least, perceive the role of the school in their overall spiritual journey.

The scope and method of the original investigation has been fully detailed in the appendix to *Teenage Beliefs*.[2] This particular study has taken the transcript data and extracted from them every reference to the world of school. These have then been analysed and categorized. Six respondents did not mention school at all. Most of these had left by the time of the interview. The other sixty-one produced a total of 349 separate references to school or associated themes. The longest uninterrupted comment ran to 66 lines in the transcript; most were 4 or 5 lines.

Two corollaries of this method are worthy of comment. First, as the original interview schedule reveals, the respondents were never asked directly about school. Their comments were always in response to some other question. It might be argued that this oblique approach has increased their validity; one does not necessarily obtain more reliable information by addressing the topic explicitly. Secondly, information about school was almost certainly embedded in comments which happened to be 'untagged' by a keyword ('school', 'teacher', 'the people in our class', 'my school friends' etc). Though it was tempting to assume that certain remarks had a school connection this information has not been used unless the linkage was made explicit.

This inquiry concedes all the weaknesses of the structured interview. The method only reveals the perceptions and understandings of the young people themselves. Their accounts are open to challenge and subject to interpretation. Nevertheless they have some validity. Whatever assessment may be made of the material this is how the young people chose to construe and present their experience.

A SCHOOL FOR SAINTS?

Where, then, might one expect the fruitful areas for spiritual development to be found? The straightforward answer would be in acts of collective worship, in religious education lessons and, in a different way, through the medium of the pupil's academic study. These are the traditional sources of 'godliness and good learning'.[3]

Collective Worship
There were no references at all to collective worship or assembly as a place where one might pray, reflect, grow spiritually, find the depth, or in any other way nourish the spirit. For the militant Christian groups assemblies offered an opportunity to proclaim the faith, often with consequent criticism. Otherwise they are unremarked upon. Even in Roman Catholic schools the mass is mentioned only as an occasion of feeling embarrassed at taking part or an opportunity for laughing at those who did participate.

Religious Education
References to general, non-examination RE were sparse. It was seen by one pupil as a forum in which an evangelical teacher might witness. Another commented on being bored and picking up a book about the Buddha; she remarked on this as a moment when she was struck by the universality of suffering. A sixth former observed, 'I didn't have much RE after the third year'. A girl said, 'I sometimes wonder how he made

the world but I think that's because of RE lessons at school'.

One account showed how an opportunity to explore the nature of conviction might arise unexpectedly. In this case, however, it was sidestepped by the teacher:

> It was in RE once, we were being taught about all these various religions and she said, 'Is there anyone here who objects to being taught these?'. So I did stand up and said that I don't want to be taught these because I've got my religion and I believe that my religion is not just a religion. It's something very real... She was stunned that anybody would stand up and admit to what they felt like... She just said, 'Right, that's fine, I'll give you some other work to do while I discuss this with the rest of the class'.

Pupils in Catholic schools did make some reference to discussing issues, largely to do with morality, but the theme was not a prominent one.

In quite a different category were those references which dealt with examination RS ('A' level or GCSE). Here there did appear to be some engagement with the Christian tradition, usually through the Bible, both intellectually and in terms of personal theology. This engagement was often stimulating, sometimes threatening but generally seen as a source of growth.

> Sometimes the way I look at it in my quiet times seeps into the way I look at it when doing my 'A' level. I don't like the way I have to study the Bible for 'A' level. It's horrible when you have to do it like a text book, but you have to look at it like that in order to do the work. I don't think I'd have chosen RE at 'A' level had I not been a Christian, I didn't know what to expect.

> Sometimes I can get really angry with the RI teacher because she's not a Christian and she's very biased. She once explained all the theories about the feeding of the five thousand, and I was so angry with her because I knew that Jesus could do it. It makes you think perhaps he didn't, but in your heart you know really that he did.

> At first it was terrible. I think I almost became un-Christian because I was so confused. I just felt terrible. At first I started not believing anything, and that Abraham was just a place or something.

I really began thinking about it at the beginning of my 'O' level course, when I really had the time to sit down and think and study questions. That course made me think all about different aspects. It made me study myself, and also my church life. You know, what I got out of going to church, and how I could make that better. You know, when you get questions put in front of you, it can make you think, but until that point really I don't think anything came before me to make me think I'd become a Christian. But when something solid is put there, well, then for me it was like the beginning.

That was one of the 'O' levels I enjoyed doing most, even though there was an examination, because all the time you had to sit and think. You weren't just studying like religious studies, you were studying yourself and what you thought and you had to bring in other people's attitudes.

It was nice to see how those parts of Jesus's life had been depicted in other gospels. At the beginning it was that I just really wanted to know, not to understand particularly, but just to know what was happening. It was curiosity more than anything else. But curiosity leads to you wanting to read it more and to broaden your knowledge.

Academic Study

Academic study may be relevant to growth as a Christian in a number of ways. It may raise difficult questions with which faith ought to grapple and so stimulate a Christian vision. Being pressed to relate the insights of Christianity to contemporary issues, questions of history, works of literature or scientific discovery ought to be one of the ways in which students develop what Blamires has called the 'Christian mind'. It has to be said, however, that examples of the young Christian striving to relate faith to secular study were difficult to find.

The only thing is in Physics. A couple of lads were arguing with us and they believed the world began with a big bang, and another lad was saying that the brain isn't thoughts, how we would think thoughts, but electronic pulses going round in a sort of electrical circuit. And I said that everyone's different inside. And if everyone was the same and had the same pulses going round everyone'd be the same, but they're not. There's got to be something inside you that makes you different. And about the big bang theory, I said that I agree with that but that doesn't mean I'm not a Christian. They say, 'What about Genesis?' and I say, 'Genesis itself, I think, people were younger, the world was younger and people were not as advanced as we are now, and they wanted to know how the world began, and God gave them a simple picture of how it happened, but now we're advanced, we know differently probably'. And I claim that God was there before the big bang. There had to be something there before the big bang, and I put it down to God being there. He caused the big bang and evolution and I think that the first few chapters of the Bible teach that.

At the moment the Warnock Report, for example. I was sitting in a lesson the other day, I study politics at school, and the teacher was going through the things that were in Parliament that week, and he brought up the Warnock Report and he said, 'Won't step on this too far, I know you're a Christian, and that means you'll support it', which I did, but he expected all Christians to do it — which they all might. If he came across one that didn't then it could give him a shock! Abortion! Not all Christians support it!

Sometimes my teacher has brought across the point with lying, in the House MPs lie when they want to get out of things, and that is the thing that you do if you are a politician. I try to explain that if I were a politician I would try my best not to do that, he would say, 'You wouldn't get very far'. I had to say, 'That's as may be, but as a Christian you would believe that God would be with you. As long as you do right then he would be with you'.

Such comments were relatively rare. In fact the life of the intellect did not loom large among respondents' expressed concerns. Little evidence of intellectual curiosity emerged from the interviews. This conclusion may be somewhat at odds with the stereotype of the questing adolescent but is in harmony with Martin and Pluck's assessment of their survey material:

Ecology, communes, oriental mysticism, anti-bourgeois existentialism are nowhere to be seen... Politics bore them even more than religion and the things about which they wax spontaneously are sex, marriage, clothes, their own plans for the future and their own images of their personal identity.[4]

Whereas the subjects of academic study might be brought only rarely alongside the concerns of faith, the same could not be said of examinations. They represent an important theme, frequently referred to. For most respondents they constitute a crisis, a stimulus to prayer or a place where God may be glorified. Faith cannot be indifferent to occasions fraught with such significance for the future. One girl confessed that she was 'like a bear with a sore head' at examination time. Others noted how the prayer rate increased dramatically even to the point of producing such agonized cries as, 'Well, God, are you going to get me my 'A's?'. Others saw faith as helping them to cope with the pressure ('I used to get uptight'; 'They're not the be-all and end-all'). One young man had a frankly utilitarian view of God's involvement. In matters of written assignments or revision:

> He literally puts the books in front of me. I sort of say, 'Ooh, that book's good, ooh, thank you'. Sometimes you can have three books in front of you and you can just write and be finished within an hour almost, and I hate writing and I can't stand most school work so it's one area where he helps me a lot.

But, examination pressure on one side, there is little evidence that what they are studying for a large part of every day provokes them to develop Christian responses or perspectives.

Worship, religious education and academic study are the areas traditionally thought to be relevant to adolescent spiritual growth. Writers on Christian education, bishops in the House of Lords and headteachers at Speech Days might all be expected to make approving reference to these aspects of school life. It is slightly disconcerting to find that their assessments are not confirmed by teenage Christians in the survey. The fairly unproductive trawl through the interview material prompts a different perspective on the question, 'What do adolescent Christians learn at school which might be connected with their spiritual development?'. When the weight of their comments is taken seriously, one is reluctantly driven to a different kind of answer.

A TRAINING GROUND FOR MARTYRS?

Put starkly, young Christians learn that they are different; that they belong to a group which in some sense is deviant and not part of the identikit picture of the teenager. Martin and Pluck summarized their interview material in these words:

> There is a very strong feeling that going to church simply isn't
> a normal, expected part of being a healthy, ordinary
> adolescent... In general they picture the churchgoer of their
> own age as ultra-academic, a swot. It was a universal point
> made in every interview, individual and group alike, that an
> adolescent who went to church would be unmercifully teased
> and probably rejected.[5]

Those who were interviewed, though themselves Christian, confirmed this stereotype. For their peers, they conceded, Christians
would be seen as 'swots, spots and glasses'. 'Only creeps get confirmed.'

> I think sadly there is still the stereotyped image...well, as I said,
> there's a CU in our school, and that's got a very sort of wet
> image. I know someone who came along to get in with the
> musical section of it, who was very unimpressed with it, because,
> I mean, people seem just to be sort of sitting there singing
> these happy Sunday choruses. Perhaps that's one image —
> that Christians are wet, and not very enthusiastic about...and
> perhaps the other image that Christianity is basically a set of
> prohibitions. That being...that cuts away freedom, that it's just
> a dull set of do's and don'ts to live by.

If this view of Christians is prevalent then it is likely to be the single
most important, school-based factor in determining the shape and
direction of adolescent spiritual development. Church, home and
youth fellowship all have their part to play but the effect of peer
attitude at school cannot be ignored.

In the interviews the sense that to be a Christian was to be seen as
different surfaced in many ways. However, one theme was so prominent that it merits extended illustration. It might be termed, in a
biblical phrase, the demand 'to give a reason for the hope which is
within you'.

Adolescent Christians, almost by definition, possess a belief-system,
a set of convictions. These may be ill-formed and incoherent but they
represent a labelled package. In this they are unlike most teenagers,
whose beliefs are seldom articulated or systematized but rather tacit
and expressed through action. This difference is sharpened up by the
fact that the beliefs in question are religious. In a society where
religion is a peripheral element and which is suspicious of the
metaphysical, religious beliefs seem to be less soundly based and more
open to challenge than others. Packages which might constitute
rough equivalents — political beliefs, being 'green', feminist or pro

animal rights — do not have to undergo the same kind of struggle for acceptance. Teenagers who hold such convictions share the deviant status of Christians but because their views are more acceptable, are not perceived as peculiar in quite the same way. Christian convictions constitute a double provocation and those who hold them must expect to be challenged.

Those who were interviewed expressed how wearying the constant need to defend a position could be. One boy said, 'I feel as if they're always trying to get one over on me'. It was 'like a competition against each other'. A girl remembered how before she had come to faith she 'went out of her way to aggravate her Christian friend'. 'That was my main ambition', she said, 'to prove her wrong'. Others commented on 'the endless discussions with the atheists'; how 'friends plagued me with questions after my baptism'; how one was 'always being confronted'. The following comment is typical:

> Often arguments come up when people know you're a Christian. They deliberately go out of their way to argue... Arguments about how people have to suffer, and why, and why God doesn't intervene, all questions like that, and about nuclear stuff and that.

It is interesting to note that the Christians themselves seem to have accepted this situation as normal. They speak about the obligation to confess Christ and acknowledge the duty even when they shirk it.

> Well, I haven't really... I've kept myself out of situations where I've been called to make a statement in front of lots of people. I mean, whenever it comes up in conversation with friends, I'll say, I always show that I've got Christian beliefs but I don't actually go on and say 'I am a Christian' to what they're saying or hope that I'm inferring that I'm a Christian but I just...possibly because I am shy but also because I just don't... I don't want to tell everyone I'm a Christian. A bit embarrassed, I suppose. I don't want to go out and share. I suppose going along to the Christian Union is in itself showing to others that you are but I find that very hard, especially when somebody looks in through the window and they are praying or something.

Other comments range from 'I hope it won't come up', to 'You should know what you're about', through 'I made a fool of myself' and 'I told God, I know I'm going to be ashamed of you'. One respondent was forced to negotiate a *modus vivendi* with his friends which consisted of, 'If you don't start preaching we won't take the mickey'.

What the adult reader finds difficult to appreciate is the pressure which this sort of confrontational relationship entails and the raw nature of the experience. Generally speaking, this is no courteous and measured inquiry for an *apologia pro vita tua*. It is about being pinned to the wall and having to fight your corner. The comments illustrate this vividly: 'You do get ridiculed a lot'; 'You get ridiculed by everybody'; 'People come up and say "Feed them to the lions"'; 'People mock me a fair bit'; 'They broke my glasses and threw them down the toilet'; 'That year nearly killed me'.

> And I remember I used to have this NT Bible — a little one. I used to love it it was so cute — in about the third year. I had it in my bag for some reason. And there was a few boys and they wanted to borrow a pencil and they went to my bag and found the Bible. They thought it was really funny and said, 'Oh yes, what is this? What are you going to do, pray and sing hymns?'. So they started skitting me.

> When I first went to college we all had to introduce ourselves. You had to say where you came from, where you lived and things like that and if I say I live in a vicarage they say, 'Oh gosh, spotless or what?', but as you go on you show them you're more of a person, not a saint. I think that's when you first have to stand up, when you first go to college. You've to say that you're not a saint, but you've really got to stand up. They ask you, 'How can you go to church?', and 'what sort of beliefs do you have to say in church, isn't it all parrot fashion?'. Quite a lot of my class have asked fairly publicly. It's embarrassing at first because you don't know what to say. You don't want to sound snotty and you have to be really careful.

The exposed nature of these situations comes out very clearly in the interviewees' descriptions of two typical scenes. The first is located in free time, outside the timetabled lesson, in the form room, at break, after a lesson or during a library period. This represents a substantial segment of school life which is easily overlooked by teachers. As one respondent put it, 'The bell goes and then you are on your own'.

> I was in the library and I've always been sort of more friendly with boys than with girls and I was with a group of eight boys or something and I started talking to them and it was really

good. They were all boys that I knew from the bad group days, they'd all mellowed slightly. They said something and we'd got into the conversation and they said, 'Well how have you become a Christian?'. As we started talking, some guys on the next table joined us, just because they like a good religious argument. They just wanted to get me going and I tried to ignore them as much as possible. Okay, it was a bit intimidating, me against eight blokes, but some were interested, some were just along for the joke and some were just sitting listening, and I've no idea what was going on in their heads.

I remember one English lesson a few of us went into the library and we just started talking about faith and I felt I was on a hot spot. There was this girl pouring questions at me and trying to sort of establish her faith. There were about six or seven others, mainly boys and they were just listening and arguing and I got quite hot under the collar but they're the sort of stands I've been making and if they make a fool of me I say, 'Well, it's up to you what you believe but I have my own beliefs', but if they ask me about it then I will certainly tell them.

We came back down to the common room and gradually more people that were not in the English set were involved and in the end I just... I was just sitting there answering a barrage of questions. 'I don't agree with you, I think you are being selfish.' In the end I just had to give up, you know. I just said, 'It is what I believe and you can believe it if you want'. I really felt out on a limb. There was nobody that was a Christian in the sixth form apart from what I know, knowledgeably there is no Christians. I really felt, oh yeah, I was fighting a losing battle at that point.

I was trying to keep — I didn't want to argue — I just wanted to show them. And one girl said to me which just ended the whole conversation, 'Don't judge others or you can expect to be judged yourself'. And I didn't have an answer... And I also remember they just left me, we were going to assembly, and nobody waited behind for me. And they all went to assembly and Jenny — she's my best friend now — I just heard her say, 'Just because she's been a Christian for umpteen years, she expects us all to be like it. I mean, who does she think she is?'. And that was such a cutting moment, I always remember it.

The second typical scene takes place within the lesson. Here the teacher plays a key role in the interrogation. In the examples which follow it is interesting to speculate about the adults' reading of the situation. They probably did not see their actions as threatening. Indeed their interventions may have been intended as no more than playing Devil's advocate, trying to inject some life into a flagging lesson, slightly debunking overbearing adolescent dogmatism or teasing affectionately. This was not how the experience was perceived by the recipients. The impact of the teachers' questions felt like persecution and victimization. They spoke of anger, anxiety, inadequacy, frustration and embarrassment.

> Well, I have done biology 'A' level and we had to study evolution. The teacher who took us for it was definitely for evolution. She said, 'There are two theories how the world began. The religious people think it is Genesis' (for she knows full well I am a Christian) 'and normal people who think it is evolution', and at that point I just let it wash over me, you know, I just didn't think about it. I just took down the notes she gave us.

> There was one time when I was sitting in this class and there were two of us who were Christians, me and Steve, and the teacher was on about the Bible, and I was just sitting there and thinking, 'Oh, I'll just hear what she has to say', and then she says, 'Does anybody believe what the Bible says?' and I looked around and I said 'Me', and Steve put his hand up. And she said, 'You two? You two believe what the Bible says?' and I says, 'Aye' and then she bombarded us with questions. All sorts of questions. And she says, 'My, this'll be something I'll have to talk about in the staff-room', so all the teachers got to know, but the teachers, they've never really said anything. But some of the kids sort of said, 'Oh, you're a Christian so-and-so', and we just used to say, 'Oh, aye'.

> In school we've got a particular English teacher, a bit mad, a man, and there are about four or five of us who are Christians in his class, and that first year of the sixth form was a superb time for witnessing with him, because he was a definite anti-Christian, you know. Oh, he was terrible. He was awful. He really used to victimize us, persecution. He was terrible, he was horrible. You see one of our set books was *Paradise Lost* so I mean that finished us off, didn't it? So he would make snide comments about Christians and a good Christian attitude, looking at us like this, you know, but it was good —

it strengthened us. Because he was the sort of person who shouts at us and abuses us but you have to answer back or else if you crumble he'll only pick on you more.

Two general observations on these excerpts seem apposite. First, the significance of situations where one has to stand alone can hardly be overestimated for the development of the adolescent Christian. The girl who said, 'But it was good; it strengthened us', was identifying the positive benefits of an otherwise taxing situation. Kitwood's influential and perceptive study of teenage values has described the difficulty which taking a stand creates for the young adult:

> There are other examples where the pressure is felt more painfully, and the consequences of not conforming may be very serious... This general picture is confirmed by the categorisation of the topics chosen in connection with item 9, 'When you were right on your own with hardly anyone taking your side'... The probably inference is that standing alone in this way is indeed rare, and almost unknown in the younger age group. This question was taken up in the validation session... The opinion of the boy who took part was that it was inconceivable for a person below the age of about sixteen to hold values in an individual way.[6]

But even while conceding this point Kitwood stresses the value of taking up a personal standpoint:

> To break away, however, means a definite choice; a movement from the unknown. It involves risk, perhaps requiring a person to rely at first upon inner resources rather than social support; and it is logically possible only in the light of reflection on what a person wishes to be or to become.[7]

The second observation is linked with this one. It should by now be obvious how, within the sub-culture of the school, the Christian teacher can play a highly significant role. The adolescent Christian, beleaguered and hard-pressed, looks for support. Teachers operate as models, as sources of comfort and reassurance ('it is not foolish to believe') or even as secret agents ('we belong to the same secret society that the outsiders know nothing about'). The situation lacks only a secret password, some equivalent to the sign of the fish. One of the important functions of the school Christian Fellowship may be to provide a safe place where the status divide may be crossed and the common allegiance acknowledged.

This survey would be incomplete without some brief reference to the area where the worlds of school and social life overlap. Apart from purely church groups and some interest groups a good deal of a teenager's social life will entail contact with some of the people he or she sees every day in the classroom. These gatherings are strictly extra-curricular but they take place in the company of one's form-mates and accounts of what has gone on flow back into the world of school.

The difficulties arise from the fact that, rightly or wrongly, many of the activities that are characteristic of the teenage lifestyle are seen as problematic for Christians. The data yielded the following list: sexual behaviour, getting drunk and drinking under age, certain types of music, swearing, smoking, 'dirty' jokes, gossiping ('being bitchy', 'dishing the dirt'). Many interviewees felt that their Christian commitment required them to behave in ways that were at least partly at variance with the norm. They often complained of being watched and questioned about their behaviour. Thus even in social settings, they were unable to escape the sense that they were different. Not surprisingly, they developed a variety of strategies for coping with this problem, ranging from avoidance ('fading into the wallpaper'), through compromise ('I just drink orange or pineapple', 'I stop after four pints'), to emphasizing alternative sources of status ('I have a hard image', 'I play in a group', 'I'm the practical joker'). However, the point to be stressed is not that adolescents are remarkably adept at coping and show considerable creativity in interpersonal encounters; it is that once again they are reminded that they are different and that it is their Christianity that makes them so.

A VALE OF SOUL-MAKING?

The interpretation of this mass of material must perforce be tentative and provisional. Space precludes anything more than the briefest identification of areas to be explored rather than hard and fast answers. Nevertheless the following conclusions are worth further consideration.

First, collective worship, religious education and academic study do little to further the spiritual development of young Christians as far as that phrase has been traditionally understood. Working for public examinations in religious studies may be the catalyst for reflection on faith but most fail to relate faith to work in any systematic manner.

Nevertheless, the life of school may contribute to spiritual development in ways unintended and unforeseen, notably by setting up a sharp separation between the adolescent Christian and his or her peers. This separation, though painful, may have a number of beneficial side effects. For example, it may be in school that some Christians first learn to engage in mission, practise apologetics and exercise some kind of ministry. Again, the distinction between Christian and non-Christian may harden the edges of one's identity. Young Christians quickly acquire what Kitwood refers to as a 'character' and a role. Reference has already been made to the possible value of being forced to break social bonds and depart significantly from what is 'normal'. If nothing else, it might be argued, this is 'character building'.

There is an alternative view to be set against this optimistic reading. It might be maintained that what has been described is emphatically not a valuable experience. Rather than contribute to spiritual growth, it just creates young churchgoers who feel abnormal and peculiar, or slightly compromised and guilty, or too unworldly and life-denying for their own good. Moreover, the school experience may colour one's view of the world for the rest of life. Here, it could be said, lie the beginnings of the polarity between church and world, the spiritual apartheid which stresses light against darkness, inside against outside, saints against sinners, in short, the unhealthy emphasis which leads to the ghetto mentality.

It is not easy to adjudicate. However, it is clear that, to a large degree, young Christians hold a common understanding of what constitutes Christian belief and lifestyle. They accept that they will be interrogated and show no surprise at being constantly called upon to justify their views. They also accept that they will be identified as different. Silence and compromise are not part of the official package, even when they happen to be the options chosen in the moment of trial. The story of Peter's denial seems never far away. What is interesting for the Christian educator is the source of these shared understandings. Does the picture of the Christian which is held by these teenagers represent the peculiar and unbalanced emphasis of a specific sub-group within Christianity? If so, then it is just one possibility among many and may be modified or rejected. The more painful possibility for young Christians is that such testing encounters and such a call to be steadfast and faithful are authentic reflections of a way of life embedded in the New Testament, exemplified by Jesus himself and undertaken by his followers throughout the history of the church. It would then be an integral part of the life (and cost) of faith. But if this is so, Christian education is faced with an urgent task, and those who are involved with young people ought not to shirk the pressing duty of helping them understand and cope with their particular version of the 'fiery trial'.[8]

NOTES

1. David Day and Philip May, *Teenage Beliefs*, Oxford: Lion Publishing, 1991.

2. *op. cit.*, pp 173-174.

3. The phrase is taken from the collect of thanksgiving for William of Wykeham, the founder of Winchester School.

4. Bernice Martin and Ronald Pluck, *Young People's Beliefs*, London: General Synod Board of Education, 1976, p 14.

5. *ibid.*, p 17.

6. Tom Kitwood, *Disclosures to a Stranger*, London: Routledge & Kegan Paul, 1980, pp 164-165.

7. *ibid.*, p 256.

8. It is interesting to note that at the time of writing Scripture Union were advertising a video called *Daniel & Co* which 'powerfully communicates the original challenge of the story of Daniel to stand up and be counted for God in a culture that's heading in a very different direction...'.

17

The Sectarian Future of the Church and Ecumenical Church Schools

PETER SEDGWICK

INTRODUCTION: PRACTICAL THEOLOGY AND CHURCH SCHOOLS

Practical theology is concerned with the church's mission to society, and the practice of the Christian faith within the church. Such a mission does not exclude a witness to individuals within society, but mission will always be aware of the wider context in which it presents the gospel of Christ, and this involves an awareness of the changing nature of our society. Equally the practice of the Christian faith within the church can be either a matter of individual response or the corporate nature of the church's response to God in worship and pastoral care. Ecumenical relationships between denominations, within the one church of those baptized in Christ, are of importance both because they seek the goal of a full reconciliation and fellowship between Christians, and because the manner of achieving this goal displays clearly how much the corporate life of a denomination reflects the true nature of Christian discipleship.

Practical theology can therefore be interested in church schools from perspectives which are not simply that of the educationalist. Educational theory and practice must always be recognized in assessing church schools, but such schools offer for the practical theologian three important perspectives on Christian mission and ecumenism today. First, and most obviously, they are one of the most visible and powerful manifestations of the practice of the Christian faith within a community during the working week. Secondly, church schools are of paramount importance in socializing the child into the Christian faith. Thirdly, church schools demonstrate very clearly what meaning the common life in the Body of Christ, or *koinonia* to use the New Testament term, actually has in the lives of church members.

For these three reasons of involvement in society, conversion and nurture, and ecumenical relationships a practical theologian will be interested in church schools without necessarily being aware of all the implications of the educational debate.

THE ARGUMENT OF THIS ESSAY

I wish to argue in this essay first, that practical theology shows how the various aspects of a church school can be united into a transformative vision of the Christian life, which itself grounds and gives authenticity to the truth of practical theology. Secondly, a liberal democracy, which has been the context of church schools in the United Kingdom since the 1870 Act, itself offers and has provided in an impressive way the means of transforming human life through the areas of liberty, social mobility, life-expectation, material affluence and self-realization. The question of the compatibility of a Christian view of transformation with that of social democracy is essentially that of the secular nature of our society and the means by which the church preserves its own Christian integrity. The third and final stage of this essay is to argue that the future of the church lies in rediscovering its own integrity and vision. This will inevitably lead to a degree of sociological sectarianism but not necessarily to that of theological sectarianism. In such a church there will be a degree of tension with the surrounding culture. I believe that the churches must all rediscover their own tradition, pay more attention to nurture and become sociologically more sectarian. Yet this is only so that witness can go on. The issues of confronting belief, personal and spiritual needs, and material deprivation remain as acute as ever. The practical implication is that the admission of pupils must reflect this openness to the world, and not simply be an invitation either to the children of practising Chrtistians or to those in the local society of comfortable background. Yet what they are invited to take part in would be a school of diverse theological views and openness to liberal culture, which was nonetheless rooted and grounded both in curriculum and ethos in the Christian tradition as handed on by the local churches: the ecumenical church school with a sectarian future of the church. I proceed with the argument in detail in three stages.

THE TRANSFORMATIVE MODEL OF PRACTICAL THEOLOGY

Practical theology is not the application of theory to human action as mere practice. It is rather reflection on what we either actually do or could achieve, and is therefore sometimes called a theology of 'praxis', although I shall keep the term practice. Any true understanding of practice demands personal commitment and involvement. Moral truth is grounded in the moral conversion of an agent who has a character which recognizes true value. Thus transformation of the agent is the essential requisite for true practical theology. Moral conversion goes with intellectual conversion. It stresses that knowing moves from experience to understanding and judgement of what is known, and the judgement of what is known will depend as much on moral values as intellectual ones. Religious conversion follows from this, and finds openness in the dynamic relationship of a person to what they see as reality: the love of God. The three sorts of conversion are not temporal, however, so much as logical analyses, of a single process, where any one change may precede the other two.[1]

A church school will bring a pupil into dialogue with this tradition. It will always allow the views of others to inform its self-understanding, and it will respect the right of a pupil or teacher to adopt a position which is outside that of the community's tradition. This will be possible because there will be a dialectic between contemporary experience in the world as a whole, made up of many different traditions, and presentations of the revelatory tradition. Disclosure and conversion are the means by which a tradition offers enculturation, but such a process is a dynamic one. Nor can a vision of truth offered by a school be presented as a particular viewpoint in a specific discipline. There can be no future whatsoever for a Christian account of history, or the novel, let alone evolution in science. The vision is rather an overall unity of truth, as argued for by philosophers as different as Geoffrey Price and Alasdair MacIntyre.[2] It would therefore be in tension with much other educational philosophy, but the exploration of these differences goes beyond my competence. Yet it is worth stressing that public discourse in academic circles does not simply work with objective, rational criteria. The historical nature of ourselves places us within some tradition or another, and the nature of art is that it can disclose truth in an event to a person willing or open for that disclosure to happen. The religious nurture of a school as socialization into a tradition is simply the disclosure of new possibilities for a human life by interpreting the existing past of that person afresh. The educational integrity of the school need not be invalidated, although religious socialization (which can be a form of evangelism) will be seen as threatening by some educational philosophers. This disagreement must be met by constructive argument from the theologian.

What is of greater concern is how such socialization is related to involvement in the community. It cannot be assumed that the transformation of an individual life will change the society in which that school is set. This society can distort any belief in personal transformation into a justification of the status quo. Educational practice, however good, is faced with the reality of profound social disadvantage for many groups. Thus the debate in practical theology between those who advocate personal conversion as the criterion for the truth of such theology and those who see practical theology as justified by its emancipatory role in society emerges anew in church schools.[3] Whatever the power of a religious tradition to speak to an individual there are massive social forces which imprison many children in an impoverished existence. So the practical theologian will see the church school as manifesting Christian love in its immediate locality. In a deprived area it can be an example of a multi-racial society in miniature, or a witness to a community where class is not determinative of a person's future. In a less deprived area it can educate those who attend about the cost for others of living in our society. The church school is about socialization into a religious tradition, and will express the faith of that church for those open to its message, but such faith is about becoming responsible personally for a relationship to God on the one hand and for the society in which we live on the other. Faith is a distinctive relationship to God in the midst of personal relationships and responsibilities. What is clear is that the church school cannot be educationally beneficent apart from the impact of that school on those from disadvantaged backgrounds.

The third area which concerns practical theology is that of ecumenical relations. What does the goal of ecumenical reconciliation, or the complex of activities that make up the seeking of that goal, have to do with practical theology? And how would such goals and activities be related to the church school? The reality of the church is not simply reducible to that of a social institution. The church as an institution is judged by the gospel of Christ, and particularly that proclamation of the kingdom revealed in Christ. So the church as an expression of the unity willed for humanity begins with the calling of the people of God in a broken world. It begins corporately and not with individuals, and looks to its final end, which is the renewal of the world. The beginnings of the church as a community were marked by death and denial, and the community was restored by resurrection and forgiveness. The eucharist is celebrated as a symbolic expression of Christ's redemptive power, which creates fellowship and reconciliation.[4]

It is therefore very striking that ecumenical relationships have frankly been so little part of church schools in the past. Much that has been written above about religious nurture and involvement in community has been true of church schools. Practical theology can find much to reflect upon in Christian education about the nature of community and the reality of social concern. The interest of practical theology in ecumenism is in seeing how sociological and theological models of the church can be correlated together. Yet ecumenism also holds up the ultimate justification of the church to the partial traditions to which the practical theologians owe loyalty. These two interests which ecumenism offers to the practical theologian can be brought together in one clear question. Given that all religious movements generate structures and procedures which are sociologically necessary to ensure the survival of that movement, what are the costs which these structures impose on a church seeking to be one, forgiving each other in reconciliation and love?[5]

Church schools have been used by Anglicans to demonstrate their concern to be involved in society, and to serve the nation as the national church. They have been used by Anglicans and Roman Catholics to socialize children into the past traditions of their faith, and to hand on and reshape that faith to a new generation. Yet service of the nation and religious nurture avoid the ecumenical questions. They avoid asking how the two traditions of Anglican and Roman Catholic church schools (with some Free Church ones as well) relate to each other. They avoid the difficult realities of practising forgiveness and reconciliation between often exclusive denominations. They avoid the sociological critique of how far the inevitable process of becoming an institution (and adapting the charisms, or gifts, of the gospel into routine ways of being and acting) destroys the reality of the vision. Yet all the time children from different denominations will meet to experience common human friendships and quarrels. The ecumenical dimension of church schools is all too often ignored.

Thus the church school brings together the transforming power of conversion which individuals and communities encounter as they meet the love of God. It takes that religious faith into the community as a whole as a sign of responsibility and overcoming of social division.

It should be a place where mutual forgiveness and reconciliation are experienced as true fellowship in the Spirit. The church school can be seen in a unified vision by practical theology. Yet all this is not simply a theoretical argument. It is time to relate this to the reality of our culture, and of social democracy and secularization. For the argument of this essay is that in changing social order the church school offers a way forward to the church which will enable it to preserve its traditions without becoming theologically sectarian.

THE SOCIAL CONTEXT OF THE CHURCH SCHOOL

The power of liberal social democracy to transform society is undoubted. Class mobility has been one of the features of our society. The proportion of adults in Halsey's study who:

> stay as adults in the social class in which they spent their childhood is little more than half (55.4%)...the middle-class man who looks at his fellows will find that nearly two out of every three of them have come from birth in another social class.[6]

It is surprising that a 1983 study, following on these quotations from the 1972 research, showed that social mobility had actually increased since 1972. Life-expectation has also risen, and indeed continues to rise. The promise of medical technology continues to diminish mortality rates, even if there are great disparities in regions. In terms of material affluence, the United Kingdom's GNP has tripled at the very least since 1900, and the same estimation can be made of the increase of the median earnings of male manual workers.[7] Furthermore, apologists for the capitalist form of liberal social democracy will point to the classic stress on individualism, independence and the worth and responsibility of each person. This tradition has recently been revived by the New Right.

> Market transactions rest on consent; they invite the widest participation by consumers and producers, and maximize the freedom all can enjoy without infringing the like freedom of others.[8]

Freedom and self-expression lead to the enrichment of individual lives from the greater opportunities for exercising personal choice.

Such social change means that the transformation of communities over this century has been very great. Yet the counter argument has been powerfully argued. These are three aspects to the disenchantment with British social democracy which is now very common among many recent reports from the churches in Britain.

First, the exclusion from prosperity and from decision making about their individual future and the future of their communities is now a sadly accepted fact for many citizens in this country. Large scale studies such as *Faith in the City* or local studies such as *Faith in Leeds* and the report on coal mining communities in County Durham entitled *Coal, Church and Community* demonstrate quite clearly both the poverty endured by many and their exclusion from decision making. Other studies include the Policy Studies Institute report on *Black and White Britain* and the National Child Development Study's report, *Born to Fail.*[9]

Secondly, in a pluralist social democracy there is no reason to believe that Christian values will be preserved or articulated. The power of advertising and the demands of an economy which requires mass consumption will increase the desire within a society for a higher and higher standard of living. Yet even if this were not the case, there will be great difficulty in a pluralist society in nurturing the altruism and disinterestedness necessary for the preservation of a social democracy.[10] And even if this were the case, and we lived in a society which both restrained the destructive tendency to increase material affluence, whatever the danger to the environment and personal morality, and also agreed on a consensual morality which would protect the weak and vulnerable (and we plainly live in a society which accepts neither of these points), it would still be a pluralist society.

There is a third reason for the disenchantment with liberal social democracy. It is that it is becoming increasingly secularist, and cannot find a place for Christian values. The argument about secularism is notoriously complex, but certain points may be made which are relevant to the position of church schools. First, it is clear that the churches on many issues have undertaken very little theological research as to why they have advocated the position which they have taken. They have been content to accept the philosophical arguments of their social allies. Raymond Plant's analysis of the uncritical adoption of the social consensus put forward by John Rawls and held by many Christian activists is that there is no alternative at the moment to:

looking for the odd bit of theological backing for one's political preferences which are held on quite other grounds.[11]

A second point that can be made is that there is a widespread disbelief in the presence and activity of God in the world. The Dutch Roman Catholic, Anton Houpeten offers six reasons why theologians have argued that this is the case:[12]

(i) There is a loss of the sense of the transcendent, and of belief in a personal God.

(ii) The values of Jesus, his movement and the response to the kingdom of God have been replaced by middle-class values and an acceptance of political compromise.

(iii) The neglect of religious experience and the Spirit has led the western churches into over-intellectualized preaching, church communities without warmth and a formal liturgy which ignores human needs.

(iv) The church has not yet responded fully to the reforms of this century. Better adult catechetics, more dialogue with other religions, improved training of clergy would all feed into a church which is prepared to accept that what is called for is a total ministry to the spiritual needs of the urbanized, industrialized West.

(v) The church is now a victim of its own catholicity. We do not live in a world which rejects religion, but rather one which has internalized Christian values to such an extent that one can no longer tell what is of God and what is not. The distinction between churchgoers and non-churchgoers is blurred, since both live in a society which accepts Christian values.

(vi) Finally there are those who see religious practice as oppressive. Morally it burdens the individual with heteronomous norms, while acting as a means of avoiding the problems of human existence, including death.

What seems clear is that in all of this the content of the Christian faith in doctrine as well as ethics is far less able to affect men and women in urban, industrialized countries than once it was. It is 'the making of post-Christian Britain'. Instead Christianity seems to exist in an uneasy relationship with the surrounding culture.[13]

Does it all matter? It is crucial to the argument of this essay that it should do so. Others will be able to pursue the logic of this claim into educational theory and practice, but I wish to maintain that at this point the unified vision seen by the practical theologian in the church school must break down in practice. The three functions of the church school are religious nurture, involvement in community and ecumenical relationships. Although weak on the third of these functions, nonetheless the church school could express a transformative model of the Christian life, with the individual converted to the love of God and acting in responsible freedom for the world. Such a vision inspired William Temple in his commitment to religious education and church schools, while he equally sought to advance the cause of British social democracy. In a Christian culture the church spoke to people as they existed before God, while the State ensured that their social relationships could be lived in a fellowship of mutual concern and justice. The transformative vision of the Christian life in personal holiness could, and did, exist for Temple alongside a great commitment to the transformation of the British society by the liberal democratic process. Yet that was over four decades ago.[14]

How incompatible then are the three failings of our contemporary society described above with the role of a church school? First, our society now has a high degree of poverty in many areas, and an even greater amount of powerlessness. It is also very pluralist, with a diminishing degree of consensus on basic values. Although remarkably stable where it is prosperous, and still astonishingly tolerant, there is also a darker side: a willingness to accept inequality and deprivation, a great deal of racial prejudice and a belief that the main function of our society is to increase material prosperity. Above all, thirdly, it is a society in which Christian practice is now a minority subculture, and where religious discourse has little meaning outside the churches.

There has been no fiercer theological argument in recent years than that between those who see religious practice as personal and private, even if critical of the faults of our society, and those who see divine action as grounding the nature of all social existence, and therefore incompatible with a society such as we have at the moment. Those who take the latter view would also often argue that a society such as that of late twentieth century Britain will subvert religious faith into a pious moralism. They would accept the first four of the six points made by Houpeten, while being critical of the last two. An outline of the opposing sides would require another essay. For myself I can only say that I am persuaded by the views of theologians with common concerns but different doctrinal positions such as Stanley Hauerwas and D. W. Hardy, and believe that an individual religious practice co-existing in a tolerant relationship with a liberal social democracy is a game not worth the candle. As Hauerwas writes in an article with the entertaining title 'Sex in Public':

The ecclesiology of most of the more liberal ethics assumes that the church is a voluntary association which exists for the spiritual enrichment of the individuals comprising it. While admitting that such a voluntaristic theory of church is inextricably bound up with a pluralist social context, [I] doubt that voluntarism can provide the countervailing power we need to counter the tremendous powers which shape and destroy our lives.[15]

He calls for a community powerful enough to protect our fragile psyche from potent cultural forces. Such a community from the perspective of this essay is the ecumenical church school in a sectarian church future. I turn to the third and final part of my argument in this essay.

RECOVERING THE INTEGRITY OF THE CHURCH

If a church becomes sectarian, it can be used as a sociological or ecclesiological concept. In this case, the connotation is sociological. Such a sect would maintain an essential ecclesiological catholicity. What I wish to argue is that the ecumenical church school will express the tradition and values of the sect which sponsors it. It will however hold beliefs which do not restrict the activity of God simply to the confines of that sect. Secondly, the primary locus of ecclesiological self-understanding will be a theology of the laity, based on the nature of baptism and Christian vocation. There will then be some provisionality about the ecclesiastical structures of authority which a church school can explore. Thirdly, a commitment to the world by a sect will have areas of particular concern and pressure. I have already argued in the first part of this essay that church schools are one such area. It is however also important that criticisms of church involvement in society, by other organizations which work alongside the church, should be carefully heard and responded to. In this connection the criticisms made by Christians against racism and fascism, the Catholic Commission for Racial Justice, and the research of Bernadette O'Keefe become crucial. There is a constant concern that church schools are significantly less multi-racial than other state schools in the same area.

The interaction with other Christians provided in church schools and in small, cohesive, mutually supportive groups in parishes gives support to the enrichment of distinctive beliefs, value and actions among church members. It is also the case, however, that without this support Christian commitment will begin to disappear. The changes within Anglican, Free Church and Roman Catholic church life in Britain in the last thirty years have allowed much greater self-expression and personal freedom in living the Christian faith. Yet it can also result in a loss of a sense of identity, a search for community, and a feeling of isolation. If the novels of David Lodge show the gradual dissipation of religious belief into greater emancipation and a concern with personal self-development,[16] it is not for the churches to attempt a nostalgic return to the years before liturgical reform and moral change. But it may well be that they should respond to the costs of greater liberalization, and note that the unacceptable alternative for them is neither a return to past decades nor greater pluralism within church life but an obsessive search for community. The growth of house churches in Britain, with strict rules of discipline and a totally uncritical acceptance of religious authority allied to a fundamentalist reading of Scripture, shows the dangers.[17] As Gregory Baum has written:

> Some people involved in the underground are eagerly looking for the perfect human community. They long for a community which fulfils all their needs and in terms of which they are able to define themselves. This search is illusory, especially in our own day when to be human means to participate in several communities and to remain critical in regard to all of them.[18]

If Christianity will survive in Britain by both adopting the position of a sociological sect and also rejecting the narrow introversion of a religious cell, it will need to refine its position further. In the absence of exclusive claims, Christians would not be socially deviant enough. They would instead be like cults and philosophical schools, which offered membership so that religious issues might be discussed. It is the Christian tradition that has constantly returned to the uniqueness of Christ and the presentation of the gospel as offering salvation. Church schools can act as the bearers of tradition, without compelling belief and without identifying tradition as simply the witness of past ages or the unchanging deposit of revelation.[19]

It is important to distinguish what is being witnessed to at this point. All the main established churches in Britain in 1945 have now passed through a period of considerable reform and liberalizing tendencies, from liturgy to organizational structure. Churches need to cope with the rapid and continuous change, high mobility and mass communications of the modern industrial society. One way to respond to the trend that makes us private individuals within a framework of highly bureaucratic structures is to create, or foster, intermediate communities of face-to-face encounters. However two options here are unacceptable. One is that of the tightly-disciplined house group. The other is that of the religious/philosophical school where people could have their tastes and needs answered without any commitment being asked for in return. I would wish to argue that church membership must have some conditions. The primary commitment required is that of exploration of Christian claims about the Incarnation, the uniqueness of Christ and the nature of humanity, as shown in the Christian tradition which is passed on in each generation yet also re-expressed in the language of that new cultural setting.

So the church school, as an intermediate community which nurtures people into faith, is not witnessing to the view that God is quite separate from the world but that certain books, rituals or institutions witness to God's transcendent reality in the world, and that without this witness God's transcendence will not be known.

Therefore the church school will be a witness to a world both secular and yet totally known by God, who is at work amongst it. This witness is to divine grace present in the secular world, where people are led to develop their own potential and the proper diversity of society is affirmed.

There are strongly practical implications for a church school which adopts a position that I am outlining. One the one hand it will insist on the religious nurture of its pupils being all important. Great care will be taken on the quality of worship, chaplaincy and religious instruction. At the same time there will be an exploration of what it means to create social relationships according to criteria which reflect the divine/human interaction, including: the integration of education between home, school and work; the fostering of artistic and cultural wholeness, as the Impasse centres in the North of England have sought to do for those without paid employment; and the creation of non-exploitative attitudes to work. As well as social relationships, there is the cognitive dimension of exploring the nature of culture, art and science as a whole.

Thus the church school will have to extend its curriculum to include a deep and careful consideration of pluralism in society and culture, including our religious traditions. It would also be a primary intermediate agency for nurturing and socializing many into the Christian faith in a secular world, where the divine activity present there becomes increasingly hard to discern. Others can develop and criticize this position from a position which is rooted in educational theory and theology. My concern is to advance the possibility of speaking of the church school as a vehicle for religious nurture, as outlined in part one of this essay, while taking account of the strongly secular tendencies discussed in part two. Lesslie Newbigin sums up the dilemma:

> That the development of the indvidual person is governed by the programme encoded in the DNA molecule is a fact every educated person is expected to know and accept. It will be part of the curriculum in the public school system. That every human being is made to glorify God and enjoy him forever is an opinion held by some people but not part of public truth. Yet, if it is true, it is at least as important as anything else in the preparation of young people for their journey through life.[20]

My second area for the development of the church school is that of relationships between established denominations. What are the implications of this proposal for developing joint church schools?

The reality of ecumenism in church schools is, to put it mildly, difficult. Although both ARCIC and the responses of the Roman Catholic Bishops of England and Wales to ARCIC both agree that:

> some difficulties will not be wholly resolved until a practical initiative has been taken and our two churches have lived together more visibly in one koinonia.[21]

The aspirations do not match the local experience of Christians. Religious education remains contentious; there are profound differences between official Roman Catholic teaching on the one hand on the role of women and the nature of family life, and non-Catholic Christian families on the other who may be deeply involved in local ecumenical discussions and action. And worship is most problematic of all, once a sacramental expression is considered.

What is the way through all of this? It must still be affirmed that there is remarkable ecumenism in some schools, and between some parishes. There has been a much greater appreciation of sacramental ministry in non-Catholic churches this century, and Roman Catholic theology no longer sees ordained ministry primarily as a priesthood with power to consecrate and forgive sins. Instead ordained ministry is placed within collegial leadership, and the sacramental role flows out of that leadership, and not *vice versa*. Furthermore, the criterion for the use of any ecclesiological model must be the needs of the church now, as a historical reality with a past and traditions to be valued, but also as a community situated in our situation and time. This community will be both a created one, with human relationships, and yet called to free love in communion with God. It is both nature and grace.[22] The church school is no different. What matters is that in religious nurture, ecumenical relations and involvement in community the church school should unify nature and grace. Worship is not simply the adoration of the wholly other, with the priest visiting the church school seen as the man apart, nor is education simply the expression of social and psychological values. Instead the church school is a Christian community that expresses nature (social and psychological values) and grace (the sacred, adoration, otherness than this world). If the church school is seen as a form of basic Christian community, made up of the baptized form of basic Christian communities, then there will be lay leadership of headteacher and a different form of leadership in the ordained minister. Both will exercise leadership within this community. But what is this community? It is a community where the baptized are growing into maturity in Christ. It is a dynamic reality, where the church is seen not so much as an institution as in terms of membership, and spiritual growth.

> The child growing up in the community is growing into the community and therefore growing in the Spirit which fills the community. There is a developing and dynamic giving of the Spirit throughout this process until it is completed.[23]

'Until it is completed.' This argument does not remove the difficulty of deciding who is or is not a full and mature member of 'the church'. But it does suggest that if the Spirit is present throughout the development of faith, then these are strong arguments for allowing full participation in the eucharist before confirmation.

> Experience of the eucharist and of union with Christ in communion is a very important and significant experience in the life of a young person and in his or her growth in faith.[24]

But can the argument stop there? Certainly John Coventry would extend the sharing of eucharistic communion to situations of serious spiritual need, and not simply dramatic physical circumstances such as concentration camps.[25] This would include situations of inter-church families. Could it not also include joint church schools?

Yet it is not simply a question of shared worship, whether sacramental or not. It is also a question of authority and the ministry of the laity. The insights of *Lumen Gentium* on the new people of God who share in Christ's work can be put alongside *Gaudium et Spes*. This latter document speaks of the place of the church in creating a Christian contribution to our modern secular culture — which is the whole theme of this paper. In this task the primary responsibility falls upon the laity.[26] The theology of baptism I am arguing for would see the church school as a form of Christian community with spiritual power. This community would be a gathering of those who were equal before God and bound in freedom to the cause of the kingdom of God. This equality would not exclude leadership and authority, but it would see this leadership as provisional and possessing social, not ontological, status. Although ordained ministerial office would remain, it would exist for the building up of the community as a place where there was explicitly an exploration of ecumenical relationships.[27]

To summarize, I am arguing for a way of seeing church schools as based on a theology of baptism, which would serve as a new way forward in ecumenical relationships. Such ecumenical church schools would not at all deny the right of children who were not Christians to attend, but they would be especially attractive to inter-church families. In a manner analogous to the development of Local Ecumenical Projects, they would be set free from some of the restrictions placed on eucharistic sharing. They would be centres of lay leadership, where community involvement of parishes could be related to the schools themselves. Thus a parish project in, say, housing or drug abuse would be seen as one aspect of mission while the school would be another. Practically they could be related by the involvement of pupils, sharing of premises, or the leadership of the same group of laity and clergy. Above all ecumenical church schools would retain close contact with their denominations, so that while they would be seen as licensed experiments some of their findings could be fed back to the churches.

What is the reality of this happening? The likelihood in terms of agreed worship must be very small. John Coventry points to the unanswered questions in inter-church marriages arising from joint churches studies of the 1970s. There are also many issues from the Liverpool 1980 National Pastoral Congress which remain undecided. On the Anglican side, there are large issues of establishment and the continuing existence of fringe membership which will not easily be decided. There are many who oppose the development of ecumenical church schools as a ghetto-like huddle.[28]

Nonetheless if my argument is sound, it should be possible to develop ecumenical church schools which nurture the faith while retaining an openness to the world.[29]

The third, and final aspect of ecumenical church schools is, then, involvement in the community. It is not a separate area from that of ecumenical relationships and shared eucharistic worship. This is so for two reasons. First, a church which is involved in the community, and a church school which is equally committed to its local area, will need to recover on a regular basis the experience of its grounding in Christ. This must be done in worship. Two separate denominations each involved in social action in an area can recognize in the eucharist of another Christian assembly the very reality of its own life. Thus it is in worship that the self-giving of a church to a community is seen for what it is in Christian terms. Secondly, there is a dynamic in worship which takes the church or school out into the community. The ecumenical document *Baptism, Eucharist and Ministry* puts it like this:

> The eucharist involves the believer in the central event of the world's history. As participants in the eucharist, therefore, we prove inconsistent if we are not actively involved in this ongoing restoration of the world's situation and the human condition. The eucharist shows us that our behaviour is inconsistent in face of the reconciling presence of God in human history. We are placed under continual judgement by the persistence of unjust relationships of all kinds in our society, the manifold divisions on account of human pride, material interest and power politics and, above all, the obstinacy of unjustifiable confessional oppositions within the body of Christ.[30]

Thus ecumenical relationships and involvement in community particularly come together in the eucharist. This section of BEM goes on to argue that 'all kinds of injustice, racism, separation and lack of freedom are radically challenged when we share in the body and blood of Christ'. It is the racial composition of church schools which has been most challenged in recent years. The Scarman Report on Brixton, the Swann Report, *Faith in the City*, and reports from the Catholic Commission on Schools have also discussed the question of race, as well as that of multi-faith education.

Ken Leech, sometime Race Relations Officer for the Church of

England's Board for Social Responsibility, has written perceptively on this. In an unpublished article he says:

> The question of the manifestation of racism in school does not raise problems specific to church schools. Racism and racist assumptions in textbooks, the effect of racist organisations and attitudes on pupils' behaviour and so on, are currently under scrutiny by a number of bodies. But the church school will need to face some specifically Christian aspects. For example, how much of the atmosphere of church worship associates whiteness (washed in the blood of the lamb, angels in white, saints in stained glass, etc) with holiness, and blackness (the colour of Cain and Ham, even of Satan, and no saints of that colour in most churches) with evil? How much do theological factors unconsciously reinforce the stereotypes of purity and gentleness against black passion and aggression?

These are general points which are given greater clarity by the Runnymede Trust's finding in 1981 that in certain multi-ethnic areas percentages of minorities were lower in Church of England (and even lower in Roman Catholic) schools than in county schools. Furthermore, the main controversy on racial policy and education in the Church of England was aroused by a leaflet from Christians Against Racism and Fascism in 1982 which noted that religion could be used as a means of racial discrimination. It pointed to the fears of minority groups that their own cultural and religious traditions could be diluted by multi-faith and multi-cultural education in Church of England schools. It noted the strong desire of some minorities for their own schools.

The Swann Report reflected this proposal, and the debate has moved on since 1981. It now needs to be seen in the context of inter-faith dialogue, where racism is a symptom of unease at the reality of a multi-cultural and ethnic society, as well as being part of the cultural tradition of English society. If church schools are to continue, then the tension will remain. Such schools can indeed socialize their members into faith, but they will need to engage in inter-faith dialogue as well. They will also need to study what racism means. Understanding racism in Christian doctrine is about experiencing the stranger who suffered and was discriminated against. Both the Old and New Testaments work with a typology of the person who is discriminated against and his or her place in the context of redemption. Thus socializing members of a church school into faith means in particular understanding what forgiveness and an awareness of evil implies in practice. Racism is part of that evil, and the answer will not always be 'reconciliation', as the immediate church response. Forgiveness and compassion include the protection of the innocent from further harm, and the intention to examine your own position in order to see if there is discrimination as well. As Ann Dummett wrote in her Runnymede study:

> The fact that the church schools are becoming multi-racial does not mean that there is no direct or indirect racial discrimination.[31]

The command to witness to Christ in the Christian tradition does not presuppose that 'we' (the Christians) have a universal truth which others implicitly own or have rejected. Rather the command to witness is a declaration of the source of power to which the Christian message points. It does not necessarily and immediately entail judgements about the beliefs of others, as an *a priori* definition of Christian witness. Honest inter-faith dialogue may raise such issues, and probably will, but Christian witness primarily contrasts the fallen nature of the whole world (including the church of Christ) with the love of God shown in Christ. The task of a Christian community is to live out the implications of that claim, and to discover a freedom based on Christ which delivers men and women from the fear which gives birth to racism, or implicit discrimination in admissions procedure. A pluralist world of religions is not tragic, but part of the mystery of divine providence, which can be explored as the opportunity arises in inter-faith dialogue from the church school. A divided world of racism and discrimination is tragic, for standing against racism may well produce conflict. Yet the Christian cannot opt out because of the risk of violence:

> For tragedy consists in the moral necessity of having to risk our lives and the lives of others in order to live faithful to the histories that are the only means we have for knowing and living truthfully.[32]

The alternative which the church offers to the world will differ from society to society and culture to culture. In this way the church decides what is and is not essential to its own life, and what is simply a cultural option. But the belief that God speaks through the stranger is not a reason for dissolving all differences into an all-embracing tolerance.

It is a basis for reviewing the cultural barriers which the church often places in the way of those it seeks to speak to.

CONCLUSIONS

In this paper church schools have been seen as offering three dimensions to the life of the church. These are the nurture of children and teachers, ecumenical relationships and community involvement. Ecumenical church schools offer a vision of religious disclosure and nurture which could be of great value in a future secular culture. It is for the churches to take their development seriously, give them greater freedom in worship and action, and learn from their discoveries. The vitality of the churches in the decades ahead could well be served by their acceptance of a sociologically sectarian role, while retaining an openness to the world and a theological breadth and pluralism. The ecumenical church school has a great part to play in such a strategy.

NOTES

1. See David Tracy, *The Analogical Imagination*, London: SCM, 1981, pp 69-79, on truth claims in practical theology. See also Bernard Lonergan, *Method in Theology*, London: DLT, 1972; and for his relationship to education, J. W. Sullivan, 'Lonergan, Conversion and Objectivity', *Theology*, Vol. LXXXVI, September 1983.

2. Alasdair MacIntyre, *After Virtue*, London: Duckworth, 1981; Geoffrey Price, 'Universities Today', in *Universities Quarterly*, Vol. 39, January 1985.

3. G. W. Ebeling, *Word and Faith*, London: SCM, 1963, and D. W. Hardy, 'Gerhard Ebeling', in *Expository Times*, Vol. 93, 1981-82.

4. *Baptism, Eucharist and Ministry*, Geneva: WCC, 1982, 'Ministry' I-VI.

5. In an unpublished paper by S. W. Sykes, 'Lutherans and Anglicans on the Catholicity of the Church', the Weberian notion of 'routinization of charisma' is applied to ecumenical relationships: 'Churches which have evolved sophisticated systems of internal communication over centuries have acquired means of discounting implications inimical to their own life and mission. Formal structures of authority as readily conceal the real exercise of power as reveal it... What is of significance for other churches to understand is the way in which effective messages are passed, not the theological legitimations of formal structures.'

6. A. H. Halsey, *Change in British Society*, Oxford: OUP, 1978, p 116.

7. Halsey, *op. cit.*, p 29.

8. Edinburgh University Centre for Theology and Public Issues, Occasional Paper No. 5, *The New Right and Christian Values*, 1985. The quotation is from Lord Harris. See also Brian Griffiths, *The Creation of Wealth*, London: Hodder & Stoughton, 1984.

9. *Faith In the City*, London: Church Information Office, 1985; *Faith in Leeds: Searching for God in Our City*, Leeds: Churches Community Involvement Project, 1986; *Coal, Church and Community*, Durham: North-East Theological Consultancy, 1986; *Black and White Britain*, 3rd PSI Study by Colin Brown, London: Heinemann/PSI, 1984; P. Wedge and H. Prosser, *Born to Fail*, National Children's Bureau, National

Child Development Study, London: Arrow Books, 1983.

10. John Habgood, *Church and Nation in a Secular Age,* London: DLT, 1983, p 47.

11. Raymond Plant, 'The Anglican Church and the Secular State', in George Moyser (ed), *Church and Politics Today: Essays on the Role of the Church of England in Contemporary Politics,* Edinburgh: T. & T. Clark, 1985, p 328, and the review article of the whole volume by S. W. Sykes, which expands Professor Plant's argument, in *Crucible,* April-June 1986.

12. See A. Houpeten, *People of God,* ET, London: SCM, 1984, pp 7-14 on alienation from church and religion.

13. For discussions of secularism see D. Martin, *A General Theory of Secularization,* Oxford: Blackwell, 1978, and for a commentary on Martin's views R. Gill, *Prophecy and Praxis,* London: Marshall, Morgan & Scott, 1981, ch 4; Habgood, *op. cit.,* ch 1. For a historical account see Alan D. Gilbert, *The Making of Post-Christian Britain,* London: Longmans, 1980.

14. W. R. Rinne, *The Kingdom of God in the Thought of William Temple,* Finland: Abo Akademi, 1966, ch 8.

15. D. W. Hardy, 'The English Tradition of Interpretation and the Reception of Schleiermacher and Barth in England', unpublished essay; S. Hauerwas, 'Sex in Public', in *A Community of Character,* Notre Dame, Ind.: University of Notre Dame Press, 1981, p 188.

16. D. Lodge, *How Far Can you Go?,* London: Secker & Warburg, 1980, and *The British Museum is Falling Down,* London: MacGibbon and Kee, 1965.

17. Ian Calvert (ed), *Wine of the Kingdom?: An Exploration into the House Church Movement in the North-East,* Diocese of Durham, 1984.

18. G. Baum, *New Horizon,* New York: Paulist Press, 1972, pp 142-43, quoted in A. Dulles, *Models of the Church,* Dublin: Gill & Macmillan, 1978, p 57.

19. George Lindbeck, 'The Sectarian Future of the Church', unpublished paper.

20. L. Newbigin, *Foolishness to the Greeks: The Gospel and Western Culture,* London: SPCK, 1986, pp 38-39.

21. Bishops Conference of England & Wales, *Response to the Final Report of ARCIC,* London: CTS, 1985, para 46, and *Response of the Holy See to the Final Report of the Anglican-Roman Catholic International Commission, 1982,* London: Catholic Truth Society, 1991.

22. Joseph Laishley, 'What is a Priest?', in *Spirituality and Priesthood,* The Way Supplement No. 47, Summer 1983.

23. T. A. Marsh, *Gift of Community — Baptism and Confirmation,* Delaware: Michael Glazier, 1984, p 191.

24. *ibid.,* p 195.

25. J. Coventry, 'Inter Church Marriage', in *Reconciling,* London: SCM, 1985, pp 54-81.

26. *Gaudium et Spes (Pastoral Constitution on the Church),* London: CTS, 1965, ch 2, 'The People of God'.

27. E. Schillebeeckx, *The Church with a Human Face,* London: SCM, 1985, pp 203-4.

28. R. Waddington, 'The Church and Educational Policy', in G. Moyser (ed), *Church and Politics Today,* Edinburgh: T. & T. Clark, 1985.

29. See the essays by P. Chadwick and M. Gladwell in *CCU Bulletin 2,* Summer 1985 and Tap Roots 5, *Schools for Unity,* London: British Council of Churches, 1985, on Dronfield St Andrew's Anglican/Methodist School. This is a community centre, church school and a church in one: 'The church is therefore seen as people involved with the wider community'. See also English Anglican/Roman Catholic Committee, *Joint Schools,* Norwich: Canterbury Press, 1987. This is an excellent survey by Priscilla Chadwick and Maria Gladwell, with chapters on liturgy, chaplaincy, curriculum, and staff policy. It is however very weak on the social context of the church school, which is one of the main arguments in this article. Nor does it explore the reluctance of the hierarchy to proceed further (it was an official document).

30. *Baptism, Eucharist and Ministry,* Eucharist II, 20, and commentary by J. M. R. Tillard, The Eucharist, Gift of God', in M. Thurian (ed), *Ecumenical Perspectives on BEM,* Geneva: WCC, 1983.

31. Ann Dummett and John MacNeal, *Race and Church Schools,* London: Runnymede Trust, 1981, p 60.

32. S. Hauerwas, 'The Church in a Divided World', in *A Community of Character,* p 106.

PART TWO

'At Eye Level':
The Contextualization of
Christian Education

SECTION THREE

The Wider Context

INTRODUCTION

Jim O'Keefe poses the question, 'Can Television Cope with Theology?' and expresses some of the tensions between an industry devoted to consumption and marketability, and reflection on the life of faith. In a wide-ranging survey of religious programmes, he considers worship, debate, documentary and entertainment, and finds that television is not a wholly suitable medium for evangelization in that its purpose, style and approach are often inimical to those of theology. Television's obsession with confrontation and conflict, with the unusual and scandalous, its preference for violent language and 'tied-up endings' are all at odds with theology's concern for dialogue, search, openness and silence.

Richard Zipfel, in 'Anti-racist Education: an Educational Task for State and Church?', explores the changing composition of British society through a survey of educational responses to its increasing diversity. He maintains that it is essential to counteract an ethnocentric approach to education in that the ethnocentric mentality warps and restricts intellectual development and is closely linked to racism. Examples of revised curriculum frameworks designed to dispel ethnocentricity are cited. A final section presents church schools with a particular challenge to develop in their pupils by their ethos and implicit religious education a sense of self and world which is guided by a wider vision.

Edward Hulmes's essay, 'Christian Education: An Instrument for European Unity?', begins with an exercise in 'discovering Christian education', understood here in a wide sense as education (whether in church schools or secular schools, whether explicitly 'religious' in content or not) whose nature is determined in relation to 'the enigmatic figure of Jesus'. The relationship of Christian education to the idea of a pluralist society, and to contemporary needs and events in Europe, is then charted. The author articulates the danger he perceives in an approach for which 'the hallmark of the mature Christian emerges as uncertainty', and argues that there is a need for Christian educators 'to encourage positive discrimination as well as reconciliation in a world fragmented by religious and cultural differences'.

In his paper, 'Growing into Christ: The Psychology and Politics of Christian Maturity', Jeff Astley discusses various images of maturity and adulthood. He relates these to psychological accounts of human development, and theological understandings of christology and Christian anthropology, arguing that 'the gospel is an overturning of values, a radical re-evaluation of what it is to be human and "successful", "mature" and "adult"'. He concludes with an attempt to show how in practice Christian formation may assist in our 'growing into Christ', and notes the relevance of social and political discussion to this central concern of formative Christian education.

18

Can Television Cope with Theology:
Hill Street Blues v James Bond?

JIM O'KEEFE

More than any other means of communication, television epitomizes the changes which have taken place in the world of communications. In 1950 only five countries had regular television services, today there are almost 140 such countries. The number of TV sets world-wide approaches 400 million, which gives some idea of the incredible impact of this invention on the lives of millions of people and on the propagation of information.[1]

CULTURAL DOMINANCE

In spite of these great developments, in at least 40% of the countries television reaches less than 10% of the population, and in more than half of all countries less than 50% of households own a TV set. So there are already questions about the danger of cultural dominance, with all the threats that this contains for cultural identity.

Some people call the post 1970 era the 'Information Era'. It is characterized by the enormous increase in our ability to extend our knowledge, store, process and produce information, and to disseminate it. Some ask whether or not our technical progress exceeds our capacity to interpret the consequences and direct it along the most profitable paths. We already have the capacity to relay messages from one satellite to another, to 'blitz' receivers with the same message throughout the world. However, the majority of people, the 'marginalized majority', will not be able either to 'receive' or to engage in debate about reception. The questions need not even be asked in theological terms, but there are massive questions emerging

within the technological advances made in communicative systems —
who owns them, what are they doing with them?

What I intend to do in this paper is simply to raise a number of
issues which I see as needing to be reflected on theologically. I think
that most of the questions are common to the mass media generally,
though I shall be using the example of television to illustrate them.

COMMODITY v PERSON

The first issue is that of non-participation at a global level of people
within the information transmission business — it could well be left in
the hands of very few. In his book *Following Christ in a Consumer Society*,
John Kavanaugh is challenging us to develop an articulated understanding of human dignity either in philosophical anthropology or
any other art or science.[2] He believes that America is pointing towards
two very different sources of inspiration — the Commodity or the
Person, The Thing god or the Person god. He explores in this book
the way television deepens belief in the Commodity, the thing,
through its massive advertising campaign. 'Buick is something to
believe in', 'Datsun saves and sets you free', 'Love is Musk', 'Wise men
ring first'. The problem here refers to advertising rather than television, though one CBC Vice President has said that programmes on
American TV were the stodge between the adverts:

> I'm not interested in culture. I'm not interested in pro-social
> values. I have only one interest. That's whether people watch
> the program. That's my definition of good, that's my definition
> of bad.[3]

Kavanaugh sees television as one of the prime movers behind the
Commodity god in a consumer society. The two pre-eminent values in
this commodity form of life are consumption and marketability.
These are most obviously seen in the quality and quantity of advertising, but also by the very fact that people consume so much time
watching TV which is marketed for that very purpose. His research
suggests that estimates of the average American TV watching time run
from 26 hours a week to 13 straight continuous years of our average
life span. 'Since up to 27% of prime time can be given to advertisement,
we could possibly spend', he suggests, 'on an average, the equivalent
of three solid years of our lives watching commercials'.[4] Fifty billion

dollars a year are not spent because they are ineffective. The message which is assaulting the nation is that you must have in order to be. Apparently the average pre-kindergartener spends 64% of his or her waking time watching television game shows (the content of which could be expressed as competition for money or commodities), soap operas, and cartooned violence sponsored by junk food.

This distinction between the Commodity form and the Person form is sometimes dismissed as the ravings of the disillusioned and those nostalgic for the past. I just open up the question and suggest it is a crucial area for debate. What effect does this consumer mentality have on the culture of a nation? What effect does it have on the few people in so-called developing countries who are exposed to it? That is the second question I should like to raise.

THE MEDIA AND EVANGELISM

I once heard Fr Jean Desautels, SJ, lecture at Hatch End, the Catholic Radio and Television Training Centre in London. He made this statement: 'The role of the church in all this is *to use the media to evangelize* and *to evangelize the media*'. I should like to raise further questions by looking at what is being done, or not being done, in these two areas.

Using the Media to Evangelize
I take evangelization to be the process whereby the churches are involved in the struggle for the fullness of life for every man and woman in the world.[5] In 1975 Pope Paul VI produced the exhortation *Evangelii Nuntiandi*, on 'The Proclamation of the Gospel'. In Section 24.2 it says:

> Evangelization is a complex process made up of varied elements: the renewal of humanity, witness, explicit proclamation, inner adherence, entry into the community, acceptance of signs, apostolic initiative.[6]

It is very challenging to ask whether or not the programmes we call 'religious programmes' actually do this.

Fortunately, in this country, religious programmes are not designed and produced by the churches. That is constitutionally impossible according to the charters of both the BBC and the IBA, though this could change in the future. The state of religious programming in the United States or Italy is a totally different question, but I should like to reflect for a few moments on some of the different kinds of what we call religious programmes in this country, keeping in mind the two texts John 10:10 ('I come that you may have life in its fullness'), and John 8:32 ('The truth will set you free').

The religious programming in the UK is presented in one of four ways — Worship, Debate, Documentary and Entertainment.

(i) *Worship*. Lord Reith once said about worship on radio that it would never be accepted, indeed, it should not be accepted. It might be heard by men in public houses, even by men with their hats on. Worship from churches must be live in this country. It is very difficult for the religious producers to get away from eavesdropping. The situation raises questions like: 'Do the viewing public actually participate in the service being broadcast?'; 'Do they share in the worship being witnessed?'. The answer is clearly 'Yes — to some extent'. When both BBC and IBA experimented with communion type services, such as *This is the Day* in which bread was broken and shared, were people at home who did the same thing — take bread and break it — entering into the same prayer and act of worship, or were they into their own? In 1980 the IBA Research Department, in conjunction with Southern Television, examined reactions to the 'Communion Service'. About half the sample questioned said they felt they were 'really making communion' when they watched the programme, and some were upset to discover that the programme was recorded beforehand.[7] The BBC equivalent — *This is the Day* — was broadcast live and invited the audience to break bread with the presenters. There are all sorts of questions surrounding Telecommunion. It challenges us once again to ask, 'What do we mean by Real Presence?' — in a context not imagined by the Reformers and their opponents.

In 1978 I attended the Sixth Religious Consultation in Bath. It asked the question, 'Who and What is Religious Broadcasting For?'. The head of the research team, Dr Ian Haldane, concluded by saying:

> Religious television has got somewhat greater patronage among the lonely than among the not so lonely people, but the outstanding finding, as ten years ago, is that in an increasing secular population, the amount of religious broadcasting which is used — and here we are talking about both television and radio — varies directly with the degree of the user's own religious commitment. Religious programmes are identified in the mind of your audiences as the conventional and the

expected, church services, hymn singing, biblical epics with very little mention of the experimental or that which would provoke thought... As far as pastoral broadcasting goes, those who seek company or comfort turn primarily to news, to light entertainment, to comedy, to stories, not I am sorry to say, to religious television.[8]

The slightly cynical could also ask, 'Do religious programme makers actually see themselves in any way responding to the challenge to evangelize, or are they responding to the needs of the audience in order to strengthen their bit of the industry?'.

(ii) *Debate.* Programmes that fall under this heading in the past include *Tell me Why, The Seven Deadly Sins* (taken off the BBC after only one programme) and *Are you taking the Tablets?*. The difficulties here are numerous. What are religious subjects as opposed to non-religious subjects? Why does Tyne Tees Television ring me to get involved in 'secular' debates on divorce, contraception and sex, but not the nuclear question, animal rights, unemployment and education? The stereotyping is legendary. A further problem is time. It takes time to explore and express the wealth of a church's traditional teaching on anything, to express the debates that took place over centuries on any subject, to share the width of belief and response held by any group of people who belong to 'a church'. But the feel of television is relentless. It wants clear lines of thought, which are available, but good television needs answers, tied up ends, confrontation if not conflict: 'The Pope's Divisions', 'The Pope versus Liberation Theologians', 'A Divided Church'. One person or view versus another makes better television than searching and dialogue — particularly when you need numbers to keep the show going. The differences between people are not seen as enriching but as divisive, and division makes better popular television.

(iii) *Documentary.* The budget for a documentary like *Everyman* is immense. It needs travel and location filming. It can include the elements of debate and worship. It now competes on the open television market with other programmes. It is minority viewing, more likely to cope with what is generally understood as 'theology' than any other mode of religious programming.

Television programme makers would also include some personality-based series in this, eg *In the Light of Experience*. This is a very inexpensive product, using a talking-head — a person telling his or her story. It verges on entertainment, although no one would call Shirley du Boulay or Angela Tilby an entertainment producer.

The problems I see here about television and theology are again in relation to time. The topic must be wrapped up in 35 or 60 minutes. The question *can* be left open, but that is rare. It is more likely that the two sides are left in parallel or growing apart. It can be something of historical interest, or a glimpse into the religious customs and practices of others. But any dialogue following the programme either takes place within the viewer or between viewers, very rarely within the content of the programme.

(iv) *Entertainment*. Not a lot of people know that in 1985 Harry Secombe received £8,900 per *Highway* programme, nor that *Stars on Sunday* is regarded as 'very good company' — above *Coronation Street*, although behind *Jim'll Fix It*, *The Generation Game* and *News at Ten*. The 'image' of the mass choirs, beautifully dressed backing groups, personalities of the stars, the 'made-it' feel of those interviewed, is communicating something about religion, church, God. But what? In the 1980s Yorkshire television was interviewing ministers for a 'religious' version of a cross between *The Krypton Factor* and *It's a Knockout*: entertainment with a 'religious' overlay, but what is it communicating?

Before we leave these thoughts on using the media to evangelize I should like to offer two further comments on one particular event. I spent five months in 1982 as the Communications Officer for the Visit of Pope John Paul II to York. As our negotiations with film makers, cameramen and photographers progressed, it became clear to me that these people were in a position almost to 'do theology for us'. Every photographer and film cameraman wanted clear, sharp, close-up pictures of the Pope, but such pictures of John Paul appearing on the screen or in newsapers take him out of context. The pictures of him standing alone emphasizes primacy, a singular power; they deny collegiality, the sharing of responsibility.

On at least two occasions in different parts of the country, Pope John Paul deliberately tried to associate the other bishops with him in what he was doing. He did this for good collegial reasons. He is not on some lofty pinnacle, solitary and remote. He wanted to show how he was 'with' his fellow bishops, and not 'over and against' them. In Southwark Cathedral during the anointing of the sick, and at Speke Airport, John Paul invited the bishops to join with him. On both occasions what the viewers actually saw was a lone Pope, in the middle of nowhere, anointing or blessing. This was very good television, but very bad theology. Television was telling us the wrong things about the Pope by the picture it showed. One journalist (Peter Hebblethwaite) noted:

The Pope was the star of the show; and the screen is not really big enough to take too many wide-angled shots of bishops who, at a distance, look like druids pursuing obscure rites.[9]

The media did not just distort the message, they broadcast the wrong one. The cameras told downright lies. In fact it is very difficult for the camera to tell the truth — it is so selective about the context. The picture media constantly confused many people about the relationship of the man who is John Paul with his office. When people saw and heard one, they saw and heard the 'infallible' other.

The second thought that emerges as a result of looking at a Papal Visit through the camera lens is that the church is presented as almost totally male. There were very few pictures of women seen in the context of the visit as a whole. But then perhaps that is not a distortion, more a reflection of the truth. So on the one hand good pictures made bad theology, but on the other, good pictures reflected bad theology.

Evangelizing the Media

I should like to move away now and look at the problem of 'evangelizing the media'. This, I believe, is a more difficult problem. It reflects some of the things said earlier: To whose benefit is the media put? What does the media in itself contribute to emerging cultures?

When Lord Northcliffe, one of the original Press Lords, said: 'News is what somebody somewhere wants to suppress; all the rest is advertising',[10] he was shrewdly compiling the elements necessary for something to be newsworthy. These elements are usually regarded as hardship and danger to the community, conflict, unusualness, scandal and individualism. News is what somebody somewhere decides to write about. Harold Evans reckons news is people: 'fires, accidents and planning decisions are only news because they involve and affect people'.[11] The questions lie in the area of which people do they involve and how does it affect them. The ultimate question lingering behind all this is, 'What is true?'. It involves every element of the process of news gathering and broadcasting from the camera lens size and angle to the editorial decisions.

Another ultimate question behind this is a question about unity, reconciliation, respect for people and growth in understanding. A rather beautiful piece broadcast in 1985 about one old Russian lady's memory of the siege of Leningrad during the war, about her memories and fear, was immediately followed by a piece on the re-signing of the Warsaw Pact. Which was true? To hint that old Russian women have fears, regrets, memories of intense suffering and pain; or that (at that time) Russia, along with others, was an enemy of NATO? Perhaps both were 'true'. But how is the unity for which Christ prayed being enhanced? Certainly not by denying the Warsaw Pact, nor by leaving it as the final memory. To evangelize the process of news gathering and editing is intensely difficult.

For something to be called news it must be chosen from a selection of stories, it has to be sudden (like violent incidents during a long drawn out coal dispute) and it must be worth reporting. Once something is defined as news it has 'made it', despite the occurrence of other, different incidents.

One element in evangelizing is the way language is used. A day of action is a day of inaction; a stoppage is a strike; the worker's 'demand', management 'offers terms'; the left 'dominates', the right 'has a majority'. Terrorists or freedom fighters; intelligence or spying; dissidents or traitors; soldiers of fortune or dogs of war (or mercenaries). Are you 'questioned' or 'interrogated'? The economy is becoming fitter, the country has tightened its belt and is in better shape, it is leaner and more able to cope — but the unemployed person is simply included in a large number. Note that the economy and the country are personified, the unwaged person is a statistic. The list of words helps to reinforce our stereotyped thinking, the political and economic vagaries help to lessen the dignity of people who tighten their belts because of poverty but are no fitter as a result. It is perhaps no wonder that the King James version of Luke 19:3, the story of Zaccheus, contains the phrase '...he could not get near Jesus because of the press'.

Circulation figures for newspapers and viewing figures for TV stations soared during the Falklands/Malvinas war in 1982. Hundreds of studies have shown that the mass media as they exist today thrive on violence and war. Media language has become more belligerent: parties are 'defeated', policies 'annihilated', verbal 'bombs' are dropped. Does this language and imagery contribute to a world of justice, love and peace; or encourage aggression to the point of violence and vanquishing? The debate about violence on television contributing to acts of violence by individuals and groups continues. It seems that heavy viewing reinforces one's prejudices — whatever they are. There is no doubt that it has an effect; the debate is about the extent of the effect.

CONCLUSION

I'd like to make four concluding remarks — about silence, symbols, and styles of television literature, and a final naive comment.

(i) Theology — the structured reflection of our faith and deepening of our awareness of God in our lives — is the third moment in a cycle. The first is experience, then reflection, then its theological structuring. The reflection stage needs silence, stillness, space. I believe that silence is pretty well impossible in television programming as it is currently developing. When Cardinal Hume is asked a question he likes to stop and think before he speaks. He only just gets away with it. You can feel the impatience.

(ii) The ultimate languages of theology are symbol and poetry. I wonder how television copes with either. After the shooting of John F. Kennedy in Dallas in 1964, the word 'blood' was subconsciously erased from the resources of the translator. Interesting things happened when people tried to translate the Scriptures. Circumlocution and inaccuracy abounded — because people saw and were struck by horrified disbelief.

I would refer you to Mike Parson's article 'Theology and the Information Society' if you should want to look at language and technology and the danger of over-simplification of meaning in order to fit it on a small screen — not literally but metaphorically.[12] Poetry points elsewhere, the box tries to contain it all.

(iii) I reckon, then, that television is like closed literature. When you read a James Bond novel, you know at the end exactly what happened. The good and the bad are obvious. The ends are all tied up. There is no chance of uncertainty. You read it once and only once. Pick up open literature, like Tolstoy or Dostoevsky, and you read it and re-read it. You live with a poem for days, years maybe. It repays a revisit. If you watch *Starsky and Hutch* or *M.A.S.H.* you have the ends tied up: you know what has happened, the programme ends — then a final 30 second burst brings humour, relief and a final explanation. It is closed literature. Like the poor religious documentary, you know whose side you are on. *Hill Street Blues* was an experiment. Michael Kozoll, one of the script writers, said: 'We raised unanswered questions — they don't like that!'.[13] There can be seven plots in one episode; a couple might disappear for weeks before returning. It is an attempt to express the mess and uncertainties in which people live and work. In that sense it is more like theology. It is not like closed literature. The actual style of programme making is different from the James Bond or *Virginian* clear ending. The steroyped figures of the Soaps are saying one thing about cultural values; the confused and the confusing figures in *Hill Street* are saying something different. Their confusion might be 'truer'. (I am not going as far as the American paranoid Left who saw network entertainment as a conspiracy to purvey capitalist values, while some on the Right saw *Dallas* as a plot to undermine the patriarchal Christian family.)

If theology or theological reflection includes processes like dialogue, search and commitment, then the style of television as we know it is unlikely to contribute to it. Programme makers do not want to leave people with open questions which need time for reflection.

(iv) Finally, I believe that television is definitely influencing the way people talk, think, and relate, in many different ways and at many different levels. So it is 'doing theology'. I suspect it is more divisive than unitive, although the potential is there for immense good. I even think that television could cope with theology as we normally understand it — it is just that nobody would watch it. At the end of the day we may be better off with radio. At least the scenery is better.

NOTES

1. *Communication and Human Promotion,* Published by OCIC/ONDA/INFO for the Nairobi Conference, 1983.

2. John Francis Kavanaugh, *Following Christ in a Consumer Society,* New York: Orbis, 1981.

3. Todd Giblin, *Inside Prime Time,* New York: Pantheon, 1983, p 31.

4. Kavanaugh, *op. cit.,* p 25.

5. John 10:10.

6. Pope Paul VI, *Evangelii Nuntiandi, 1975,* in Michael Walsh and Brian Davies (eds), *Proclaiming Justice and Peace;* London: Cafod/Collins, 1984.

7. *The Times,* August 18th 1980, quoting the IBA Research Department.

8. *Report of IBA's Sixth Consultation on Religious Broadcasting,* London, 1978.

9. Peter Hebblethwaite in *The Catholic Herald,* June 1982.

10. Quoted in Denis MacShane, *Using the Media,* London: Pluto Press, Workers Handbooks, 1979, p 46.

11. MacShane, *op. cit.,* p 46, quoting Harold Evans, *The Practice of Journalism,* London: Heinemann, 1963.

12. Mike Parsons, 'Theology and the Information Society', *Media Development,* Vol. XXX, No. 4, 1983.

13. Giblin, *op. cit.,* p 303.

19

Anti-Racist Education:
An Educational Task for
State and Church?

RICHARD ZIPFEL

(This paper was delivered as a Hild/Bede Lecture under the auspices of NEICE in 1987)

INTRODUCTION

Perhaps it is obvious why the church in the North of England should be hosting a lecture on the racial and cultural foundations of the education we offer in our schools, especially on an occasion dedicated to two great pillars of the church in this country — Hild, the Abbess of Whitby, and Bede, monk of Jarrow and author of *The Ecclesiastical History of the English Nation.* However, in case it is not obvious, let me remind you that Hild and Bede were on different sides of an argument between opposing cultural traditions in the English church in the 7th century. The argument, between the Celtic party represented by Hild and the Roman party greatly influenced by Bede, culminated in the Synod of Whitby in AD 663. Under Bede's influence the day was won for Rome and the church in this country was given a character and orientation which 'ended only with the English Reformation in the 16th century'.[1]

We are today involved in similar discussions concerning the racial and cultural identity of the British people and the nature of the education we offer our children. These questions have been prompted in part by the emergence of a significant black population in this country.

Although black people have lived here for centuries, the migration of people from the Caribbean, Africa and the Indian sub-continent since the Second World War has significantly altered the racial and cultural face of Britain. Today about two million black people live here, representing a diversity of cultures and faiths. Almost half our black population is now British born. We also have a relatively large Chinese community, and smaller but significant numbers of Philippinos, Vietnamese, Cypriots, Arabs and people from a variety of European backgrounds. Although we still think of this as a 'Christian country', our people are also Jewish, Muslim, Hindu, Sikh, Buddhist and from many less well-known traditions.

In July 1979, the Roman Catholic bishops of England and Wales, in their comments on the proposed changes in nationality law, summarized this process of racial and cultural diversification. They said:

> Britain has traditionally been a multicultural society made up of diverse national cultures — English, Scottish, Welsh and Irish, etc. Our history of Empire and Commonwealth has accentuated this characteristic by bringing people of many races and backgrounds to these islands. We accepted into our society other communities who sought refuge from persecution. All have been changed in coming here and we have been changed in welcoming them. Through a long and constant process, therefore, Britain has become irreversibly a multiracial, multicultural society.[2]

These developments have important implications for British education, and since the early 1960s education authorities have been conscious of the need to address them.

EARLY EDUCATIONAL INITIATIVES

One of the first attempts to cope with the growing black presence was a process of 'dispersal' of black pupils from areas of high concentration. In 1965 a circular from the Department of Education and Science entitled *Education of Immigrants* discussed the 'difficulties which could arise in schools with large numbers of immigrants' and suggested that a school could not meet the educational needs of its pupils if more than a third were 'immigrant'. This advice was later modified and then dropped because of opposition from black parents whose young children were in some places being bussed to schools in totally unfamiliar neighbourhoods.

In 1965 as well the Plowden Report — *Children and their Primary Schools* — was published. It pointed to the need for a programme of 'positive discrimination' to make schools in areas of multiple deprivation 'as good as the best in the country'. Though this was not exclusively aimed at black children it was obviously relevant because of the concentration of ethnic minorities in poor inner city areas.

In 1966, Section 11 of the Local Government Act gave local authorities the right to claim grant aid if they were required to employ extra staff because of the presence in their areas of substantial numbers of 'immigrants' from the Commonwealth whose language or customs differed from those of the larger community.

In 1972-73 the House of Commons' Select Committee on Race Relations and Immigration devoted its session to 'Education'. Their report was aimed primarily at the educational needs of immigrants, though they also raised some of the larger issues, such as what contribution the educational services might make towards the multicultural society; whether the unity of society should be conceived as 'uniformity' or 'unity in diversity'; whether there was yet a consensus concerning the multi-racial society; and, in the absence of such a consensus, what role the school might legitimately play.

In 1974, in response to the Select Committee Report, a government White Paper was published entitled, *Educational Disadvantage and the Educational Needs of Immigrants.* The White Paper stated explicitly that:

> The educational service has important contributions to make both to the well-being of the immigrant communities in this country and to the promotion of harmony between the different ethnic groups of which our society is now composed.[3]

As a result of recommendations made in the White Paper, in 1975 the Centre for Information and Advice on Educational Disadvantage was established to provide information and advice to schools, education authorities and government. The 'problems of West Indian children' was included as one of its specific areas of inquiry.

In July 1977 the DES published a Green Paper entitled *Education in Schools: A Consultative Document,* in which they made a clear and unequivocal statement about education in a multi-racial society:

> The education appropriate to our imperial past cannot meet the requirements of modern Britain. (1:11)

The curriculum of the schools must also reflect the needs of this new Britain. (1:12)

Our society is a multicultural, multiracial one and the curriculum should reflect a sympathetic understanding of the different cultures and races that now make up our society... We also live in a complex, interdependent world and many of our problems in Britain require international solutions. The curriculum should therefore reflect our need to know about and understand other countries. (10:11)

In the same year the House of Commons' Select Committee on Race Relations and Immigration published a report on *The West Indian Community*. One of the recommendations in that report was that the government 'as a matter of urgency' should institute a 'high level and independent inquiry into the causes of the underachievement of children of West Indian origin in maintained schools'.

The government recognized the need for an inquiry; but while giving priority to the question of West Indian underachievement it gave the inquiry wider terms of reference — ie to look at the achievement of all ethnic minorities and the preparation of all children for life in a society which is multi-racial and culturally diverse.

In 1979, therefore, the Committee of Inquiry into the Education of Children from Ethnic Minority groups was established. Two years later, under the chairmanship of Anthony Rampton, the Committee produced an Interim Report, *West Indian Children in our Schools*. Finally in 1985, after another four years working under the chairmanship of Lord Swann, the Committee finally produced its 800-page report, *Education for All*, which is more commonly known as *The Swann Report*.

THE SWANN REPORT

It will be obvious from even this brief historical sketch that the racial and cultural diversity of contemporary British society faces educators with two separate tasks:

(i) to provide very specifically for the educational needs of ethnic minority pupils; and

(ii) to prepare all pupils for life in a racially mixed and culturally diverse society.

In the 1960s and 1970s the focus was on the first of these; and it was the particular needs of West Indian children which gave rise to the inquiry that eventually produced the Swann Report. Nevertheless, with the publication of that report a new balance was struck which gave equal value to these two tasks. In fact, in the concept of 'Education for All' the Swann Committee felt that it had combined the two tasks into a single educational approach:

> Whilst these two issues are clearly inter-related and, in our view, complementary, we believe it is now possible and indeed essential to see them within a new and broader perspective — that of offering *all* pupils a good, relevant and up to date education for life in Britain and the world as it is today.[4]

According to Swann, therefore, a good education must meet each child's individual needs; and in Britain today it must also 'reflect the diversity of British society and indeed the contemporary world' for all pupils. Anything less would 'prepare pupils for an unreal world'. Narrow education is bad education. Good education must move beyond the confines of an outdated ethnocentric bias:

> The replacement of teaching materials which present an anachronistically Anglo-centric view of the world, and the development, for example, of history and geography syllabuses which are both multicultural in their content and global in their perspective, would remain equally valid from an educational point of view whether there were ethnic minority pupils in our schools or not.[5]

THE CHURCH REPORTS

At about the same time as *The Swann Report* was published, the churches were also taking up these issues. The Church of England General Synod's Board of Education published a report entitled *Schools and Multicultural Education*. A short time later a Department of the Catholic Bishops Conference published *Learning from Diversity*, the report of a working party on Catholic Education in a multi-racial, multi-cultural society based on visits to fifty Catholic schools, five colleges of education and four seminaries.

Looking at *Learning from Diversity*, the Roman Catholic report, one is struck by the remarkable consensus that exists between it and the Swann Report:

(i) both reject the extremes of assimilationist and separatist approaches to diversity and both put forward a model of the pluralist society which would allow considerable diversity within a basic unity;

(ii) both call attention to the complex phenomenon of *racism* and its impact on education;

(iii) both accept the central educational task of preparing all pupils for life in a racially and culturally diverse society;

(iv) both attach particular importance to predominantly white schools in predominantly white areas.

Let me dwell on this last point for the moment. Both *Learning from Diversity* and *The Swann Report* point with some concern to the fact that white schools, on the whole, *have not accepted* the task of preparing pupils for life in a diverse society as part of their educational responsibility. The typical attitude of teachers in such schools is 'we have no problem here'. Both reports criticize this tendency to equate black children with 'the problem'.

In fact, the *real problem* is not black people or black children but racism, prejudice, ignorance, and narrowness of outlook — and this problem is clearly present in white schools as well as other schools. If one were to have doubted this fact the Swann Report has done us the service of looking into the question.

The Swann Committee went to the trouble of commissioning a special research project into all white schools. The results of this research are contained in the report. Swann finds racism 'widespread' in these white schools:

> ranging from unintentional racism and patronizing and stereotyped ideas about ethnic minority groups combined with an appalling ignorance of their cultural backgrounds and lifestyles and of the facts of race and immigration, to extremes of overt racial hatred and 'National Front'-style attitudes.

Even among *teachers* in all white schools Swann finds:

> The whole gamut of racial misunderstandings and folk mythology was revealed, racial stereotypes were common and attitudes ranged from the unveiled hostility of a few, to the apathy of many and the condescension of others, to total acceptance and respect by a minority.[6]

BEYOND ETHNOCENTRIC EDUCATION

This then is the heart of the matter — the central question. Given the presence of racism and the whole range of prejudiced views and misunderstandings, even in all white areas, are we willing to accept that *all* schools must take on the task of preparing all pupils for life in a racially mixed and culturally diverse society?

There are of course many arguments one could use to support the thesis that this is an important part of our educational task. One could argue *morally* that education cannot be divorced from values and it is part of the school's task to teach a respect for values such as freedom, democracy, and the fundamental equality of all human beings. One could go on to argue that church schools especially must offer a value-based education which embodies the Christian gospel.

Or one could use a *pragmatic* argument. Our children will not be well served if we fail to prepare them for society as it exists. In tomorrow's world they will be required to compete for jobs as teachers, social workers, journalists, civil servants, or business people working in a multi-racial and multicultural environment. If they are prejudiced and ill-informed about that diverse world they may well be passed by for such jobs.

However, I would like to concentrate on a more purely educational argument about the *quality of knowledge* we are offering our children. For education, if it is about anything, is about knowledge, and I want to argue that the knowledge systems which our schools seek to impart are fundamentally skewed with an ethnocentric bias, permeated by an ethnocentric mentality — a way of thinking or a pervasive limitation to thinking which is more than any single idea or even any series of connected ideas. This ethnocentric mentality warps and restricts intellectual development. It is a self-deceiving myth that runs deep in the culture and affects both our common sense notions and our academic insights as well as distorting the education we offer. And because of the peculiar nature of British racism — tied, as it is, to a history of colonialism and empire — this ethnocentric mentality reinforces and is closely linked to the racism of this society.

Let us look at a few examples of this ethnocentric bias in our knowledge systems. I begin with a simple example pointed to by Claude Lévi-Strauss. He is speaking of the misconceptions which continue to be common even in academic circles concerning the intelligence and inventiveness of so-called 'primitive' peoples:

Treatises on ethnology, including some of the best, tell us that man owes his knowledge of fire to the accident of lightning or of a bush fire; that the discovery of a wild animal accidentally roasted in such circumstances revealed to him the possibility of cooking his food; and that the invention of pottery was the result of someone's leaving a lump of clay near a fire. The conclusion seems to be that man began his career in a sort of technological golden age, when inventions could, as it were, be picked off the trees as easily as fruit or flowers. Only modern man would seem to find it necessary to strain and toil; only to modern man would genius seem to grant a flash of insight... Chance played no more important a part in the invention of the bow, the boomerang or the blow-pipe, in the development of agriculture or stock rearing, than in the discovery of penicillin...[7]

Misconceptions of 'primitive' cultures only serve to give us an inflated view of contemporary western civilization which is untrue. Moreover, they reinforce a range of stereotypes of Africa and of black peoples who are too often connected in people's minds with the notion of 'primitive'.

Turning to history, as long ago as 1967 the Department of Education and Science questioned the traditional bias towards British constitutional and social history. In Education Pamphlet No. 52, *Towards World History*, the following point was made:

The question today is whether, now that we have so evidently become 'one world', the study of our own constitutional and social history in isolation is sufficient. If we have become part of one world (a twentieth century development) must we not concern ourselves with the history of that world, as the only proper approach to understanding it?[8]

Basil Davidson makes a slightly different point in an article entitled 'British History in British Schools'. After describing some of the recent scientific advances in our knowledge of African history, he reflects on how little of this new knowledge reaches our schools:

There is a final point to be made.... It relates to the extraordinary delay which seems to obstruct the dissemination of new knowledge in our culture. What I have been saying in this article [concerning the history of Africa] is common knowledge now to a very wide and international community of scholars.

It is accepted, taught, and worked on in many universities. It is the subject of whole libraries of specialised books, and more come out with every week that passes... And yet somehow it 'sticks' at the level of advanced research and teaching. With some very honourable exceptions, none of our schools makes use of all this new knowledge. On the contrary, the old textbooks presenting the old stereotypes continue to be used, just as though no more were known about the Africans and their past than fifty years ago. The old and wrong ideas continue in circulation. So long as this remains the case, just so long will our cultural racism continue to feed on these old and wrong ideas.

It stands on the record that British historians and archeologists were pioneers in the modern reassessment of Africa's contribution to civilisation and development in the world. Why is it, then, that British schools remain so slow, even so reluctant, to follow where those pioneers have led?[9]

To take a third example, anyone looking closely at English literature realizes that it often tends to justify the culture of its day. Defoe's *Robinson Crusoe* can be seen as an adventure story which also embodied the self-justifying myth of English imperialism. Crusoe is the hero of white, Anglo-Saxon, Protestant mercantilism. However, there are other strands in our literature. Swift, for instance, could be devastating in his satirical critique of the colonial mentality. In the following paragraph he derides the typical pattern of the adventure tale of the period:

> A crew of pirates are driven by a storm, they know not whither; at length a boy discovers land from the topmast; they go on shore to rob and plunder; they see a harmless people, are entertained with kindness; they give the country a new name; they take formal possession of it for their king; they set up a rotten plank or a stone for a memorial; they murder two or three dozen of the natives, bring away a couple more by force for a sample, return home, and get their pardon. Here commences a new dominion, acquired with a title by divine right. Ships are sent with the first opposition; the natives driven out or destroyed; their princes tortured to discover their gold; a free licence given to all acts of inhumanity and lust; the earth reeking with the blood of its inhabitants; and this execrable crew of butchers employed in so pious an expedition is a modern colony sent to convert and civilise an idolatrous and barbarous people.[10]

It is important that students understand that English literature contains these contrary threads. On the one hand it embodies the myth that enshrined and justified British culture, colonialism and empire. On the other hand, it sees through hypocrisies and self-deception, criticizes culture, and satirizes the self-justifying myth. These two impulses are present again in the different novels of empire. Kipling's popular novels generally embody the myth, although his last novel *Kim* is more ambivalent. The novels that are critical of the colonial enterprise from various points of view could be the subject of a study in themselves. They include Conrad's *Heart of Darkness* and *Nostromo,* and some of the novels of Joyce Cary and Graham Greene. Perhaps the single most successful and insightful novel criticizing the imperial mentality is Forster's *Passage to India,* which, studied alongside the history of its time, could provide students with a profound perspective on their own history and prepare them to confront the multicultural society they live in with greater than average humility and understanding.

So you see that what I am advancing is not a crude theory of an ethnocentric bias of the past, there are now and always have been people and ideas which break beyond the limits of that narrow mentality. Moreover, to speak of an ethnocentric bias to our thinking is not to accuse our society of some special sin. For it is of the nature of knowledge to be rooted in the history of people; and while Britain has for some years divested herself of most of her empire and colonies, the process of divesting ourselves of the mentality which was formed during those centuries of empire is still going on.

We can thank a scientist, Michael Polanyi, for having so clearly demonstrated the contingent, personal element in all knowledge. In his seminal work, *Personal Knowledge: Towards a Post-critical Philosophy,* he argued cogently that even science is rooted in a framework of assumptions, in a tradition, in belief and intellectual passion — none of which can be fully articulated or verified.

> The curious thing is that we have no clear knowledge of what our presuppositions are and when we try to formulate them they appear quite unconvincing... When we accept a certain set of presuppositions and use them as our interpretative framework, we may be said to dwell in them as we do in our own body. Their uncritical acceptance for the time being consists in a process of assimilation by which we identify ourselves with them. They are not asserted and cannot be asserted, for

assertion can be made only within a framework with which we have identified ourselves for the time being.[11]

The ethnocentric mentality is part of such a framework. We only move out of it slowly as fundamental new questions and new insights alter the framework itself, as a passion for a larger truth and for ignored aspects of the truth move us to a wider perspective.

Let me tell you a brief story about the beginnings of such a move towards a new framework and a new vision in one person. A friend of mine tells of himself as a young teacher going to teach at Tulse Hill school in Brixton. One day after class a black youngster came up to him and asked whether he had made any links between the French Revolution and what was happening in the Caribbean at the time. He was dumbfounded; and admitted that he had not. The youngster then pulled from his bag a copy of C. L. R. James's *The Black Jacobins* which tells the story of the 1791-1803 successful slave revolt in France's most profitable colony of San Domingo, which ended in the establishment of the black state of Haiti. My friend borrowed the book from the youngster. Thus began a period of reading and making links which culminated some years later in his authorship of a history textbook for secondary schools, *The History of Black Settlers in Britain 1555-1958.*

Others are also searching for a new framework. Consider the simple example of what one school did with its geography syllabus. Quintin Kynston School has used a geography syllabus which centres around the concept of 'development'. Among the skills it attempts to impart are all the traditional skills appropriate to geography study, for example: interpretation of maps, graphs and statistics; construction of maps; visual correlation of maps; note-taking; analysis of evidence; making generalizations; essay-writing. However, the 'key ideas' which are to guide the choice and treatment of content focus on the contrast between the 'developed' and the 'underdeveloped' world. They examine the roots of the divide between these two worlds and the meaning of 'development'. Included in the 'key issues' which are to guide the syllabus are the following:

> the level of well-being in a country can be quantified;
> there are different patterns of well-being;
> the concept of development has a range of meanings;
> problems in developing countries are related to the country's
> structure;

problems facing developing countries are related to the world
  political and economic situation;
underdevelopment is a process;
common notions of development may not be in the best
  interests of developing countries.

Such a syllabus can lead children beyond ethnocentric views in a
number of ways. First of all, it will challenge the common stereotype
that assumes 'third world' countries are poor because the people
living there are inferior. In place of this stereotype, such a syllabus
encourages the students to explore the political, social and economic
causes of 'underdevelopment' and to understand the relationship
between 'third world' poverty and western affluence. Secondly, by
examining the various meanings of the word 'development' and by
coming to understand that common notions of development may not
be in the interest of 'third world' countries, the student can move
beyond a simple, western, ethnocentric notion of development to a
more complex and intellectually challenging concept.

Or consider another example of what a London secondary school
did with a very traditional second year history syllabus to bring in a
wider perspective. Before the changes were introduced the syllabus
began with 1066 and included the Norman Conquest, the Crusades,
Doomsday Book, the medieval village and town, Henry II and Thomas
Becket, the Black Death, Marco Polo, Portuguese voyages of discovery, Magellan, Cortez and Tudor London. With some carefully selected changes, the same syllabus began by looking at the world as a
whole in 1066 and ended by looking at the world as a whole during the
Tudor period. The Crusades included a look at the Muslim world. The
voyages of Marco Polo were taken in conjunction with the voyages of
Cheng Ho and Ibn Batutu; and the study of Cortez was linked to a
study of Aztec civilisation before and after the arrival of Cortez.

RELIGIOUS EDUCATION

Why is it important to move beyond the ethnocentric framework of
the past into a wider framework for our thinking and our teaching? In
answering this question, which will be the final part of this paper, I
want also to say something about religious education and church
schools.

I am not here going to discuss religious education as a separate
subject in the curriculum; but I want to discuss a broader notion of

religious education as something which permeates the whole curriculum and the ethos of the school in a church school. I will call this the *implicit process of religious education* which goes on continually throughout the school.

Now there are many things that are important religiously in the growth and development of our children; but I want to focus on two fundamental aspects of their religious development — namely their *sense of self* and their *concept of the world* in which they live. This development of a sense of self and world is going on all the time in a child; and it is influenced by the school and by the knowledge he or she is exposed to in history, literature, geography, science and other subjects. In all these disciplines the child's outlook is taking form implicitly and the formation of that outlook on self and world is a profoundly important base for any more explicit approach to religious education. To the extent that young people take on, consciously or unconsciously, an ethnocentric or racist view of themselves and the world, to that extent their outlook will tend to contradict the gospel message; their minds will be infertile soil in which the seed of the gospel message will have difficulty taking root.

Let me try to illustrate this with a simple story from real life. One day, two five-year-old children were playing together. One child was white. The other was black. They had grown up together and were almost as close as sisters. The two children were quiet for a long time while playing with their Paddington Bears. Then at some point the white child spoke out of her reverie: 'Paddington Bear doesn't like black people — Paddington Bear only likes white people'. The black child was disturbed, looking around for support against what had been said. An adult who had overheard intervened.

How that particular incident ended is not important for our consideration; but the story is worth further reflection. First of all, we might ask what is happening here. A white child is trying out a thought, a thought about herself and her friend and the wider world which runs contrary to her own experience of friendship but which has occurred to her from things she has seen and heard. The black child is hearing from her friend a sentiment that she may hear many times in her life, a sentiment which tends to undermine her sense of self-worth and her place in the world. It also, obviously, runs contrary to the most fundamental message of the gospel that God loves us all.

We might ask: as these two children grow into adulthood and each in her own way has to wrestle with this question in more subtle and sophisticated forms, what do they each need from education? An ethnocentric education will be a dis-service to both, for it will further undermine the black child's sense of self while it will reinforce in the white child a false sense of superiority. Polanyi reminds us that all knowledge is shaped by vision and the passion for understanding. Both these young people will be best served, whether in a church school or a state school, by an education which is guided by the vision of a wider world and the search for the neglected areas of our past and the various traditions which gave birth to our own.

Let me end with a quotation from a little known booklet published in 1983 by the Catholic Commission for Racial Justice. The quotation summarizes what I have been trying to say in this paper about the diversity of society, racism, knowledge and the church's commitment to the truth:

> Racism is at heart a lie — or more precisely a series of lies, about ourselves, about other people, about relationships, about human nature, and about history and culture. Originating in racial myths and the rationalisations of the slave trade and colonial subjugation, the lies of racism remain alive centuries later, woven in complex patterns throughout the whole of western culture and closely linked to the specific alienations of western society. The lies involved in western racism are manifold. They include the lies of the cultural superiority of western industrialised civilisation, the racial superiority of white people, the prejudices which stereotype people from certain groups or make them scapegoats for the deeper ills in ourselves and our society which we cannot bear to face, the lies that rationalise collusion and discriminatory practices of individuals and institutions.
>
> The truth of Jesus as spoken by the church cuts through all this and speaks the truth, denounces the lie, names the injustice, directs people's attention to the real problems of society, perceives and speaks to the complex reality of the particular situation. In doing all this, the church continually undermines the self-deception which makes up the mental framework of racism.[12]

NOTES

1. P. H. Blair, *Anglo Saxon England*, London: Cambridge University Press, 1956, p 131.

2. *Concerning the Revision of British Nationality Law*, A statement by the Roman Catholic bishops of England and Wales, July 1979.

3. *Educational Disadvantage and the Educational Needs of Immigrants*, London: HMSO, 1974.

4. The Report of the Committee of Inquiry into the Education of Children from Ethnic Minority Groups, *Education for All*, Chairman Lord Swann, London: HMSO, March 1985, p 315.

5. *ibid.*, p 318.

6. *ibid.*, pp 234, 236.

7. *Race, Science and Society*, ed Leo Kuper, New York: UNESCO, 1975, pp 119-120.

8. Department of Education and Science, *Towards World History*, Education Pamphlet No. 52.

9. Basil Davidson, 'British History in British Schools', *New Approaches in Multiracial Education*, Vol. 7, No. 3, Summer 1979.

10. Jonathan Swift, *Works*, Vol. XII, pp 378f.

11. Michael Polyani, *Personal Knowledge*, London: Routledge & Kegan Paul, 1958, pp 59-60.

12. *All God's People*, a Report from a Series of Consultations on the Future of the Church and Racial Justice, London: Catholic Commission for Racial Justice, December 1983, p 31.

20

Christian Education:
An Instrument for European Unity?

EDWARD HULMES

DISCOVERING CHRISTIAN EDUCATION

'Discovering', or better perhaps *dis*-covering, is the appropriate word. The problem is not to define Christian education but to find it. Even when there is a measure of agreement about its theoretical aspects, about what it might be or, perhaps, about what it ought to be, there is a reticence to claim that *this* is what Christian education is, and that *here* is where you will find it if you choose to look. Such is the theological confusion at present that it may prove to be difficult to attach to the word 'Christian' a meaning which finds general acceptance. In consequence the adjective may be used indiscriminately, without precision, and for all its vagueness. 'Those who wish to succeed must ask the right preliminary questions', said Aristotle. He continued, 'What we learn from experience depends on the kind of philosophy we bring to experience. It is therefore useless to appeal to experience before we have settled, as well as we can, the philosophical question.'[1] I acknowledge the truth of this, and readily admit that my approach to education, as well as to every consideration of unity, is influenced by my understanding of the claims laid upon me by the faith that I profess. The primary question remains. What is Christian education? It is only when an attempt has been made to answer *this* question, however tentative and personal the answer may be, that the secondary question about unity can be considered. It is prudent, therefore, to begin by stating briefly what I take authentic Christian education to be.

In a chapter contributed recently to a book of essays about education in a pluralist society I wrote:

Christian education has three essential features. First, it establishes faith in Christ as the foundation and guide for correct thinking and right action. Second, it is integrative, serving to bring together elements in individuals and in society that tend towards fragmentation. It is thus concerned with human beings, whole and entire, catering for their moral, as well as for their intellectual, needs at each succeeding stage of life. Third, it enables individuals to decide for themselves whether they will believe or not, by exercising their capacity for reason as well as for faith. From an educational point of view there is one aspect of Christian education which is of special interest in a situation where the unity of any society threatens to crack along the fault-lines of cultural diversity. It may be that the most significant task for Christian education at the present time is to provide bridges, not cement. Ideally, if not always in practice, Christian education promotes more than an understanding of one particular kind of religious faith. From the theology of dereliction which is at the heart of Christian faith and experience, Christian education proposes an understanding of human vulnerability, and *difference*. It encourages the exploration of pluralism, with regard to doubt as well as to faith. The image of the suffering God is more than an icon. Christian education begins where it ends, with the enigmatic figure of Jesus. In every generation it focuses attention on a startling claim which might otherwise remain unknown.[2]

In an increasingly secular society (it may be said) any educational system predicated on a particular set of religious beliefs can only be divisive. If there is to be Christian education (so the argument may run) this must be a matter for the communities of Christians within their own institutions, and for these institutions there can be no special provision by the state. What is true for Christians should also be true (so it may be said) for Jews in the privacy of their synagogues and for Muslims in the sanctuary of their mosques. It is difficult to see how an educational service can best serve the interests of a pluralist society without discouraging sectional religious interests from insisting on their rights to provide a suitable education for members of their own communities, but recent experience provides little evidence that a secular alternative philosophy of education is without its own ideological bias, a bias which can be all the more dangerous in education because it is rarely noted and seldom challenged.

Is Christian education to be found even in the churches, however?

How far does liturgy for instance — in all its aspects — contribute to
the continuing education of Christians? Is Christian education to be
found in 'Christian' schools, and recognized there not as a 'subject'
to be studied but as the prevailing attitude to teaching and to learning
which informs the curriculum as a whole? In churches and Christian
schools is Christian education an instrument for reconciliation and
unity which *demonstrably* helps to create and to build up a distinctively
Christian community? Is Christian education necessarily confined to
Christian institutions? Or is it also to be found (for example) in state
schools where the dominant philosophy of education — though
consciously secular, and by no means explicitly anti-Christian — does
not require Christians to be excluded for their beliefs, provided that
as teachers or students their personal religious convictions are not
permitted to interfere with professional educational obligations? Is
there, in point of fact, any fundamental difference between 'secular'
education and 'Christian' education today? If not, why maintain the
fiction that there is by continuing to use either of these redundant
adjectives? On the other hand, if there are substantial differences is it
educationally defensible to argue that children be subjected to one
kind of education in the state school and another at home and in their
community of faith?

THE PURSUIT OF UNITY AND THE ACCOMMODATION OF
DIFFERENCE

Events are moving fast in Europe. From the Balkans to the Baltic, from
Belfast to Belgrade, from Madrid to Moscow — one might say from
one end of Europe to the other, from Amsterdam to Zaghreb so to
speak — disunity and conflict between sectional (and even warring)
factions give cause for concern. The pursuit of political independence
goes hand in hand with the expression of nationalistic sentiments.
Where differences of opinion cannot be accommodated the result is
often violence of unspeakable ferocity. In theory the case for unity in
Europe seems to be unassailable. In practice it is not so simple. Talk
of federation, of monetary union, of the surrender of sovereignty, of
'going it alone', often conceals deeper fears about what might happen
if we do not sink our differences and learn to co-operate in political
as well as economic self-interest. Could Britain, alone and isolated
from Europe, long survive the consequences of international economic competition? Is the answer, whether it be in the Union of

Sovereign States (formerly USSR), or in Croatia, or in Britain, a suitably sanitized form of *apartheid,* that is to say a form of separate development? In default of organic unity, are there not increasing dangers of another catastrophic armed struggle between independent nation-states who have fought twice before this century, a war fought this time with arsenals of unimaginable destructive power? It is not hard to see why there are so many who think it unreasonable to expect that anything other than a superficial unity can ever be achieved in Europe, a continent which continues to suffer from the wounds inflicted by centuries of conflict between feuding parties and sectional interests. There are good grounds for scepticism about the prospects for unity. The ideal of peaceful co-operation between nations and communities which were once engaged (or which, sadly, are now engaged) in armed conflict remains what it always was, namely an aspiration. Experience confirms the truth of a universal insight expressed, in the culture in which I have been reared, as original sin — that is, a potentially fatal disposition to choose the lower rather than the higher course even when one holds a considered preference for the latter — so much so that the solutions of conflict are, at best, provisional and temporary.

From the day on which I began teaching I have always worked in secular educational institutions. That is to say I have been involved in the life of communities in which the influence of *any* form of over-riding religious conviction is discouraged, where it is not explicitly excluded. In practice it is not easy to remove confessional bias from the classroom or the lecture room, and it is probably unwise to try. The attempt to do so is certainly misguided if, as often happens, the identification of 'confessionalism' is too selective. Such is likely to be the case whenever a so-called 'confessional' approach to education (let us say, a *Christian* approach) is purged, only to be replaced by a 'non-confessional' approach which, when looked at carefully, turns out to be merely another form of confessionalism. In the state system of education in Britain, and this includes education at all levels from primary school to the university, the dominant philosophy of education is based upon a set of assumptions which may be far from consistent with Christian principles. Fortunately, for most teachers — and it is not just Christian teachers who are affected — the conflict between private convictions and professional educational obligations seldom, if ever, presents itself. But it could easily do so. I sense that in the not too distant future the dilemma will become real enough, especially in those societies in Europe and elsewhere which are now being described, prematurely and inaccurately in my view, as 'pluralist'. 'Pluralism', as it is understood in the West, is not as accommodating as it sounds, or as it is often assumed to be. Nowhere is this to be seen more clearly in Europe than in education where, despite all the rhetoric of multi-culturalism, and despite repeated expressions of gratitude for the distinctive contributions which ethnic minorities are said to be uniquely able to contribute to the cultural diversity of the societies to which they now belong, educational praxis remains unassailably secular, ideo-logically exclusive, effectively *monocultural* in its implementation, and apparently immune from 'cultural enrichment' in all but a superficial way.

COPING WITH UNCERTAINTY

The German Nobel prize-winning physicist Werner Heisenberg, who formulated his Uncertainty Principle in 1927, spoke about the need to guide students at a time when nothing can be taken as certain, and when everything seems to be the result of random and unpredictable relations. In the course of an address which he gave in Munich after receiving the Romano Guardini Prize of the Catholic Academy in Bavaria in 1973, he said:

> Perhaps today we can again distribute more correctly the weights which have been put out of place by the enormous spread of science and technology in the last hundred years. I mean the amount of weight which we accord to the material and spiritual considerations in human society. Material considerations are important, and it was the duty of society to remove the material need of great masses of people when technology and knowledge afforded the opportunity. But when this had happened there was still a great deal of misery left, and we have seen how much the individual, whether he consciously asks for it or takes it for granted, needs the protection which the spiritual side of a community can afford him. It is here that perhaps our most important tasks lie. If there is a great deal of unhappiness in today's young students, then the reason is not material need, but the lack of trust which makes it hard for the individual to give his life a purpose. So we must try to overcome the isolation which threatens the individual in a world dominated by the practical demands of technology. Theoretical consideration of questions of psychology or the structure of society will

not be much help unless we succeed in regaining a natural balance in the intellectual and material spheres of life, through practical action. It will be a matter of reviving in everyday life the values enshrined in the spiritual side of the community and giving them so much illuminating power that people take them as a guide for their own individual lives.[3]

This situation, with all its uncertainty, seems to me to offer new opportunities for Christian education in the wider setting of Europe. That so many people today are ignorant of the Christian faith and incapable of giving a reasoned account of the hope that is in them (or, indeed, a reasoned account of the faith which they deny) is a fact of life which owes at least something to the shift in emphasis in Christian education. This shift redirects attention from the particular ('Christianity', in this case) to the general (in order to include 'world religions', let us say, or 'non-theistic life-stances', without necessarily neglecting Christianity as a major world religion). Students can, therefore, no longer expect (as they might not wish) to be provided with a grounding in Scripture, in doctrine, in catechesis, and even in apologetics, from an explicitly Christian viewpoint. The *authentically* Christian approach is, apparently, to be less dogmatic, less certain about former doctrinal and ethical absolutes, more sympathetic to the value of other faiths, essentially descriptive in considering alternative religious beliefs and practices, non-judgemental, ostensibly non-directive with regard to student responses, existential, and personalist. The hallmark of the mature Christian emerges as uncertainty. It is unquestionably true that in some Christian circles today uncertainty has been elevated to a credal status, and orthodoxy redefined in terms of doubt.

In an atmosphere of studied neutrality the vital cutting edge of Christian education may soon be blunted. Students are unlikely to learn how to distinguish the life-enhancing option from the licensed insanity when all religious points of view are accorded a parity of esteem. Students are less likely, in my opinion, to see how, when, and why the prospects of reconciliation (and thus of unity) can be compromised by failing to note the substantial differences which exist about the various ways in which life is to be regulated in a society which is religiously and culturally diverse. Yet it is precisely at this point of difficulty that there is an opportunity for Christian education which, by definition, cannot be true to its title deeds without meeting the universal needs and serving inclusive interests. If Christians are looking for scriptural guide-lines they can do no better than note both the programme and the method advocated by the writer of 1 Peter 3:15, 'But in your hearts reverence Christ as Lord. Always be prepared to make a defence to anyone who calls you to account for the hope that is in you, yet do it with gentleness and reverence.' There is a need for Christian education to encourage positive discrimination as well as reconciliation in a world fragmented by religious and cultural differences. One of the neglected tasks in education in general, and of Christian education in particular, is that of developing the critical faculty in students just when and where they need most help, namely in choosing for themselves a set of values and principles by which to live. Cardinal Newman made this a matter of prayer:

> Give me the gift of discriminating between true and false in all discourse of mind... Give me that wisdom, which seeks Thy will by prayer and meditation, by direct intercourse with Thee, more than by reading and reasoning.[4]

THE CRITICAL MOMENT

Newman's response to those who wanted to know what he meant by 'discriminating between true and false in all discourse of mind' was to link faith and reason in such a way as to describe both, not just the former, as a 'gift' that comes from God. In this he reminds Christian teachers that their efforts are in vain if they are not undertaken in the conviction that all true knowledge is of God and comes from God. His thoughts turn to practical issues when he writes about the education of the intellect:

> ...one main portion of intellectual education, of the labours of both school and university, is to remove the original dimness of the mind's eye; to strengthen and perfect its vision; to enable it to look out into the world right forward, steadily and truly; to give the mind clearness, accuracy, precision; to enable it to use words aright, to understand what it says, to conceive justly what it thinks about, to abstract, to compare, analyse, divide, define, and reason, correctly. There is a particular science which takes these matters in hand, and it is called logic; but it is not by logic, certainly not by logic alone, that the faculty I speak of is acquired. The infant does not learn to spell and read the hues upon his retina by any scientific rule; nor does the student learn

accuracy of thought by any manual or treatise. The instruction given him, of whatever kind, if it be really instruction, is mainly, or at least pre-eminently, this — a discipline in accuracy of mind... It is an acquisition quite separate from miscellaneous information, or knowledge of books.[5]

Logic, as Newman points out in *The Grammar of Assent*, is insufficient for the task, arguing that inference is conditional whereas assent, by contrast, is unconditional. 'Daily life', he wrote, 'is based not upon inferences logically thought out, but upon concrete assents resting on countless *probabilities*; daily life is a constant act of faith'.[6] Despite its importance, however, the education of the intellect can only be a part of Christian education. The role of the Christian teacher is not only to inform but to exercise the critical faculty of students in pursuit of 'inferences logically thought out' whilst leaving room for the mind to follow other laws which bring certitude by transcending logic. This is a role that Christian teachers share with their non-Christian colleagues, though they approach it from a radically different perspective which allows for advocacy, but not for proselytism.

Secularism, inside as well as outside the different religious traditions, has contributed in at least two ways to the present uncertainty about the distinctiveness of Christian education of the type which Newman had in mind. In the first instance it has fostered a massive indifference to the claims of institutionalized religion, especially, perhaps, to the claims of Christianity. It is not that religion has been decisively rejected in so many cases because of the sophisticated disinclination on the part of modern man to accept outdated metaphysics. To judge from the evidence (even in some sophisticated places), the rejection of the claims of religion is often the consequence of an idle pragmatism nourished by impenetrable ignorance. Put in another way, it seems to be widely believed that in order to live a 'reasonable' and a 'reasonably successful' life one does not need to bother oneself with the claims and counter-claims of religion. Secondly, and more menacingly, secularism has encouraged a counter-ideology of fundamentalism, anti-intellectual in its formulations and credulous in its dogmas.

The opponents of any religious belief which retains a transcendental reference to God (or to some unspecified 'higher power') have always insisted that human beings are alone in the universe. They have asserted that the invocation of deity, whether inscrutably benign or not, is delusory; and that human beings have to settle their own affairs individually and collectively as best they can, without denying the spiritual dimension of their common humanity, yet without recourse to 'God'. In any case, it is quite different from the message of the Christian gospel. Thoroughgoing secularists aver that if there is to be a 'universal religion' by which men and women seek to regulate their present and future relationships it can only be founded upon human solidarity in the face of cosmic indifference. This is a bleak view of human existence which inexorably gives rise to a universalism that requires of its adherents not only a preliminary denial of the reality, but of the possibility, of supernatural intervention. This admission (so atheists the world over have averred) is, however, the beginning of wisdom. It brings into a formidable anti-theistic alliance two quite separate groups. On the one hand are the self-conscious and dogmatic atheists, with their own counter-gospel to propagate in a generally unbelieving world. On the other hand are those whose practical atheism has never been subjected to critical scrutiny, and whose lives appear to stand in no need of spiritual inquiry, except at infrequent moments of particular stress. They are indifferent rather than hostile to 'religious' questions. This suggests that another important priority for Christian education in a 'pluralist' society is, in the strictest sense, apologetic. It is to meet head-on the challenge presented to Christian humanism by its secular alternative. One of the best informed advocates of the latter expressed the challenge like this. Secular humanism, he claimed:

> ...is about the world, not about humanism. It would be perfectly possible to write about humanism without a mention of Christianity, but in this country with centuries of Christian tradition and a Christian establishment, that would be irresponsible. Humanism in Europe or America has to be in a preliminary way justification of a rejection of Christianity. In other cultures also humanism has been the alternative to the dominant religious outlook. Indeed, humanism is the permanent alternative to religion, an essentially different way of taking and tackling human life in the world.[7]

CHRISTIAN EDUCATION IN THE SERVICE OF UNITY

The impressively unified triumphs of science and technology present an interesting comparison with the disunity and the uncertainty that arise out of religious diversity. The claims of scientific investigation can be put to the test. Its methods are universally discernible, as-similable, and applicable. Scientific knowledge is, in short, *real* knowledge. Are not the roots of European (as of world-wide) unity to be found in science? The universality of science is taken to be exemplary. If science can be universal, why not religion, and why not the religion of science? Why should it prove impossible to adopt in religion those beliefs and practices that correspond to the universally felt needs of mankind? One way of coping with conflicting truth-claims and universal human needs, real or apparent, is to relativize them. This, however, is a Hindu rather than a Christian view. The nineteenth century Bengali Brahmin, Sri Ramakrishna, having spent twelve years of his life discovering the universal truth which he claimed to have found concealed beneath the different names and forms of all religions, put it like this:

> As one can ascend to the top of a house by means of a ladder or a bamboo or a staircase or a rope, so divers are the ways and means to approach God, and every religion in the world shows one of these ways. Different creeds are but different paths to reach the Almighty.[8]

In the light of recent events in south-eastern Europe and Northern Ireland we cannot be certain that reconciliation and peace are as universally desired as is often assumed. Christians in both these areas of conflict have not always distinguished themselves by their attitudes to reconciliation, although the many known acts of personal heroism in the face of personal suffering and grief (and, no doubt, the similar acts about which we may never know) stand out as examples of the cost of true Christian discipleship. The point is that Christian education is precisely a life-long pilgrimage of learning what the cost of Christian discipleship really is. To deny this is to trivialize Christian education. The sufferings of the innocent appear to be of no account in the calculations of those who murder and kill indiscriminately in pursuit of their goals. Yet it is in the depths of human suffering that Christians are reminded of the staggering claim that God took it upon himself to suffer in human form. There is no explanation of suffering in the mystery of the cross, but there is the testimony of faith which even springs out of the cry of dereliction, 'My God, my God, why have you forsaken me?'.[9] Despite the formidable difficulties the task of reconciliation must go on, and it is a task which specifically, though by no means uniquely, devolves upon Christians, whether or not they are formally engaged in education. In short (and not least) it is a task with far-reaching educational implications. Sympathy and compassion, in the most literal sense, are at the centre not at the edge of Christian education.

> One weakness of our present situation is that men appear to be faced with choice between two evils, on the one hand such a rediscovery of community as enslaves the individual to the state or nation, and on the other an individualism which is powerless to resist such totalitarianism both because it is weak in itself and because it fails to provide satisfaction for that returning hunger for solidarity which undoubtedly characterizes the youth of the present generation. I see no way out of this predicament save by the reintegration of the ideals, which even in our individualism we continue to cherish, in a community of a genuinely universal kind. Only in the fellowship of the Eternal can we escape *both* the totalitarian *and* the individualistic heresies... The Church of Christ is such a universal community: it amply provides the corrective for individualism, and at the same time delivers us from earthly totalitarianisms by directing our sovereign allegiance to God alone; while it further discourages us from taking precarious stand upon virtues which men see that we do not possess, and inclines us rather to stand before men as sinners who have found forgiveness and who are called upon, not merely to defend their own rights, but to love and serve their fellows and to forgive as they themselves have been forgiven.[10]

The role for Christian education in encouraging these processes of reintegration and reconciliation needs to be reassessed. The theory and the practice of Christian education have been influenced in recent years by what might be termed 'the principle of theological uncertainty'. Not surprisingly this has had its effects on Christian teachers who, in the eyes of some of their critics, are singularly guilty of indoctrination rather than of education. Responses to the charge of indoctrination have been somewhat evasive and confusing, at least with regard to religious education and moral education. Neither religious nor moral education has ever been understood by Christians as a discrete 'subject area' which may, or may not, be included in the curriculum. Christian education has always been a comprehensive enterprise in which, ideally if not always in practice, 'religious' and 'moral' education are integral parts of the whole, not optional extras. In other words one might fairly expect that in a Christian school every teacher, of whatever subject, is to some extent involved in the common task of relating religious faith to life and work. But by no means all Christian teachers teach in Christian institutions. That the uniqueness of the Christian faith, its supernatural origins, its dogmatic basis, its doctrinal development, not to speak of its institutional organization, should be called into question by its opponents is to be expected. More confusing, more disturbing perhaps, is the fact that such criticisms are voiced by Christians who appear to argue that agnosticism is no longer the enemy of faith but its standard-bearer; that the Christian agnostic is one who takes the honourable as well as the prudent course in response to the vagaries of human existence. All of this suggests that the time is ripe for a thorough review of education from Christian points of view. It may be that Christians still have a long way to go before they are in a position to claim as much as my title implies. Whether or not Christian education can serve as an instrument for reconciling and for accommodating the differences between individuals and groups in this country not to speak of the wider world of Europe and beyond depends, humanly speaking, on the determination of Christians to reflect in their own lives something of the dynamic unity of God who not only wills that human beings be at one with each other, but also provides the means. In a divided world, in which divisions are likely to persist even after political and economic 'unity' is achieved, Christian education will still have its distinctive part to play in *dis*-covering in human beings the image of God.

NOTES

1. The words — from Aristotle, *Metaphysics*, II (iii) i — are quoted by C. S. Lewis in the first chapter of his 'preliminary study' on the subject of *Miracles* (London: Collins, Fontana Books, 1968, p 7).
2. Edward Hulmes, in V. Alan McLelland (ed), *Christian Education in a Pluralist Society*, London: Routledge, 1988, pp 88-89.
3. Werner Heisenberg, 'Scientific Truth and Religious Truth', *Universitas*, English edition, Vol. 16, No. 1, 1974, pp 1-14.
4. Quoted by Meriol Trevor in her introduction to Newman's *Meditations and Devotions*, London: Burns & Oates, 1964 edition, first published 1893, pp v-vi.
5. J. H. Newman, *The Idea of a University*, London: Longmans, Green & Co, 1912 edition, pp 331-333.

6. J. H. Newman, *A Grammar of Assent*, edited by C. F. Harrold, London: Longmans, Green & Co, 1947 edition, p xiii.

7. H. J. Blackham, *Humanism*, Harmondsworth: Penguin Books, 1968, from the Preface.

8. 'The Sayings of Sri Ramakrishna', quoted in Robert O. Ballou, *The Bible of the World*, London: Kegan Paul, Trench Trubner & Co, 1946, p 161.

9. Psalm 22:1; Mark 15:34.

10. John Baillie, *Invitation to Pilgrimage*, Harmondsworth: Penguin Books, first published by Oxford University Press, 1942, pp 153-154.

21

Growing into Christ: The Psychology and Politics of Christian Maturity

JEFF ASTLEY

> ...until we should all attain to the unity of the faith and of the full knowledge of the Son of God, to maturity, to the measure of the stature of the fullness of Christ... speaking the truth in love, we are to grow up in every way into him who is the head, into Christ. (Ephesians 4:13ff)

This paper is an attempt to answer the question, What is — humanly and Christianly speaking — 'maturity', 'adulthood', 'growing up'? We need to answer that question both from a human *and* from a Christian perspective, recognizing that to be fully Christian implies being fully human and accepting, with Hans Küng, that being Christian 'is not an addition to being human' but 'an elevation — or better a — transfiguration of the human'.[1] Küng notes that being Christian is not the same as being human, but 'everything can be called Christian which...has an explicit, positive reference to Jesus Christ'.[2] So this paper will offer models of what it is to be a mature, adult human being, and then try to relate this discussion to the Christian tradition about Jesus (the 'explicit positive reference').

IMAGES OF MATURITY AND ADULTHOOD

According to the dictionary, to be mature is to be fully grown, fully developed, 'ripe'. The word 'adult' is defined in terms of such maturity. An adult is one who has reached maturity. Etymologically the word derives from the Latin *adultus*, the past participle of *adolescere*, 'to grow up' — we may compare the word 'adolescent'.

The social sciences have offered us many developmental schemes that provide an overview of growing up. It is tempting to present such schemes as essentially descriptive: straightforward factual accounts of how people actually develop. But they invariably contain a normative element as well, or at least we cannot stop ourselves treating them as normative, for where you get to in development is surely where you should end up. It is better to have arrived than still to be on the way. So Ronald Goldman's account of the development of religious thinking designated most five- to seven-year-olds as 'pre-religious', and eight- to eleven-year-olds as 'sub-religious', because they represented immature stages on the way to 'getting it right'.[3]

Thus ideas of human development, like ideas of biological or social evolution, posit for us an image of a future that operates like a sort of 'final cause' pulling us on to itself. It is the good-time-coming, or the good-thing-we-are-becoming, and to know it is to love it. It serves us as an image or symbol of what it is to have arrived, to have succeeded in development. It is no wonder that James Fowler found that, although only 0.3% of his sample were at the 'final' Stage 6 of his 'stages of faith', every group he spoke to showed most interest in this stage.[4]

Presumably such an image of maturity or adulthood connects with what has been called a person's *project*, which includes what I have uniquely to do and to become: my image of myself that has to be realized, actualized, or 'individuated'.[5] This is my possible future state. It is what I aspire to. And 'image' is the right word for it, for it has its home in the imagination. There it is fed not only by my sober observations of facts about my development and the nature of other adults; but also by stories and myths, fiction and fantasy — by Clint Eastwood as much as by Thomas Merton.

Even very young children form some idea of what it is to be grown up. They express this imaginatively in their play, modelling themselves on what they selectively know about their parents and others. This idea changes over time, of course, and is eventually overtaken by events as the adolescent grows up through it. Particularly in the case of adolescents, with their deep need to think of and look to a future for themselves, the image is not only alluring and entrancing, but daunting and fearful also — for who wants to be middle-aged? This description of the paradoxical combination of emotions associated with growing up is of course stolen from Rudolf Otto's account of the 'numinous' experience: the captivating but dreadful experience of the holy. That is proper, for the image of maturity has some of these religious overtones implicitly associated with it. It is the End of the storm and stress of adolescence, it is the end-that-justifies-the-means, and it is inevitable. Like many a god, devotion to it either frees us or enslaves us. (So in the second half of my life, Daniel Levinson has suggested, I — like most men — must live with my failure to become Clint Eastwood, and coping with that may cripple my middle years.[6])

Gabriel Moran suggests that there are four uses of the word 'adult'.[7] The first is the *pornographic* use ('adult movie' etc), an interesting modern debasement and restriction of the notion.[8] The second usage denotes a *chronological or biological* point in time, when we reach a certain age (legal notions of 'adult') or a particular stage of physical and sexual development. The remaining two meanings are more interesting to Moran and to us because they relate to psychosocial criteria.

The third in Moran's list is perhaps the most popular received meaning: that of an *independent, autonomous man*. (Here 'man' is more appropriate than 'person', as we shall see.) This is the adult as a rational, objective, productive individual who is strong, healthy, liberated and successful. In the language of Transactional Analysis he might be described as 'O.K.'.[9] The development of such an ideal is well displayed by a piece of longitudinal research done in the United States on male managers in industry. This showed that over a period of twenty years they became more motivated by achievement, aggression and autonomy, and progressively less motivated by affiliative (interpersonal) goals.[10] This was particularly marked among the most 'successful' (ie most promoted). Also relevant is the work of Roger Gould whose developmental scheme for sixteen- to forty-five-year-olds is explicitly described as showing a movement from 'worse' to 'better' through growing up. As we become adult, Gould claims, we are 'no longer dependent, powerless children, and we can now view life from the independent vista of adulthood'.[11]

Many would be willing to criticize such an image of maturity as being sexist, ageist, and perniciously intellectualist and middle-class. It clearly fits most closely a male stereotype of adulthood and excludes the old who are no longer independent. Its stress on autonomy and rationality, on deciding for one's self and being in charge of one's own life, excludes a large percentage of the chronologically adult population. We may note that one third of the males in their thirties interviewed by Fowler (and, significantly, over 40% of the females) were at his Stage 3, showing a heteronomous faith highly dependent on the authority of other people.[12] Fowler recognizes that on his scheme movement on to Stage 4 (the autonomous stage of having a faith of one's own) involves a 'critical distancing' from one's previous assumed value system, and is dependent on the development and use of a certain sort of abstract reasoning.

It is interesting that Tom Kitwood's excellent study of English fifteen- to nineteen-year-olds shows very little evidence of any assertion of autonomy in adolescence.[13] The shift that he noted was not from heteronomy to autonomy, but from one sort of authority to another — to the authority of the social worlds of peer groups. Very few of the teenagers he talked to had much interest in ideas or abstract thinking; they did not appear to be self-consciously searching for or choosing an identity or value-system.[14] This may come later, but even then perhaps it will do so only for a minority. It is very easy to put too much stress on autonomous decision-making and the rational element in both human development and religious conversion. The literature often points to the 15/16 age group as the most likely time for conversion.[15] Yet sixteen-year-olds are not the individuals who are most able to stand alone. The adolescent convert desperately needs the support of a new social world, and probably of a new (religious) peer group.

We may see religious conversion as a change mainly in the content of faith, but it is also closely related to a shift in the form or structure of faithing.[16] In particular it has been seen as a subspecies of the identity change whereby I come to know where I fit in: who I am and who loves me.[17] But neither of these dimensions should be over-intellectualized. We are all less capable than we think we are of climbing up to some Archimedean standpoint from which we coolly choose from a variety of worldviews. At the core of all theories of knowledge lies some account of the way truth or reality forces itself on us. We do not decide what to believe; rather our beliefs are forced out of us (or into us) by the evidence, self-evident intuition, or whatever. If I were to point a revolver at you, what 'cognitive freedom' would you really have left with regard to the truth-claim that 'a revolver is being pointed at me'? We believe because we cannot help believing. If we were really to choose what to believe we should be less rational, not more.[18] I do not choose my gods; the gods choose me.

So autonomy is perhaps not all it is cracked up to be. It is not always self-evidently an intrinsically good thing: a virtue of the Reason and the Will. And it is, in any case, a minority option. Don Cupitt's autonomous man-come-of-age, who cherishes above all 'that unique inner kernel of loneliness, scepticism and freedom', is a rarity.[19]

So in talking about conversion — and it is important to talk about conversion — we must not treat it in too intellectualist a fashion. Some psychologists of religion have attempted to distinguish intellectual conversions from other types (eg 'moral' and 'social'), but the typology is somewhat strained.[20] A more holistic view would see conversion as a shift in an interrelated set of attitudes, emotions and beliefs. Deeply embedded within this complex are the values by which every person lives, and we may see conversion primarily as a shift in — or discovery of — a new ideal, a new image of what it is to be truly human. L. W. Lang described Christian conversion as the adoption of a Christian personality. He wrote that:

> the main religious appeal should be to gain a decision to have a Christian character....a conversion-decision is a choice between personal types or values.[21]

Here perhaps we *can* use an insight from Don Cupitt, his claim that:

> the essence of the matter is that you are not fully human unless there is something that is dearer to you than your own life.[22]

This brings us back to values, including the image or ideal of maturity and adulthood, and in a Christian context to the Christian redaction of this ideal.

THE CHRISTIAN IMAGE OF MATURITY AND ADULTHOOD

In Moran's list we are left with the understanding of adult that he himself opts for, designating it '*maturity/wholeness*'. This is the synthesizing of opposites, the integration of very different elements.[23] Children and adolescents can be one-sided, but adulthood demands wholeness and a holding together of what might otherwise fly apart. Like orthodoxy, and unlike the heretics, disparate truths are held in tension; the tension is not 'resolved' by giving up one of them and running the other to death. Maturity is a matter of balance. Moran recognizes three areas of integration: the rational and the non-rational, dependence and independence, and life and death.

Rational/non-rational

Split-brain theory regards the left lobe of the brain as controlling our rational, verbal and intellectual activities, whereas the right lobe controls the more intuitive, artistic and non-verbal functions. In the healthy, whole adult person one lobe does not dominate at the expense of the other.

Dependence/independence

Research into the development of moral thinking (Kohlberg's 'justice reasoning'[24]) may be sex-biased. Males score better than females in the application of universalizable rules to hypothetical 'moral cases'. Females tend to reject the format of such discussions, asking first about interpersonal relationships within the example.[25] They would argue for the general principle that adulthood implies interdependent relationships. Such a view is paralleled in theology by the difference between the traditional theistic model of God creating a somewhat independent world 'outside himself' (as in male procreation), and a panentheistic model of God creating the universe as a mother does, within her own being.[26] Independence is not the highest state of being, either for God or for us.

Life/death

It is Jung who writes most powerfully of the religious importance of the second half of life, when we begin to face its end:

> Ageing people should know that their lives are not mounting and unfolding, but that an inexorable inner process forces the contraction of life. For a young person it is almost a sin — and certainly a danger — to be too much occupied with himself; but for the ageing person it is a duty and a necessity to give serious attention to himself. After having lavished its light upon the world, the sun withdraws its rays in order to illumine itself. Instead of doing likewise, many old people prefer to be hypochondriacs, niggards, doctrinaires, applauders of the past or eternal adolescents — all lamentable substitutes for the illumination of the self, but inevitable consequences of the delusion that the second half of life must be governed by the principles of the first.
>
> I said just now that we have no schools for forty-year-olds. That is not quite true. Our religions were always such schools in the past, but how many people regard them as such today? How many of us older persons have really been brought up in such

a school and prepared for the second half of life, for old age, death and eternity?[27]

Nothing is more potent or religious than the recognition that we are in time and, like all temporal objects, passing away. This is an insight that cannot be taught to the young, for each must discover it for himself or herself. The old have a better chance of learning it, along with other aspects of this 'wisdom of time'. As the theologian Sam Keen puts it:

> It is only after the tragedy of disease, evil, and death has been wrestled with that authentic love begins to emerge. I suspect the 'wisdom' of twenty-year-old children who have had no encounter with the raw side of life. When they say 'All is one', they don't know what they are talking about... You cannot lose an ego that you have not constructed. Character armor must be built before it can be destroyed. *Karma* must be accumulated before it can be burnt. The whole notion of teaching young people to be saints before they have been sinners is ridiculous. The yogis and spiritual masters who advocate wall-to-wall spiritual disciplines for adolescents have no respect for the wisdom of time. They try to teach wisdom before folly has been tasted. They train children to give Sunday school affirmations of love before they have discovered the depths of their untrust.[28]

Experience and age must be allowed back into our image of adulthood. Twenty- and thirty-year-olds need to have such an image, an image which transcends themselves. A society which sees the middle-aged and elderly as failed adults should not be taken seriously.

Do we have here a more authentically Christian notion of adulthood? It is certainly more balanced and integrating. Is it not also more vulnerable, more open, more paradoxical — and *weaker*? Keen describes his final stage of maturity as *the lover/fool* for whom 'vulnerability and compassion have replaced defensiveness and paranoia'. I warm to this 'weak' image of adulthood; for the Christian insight is surely that Christian strengths are what the world calls weaknesses, and that true strength only comes from weakness. Such a view is deeply embedded in the gospel, for the gospel is primarily about the *poor*.

This claim calls for some elaboration. First, the gospel is about serving the poor. Christian ministry has been described in these words:

> noticing the unnoticed [contrast most parties];
> celebrating the noncelebrity [contrast most television];
> questioning the unquestioned [contrast most education];
> empowering the powerless [contrast most politics];
> and putting in touch the out of touch.[29]

Secondly, the gospel is given to the poor. The rich, healthy and successful have their rewards already. (What rewards? Riches, health and success of course.) Jesus is physician to the sick. 'The poor' of the Psalms and Beatitudes and 'the humble' of the Magnificat are those of low status, those who are 'no people'. And the gospel, we note, is *given* to them; their poverty starkly symbolizes the fact that no one could afford it or demand it. 'Fear not, little flock, for it is your Father's good pleasure to give you the kingdom.'[30]

Thirdly, the gospel celebrates the poor. We must beware of a danger here. It is easy to be patronizing. It is tempting to keep the poor poor for their symbolic effect. But this would be to miss the point. The gospel is an overturning of values, a radical re-evaluation of what it is to be human — and 'successful', 'mature' and 'adult'.

This spiritual overturning is very marked in the ministry and teaching of Jesus. He points to the widow donating her mite and tells the disciples that she has given more than any of the others. He puts a child in the midst of his followers to present them with a model for being a disciple: a model of one who is without status. In his words and lifestyle Jesus gives recognition to the unchurched, the unrespectable, the sinner and the poor as those who enter the kingdom of God first. This is not because they are sinful, disreputable or penniless; but because they are without social or religious status. Hence his 'ministry to women', and so on.

Such a reading of Christ should give us pause in our consideration of what it is to become mature or adult, to grow up into Christ. At the very least it must be something about letting go of status, strength, power, freedom, possessions, and autonomy. This has to be a less macho image that allows for maturity to be defined more in terms of self-giving and giving up (compare C. Day Lewis's 'love is proved in the letting go'), than in terms of arguments won and opponents beaten.

Perhaps the best text for such an account is to be found in Philippians 2:5ff, where the context — significantly — is the imitation of Christ. We read there of the kenosis of the Son of God 'who did not count equality with God a thing to be grasped, but emptied himself, taking the form of a servant' and 'humbled himself'. In C. F. D.

Moule's suggested translation, the christology is even more pointed:

> 'Jesus did not reckon that equality with God meant snatching:
> on the contrary, he emptied himself...' This would mean that,
> whereas ordinary human valuation reckons that God-likeness
> means having your own way, getting what you want, Jesus saw
> God-likeness essentially as giving and spending oneself out.[31]

Divinity — and therefore humanity? — means giving up power and
letting-be, not holding on to power and thus building up one's own
being. The motto of the Christian is not 'What I have I hold', but 'What
I am I give'.

Donald Evans convincingly describes human life as a struggle of
attitude-virtues over the corresponding attitude-vices.[32] Human fulfilment obtains when the virtues predominate. His list of such virtues
is interesting: trust, humility, self-acceptance, responsibility, self-
commitment, friendliness, concern and contemplation. These
strengths of character are surely paradoxical strengths: strengths that
come through weakness. *Trust* will only develop in the weak, for what
need have the strong for it? *Self-acceptance* means accepting myself warts
and all, without the warts there is nothing that needs to be accepted.
And my willingness to be a *friend* and to show *concern* (both are species
of love) is surely a function of my willingness to be vulnerable and to
eschew independence.

There is also a point to be made about *humour* here. Evans makes
it well:

> What is the way of liberation from being dominated by either
> pride or self-humiliation in our responses to people and
> situations? Sometimes what is needed is not 'struggle' in the
> sense of intensely serious effort, but humor. Sometimes humor
> can expose the fantasies which underlie my pride or my self-
> humiliation, rendering them vulnerable to an insight in which
> they lose their power over me — for a crucial moment at least.
> The fantasies are ludicrous, and I can see this if they are
> described in a witty way. I am seated neither on a celestial
> throne at the center of the universe nor on a 'one-holer' in an
> outhouse at the edge of the universe. A sharp, penetrating
> joke can prick my pompous pretensions, bringing me down to
> earth. Or, alternatively, it can pierce through the prison walls
> of my somber self-abasement, jolting me into an initiative
> towards freedom..... At its best, humor can liberate our
> humanity, freeing us from our obsession with comparative

power and status. Together we mock the obsession so that it loses its spell.[33]

Humility and humour are intimately related. Both bring us down to earth (*humus*) where we can realize our true humanity. Humour is both realistic and paradoxical, and therefore a good medium in which to articulate the Christian doctrine of *human* being: created from (and in) the mud, but made a little lower than the angels. Humour can be revelatory and salvific. In *Steppenwolf* Herman Hesse writes:

> Humour alone, that magnificent discovery of those who are cut short in their calling to highest endeavour, those who falling short of tragedy are yet as rich in gifts as in affliction, humour alone (perhaps the most inborn and brilliant achievement of the human spirit) attains to the impossible and brings every aspect of human existence within the rays of its prism. To live in the world as though it were not the world, to respect the law and yet to stand above it, to have possessions as though 'one possessed nothing', to renounce as though it were no renunciation, all these favourite and often formulated propositions of an exalted worldly wisdom, it is in the power of humour alone to make efficacious.[34]

As Garp puts it in John Irving's novel, 'Laughter is my religion'.[35] Certainly those who do not appreciate humour may find it hard to appreciate religion. Spirituality can often best be captured in a joke. What better explanation can there be of the survival of the Jews than the power of their faith and of their jokes?

It should be noted that Evans's virtues have their corresponding vices, which makes his notion of human fulfilment one that is vulnerable in another sense. His character strengths are not incompatible with character weaknesses, in the way that power and success are incompatible with powerlessness and failure. Rather the character strength is forged in the struggle with the ever-present correlative weakness. As J. D. G. Dunn notes, with reference to St Paul's account of the Spirit-filled life:

> It is a religion...of faith always assailed by question and doubt, of life always assailed by death, of Spirit always assailed by flesh (Galatians 5:16f)... It is a *life-long tension* [between flesh and Spirit]... It is important to realize that conversion, experience

of Spirit, charismatic experience, does not raise the believer above and beyond this conflict — rather the presence and activity of the Spirit sharpens the conflict.[36]

According to Daniel Jenkins, the Christian life as a 'realization of mature humanity' includes such qualities as meakness, peacemaking, generosity, joy and magnanimity. Jenkins notes that the temptations of such a maturity are more deadly than those of either childhood or adolescence: 'to the extent that we grow into the fullness of the stature of Christ, we make a very large target'.[37] As a target for the temptations of pride, complacency and sloth, Christian maturity is a most vulnerable and insecure entity.

CHRISTIAN MATURITY AND CHRISTIAN EDUCATION

If we understand Christian education in its widest sense it may be said to include both the formation of a Christian worldview and lifestyle, and also some self-critical reasoning about Christianity from within that position. Formative Christian education — 'Christian formation' — captures the first element, denoting the processes whereby we structure and change a person's learning environment so that her attitudes, values, beliefs, emotions, dispositions to act, etc are shifted in a more Christian direction.[38] Social psychology suggests two ways in which this might most effectively happen:

(a) *Modelling*. If we are presented with an example of behaviour being displayed by a person we admire and respect, we are very likely to change our attitudes to correspond with those shown by the model.[39] I would suggest that 'growing into Christ' is not so much a metaphysical mystery as a psychological reality. It is learning to be Christian through the imitation of (or 'conformity to') Christ. The most effective place for such an attitude-change is in the worshipping community. For there we celebrate Christ as the model of humanity and the incarnation of the values of maturity. In the church we are also meant to learn from other people (sub-models) what it is to be Christian: 'Be imitators of me, as I am of Christ'.[40]

(b) *Roleplaying and Commitment*. I can change my attitudes most effectively by playing out the behaviour which those attitudes should engender. To develop trust in you I can behave 'as if' I trust you; to develop the attitude of love I may need to go through the behaviour of love. H. H. Price has called this ploy in religion 'assiduous supposing';

Peter Baelz describes it as an 'experiment with life'.[41] In John Westerhoff's phrase, we make believe in order to believe as we make love in order to love. Prayer is central to all of this. In religion prayer comes first, belief follows. To cease to pray is to cease to believe. To 'role-play' the role of a pray-er is to put oneself in the place where belief will come most easily.

These two suggestions may be merged. Among the laboratories for Christian learning that we need, should we not have places where people can experiment with prayer? These may be groups on the borders of the church which are open to outsiders or the twentieth century equivalent of 'God fearers', where people can come to the threshold of worship and try it out.[42] There they will find the Christian model of maturity being celebrated, and hopefully its attractiveness will have its effect.

A POLITICAL CONCLUSION

A final word may be appropriate here, relating this discussion to current social and political concerns. According to Westerhoff:

> we cannot gradually educate persons to be Christians, not in this world. Christian faith runs counter to our ordinary understandings and ways. It is hardly possible to grow up in our sort of society and have the eyes and ears of Christian faith. Transformations, reorientations of life, conversions are necessary... Nurture and conversion, conversion and nurture, belong together...[43]

Christianity stands *contra mundum*, over against the world. In the language of St John's Gospel 'the world' is the secular in its orientation towards the flesh rather than the Spirit. It is the world in bondage to the powers of darkness: the world as subhuman, inhuman or anti-human. It is to such a worldly world that Christianity is opposed.

So the gospel inevitably carries political implications, as politics inevitably implies a view of the human — an anthropology. Christianity must stand opposed to any political view, whether of the Left or of the Right, that is inadequate in its anthropology. We must ask ourselves whether the political stances we embrace and the social policies we encourage allow a fully human maturity.

Back in 1985 the White Paper *Education and Training for Young People* informed us that in such areas a government will do well to 'ensure that the interests of employers and other consumers are to the forefront of the concerns of the providers'.[44] Doubtless this is entirely right, proper and economically important. It might, however, have been worded differently. For the 'providers' and 'consumers' mentioned here are providers and consumers of *people.* There is always a temptation to see education in less than fully human terms, as a production line moulding people into the right shapes to fit empty holes in the economy. But if one of the aims of education is the person-making function, teaching me to be more fully human, then it needs to develop more than my technical skills and economically-valuable technological knowledge. Certainly power, competence, skill and knowledge *will* get the bairn a new coat, as they say in the North East. But they will not themselves nurture the bairn into the measure of the stature of the fullness of Christ. Something more is needed for that. It is something that is rather low-tech and difficult to quantify, and therefore embarrassing to mention in economic debates. But it is crucial to the development of mature personhood, and can only be provided by those who have attained a certain sort of maturity. It is *love,* and knowledge directed by love.

The concept of Christian maturity is integrally related to the power and possibility of love: of growing up through love into love. This is a difficult thing to hear, because it is hard to hear a soft thing. These are hard times, we are told, and the corollary is that we must be hard people. Progress, success, even survival, depends on our being hard. It is time that we all grew up.

But if we sell out completely to such rhetoric we do not just give up Christianity, we give up our humanity. Biological success and evolution, in mammals at least, are often as much dependent on caring and cooperation as they are on the hard laws of a Nature red in tooth and claw. Many of Kitwood's adolescent interviewees seemed hard and uncaring enough, but as the sessions proceeded their bravado faded. They may not have universalized their virtues, but virtues they were: loyalty, mutual help and cooperation. But who dare admit to such softness outside the immediate peer group? Outside we all need to be hard and to develop strong carapaces to protect the vulnerable tissues of our humanity. Males learn this early. I understand that some recent research has shown that teenage boys and girls display identical physiological responses when shown pictures of babies, but their external verbal behaviour is radically different — 'Ooh' and 'Aaah' from the girls, and 'push them out of the pram' jokes from the boys. But beneath lies the common humanity.

Our hope as a society lies in that common humanity. But it needs nurture, and it needs expression. What is required is social support for the values of our true humanness. To put it bluntly: if Christianity is soft — if it is the expression of a soft model of maturity — then it needs soft societies to allow its full growth.

It would then be a mistake to harden society too much: a religious mistake and a mistake about human beings. Perhaps psychologically we need our quota of short, sharp shocks. Things can be too easy. For the good of our spiritual and moral health, as well as our economic health, they must not be *too* easy. But nor must they become too hard. We need help in becoming fully human, for it is a difficult thing and those who fully achieve it often seem to end up naked on a cross. In a hard society where soft flesh is faced by hammers and nails, it will be a fearfully difficult option. Humankind simply cannot stand too much hardness; not without disastrous consequences.

According to the psychologists, adults need to love and to work. In the broadest sense of these terms they need a sexual identity and an occupational identity. To be fully human they need to care and to produce, and to be needed in both these roles. Growth to maturity demands an environment that makes both activities possible. We do not really know what will happen in a society where such growth is curtailed. But if there is any alternative to such a curtailment, our humanity and our Christianity both demand that it should be explored.

NOTES

1. H. Küng, *On Being a Christian*, trans E. Quinn, London: Collins, 1977, pp 601f.
2. *ibid.*, p 125.
3. R. Goldman, *Readiness for Religion*, London: Routledge & Kegan Paul, 1965, p 196.
4. J. W. Fowler, *Stages of Faith*, San Francisco: Harper & Row, 1981, p 318. The literature on human development is often described as heavily biased to cognitive, rationalistic conceptions of growth, and to liberalism. See K. Stokes (ed), *Faith Development in the Adult Life Cycle*, New York: W. H. Sadlier, 1982, p 29. This is a criticism that is sometimes made of Fowler's work, see G. Moran, *Religious Education Development*, Winston Press: Minneapolis, 1983, ch 6. For a sympathetic introduction to faith development theory see J. Astley *et al.*, *How Faith Grows: Faith Development and Christian Education*, London: National Society, 1991. A few paragraphs in the present paper overlap with the text of that book, and are reproduced with permission. On the vexed issue of the normative status of faith development theory see J.W. Fowler, K.E. Nipkow and F. Schweitzer (eds), *Stages of Faith and Religious Development*, London: SCM, 1991, pp 25f, 35f, 92ff.
5. R. Ruddock, 'Conditions of Personal Identity', in Ruddock (ed), *Six Approaches to the Person*, London: Routledge & Kegan Paul, 1972, pp 114ff.
6. D. J. Levinson *et al.*, *The Seasons of a Man's Life*, New York: Knopf, 1979, chs 13 and 16.

7. G. Moran, *Education toward Adulthood*, New York: Paulist Press, 1979, ch 2.

8. Pornography has been described as the public exposure of a part of a human being at the expense of the whole.

9. Or so Moran claims: see T. A. Harris, *I'm OK — You're OK*, New York: Avon, 1967.

10. D. W. Bray and A. Howard, 'Keeping in Touch with Success', *The Wharton Magazine*, Vol. 3, No. 2, 1979.

11. R. L. Gould, *Transformations: Growth and Change in Adult Life*, New York: Simon & Schuster, 1978, p 21.

12. Fowler, *Stages of Faith*, pp 318, 322.

13. T. Kitwood, *Disclosures to a Stranger*, London: Routledge & Kegan Paul, 1980, especially pp 131, 260.

14. *ibid.*, pp 258, 274f.

15. See V. B. Gillespie, *Religious Conversion and Personal Identity*, Birmingham, Ala.: Religious Education Press, 1979, p 78, and his *The Dynamics of Religious Conversion*, Birmingham, Ala.: Religious Education Press, 1991, ch 5.

16. Fowler, *Stages of Faith*, pp 281ff.

17. Gillespie, *Religious Conversion and Personal Identity*, ch V, and *The Dynamics of Religious Conversion*, chs 6 and 7.

18. Compare L. P. Pojman, *Religious Belief and the Will*, London: Routledge & Kegan Paul, 1986, chs XI, XIII, XIV.

19. D. Cupitt, *Only Human*, London: SCM, 1985, p 72. Compare his *Taking Leave of God*, London: SCM, 1980, ch 1.

20. R. H. Thouless, *An Introduction to the Psychology of Religion*, Cambridge: Cambridge University Press, 1971, ch 14. For a more satisfactory account of the moral, cognitive and affective species of conversion, their place in human development and their contribution to what he calls 'religious conversion', see Walter Conn's perceptive study, *Christian Conversion*, Mahwah, N.J.: Paulist Press, 1986.

21. L. W. Lang, *A Study of Conversion*, London: Allen & Unwin, 1931, p 189.

22. Cupitt, *Only Human*, p 170.

23. Moran, *Education toward Adulthood*, pp 28ff. For a very similar emphasis, described as a hallmark of the transition to the stage of 'Conjunctive Faith', see J. W. Fowler, *Becoming Adult, Becoming Christian*, San Francisco: Harper & Row, 1984, p 65.

24. L. Kohlberg, 'Stage and Sequence: The Cognitive-Developmental Approach to Socialization', in D. A. Goslin (ed), *Handbook of Socialization Theory and Research*, Chicago: Rand McNally, 1969.

25. C. Gilligan, *In a Different Voice*, Cambridge, Mass.: Harvard University Press, 1982. Feminist authors have pointed out the way in which male interpretations have hijacked even the notion of 'reason': see G. Lloyd, *The Man of Reason: 'Male' and 'Female' in Western Philosophy*, London: Methuen, 1984. See also M.F. Belenky *et al.*, *Women's Ways of Knowing*, New York: Basic Books, 1986 and J.W. Fowler, 'Foreword' to J. Astley and L.J. Francis (eds), *Christian Perspectives on Faith Development*, Leominster: Fowler Wright, 1992.

26. See A. R. Peacocke, *Creation and the World of Science*, Oxford: Clarendon, 1979, pp 141ff.

27. C. G. Jung, *Modern Man in Search of a Soul*, London: Routledge & Kegan Paul, 1961 (first published 1933), p 125.

28. J. Fowler and S. Keen, *Life Maps*, Waco, Texas: Word, 1978, p 123.

29. Amended from a Winchester Diocesan Newsletter.

30. Luke 12:32, RSV.

31. C. F. D. Moule in S. W. Sykes and J. P. Clayton (eds), *Christ, Faith and History*, Cambridge: Cambridge University Press, 1972, p 97. See also J. Moltmann, *The Church in the Power of the Spirit*, trans M. Kohl, London: SCM, 1977, pp 102ff.

32. D. D. Evans, *Struggle and Fulfillment*, Cleveland: Collins, 1979.

33. *ibid.*, pp 115f.

34. H. Hesse, *Steppenwolf*, Harmondsworth: Penguin, 1965, p 67.

322   JEFF ASTLEY

35. J. Irving, *The World according to Garp*, London: Corgi, 1979, p 224.
36. J. D. G. Dunn, *Jesus and the Spirit*, London: SCM, 1975, pp 338f.
37. D. Jenkins, *Christian Maturity and the Theology of Success*, London: SCM, 1976, p 21.
38. Compare J. M. Lee, *The Flow of Religious Instruction*, Birmingham, Ala.: Religious Education Press, 1973, and *The Content of Religious Instruction*, Birmingham, Ala.: Religious Education Press, 1985, *passim*.
39. See A. Bandura, *Principles of Behavioral Modification*, New York: Holt, Rinehart & Winston, 1969, ch 3.
40. 1 Corinthians 2:1.
41. H. H. Price, *Belief*, London: Allen & Unwin, 1969, pp 482ff; P. R. Baelz, *The Forgotten Dream*, London: Mowbrays, 1975, ch 8.
42. Compare J. Hull, *School Worship: an Obituary*, London: SCM, 1975, p 125 on the 'threshold of worship', and the comments on p 401 of chapter 26 below.
43. J. H. Westerhoff in J. Ferguson (ed), *Christianity, Society and Education*, London: SPCK, 1981, pp 192, 194.
44. London: HMSO, 1985, p 10. The use of metaphors and jargon drawn from industry and commerce has continued into the 1990s, with talk of the 'products' of 'value-added' educational processes, quantitatively assessed through 'performance indicators' and 'league tables'.

PART THREE
'Among the Grass Roots':
Empirical Investigation in
Christian Education

INTRODUCTION

'What is a Christian?: Investigating the Understanding of 16- to 19-year-olds',
by Leslie Francis, Carolyn Wilcox and Jeff Astley, studies data provided by
over 200 sixth formers who responded to 65 descriptions of what it means to
be a Christian. Their responses indicate that the young person's concept of
a Christian involves four empirically distinct dimensions, and that one of
these (religious beliefs) is given much more salience than one of the others
(public religious practice). The relevance of this research for religious
education about Christianity, and for further research, is discussed.

In 'Christianity Today: The Teenage Experience', Leslie Francis surveys
the responses of nearly four thousand 12- to 16-year-olds in English schools
to questions about their attitudes to issues relating to God, Jesus, prayer, the
church, Christians, science and RE, science and the Bible, and personal
wellbeing. The paper explores the relationship between these attitudinal
areas and the teenagers' sex, age and frequency of church attendance. It
provides important data both for those concerned with religious education
in schools, and for those with a responsibility for the Christian formation of
young people.

Leslie Francis and Harry Gibson's paper, 'Popular Religious Television
and Adolescent Attitudes towards Christianity', explores data from over
5,000 secondary school pupils in Scotland. This material shows that nearly
a third of them watch popular religious television, at least from time to time,
and that such religious programmes — contrary to the assumptions of many
Christian educators — seem to help to reinforce a positive attitude towards
Christianity.

In 'A Survey of Bible Reading Practices and Attitudes to the Bible Among Anglican Congregations', Elizabeth Fisher, with Jeff Astley and Carolyn Wilcox, describes a piece of research surveying 445 Anglican churchgoers. The results show that a majority of these read their Bibles at home less than once a month. Their responses to questions about the historical, scientific, theological and moral 'accuracy' of the Bible, and its relevance today, are also charted; together with their positions on a spectrum of views ranging from the fundamentalist option through to an extreme rejectionist view of Scripture. A substantial group 'found it very difficult to identify or articulate their own attitudes to the Bible'. Those who did seem to know what they believed adopted in the main one or other 'liberal' views of Scripture. Some suggestions as to the relevance of these data for Christian educators are appended.

'Learning and Believing in an Urban Parish' by Guy Buckler and Jeff Astley is an interim report of a research project which includes surveys of the general population of a predominantly working-class parish and its Anglican churchgoers. Their Christian beliefs and practices are reviewed, together with their attitudes to 'further education'-type Christian education and more implicit forms of Christian learning. A study of a small group of churchgoers and their evaluation of various Christian education materials and methods is also reported. Some implications are drawn for the Christian education activities of the churches.

22

What is a Christian?
Investigating the Understanding
of 16- to 19-year-olds

LESLIE J. FRANCIS, CAROLYN WILCOX AND JEFF ASTLEY

INTRODUCTION

According to the Acts of the Apostles, it was in Antioch that the followers of Christ first got the name of Christians (Acts 11: 26). The significance of this epithet has been a matter of theological and social debate ever since. Theologically the term has been applied narrowly to small exclusive sects, or broadly to whole nations supporting an established church. Socially the term has led variously to persecution and martyrdom, or to security, wealth and status.

In England today, social commentators are divided between two rather different views regarding the significance of Christianity in shaping contemporary culture and values. One view speaks of a 'doggedly persistent faith in Christianity' (Bailey, 1986) or the 'unexpressed, inarticulate, but often deeply felt, religion of ordinary folk' who 'feel themselves to have some sort of Christian allegiance' (Habgood, 1987). The other view speaks of growing secularization as 'that process by which religious institutions, actions, and consciousness, lose their social significance' (Wilson, 1982) or 'the making of post-Christian Britain' (Gilbert, 1980).

Nevertheless, the 1988 Education Reform Act is clear in its insistence that Christianity should continue to play a significant part in the education of pupils within the state maintained system of schools (Department of Education and Science, 1989). The Act explicitly states that:

the collective worship in county schools must be wholly or mainly of a broadly Christian character, though not distinctive of any particular Christian denomination.

The provisions of this Act have been variously perceived by different groups of Christians who evaluate the Christian emphasis of the legislation as presenting either opportunities, challenges or problems for the churches (Cooling, 1990; Hull, 1989; British Council of Churches, 1989). Such research as exists among school children themselves suggests that religious education in school is not a popular option (Francis, 1987), that there is a steady movement away from the churches during the years of secondary schooling (Francis, 1989a) and that young people's attitudes towards Christianity have become increasingly less favourable during the 1970s and the 1980s (Francis, 1989b).

Currently little is known, however, about the significance associated with the word 'Christian' by young people in England today. The aim of the present study, therefore, is to explore three specific theories regarding school pupils' perceptions of what it means to be a Christian.

The first theory suggests that the word 'Christian', like the wider term 'religion', functions in a multidimensional way. Several commentators have explored the multidimensional nature of religion from both conceptual (Glock and Stark, 1965; Smart, 1969) and empirical perspectives (King and Hunt, 1975; Batson and Ventis, 1982). Although no generally agreed consensus has emerged from these studies, distinctions are often developed between such dimensions as belief and practice, public and private expressions, ideas and lifestyles. Preliminary conversations with young people suggest that they employ four particular sets of descriptors to describe their use of the word Christian. These involve aspects of religious beliefs, public practices, personal spirituality and personal morality (especially relationships). If these aspects are truly distinct, they should be recoverable by means of factor analysis.

The second theory suggests that within secular societies religion becomes increasingly privatized (Wilson, 1982). As a consequence of this process, personal aspects of religiosity should emerge as more salient descriptors of a Christian than public or community expressions of religion. In other words, in defining 'Christian' more emphasis should be given to personal religious beliefs than to church-related practices. If this is so, more young people should wish to define a Christian in terms of what he or she believes than in terms of his or her relationship with a church.

The third theory suggests that young people who classify themselves as Christians or who display Christian commitment by attending church may tend to profile a 'Christian' in a different way from young people who do not classify themselves as Christians or who do not attend church. In particular churchgoers are likely to give more importance to the role of public practice in defining a Christian. This theory can be tested by comparing the responses of regular churchgoers with pupils who never attend church.

METHOD

Questionnaire

A bank of descriptors of a Christian was generated from discussions conducted among two groups of adult 'professing' Christians: ordinary churchgoers from a variety of congregations and more theologically-articulate educators, scholars and church leaders. The original list of descriptors was pilot-tested among a small sample of both groups to identify terms that were regarded as ambiguous, synonymous or lacking in clarity. The final list of 65 descriptors clearly included examples of religious beliefs, public practices, personal spirituality and personal morality. Subjects were asked to indicate how important a part they thought each of these 65 descriptors played 'in what it means for a person to be a Christian', on a five point scale ranging from 'no part of/completely irrelevant', through 'unimportant', 'neither important nor unimportant' and 'quite important', to 'essential/very important'.

Subjects

The questionnaire was completed by 202 sixth form pupils taking 'A' level religious studies courses attending a study day conference at the North of England Institute for Christian Education. The sample comprised 44 sixteen-year-olds, 89 seventeen-year-olds, 63 eighteen-year-olds and 6 nineteen-year-olds; 38% were weekly churchgoers, a further 11% attended church at least once a month, 33% attended from time to time, and 18% never attended church.

Data analysis

The data were analysed by means of the SPSSX statistical package, using the factor, reliability, correlation and breakdown facilities (SPSS Inc., 1988).

RESULTS

The first statistical procedure to be applied to the data was factor analysis. This procedure attempts to make sense of data by examining relationships between all the different variables (in this case the descriptors), and then attempting to group related variables into a relatively small number of factors. The basic assumption underlying factor analysis is that complex constructs, such as what it means to be 'Christian', may be explained in terms of underlying factors or dimensions. The aim of the process is to represent the relationships among variables using as few factors as possible. The results of factor analysis can be checked and refined by reliability analyses which confirm how well the identified factors hang together. A series of factor analyses and reliability analyses identified a clear four factor structure among the 65 items. Table 1 (see Appendix) presents the resultant varimax rotated solution in which each of the four dimensions is represented by nine items. This solution suggests that the four dimensions measured by the original batch of 65 items can be more economically and more clearly expressed in terms of 36 items.

Table 2 explores the four dimensions identified by factor analysis in terms of the item rest of scale correlations. Each of these nine item scales produces an alpha coefficient of 0.89 which is a most satisfactory index of scale homogeneity and unidimensionality for measures of this length (Cronbach, 1951). In other words the items which have been grouped together to form each scale are clearly measuring the same dimension. The item rest of scale correlations show how closely each item is related to the scale in which it has been placed. The larger the correlation coefficient the closer the relationship.

The first scale, characterized by the descriptor 'a regular churchgoer', is clearly an index of *public religious practice*. The second scale, characterized by the descriptor 'believes in Jesus', is clearly an index of *individual belief*. The third scale, characterized by the descriptor 'has committed his/her life to Christ' and including references to personal prayer and bible study, is clearly an index of *personal spirituality*. The fourth scale, characterized by the descriptor 'tries to treat people equally', is clearly an index of *personal morality/relationships*. These findings give empirical support to the theory that the word 'Christian' functions in a multidimensional way among young people, involving the four distinct components of religious belief, public practice, personal spirituality and personal morality/relationships.

Table 2   Item rest of scale correlations for the four scales of Christian identity

scale items	correlations
public practice	
is baptized	0.4902
supports church activities	0.5593
goes to a place of worship	0.7216
is a regular churchgoer	0.7483
frequently receives communion	0.7279
attends church at Christmas	0.6165
encourages his/her children to attend church/ Sunday school	0.6781
supports the church financially	0.6032
regularly receives communion	0.7471
(alpha = 0.8940)	
religious belief	
finds God in Jesus	0.6531
believes that God exists	0.5615
loves God	0.6403
believes in Jesus	0.7485
follows God's word	0.6719
believes that he/she will enter heaven through Christ	0.6641
believes that Jesus is worthy of worship	0.6425
believes in the resurrection of Jesus	0.6433
believes that Jesus is the Son of God	0.7364
(alpha = 0.8928)	
personal spirituality	
is humble	0.4461
prays to God (individual prayer)	0.5664
has committed his/her life to Christ	0.7351
tells other people about Christianity	0.6515
has received the Holy Spirit	0.6180
reads the Bible	0.7111
believes that he/she has been saved	0.6548
seeks to know God better through reading the Bible	0.6447
allows the Spirit to change his/her life	0.7382
(alpha = 0.8860)	
personal morality/relationships	
is considerate of others' feelings and views	0.6695
is friendly	0.7343
is hopeful	0.5217
tries to treat people equally	0.7913
helps others	0.6792
tries to lead a good life	0.6301
forgives other people	0.6920
orients his/her life towards the needs of others	0.5872
is a good person	0.5968
(alpha = 0.8906)	

Although factor analysis has demonstrated the objective existence of these four dimensions, the fact that they emerged from a rotated solution indicates that the dimensions are interrelated. Table 3 (see Appendix) explores the extent of these interrelationships in terms of the Pearson product moment correlation coefficients. This provides a measure of linear association between two variables, in this case the four dimensions identified by the factor analysis. Once again the larger the correlation coefficient the more closely the dimensions are associated. These statistics demonstrate that public practice is clearly associated with personal spirituality and religious belief, but not with personal morality/relationships. Similarly while this last factor is unrelated to public practice, it is related to religious belief and personal spirituality. These findings give further support to the view that sixth form pupils' images of a Christian cannot be adequately summarized in less than four dimensions.

Table 4 presents the 36 descriptors ranked in order according to the proportion of respondents who rated them as playing an 'essential/very important' part in what it means for a person to be a Christian. This table reveals wide variation from 82.2% who regard belief that God exists as an essential descriptor to 2.0% who regard financial support for the church as an essential descriptor. Identification of the scales to which each of these 36 descriptors belongs makes the point very clearly that personal belief is rated much more highly than public practice. This finding gives empirical support for the theory that within secular societies personal aspects of religiosity emerge as more salient descriptors of a Christian than public or community expressions of religion.

Table 5 contrasts the scores recorded on four scales by the subjects who attend church weekly, those who attend church less than weekly but at least very occasionally, and those who never attend church. This table demonstrates that the strongest relationship exists between church attendance and the salience given to descriptors concerned with the public practice of religion. A significant relationship also exists between church attendance and the salience given to descriptors concerned with religious belief and personal spirituality. No significant relationship exists, however, between church attendance and the salience given to descriptors concerned with personal morality/relationships.

Table 4 Rank order of descriptors rated as 'essential or very important'

rank order	% endorse- ment	scale	descriptor
1	82.2	BELIEF	believes that God exists
2	74.1	BELIEF	believes in Jesus
3	69.2	BELIEF	loves God
4	62.0	BELIEF	believes that Jesus is the Son of God
5	60.5	BELIEF	believes that Jesus is worthy of worship
6 =	53.2	BELIEF	finds God in Jesus
6 =	53.2	RELATIONSHIPS	forgives other people
8	53.0	BELIEF	follows God's word
9	52.5	BELIEF	believes in the resurrection of Jesus
10	50.2	BELIEF	believes he/she will enter heaven through Christ
11	42.8	RELATIONSHIPS	tries to lead a good life
12	38.3	SPIRITUALITY	prays to God (individual prayer)
13	37.1	RELATIONSHIPS	is considerate of others' feelings and views
14	37.0	RELATIONSHIPS	helps others
15	36.2	RELATIONSHIPS	tries to treat people equally
16	33.7	SPIRITUALITY	has committed his/her life to Christ
17	32.2	RELATIONSHIPS	is a good person
18	24.1	SPIRITUALITY	allows the Spirit to change his/her life
19	23.7	SPIRITUALITY	has received the Holy Spirit
20	23.1	SPIRITUALITY	believes he/she has been saved
21	22.3	RELATIONSHIPS	is friendly
22	18.5	RELATIONSHIPS	is hopeful
23 =	15.9	SPIRITUALITY	seeks to know God better through reading the Bible
23 =	15.9	SPIRITUALITY	reads the Bible
23 =	15.9	SPIRITUALITY	tells other people about Christianity
23 =	15.9	PRACTICE	is baptized
27	14.6	RELATIONSHIPS	orients his/her life towards the needs of others
28	13.5	PRACTICE	goes to a place of worship
29	13.4	SPIRITUALITY	is humble
30	12.6	PRACTICE	encourages his/her children to attend church/Sunday school
31	11.6	PRACTICE	attends church at Christmas
32	10.0	PRACTICE	frequently receives communion
33	9.1	PRACTICE	regularly receives communion
34	7.4	PRACTICE	supports church activities
35	5.5	PRACTICE	is a regular churchgoer
36	2.0	PRACTICE	supports the church financially

Table 5   Scale scores by frequency of church attendance

scale	weekly mean	sd	sometimes mean	sd	never mean	sd	F	P<
public practice	31.5	6.9	23.6	6.8	22.1	5.5	36.2	.001
religious belief	41.7	5.0	39.1	5.9	36.7	6.5	10.0	.001
personal spirituality	34.6	7.8	29.0	7.5	27.4	6.4	15.4	.001
personal morality/ relationship	37.0	4.6	35.1	7.0	34.8	7.1	2.5	NS

Table 6 explores the trends identified by the overall analysis of differences in scale scores in greater detail by comparing the responses of those who attend church weekly and those who never attend church in relationship to each of the 36 individual descriptors. Four features of this table are particularly worthy of comment.

First, the data indicate that public religious practice plays a very minimal part in the definition of a Christian advanced by young people who do not themselves attend church. For such young people being a Christian is defined almost entirely in terms of private rather than public features. Even weekly churchgoers understand public practice as relatively marginal to being a Christian, with less than a third (29%) feeling that baptism is essential, less than a quarter (24%) feeling that going to a place of worship is essential, and only one in twenty (5%) feeling that financial support for the church is essential.

Second, the data indicate that, while young people who do not themselves attend church recognize that belief in the existence of God is an essential descriptor of a Christian, they are much less certain about the role of other traditionally formulated beliefs concerned with areas like the divinity of Jesus or his resurrection. Thus, less than a half (47%) of non-churchgoing young people consider that belief in Jesus as the Son of God is essential and just a quarter (25%) consider that belief in the resurrection of Jesus is an essential component of being a Christian.

Third, the majority of young people who never attend church seem to have little appreciation of the role of personal spirituality in shaping a Christian. Thus only a quarter (27%) of non-churchgoing young people consider that individual prayer is essential, and less than one in ten (8%) consider that Bible reading is an essential component

Table 6 Descriptors rated as 'essential or very important' by church attendance

scale items	church attendance weekly %	never %
public practice		
is baptized	28.6	0.0
supports church activities	11.7	0.0
goes to a place of worship	23.7	8.3
is a regular churchgoer	12.0	2.8
frequently receives communion	23.4	2.8
attends church at Christmas	22.7	5.6
encourages his/her children to attend church/Sunday school	26.7	0.0
supports the church financially	5.3	0.0
regularly receives communion	21.6	0.0
religious belief		
finds God in Jesus	70.1	36.1
believes that God exists	87.0	83.8
loves God	76.6	58.3
believes in Jesus	85.7	61.1
follows God's word	66.2	47.2
believes that he/she will enter heaven through Christ	63.6	16.7
believes that Jesus is worthy of worship	74.0	47.2
believes in the resurrection of Jesus	75.0	25.0
believes that Jesus is the Son of God	77.6	47.2
personal spirituality		
is humble	18.4	10.8
prays to God (individual prayer)	50.6	27.0
has committed his/her life to Christ	48.1	13.5
tells other people about Christianity	30.3	8.1
has received the Holy Spirit	42.1	14.3
reads the Bible	24.7	8.3
believes that he/she has been saved	40.0	5.6
seeks to know God better through reading the Bible	23.4	8.3
allows the Spirit to change his/her life	44.7	8.3
personal morality/relationships		
is considerate of others' feelings and views	40.3	43.2
is friendly	27.3	13.5
is hopeful	24.7	22.2
tries to treat people equally	43.4	31.4
helps others	36.4	31.4
tries to lead a good life	46.8	44.4
forgives other people	62.3	41.7
orients his/her life towards the needs of others	14.5	11.4
is a good person	27.6	36.1

of being a Christian. More surprisingly, weekly churchgoers also seem to ascribe a relatively marginal role to these practices, with half (51%) feeling that individual prayer is essential and a quarter (25%) feeling that Bible reading is essential.

Fourth, there is much closer convergence between weekly churchgoers and young people who never attend church in their views regarding the personal morality/relationships which characterizes a Christian. Thus, around two-fifths of both groups regard as an essential component of being a Christian the quality of being considerate of others' feelings and views. Slightly more than two-fifths of both groups regard the quality of trying to lead a good life as an essential marker of a Christian. More non-churchgoers (36%) regard being a good person to be an essential characteristic of a Christian, compared with 28% of those who attend church weekly.

Table 7   Scale scores by self perceived status as a Christian

scale	affirmed mean	sd	not affirmed mean	sd	F	P<
public practice	28.2	8.0	23.3	6.4	19.9	.001
religious belief	41.0	5.2	37.6	6.5	16.7	.001
personal spirituality	32.6	7.8	27.9	7.4	17.2	.001
personal morality/relationships	36.4	5.2	34.6	7.7	3.7	NS

Tables 7 and 8 present a similar model of analysis to explore the differences in perceptions of what is a Christian held by young people who clearly identify themselves as being a Christian and those who do not identify themselves as a Christian. Two main features emerge from these tables in comparison with the information presented in tables 5 and 6. First, both sets of tables reveal the same basic points of difference in perception. Young people who classify themselves as Christians, like young churchgoers, are more likely to give salience to descriptors concerned with the public practice of religion, religious belief and personal spirituality. Overall, they do not differ significantly from young people who do not claim the epithet 'Christian' for themselves in relationship to the emphasis they place on personal morality/relationships as essential descriptors of a Christian. Second,

Table 8   Descriptors rated as 'essential or very important' by self perceived
status as a Christian

scale items	yes %	no %
public practice		
is baptized	23.1	6.2
supports church activities	9.3	4.9
goes to a place of worship	15.3	11.3
is a regular churchgoer	7.7	2.5
frequently receives communion	16.1	1.2
attends church at Christmas	16.9	3.8
encourages his/her children to attend church/Sunday school	18.8	2.5
supports the church financially	3.4	0.0
regularly receives communion	15.4	0.0
religious belief		
finds God in Jesus	61.0	41.3
believes that God exists	83.9	80.2
loves God	73.7	63.0
believes in Jesus	81.4	64.2
follows God's word	61.0	41.3
believes that he/she will enter heaven through Christ	58.5	38.3
believes that Jesus is worthy of worship	70.3	46.3
believes in the resurrection of Jesus	65.3	33.8
believes that Jesus is the Son of God	72.0	47.5
personal spirituality		
is humble	13.7	12.3
prays to God (individual prayer)	44.1	30.0
has committed his/her life to Christ	39.8	24.7
tells other people about Christianity	21.2	7.5
has received the Holy Spirit	31.6	12.7
reads the Bible	20.3	9.9
believes that he/she has been saved	29.9	12.5
seeks to know God better through reading the Bible	18.6	11.1
allows the Spirit to change his/her life	34.2	8.8
personal morality/relationships		
is considerate of others' feelings and views	35.6	38.3
is friendly	22.9	22.2
is hopeful	19.5	17.5
tries to treat people equally	39.3	31.3
helps others	33.9	41.3
tries to lead a good life	47.0	37.0
forgives other people	57.6	46.9
orients his/her life towards the needs of others	14.5	15.2
is a good person	31.4	34.2

however, comparison between the two sets of tables makes it clear that the public practice of the faith through personal church attendance is a stronger predictor of individual differences in perception of what it is that characterizes a Christian than the personal ownership of the epithet Christian itself. In other words, it is regular association with the worshipping practices of the Christian community that has the strongest influence on the young person's perceptions of 'what is a Christian'.

CONCLUSION

This study has examined the way in which a sample of 202 16- to 19-year-old pupils conceptualize what it means to be a Christian. Analyses of the data demonstrate three key features of this conception.

First, factor analysis confirms the view that there are four main dimensions underlying contemporary understanding of what it means to be a Christian. These dimensions have been characterized as *religious belief, personal spirituality, public practice* and *personal morality/ relationships*.

Second, examination of the responses to the individual items which illustrate the four main dimensions confirms the view that, in today's secular society, personal and individual aspects of religiosity emerge as more salient descriptors of what it means to be a Christian than public and communal expressions of religiosity. Much more importance is given to religious beliefs than to church attendance as essential characteristics of being a Christian.

Third, comparison of the responses of the subjects who attend church weekly with those who never attend church confirms the view that these two groups hold very different ideas about what it means to be a Christian. For example, public expressions of religiosity play very little part in the non-churchgoing respondents' understanding of what it means to be a Christian.

Important pointers emerge from this study for further research into adolescents' understanding of what it means to be a Christian. The 36 item four-dimensional index developed in the present study is now ready for re-application in other projects. In particular appropriately designed studies could now employ this index to model the relationships between views on what it means to be a Christian and such factors as attitudes towards Christianity; to assess the differences in understanding among pupils' educated in county, Church of

England or Catholic schools; and to monitor the impact of curriculum materials in promoting understanding of what it means to be a Christian. Similar research also needs to be undertaken to develop measures of adolescents' understanding of what it means to be a member of other faith communities.

Important pointers also emerge from this study for the practice and content of religious education. The data clearly demonstrate that there is considerable uncertainty and ignorance among 16- to 19-year-olds regarding what it means to be a Christian. Given the religious provisions of the 1988 Education Reform Act, there remains an urgent need to improve teaching about the Christian tradition within religious education, through curriculum development and in-service training of teachers. The present study not only sharpens perception of the need, but provides a method for assessing the effectiveness of remedies implemented.

REFERENCES

Bailey, E. I. (1986), 'The religion of the people', in T. Moss (ed), *In Search of Christianity*, London: Firethorn Press, pp 178-188.

Batson, C. D. and Ventis, W. L. (1982), *The Religious Experience*, New York: Oxford University Press.

British Council of Churches (1989), *Worship in Education*, London: British Council of Churches.

Cooling, M. (1990), *Assemblies for Primary Schools*, Exeter: Religious and Moral Education Press.

Cronbach, L. J. (1951), 'Coefficient alpha and the internal structure of tests', *Psychometrika*, Vol. 16, pp 297-334.

Department of Education and Science (1989), *The Education Reform Act 1988: religious education and collective worship*, London: DES, circular 3/89.

Francis, L. J. (1987), 'The decline in attitudes towards religion among 8-15 year olds', *Educational Studies*, Vol. 13, pp 125-134.

Francis, L. J. (1989a), 'Drift from the churches: secondary school pupils' attitudes towards Christianity', *British Journal of Religious Education*, Vol. 11, pp 76-86.

Francis, L. J. (1989b), 'Monitoring changing attitudes towards Christianity among secondary school pupils between 1974 and 1986', *British Journal of Educational Psychology*, Vol. 59, pp 86-91.

Gilbert, A. D. (1980), *The Making of Post-Christian Britain*, London: Longman.

Glock, C. Y. and Stark, R. (1965), *Religion and Society in Tension*, Chicago: Rand McNally.

Habgood, J. S. (1983), *Church and Nation in a Secular Age*, London: Darton, Longman and Todd.

Hull, J. M. (1989), *The Act Unpacked*, London: Christian Education Movement.

King, M. B. and Hunt, R. A. (1975), 'Measuring the religious variable: national replication', *Journal for the Scientific Study of Religion*, Vol. 14, pp 13-22.

Smart, N. (1969), *The Religious Experience of Mankind*, New York: Charles Scribner's Sons.

SPSS Inc (1988), *SPSSX User's Guide*, New York: McGraw-Hill.

Wilson, B. (1982), *Religion in Sociological Perspective*, Oxford: Oxford University Press.

APPENDIX

Table 1   Factor pattern proposed by varimax rotated solution

item	factor 1	factor 2	factor 3	factor 4
finds God in Jesus	.11	**.63**	.16	.32
is baptized	**.53**	.20	.04	.10
is considerate of others' feelings and views	-.13	.10	**.74**	.06
is humble	.04	.02	.41	**.52**
is friendly	.01	.01	**.80**	.05
prays to God (individual prayer)	.10	.29	-.04	**.60**
believes that God exists	-.05	**.73**	-.07	.13
supports church activities	**.61**	.07	.10	.15
has committed his/her life to Christ	.18	.33	.07	**.71**
tells other people about Christianity	.32	.19	.06	**.66**
goes to a place of worship	**.76**	.09	-.12	.18
loves God	.11	**.62**	.13	.36
is a regular churchgoer	**.79**	.06	-.06	.24
has received the Holy Spirit	.43	.31	.01	**.48**
reads the Bible	.33	.19	.02	**.70**
frequently receives communion	**.76**	.18	-.07	.20
attends church at Christmas	**.74**	.01	.05	-.07
encourages his/her children to attend church/ Sunday school	**.73**	.11	.09	.18
believes in Jesus	.06	**.79**	.12	.17
follows God's word	.16	**.69**	.16	.34
is hopeful	.26	.23	**.59**	.11
supports the church financially	**.65**	.01	.11	.29
believes he/she has been saved	.30	.24	.06	**.62**
regularly receives communion	**.79**	.24	.01	.16
tries to treat people equally	.01	.10	**.84**	.03
seeks to know God better through reading the Bible	.26	.20	.16	**.65**
helps others	.03	-.03	**.74**	.08
believes that he/she will enter heaven through Christ	.25	**.68**	.10	.07
tries to lead a good life	.13	.22	**.68**	-.03
believes that Jesus is worthy of worship	.05	**.67**	.19	.24
forgives other people	.01	.11	**.73**	.29
believes in the resurrection of Jesus	.39	**.62**	-.05	.23
allows the Spirit to change his/her life	.15	.42	.09	**.69**
orients his/her life towards the needs of others	-.16	.04	**.62**	.37
is a good person	.06	-.06	**.72**	-.19
believes that Jesus is the Son of God	.21	**.77**	.03	.11

Table 3   Correlation matrix

	personal morality/ relationships	personal spirituality	religious belief
public practice	+0.1060 NS	+0.5486 .001	+0.3777 .001
religious belief	+0.1982 .01	+0.6605 .001	
personal spirituality	+0.2584 .001		

23

Christianity Today: The Teenage Experience

LESLIE J. FRANCIS

WORDS INTO ACTION

The prominence given to Christianity in the religious clauses of the 1988 Education Act is reflected in a new generation of religious education programmes produced by BBC Schools Television, first through the series *Words into Action* developed in association with the Christian Education Movement (Lealman, 1988) and more recently through the series *Christianity in Today's World* developed in association with the Christianity in RE Programme (Lazenby, 1991).

As part of the fundamental research underlying the *Words into Action* series, the production team undertook a review of recent and relevant studies into teenage attitudes towards Christianity, as exampled by Francis (1989a, 1989b), and included reference to such empirical findings in the programmes. A key aim of this exercise was to reflect back to teenage viewers the views of their peers.

At the same time the *Words into Action* production team recognized that it would be helpful to enable individual teachers to undertake their own surveys among the pupils in their school. With this end in mind, Leslie Francis was asked to design a self-completion questionnaire for publication in the teachers' handbook (Lealman, 1988) which accompanied the television programmes. Teachers were invited to use the questionnaire to discover what their school or class thought about the Christian faith today and to employ the findings as a resource for their own teaching.

This questionnaire contained two main sections. The first section used multiple choice questions to profile the pupils' age, sex, background, religious affiliation and religious practice. It included questions on denomination, prayer, Bible reading, and various aspects of church attendance. The second section used Likert type questions, according to which the pupils were invited to express their level of agreement with clear well-focused statements on a five point scale, ranging from 'agree strongly', through 'agree', 'not certain' and 'disagree', to 'disagree strongly' (Likert, 1932).

The sixty-two attitude statements incorporated in the questionnaire were designed to produce information about the pupils' attitudinal response to eight main issues or concepts: God, Jesus, prayer, church, Christians, science and religious education, science and the Bible, and personal wellbeing. All the statements had been previously employed in other research studies and were known to function appropriately among pupils of the secondary school age range. In particular, the battery of questions included the twenty-four item scale of attitude towards Christianity developed by Francis (1978, 1989c) and employed in a wide range of other studies. The inclusion of this scale enables the new findings to be compared more generally and to be anchored within a wider context.

Through the teachers' handbook the Christian Education Movement also invited teachers to send in their completed questionnaires so that information could be assembled from a number of schools, professionally analysed, and the findings made more generally available. A number of teachers accepted this invitation, and the present report is written on the basis of the first schools to have submitted data for analysis.

It needs to be stressed that a sample built up in this way does not constitute a representative sample of schools or of pupils. It is dangerous, therefore, to generalize too confidently from these findings to the more general situation. Nevertheless, the replies have come from a sufficiently wide range of geographical areas and social backgrounds to encourage considerable confidence to be placed in them.

The results are presented here with two particular purposes in mind. First, a general overview is presented of the views of all the pupils whose questionnaires have been processed. When other schools now invite their pupils to complete the questionnaire, they can compare their situation with these published findings. On this basis they can judge whether their pupils hold a more or less favourable attitude towards Christianity than the pupils who participated in the present survey. Second, some careful comparisons are made to explore the relationships between attitudes towards Christianity and such factors as sex, age, and church attendance. Such comparisons are robust and provide insights into the personal and social correlates of adolescent religiosity which can be generalized with greater confidence to young people in general.

The questionnaire itself is able to generate considerably more information than the present paper is able to report. Further analyses will emerge in due course. It is also important to recognize that the conceptual areas in which the attitude items have been grouped for the present paper represent only one framework through which the empirical data may be usefully presented.

THE RESPONDENTS

The first batch of questionnaires prepared for analysis provided information on 3,863 pupils from all over England. These respondents comprised 1,706 males and 2,157 females, 766 12-year-olds, 802 13-year-olds, 958 14-year-olds, 955 15-year-olds and 382 16-year-olds. Pupils below or above this age range were not included in these initial analyses.

Four out of every nine (45%) of the respondents claimed to have no denominational affiliation. The majority of those who identified with a Christian denomination mentioned the Church of England (38%), with 5% mentioning the Roman Catholic church and 12% mentioning one of the Free Churches. Pupils affiliated to other world religions were not included in these initial analyses.

Two-fifths (40%) of the respondents claimed never to have contact with the churches on a Sunday. Just under two-fifths (36%) claimed to have occasional contact, and nearly a quarter (24%) claimed to have regular contact by attending services at least once a month.

A similar pattern emerged in relationship to personal prayer. Two-fifths (41%) of the respondents claimed never to pray. A further two-fifths (39%) claimed to pray from time to time, and the remaining one-fifth (21%) claimed to pray regularly, at least once a week.

Considerably fewer of the respondents read the Bible than have contact with the churches or pray. Three-fifths (59%) of them claimed never to read the Bible, while only one-in-twenty (5%) claimed to read the Bible as regularly as once a week. The remaining 36% claimed to read the Bible occasionally.

ATTITUDE TOWARDS GOD

Table 1.1 presents an overview for the whole sample in relationship to the seven items concerned with God.

Table 1.1 Attitude towards God: overview

	Agree %	Not Certain %	Disagree %
I believe in God	56	31	13
Most of my best friends believe in God	29	38	33
I know that God helps me	32	41	27
God is very real to me	31	37	32
I feel that my life is being guided by God	19	37	44
Sometimes I am very aware of God's presence	22	38	41
I find it hard to believe in God	33	25	43

This table demonstrates that between half and three-fifths (56%) of the 12- to 16-year-old respondents professed belief in God. Just under a third of them claimed to be agnostic and about one-in-eight (13%) claimed to be atheist. The fact that such a high proportion of young people believe in God would come as a surprise to many of the respondents. The statistics show that young people are much more likely to believe in God themselves than to imagine that their friends believe in God. To confess belief in God may, therefore, be unnecessarily unfashionable in teenage culture.

Considerably more young people believe in God than are able to immediately recognize the presence or influence of God in their daily lives. Thus, while nearly three-fifths (56%) believed in God, only one-fifth felt that his or her life is being guided by God (19%) or experienced awareness of God's presence. Just under a third of them claimed that God is very real to them (31%) or expressed knowledge that God helps them (32%).

Another significant feature of these statistics concerns the large number of pupils who check the 'not certain' category. More young people are unclear, for example, of how real God is to them than give outright rejection to the proposition. Clearly young people need to be enabled to think more clearly about such issues and to come to their own decisions.

Table 1.2 presents the differences in responses between male and female pupils in their attitude towards God. As is consistent with much research in the psychology of religion (Argyle and Beit-Hallahmi, 1975; Brown, 1987), females are much more inclined to demonstrate belief in God than males. The statistics also demonstrate that females

Table 1.2   Attitude towards God: sex differences

	Male % agree	Female % agree	P<
I believe in God	48	62	***
Most of my best friends believe in God	20	36	***
I know that God helps me	23	38	***
God is very real to me	25	36	***
I feel that my life is being guided by God	16	21	***
Sometimes I am very aware of God's presence	19	25	***
I find it hard to believe in God	38	27	***

Note: In this and the following tables statistical significance levels are expressed:
* = P<.05;   ** = P<.01;   ***= P<.001

are more likely to be aware of God's presence and to feel that their life is being guided by God. They are more likely than males to feel that God is very real to them and to experience God's help in their lives. Females are also more likely to believe that their best friends believe in God.

Table 1.3 presents the differences in responses between 12-year-old and 15-year-old pupils in their attitude towards God. As is consistent with much research in the psychology of religious development (Mark, 1982; Francis, 1987a), the older subjects are significantly less likely to express belief in God, to experience God's presence or guidance in their daily lives, or to be aware of the reality of God. They are also significantly less likely to imagine that their best friends believe in God.

Table 1.4 presents the relationship between frequency of church attendance and attitude towards God. The comparison is made between those who never attend church, those who attend less frequently than once a month and those who attend regularly at least once a month. Although attitude and practice are properly studied as distinct dimensions of religiosity, much previous research has confirmed the importance of church attendance in predicting religious attitudes among children (Francis, 1987b), young people (Francis, 1982a) and adults (Francis, 1982b). The present data

Table 1.3   Attitude towards God: age differences

	12 years % agree	15 years % agree	P<
I believe in God	62	53	***
Most of my best friends believe in God	37	24	***
I know that God helps me	41	28	***
God is very real to me	43	27	***
I feel that my life is being guided by God	24	17	***
Sometimes I am very aware of God's presence	26	20	***
I find it hard to believe in God	29	34	***

are clearly consistent with this trend. They also serve to highlight the importance of distinguishing between attitude and practice. For example, as many as one-in-seven (14%) regular churchgoers was unsure of his or her belief in God, while as many as one-in-three (34%) young people who never go to church was firm in his or her belief in God. Similarly, as many as three-fifths (57%) of the young people who regularly attend church had little awareness of God's presence in their lives, while one in ten (11%) of the young people who never attend church was very aware of God's presence.

Table 1.4   Attitude towards God: relationship with church attendance

	never %	sometimes %	monthly %	P<
I believe in God	34	61	8	***
Most of my best friends believe in God	19	30	44	***
I know that God helps me	15	30	63	***
God is very real to me	15	31	59	***
I feel that my life is being guided by God	8	15	43	***
Sometimes I am very aware of God's presence	11	20	43	***
I find it hard to believe in God	46	27	19	***

ATTITUDE TOWARDS JESUS

Table 2.1 presents an overview for the whole sample in relationship to the six items concerned with Jesus. This table demonstrates that attitude towards Jesus follows a very similar pattern to attitude towards God. In both cases just under three-fifths believed in God or believed that Jesus is the Son of God; just under a third were agnostic about belief in God or about belief that Jesus Christ is the Son of God. In both cases just under a third knew that God helps them or knew that Jesus helps them; about two-fifths were unclear about whether God or Jesus helps them; just over a quarter denied that God helps them or that Jesus helps them.

Table 2.1   Attitude towards Jesus: overview

	Agree %	Not Certain %	Disagree %
I believe that Jesus Christ is the Son of God	57	29	14
I believe that Jesus really rose from the dead	40	39	21
I know that Jesus helps me	31	41	28
I know that Jesus is very close to me	26	40	34
I want to love Jesus	33	36	31
Jesus doesn't mean anything to me	17	26	57

Young people find the resurrection of Jesus considerably more difficult to believe in than the theological idea that Jesus is the Son of God. While nearly three-fifths (57%) of the respondents professed belief that Jesus is the Son of God, the proportion fell to two-fifths (40%) who professed belief that Jesus really rose from the dead.

The statistics also show that comparatively few of the respondents had adopted a really negative attitude towards Jesus. About one-in-six (17%) agreed with the negative statement that Jesus did not mean anything to him or her, while more than three times this number (57%) firmly rejected such a statement.

Table 2.2 presents the differences in responses between male and female pupils in their attitude towards Jesus. These sex differences demonstrate that females were more likely to believe that Jesus really rose from the dead and that he is the Son of God. They were more likely than males to experience the closeness of Jesus and his help in their lives. The were more likely to express commitment to love Jesus.

Table 2.2 Attitude towards Jesus: sex differences

	Male % agree	Female % agree	P<
I believe that Jesus Christ is the Son of God	48	65	***
I believe that Jesus really rose from the dead	32	46	***
I know that Jesus helps me	24	37	***
I know that Jesus is very close to me	20	31	***
I want to love Jesus	25	39	***
Jesus doesn't mean anything to me	26	11	***

Table 2.3 presents the differences in responses between 12-year-old and 15-year-old pupils in their attitude towards Jesus. These age differences demonstrate that the older age group was less likely to express a positive attitude towards Jesus than the younger age group.

Table 2.3 Attitude towards Jesus: age differences

	12 years % agree	15 years % agree	P<
I believe that Jesus Christ is the Son of God	64	55	***
I believe that Jesus really rose from the dead	44	37	***
I know that Jesus helps me	44	26	***
I know that Jesus is very close to me	37	23	`***
I want to love Jesus	44	28	***
Jesus doesn't mean anything to me	14	18	***

The statistics also suggest that there is a greater decline in the proportion of pupils between the two age groups who express positive experience of Jesus than in the proportion of pupils who express belief in Jesus. For every six 12-year-olds who believed that Jesus really rose from the dead, there were five 15-year-olds who believed the same thing, while for every six 12-year-olds who felt that Jesus is close to them, there were only four 15-year-olds who felt the same way.

Table 2.4 presents the relationship between frequency of church attendance and attitude towards Jesus. These statistics confirm the extent of residual Christian belief outside the churches. Nearly two in every five young people who never attend church acknowledged Jesus as the Son of God and one-in-five of them shared the belief that Jesus really rose from the dead. One-in-seven of the young people who never attend church expressed the wish to love Jesus. Two-thirds of the young people who never attend church clearly refused to accept the idea that Jesus does not mean anything to them.

Table 2.4   Attitude towards Jesus: relationship with church attendance

	never %	sometimes %	monthly %	P<
I believe that Jesus Christ is the Son of God	38	63	84	***
I believe that Jesus really rose from the dead	21	42	68	***
I know that Jesus helps me	15	30	62	***
I know that Jesus is very close to me	11	25	55	***
I want to love Jesus	14	33	64	***
Jesus doesn't mean anything to me	32	10	4	***

At the same time, these statistics also confirm the extent to which traditional christological belief is alien to some young churchgoers. One-in-six young regular churchgoers was not willing to own the credal statement that Jesus Christ is the Son of God. One-in-three young regular churchgoers was not willing to ascribe to the belief that Jesus really rose from the dead. Between one-third and one-half of the young regular churchgoers were unclear about the personal experience of Jesus in their lives.

ATTITUDE TOWARDS PRAYER

Table 3.1 presents an overview of the whole sample in relationship to the six items concerned with prayer. This table demonstrates that nearly half (47%) of the 12- to 16-year-old respondents believed that God listens to prayers, compared with one-fifth (21%) who did not believe that this is the case. The other third (33%) did not know what

Table 3.1 Attitude towards prayer: overview

	Agree %	Not Certain %	Disagree %
I believe that God listens to prayers	47	33	21
Most of my best friends believe in prayer	16	40	45
Saying my prayers helps me a lot	31	30	39
Prayer helps me a lot	30	30	40
I think saying prayers in school does no good	32	33	35
I think people who pray are stupid	5	11	84

to believe about this issue. Only one-in-three of the young people who believed that God listens to prayers themselves reckoned that their best friends also believe that God listens to prayers. These figures continue to demonstrate the extent to which young believers feel that they are different from their friends. Such feelings of differences easily promote reticence about faith and may lead to the suppression of faith.

These statistics also indicate that for every three young people who believed that God listens to prayers, only two derived personal benefit or help from prayer. For every three young people who derived personal benefit or help from prayer, four were quite clear that prayer was of no help to them at all and another three kept an open mind on the matter.

Although the young people who felt that they derive help from prayer are clearly in the minority, very few were totally disparaging of prayer and dismissed people who pray as stupid (5%). If the majority of 12- to 16-year-olds remain somewhat sceptical about prayer, they also seem to respect the right of others to believe in a more positive way.

Table 3.2 presents the differences in responses between male and female pupils in their attitude towards prayer. These sex differences

Table 3.2   Attitude towards prayer: sex differences

	Male % agree	Female % agree	P<
I believe that God listens to prayers	36	55	***
Most of my best friends believe in prayer	9	21	***
Saying my prayers helps me a lot	22	38	***
Prayer helps me a lot	21	38	***
I think saying prayers in school does no good	36	28	***
I think people who pray are stupid	10	26	***

demonstrate that females were much more likely to believe that God listens to prayers. They were more likely than males to feel that they derive personal benefit from prayer. They were more likely to assume that most of their best friends believe in prayer. They were less likely to dismiss people who pray as being stupid.

Table 3.3 presents the differences and responses between 12-year-old and 15-year-old pupils in their attitude towards prayer. These age differences demonstrate that the older age group was less likely to believe that God listens to prayers and less likely to derive personal benefit from prayer. Pupils in the older age group were much less likely to believe that their best friends believe in prayer, but they were

Table 3.3   Attitude towards prayer: age differences

	12 years % agree	15 years % agree	P<
I believe that God listens to prayers	55	43	***
Most of my best friends believe in prayer	21	13	***
Saying my prayers helps me a lot	35	31	***
Prayer helps me a lot	36	28	***
I think saying prayers in school does no good	23	37	***
I think people who pray are stupid	5	7	

not significantly more likely to dismiss people who pray as stupid. These statistics also show a significant hardening of attitude towards saying prayers in school among the older age group.

Table 3.4 presents the relationship between frequency of church attendance and attitude towards prayer. Once again these statistics confirm the presence of clear religious belief among young people

Table 3.4   Attitude towards prayer: relationship with church attendance

	never %	sometimes %	monthly %	P<
I believe that God listens to prayers	28	49	76	***
Most of my best friends believe in prayer	8	16	28	***
Saying my prayers helps me a lot	16	31	55	***
Prayer helps me a lot	15	30	57	***
I think saying prayers in school does no good	44	26	20	***
I think people who pray are stupid	10	3	2	***

who never associate themselves with the churches. More than one-in-four (28%) of the young people who never attend church nonetheless believed that God listens to prayers and one-in-six (16%) of them derived help from praying.

At the same time one-in-four (24%) of the regular churchgoers remained unconvinced that God listens to prayers and about one-in-two (45%) of them remained unconvinced that prayer actually helps them. It is also interesting to note that between two-thirds and three-quarters (72%) of the regular churchgoers felt that most of their best friends do not believe in prayer.

These statistics also draw attention to the relationship between church attendance and attitude towards saying prayers in school. School worship and church worship clearly remain associated in pupils' minds. However, the relationship is not that close. It is by no means the case that school prayers were supported by all regular churchgoers. One-in-five regular churchgoers voted clearly against the value of school prayers.

ATTITUDE TOWARDS CHURCH

Table 4.1 presents an overview for the whole sample in relationship to the seven items concerned with church. This table demonstrates that young people in general have a much less positive attitude towards the church than towards belief in God or the practice of prayer. It is clear from these statistics that the Sunday worship of the church is seen by many young people as boring or unimportant. Half (50%) of the respondents dismissed church services as boring, twice as many as those who felt that church services were not boring (28%). Nearly half (46%) of the respondents dismissed the church as unimportant to them, twice as many as those who felt that the church was important to them (22%). Three-fifths (62%) of the respondents felt clear that most of their best friends do not go to church, more than three times as many as those who felt clear that most of their best friends go to church (18%).

Table 4.1 Attitude towards church: overview

	Agree %	Not Certain %	Disagree %
The church is very important to me	22	32	46
Most of my best friends go to church	18	20	62
I think going to church is a waste of my time	23	27	50
I think church services are boring	50	22	28
People who go to church are hypocrites	7	16	77
I want to get married in church	83	13	4
I want my children to be baptized/ christened in church	66	21	12

In spite of not having a high regard for the church themselves, the majority of young people adopt a sympathetic attitude towards churchgoers. For every young person who accused churchgoers of being hypocrites, eleven young people clearly distanced themselves from this view and two others refused to align themselves with it.

The statistics also demonstrate that young people continue to have a high regard for some of the social functions of the Christian churches and for the churches' involvement in the major rites of passage. Four out of every five (83%) 12- to 16-year-olds professed that they want to get married in church and two out of every three (66%) professed that they want their children baptized or christened in church.

Table 4.2 presents the differences in responses between male and female pupils in their attitude towards church. These sex differences demonstrate that females hold a less negative attitude towards the church than males. Females were more likely to think of the church as having importance to them and less likely to think of church services as boring or church attendance as a waste of time. Females were more likely than males to judge that most of their best friends go to church. While six out of every eight males (76%) said they want to get married in church, the proportion rose to seven out of every eight females (88%). While seven out of every twelve males (57%) said that they want to have their children baptized or christened in church, the proportion rose to nine out of every twelve females (73%).

Table 4.2   Attitude towards church: sex differences

	Male % agree	Female % agree	P<
The church is very important to me	18	25	***
Most of my best friends go to church	13	22	***
I think going to church is a waste of my time	31	16	***
I think church services are boring	58	43	***
People who go to church are hypocrites	11	4	***
I want to get married in church	76	88	***
I want my children to be baptized/ christened in church	57	73	***

Table 4.3 presents the differences in response between 12-year-old and 15-year-old pupils in their attitude towards church. These age differences demonstrate a considerable hardening in attitude towards the worship of the church during this three year age span. While 38% of the younger age group considered church services to be boring, the proportion rose to 54% among the older age group. While 30% of the younger age group considered the church important to them, the proportion fell to 19% among the older age group. While one-in-four (23%) of the younger age group judged that most of their best friends go to church, the proportion fell to one-in-six (15%) among the older age group. This growing alienation from the church, however, is not reflected in a greater rejection of the churches' role in the major rites of passage. More than four-fifths (82%) of the 15-year-olds still

Table 4.3   Attitude towards church: age differences

	12 years % agree	15 years % agree	P<
The church is very important to me	30	19	***
Most of my best friends go to church	23	15	***
I think going to church is a waste of my time	18	25	***
I think church services are boring	38	54	***
People who go to church are hypocrites	7	8	
I want to get married in church	83	82	
I want my children to be baptized/ christened in church	67	64	**

expressed the desire to get married in church and almost two-thirds (64%) of them still expressed the desire to have their children baptized or christened in church.

Table 4.4 presents the relationship between frequency of church attendance and attitude towards church. These statistics confirm the expected relationship between religious practice and religious attitude.

Table 4.4   Attitude towards church: relationship with church attendance

	never %	sometimes %	monthly %	P<
The church is very important to me	5	16	56	***
Most of my best friends go to church	6	16	41	***
I think going to church is a waste of my time	40	15	6	***
I think church services are boring	66	48	27	***
People who go to church are hypocrites	11	4	4	***
I want to get married in church	74	87	91	***
I want my children to be baptized/ christened in church	49	74	84	***

Young people who never attend church hold a much more negative view of the church than those who attend regularly. Two out of every three (66%) non-attenders hold the firm image of church services as boring. Nonetheless, comparatively few non-attenders (11%) dismissed those who do attend church as hypocrites. Three-quarters (74%) of the non-attenders still wanted to get married in church and half (49%) of the non-attenders still wanted to have their own children baptized or christened in church. The statistics also reveal discontent with the church among regular attenders. Over a quarter (27%) of the young people who attend church at least once a month reported that they were bored by the services they attend. Over two-fifths (44%) of the young people who attend church at least once a month clearly did not affirm that the church is very important to them. A significant minority of the regular attenders were not clear that they wished to get married in church (9%) or to have their children baptized or christened in church (16%).

These statistics also confirm the role of church attendance in the formation of peer relationships. Thus, 41% of the regular attenders felt that most of their best friends go to church, compared with 16% of the occasional attenders and 6% of those who never attend. According to these data young people who never attend church themselves appear very unlikely to form close friendships with young people who are churchgoers.

ATTITUDE TOWARDS CHRISTIANS

Table 5.1 presents an overview for the whole sample in relationship to the six items concerned with Christians. This table demonstrates that

Table 5.1   Attitude towards Christians: overview

	Agree %	Not Certain %	Disagree %
People who believe in God are more honest	32	27	41
People who believe in God are kinder to others	32	31	37
People who believe in God live happier lives	26	34	40
Christians do not smoke	6	15	79
Christians do not drink	5	16	79
Christians do not swear	10	17	73

a significant minority of young people feel that the Christian faith promotes good personal qualities among its adherents. Between a quarter and a third of the sample thought that people who believe in God live happier lives, are kinder to others, and are more honest. A larger proportion of the sample, around two-fifths, was clear that this is not the case, and about a third was uncertain.

At the same time these statistics also demonstrate that only a handful of young people hold a 'holier than thou' view of Christian believers. Very few of the sample hold to the view that Christians do not smoke, drink, or swear, with between three-quarters and four-fifths of the young people making it clear that they do not associate this kind of abstinence with Christians today. In other words, considerably more young people hold a positive view of the influence of Christianity on people's lives than hold a negative view.

Table 5.2   Attitude towards Christians: sex differences

	Male % agree	Female % agree	P<
People who believe in God are more honest	35	29	**
People who believe in God are kinder to others	36	29	***
People who believe in God live happier lives	27	26	*
Christians do not smoke	7	4	***
Christians do not drink	6	4	
Christians do not swear	11	9	

Table 5.2 presents the differences in responses between male and female pupils in their attitude towards Christians. These sex differences demonstrate that males were more likely to believe that religion has a positive influence on people's lives, in the sense of making them more honest, kinder and happier. They were also more likely than females to believe that Christians do not smoke, although sex differences were not significant in relationship to the proportions of young people who perceived Christians as neither drinking nor swearing.

Table 5.3 presents the differences in responses between 12-year-old and 15-year-old pupils in their attitude towards Christians. These

Table 5.3   Attitude towards Christians: age differences

	12 years % agree	15 years % agree	P<
People who believe in God are more honest	44	25	***
People who believe in God are kinder to others	42	25	***
People who believe in God live happier lives	37	22	***
Christians do not smoke	11	4	***
Christians do not drink	8	4	***
Christians do not swear	16	7	***

age differences demonstrate that the older age group was significantly less likely to maintain that religion has an impact on the personal lives of believers. While more than two-fifths of the 12-year-olds considered that people who believe in God are more honest or kinder to others, the proportion fell to one-quarter of the 15-year-olds. Similarly, less than half the number of 15-year-olds believe that Christians do not drink, smoke and swear than is the case among the 12-year-olds.

Table 5.4   Attitude towards Christians: relationship with church attendance

	never %	sometimes %	monthly %	P<
People who believe in God are more honest	28	31	38	***
People who believe in God are kinder to others	26	31	41	***
People who believe in God live happier lives	16	24	48	***
Christians do not smoke	7	5	5	**
Christians do not drink	6	4	5	***
Christians do not swear	10	8	11	

Table 5.4 presents the relationship between frequency of church attendance and attitude towards Christians. These statistics demon-

strate a positive relationship between frequency of church attendance and the view that religion promotes personal life satisfaction and pro-social attitudes. For every two non-churchgoers who maintained that people who believe in God live happier lives, this view was held by three occasional attenders and by six regular attenders. For every three non-churchgoers who maintained that people who believe in God are kinder to others, this view was held by four occasional attenders and by five regular attenders.

On the other hand, churchgoers were less likely than non-church-goers to believe that Christians neither smoke nor drink. Being on the inside of the faith themselves, churchgoers may be in a position to make more realistic judgements about the implications of Christianity for personal living. At the same time, the statistics demonstrate that regular churchgoers are more likely to regard swearing as something from which Christians abstain than either drinking or smoking.

ATTITUDE TOWARDS SCIENCE AND RELIGIOUS EDUCATION

Table 6.1 presents an overview for the whole sample in relationship to the seven items concerned with religious education and science education. This table demonstrates just how much more interest 12- to 16-year-olds take in science education than in religious education. Overall two in every three pupils reported a positive interest in science education, compared with one-in-three who reported a positive interest in religious education. Thus, 65% claimed to be interested in science, compared with 34% who claimed to be interested in religion. Similarly, 67% reported that they liked science lessons in school,

Table 6.1   Attitude towards science and religious education: overview

	Agree %	Not Certain %	Disagree %
I am interested in religion	34	29	37
I like finding out about Christianity	31	27	43
I like finding out about the religions of the world	37	23	39
I like religious education lessons in school	31	26	43
I am interested in science	65	16	19
I like finding out about science	61	19	20
I like science lessons in school	67	13	20

compared with 34% who reported that they liked religious education lessons in school. Looked at from a different perspective, two in every five pupils were clear that they did not like religious education lessons, twice as many as were clear that they did not like science lessons in school.

Within the area of religious education itself, a slightly higher proportion of the pupils reported interest in finding out about the religions of the world (37%) than reported interest in finding out about Christianity (31%).

Table 6.2 presents the differences in responses between male and female pupils in their attitude towards religious education and science education. These sex differences confirm the consensus of earlier studies that, while females show a more positive attitude towards religious education, males show a more positive attitude towards science education (Francis, Gibson and Fulljames, 1990). Thus, more than a third of the females reported liking religious education lessons, compared with a quarter of the males. Less than two-thirds of the females reported liking science lessons, compared with three-quarters of the males. For every two males who reported an interest in religion, six reported an interest in science. By way of comparison, for every two females who reported an interest in religion, three reported an interest in science.

Table 6.2 Attitude towards science and religious education: sex differences

	Male % agree	Female % agree	P<
I am interested in religion	25	40	***
I like finding out about Christianity	24	36	***
I like finding out about the religions of the world	29	44	***
I like religious education lessons in school	24	37	***
I am interested in science	73	59	***
I like finding out about science	68	56	***
I like science lessons in school	74	62	***

Within the area of religious education, both males and females demonstrated a greater interest in finding out about the religions of the world than in finding out about Christianity.

Table 6.3 presents the differences in responses between 12-year-old and 15-year-old pupils in their attitude towards religious education and science education. These age differences confirm the consensus of earlier studies that attitude towards science education deteriorates during the years of secondary schooling as well as attitude towards religious education (Francis, Gibson and Fulljames, 1990). During the three year period represented by the present statistics, the proportion of pupils who reported liking science lessons fell from 72% to 62%; the proportion of pupils who reported liking religious education lessons fell from 42% to 29%. This hardening of attitude towards the school lessons is also reflected in a loss of interest in the subject-matter more generally. During the three year period the proportion of pupils who reported an interest in science fell from 70% to 61%; the proportion of pupils who reported an interest in religion fell from 39% to 33%.

Table 6.3   Attitude towards science and religious education: age differences

	12 years % agree	15 years % agree	P<
I am interested in religion	39	33	***
I like finding out about Christianity	39	27	***
I like finding out about the religions of the world	47	33	***
I like religious education lessons in school	42	29	***
I am interested in science	70	61	***
I like finding out about science	66	58	***
I like science lessons in school	72	62	***

Within the area of religious education itself this three year period witnessed a similar loss of interest in finding out both about Christianity and about the religions of the world. In both cases it seems that about a third of the 12-year-olds who show an interest will have lost this interest by the age of 15 years.

Table 6.4 presents the relationship between frequency of church attendance and attitude towards religious education and science education. These statistics confirm the clear relationship between church attendance and interest in religious education at school. Well over twice as many regular churchgoers reported that they liked

Table 6.4 Attitude towards science and religious education: relationship with church attendance

	never %	sometimes %	monthly %	P<
I am interested in religion	14	34	68	***
I like finding out about Christianity	12	32	61	***
I like finding out about the religions of the world	23	41	58	***
I like religious education lessons in school	19	35	46	***
I am interested in science	62	68	67	*
I like finding out about science	57	64	64	*
I like science lessons in school	64	69	69	

religious education lessons in school than pupils who never attend church. The statistics also clearly demonstrate that the interest shown by regular churchgoers in religion is not restricted to Christianity. While regular churchgoers are twice as likely as occasional churchgoers to express an interest in finding out about Christianity, they are also much more likely to express an interest in finding out about the religions of the world. While only one-in-seven of the non-churchgoers express a general interest in religion, what interest they have is twice as likely to be expressed in the religions of the world than in Christianity.

Far from detracting from interest in science, church attendance is actually associated with a greater interest in science and in finding out about science.

ATTITUDE TOWARDS SCIENCE AND THE BIBLE

Table 7.1 presents an overview for the whole sample in relationship to the seven items concerned with attitude towards science and the Bible. This table demonstrates how many young people have failed to think through clearly their understanding of the relationship between science and religion. More young people have checked the 'not certain' category in answer to the first three questions in this table than to any other questions in the survey. About half of the sample has no clear view on whether or not science has disproved religion,

Table 7.1 Attitude towards science and the Bible: overview

	Agree %	Not Certain %	Disagree %
Science has disproved religion	16	51	33
Science disproves the Bible account of creation	30	47	22
Scientific laws make miracles impossible	20	46	33
I think the Bible is out of date	22	32	47
Christians have to believe that every word of the Bible is true	20	27	53
Christians have to believe that Jesus walked on water	15	34	51
Christians have to believe that God made the world in six days and rested on the seventh	20	33	48

whether or not science disproves the Bible account of creation, or whether or not scientific laws make miracles impossible. Among those who had made up their minds on such issues, three young people had come to the conclusion that science disproves the Bible account of creation for every two who had come to the conclusion that science does not disprove the Bible account of creation. On the other hand, more rejected the view that scientific laws make miracles impossible than accepted that view.

Up to one-in-five young people perceive Christianity as being essentially fundamentalist. Thus, 20% of them imagined that Christians have to believe that every word of the Bible is true or that God made the world in six days. Overall, however, two and a half times this number of young people recognized that Christianity does not necessarily involve fundamentalism. Thus, around 50% of them understood that some Christians adopt a more liberal understanding of biblical truth. Still as many as one-in-three 12- to 16-year-olds were uncertain what Christianity implied about creation, miracles and biblical truth.

Table 7.2 presents the differences in responses between male and female pupils in their attitude towards science and the Bible. These sex differences demonstrate that females were less likely to believe that science creates difficulties for religion. They were less likely than males to have agreed that science has disproved religion, that scientific laws make miracles impossible, or that science disproves the Bible

Table 7.2   Attitude towards science and the Bible: sex differences

	Male % agree	Female % agree	P<
Science has disproved religion	22	11	***
Science disproves the Bible account of creation	38	24	***
Scientific laws make miracles impossible	28	15	***
I think the Bible is out of date	30	15	***
Christians have to believe that every word of the Bible is true	22	18	
Christians have to believe that Jesus walked on water	16	14	
Christians have to believe that God made the world in six days and rested on the seventh	21	18	

account of creation. Females were less likely to reject the Bible as out of date. On the other hand, while females were slightly less likely to endorse the view that Christians need to espouse fundamentalist views, this difference was not statistically significant.

Table 7.3   Attitude towards science and the Bible: age differences

	12 years % agree	15 years % agree	P<
Science has disproved religion	17	16	
Science disproves the Bible account of creation	27	32	**
Scientific laws make miracles impossible	22	18	**
I think the Bible is out of date	19	22	
Christians have to believe that every word of the Bible is true	29	18	***
Christians have to believe that Jesus walked on water	19	13	***
Christians have to believe that God made the world in six days and rested on the seventh	25	18	***

Table 7.3 presents the differences in responses between 12-year-old and 15-year-old pupils in their attitudes towards science and the Bible. These age differences demonstrate that the older age group was less likely to imagine that Christians had to endorse a fundamentalist view of Scripture. It seems that one in every three 12-year-olds who hold to this view of what it means to be a Christian had adopted a more open view by the age of 15 years. On the other hand, no consistent changes have taken place between the ages of 12 and 15 years in relationship to perceptions about the conflict between science and religion. If 15-year-olds were slightly less likely to believe that scientific laws made miracles impossible, they were also slightly more likely to believe that science disproves the Bible account of creation. No change takes place between these two age groups in the proportions of young people who believed that science has disproved religion.

Table 7.4 presents the relationship between frequency of church attendance and attitude towards science and the Bible. These statistics demonstrate a complex relationship between church attendance and attitudes towards science and the Bible. To begin with, regular churchgoers are no less likely than non-churchgoers to believe that Christians have to accept the biblical account of creation. At the same time, regular churchgoers are no less likely than non-churchgoers

Table 7.4   Attitude towards science and the Bible: relationship with church attendance

	never %	sometimes %	monthly %	P<
Science has disproved religion	18	15	13	***
Science disproves the Bible account of creation	32	29	30	***
Scientific laws make miracles impossible	25	19	15	***
I think the Bible is out of date	33	17	9	***
Christians have to believe that every word of the Bible is true	22	17	21	
Christians have to believe that Jesus walked on water	13	14	21	***
Christians have to believe that God made the world in six days and rested on the seventh	19	17	23	***

to believe that science disproves the Bible account of creation. Second, regular churchgoers are less likely than non-churchgoers to argue that scientific laws make miracles impossible. At the same time, regular churchgoers are more likely than non-churchgoers to argue that Christians have to believe that Jesus walked on water.

PERSONAL WELLBEING

Table 8.1 presents an overview for the whole sample in relationship to the three items concerned with personal wellbeing. This table demonstrates that seven out of every ten young people in the sample found their life really worth living. One-in-ten found his or her life not worth living and two-in-ten were unsure. Considerably fewer young people were sure of a sense of purpose in their lives than found life really worth living. Half of the young people in the survey often felt depressed.

Table 8.1   Personal wellbeing: overview

	Agree %	Not Certain %	Disagree %
I find life really worth living	69	21	10
I often feel depressed	50	19	31
I feel my life has a sense of purpose	55	33	12

Table 8.2 presents the differences in response between male and female pupils in their personal wellbeing. These sex differences demonstrate that there is no significant variation in the proportions of male and female pupils who find their life really worth living.

Table 8.2   Personal wellbeing: sex differences

	Male % agree	Female % agree	P<
I find life really worth living	69	70	
I often feel depressed	44	54	***
I feel my life has a sense of purpose	53	57	***

Female pupils, however, were more inclined than male pupils both to feel that their lives have a sense of purpose and to suffer from feelings of depression.

Table 8.3 Personal wellbeing: age differences

	12 years % agree	15 years % agree	P<
I find life really worth living	75	72	*
I often feel depressed	49	50	
I feel my life has a sense of purpose	51	58	**

Table 8.3 presents the differences in responses between 12-year-old and 15-year-old pupils in their personal wellbeing. These age differences reveal a small tendency for a growth in a sense of purpose with age, but a reduction in finding life really worth living. There is no significant difference in the proportions of the two age groups who reported that they often feel depressed.

Table 8.4 Personal wellbeing: relationship with church attendance

	never %	sometimes %	monthly %	P<
I find life really worth living	65	70	75	***
I often feel depressed	50	51	48	
I feel my life has a sense of purpose	44	58	68	***

Table 8.4 presents the relationship between frequency of church attendance and personal wellbeing. These statistics confirm the findings of some previous research (Hay and Heald, 1987) that religion is associated with higher levels of wellbeing. While 65% of the non-churchgoers found life really worth living, the proportions rose to 70% among the occasional churchgoers and to 75% among the regular churchgoers. While 44% of the non-churchgoers felt their lives had a sense of purpose, the proportions rose to 58% among the occasional churchgoers and to 68% among the regular churchgoers.

On the other hand, there was no significant difference in the proportions of young people who reported feelings of depression among churchgoers and non-churchgoers.

CONCLUSION

The foregoing analysis has provided a window into adolescent perceptions of Christianity today. It has done so through the administration of a straightforward Likert-type self-completion questionnaire, using a battery of sixty-two attitude statements developed from previously well tested instruments. The responses of 3,863 12- to 16-year-old adolescents from all over England have been presented to provide an overview of their attitudes towards God, Jesus, prayer, church, Christians, science and religious education, science and the Bible, and personal wellbeing. Then the relationship has been explored between these eight attitudinal areas and sex, age and church attendance.

Other schools are now invited to employ the same questionnaire among their own pupils. The questionnaire can be photocopied from the teachers' handbook, *Words into Action* (Lealman, 1988), or obtained directly from the author. Schools which decide to do this can calculate the profile of their own pupils and compare this with the data published in this chapter. They can also contribute to the growing database on Christianity during childhood and adolescence, being developed by Trinity College, Carmarthen, and the North of England Institute for Christian Education, by sending in the completed questionnaires for further analysis.

While the present chapter provides a window into adolescent perceptions of Christianity today, the developing database already contains the potential for generating further crucial insights into the relationships between such issues as science, religion and personal wellbeing, and for identifying the personal and environmental correlates of key individual differences in these areas.

END NOTE

Professor Leslie J. Francis and Dr Jeff Astley are interested, through their collaborative work at the Centre of Theology and Education, Trinity College, Carmarthen, and the North of England Institute for Christian Education, Durham, to assist individual schools in developing this kind of survey work further and welcome enquiries from teachers in the primary and secondary sectors. They may be contacted by writing to:

Revd Professor Leslie J. Francis
Trinity College
Carmarthen
Dyfed SA31 3EP

Revd Dr Jeff Astley
North of England Institute for
  Christian Education
Carter House
Pelaw Leazes Lane
Durham DH1 1TB

ACKNOWLEDGEMENTS

I am grateful to John Forrest, producer BBC Schools Television, for originally suggesting this project; to Brenda Lealman, Christian Education Movement, for promoting and encouraging the survey; to the teachers and pupils who responded to the invitation to provide data; to the trustees of the Foundation of St Matthias and the trustees of the North of England Institute for Christian Education, for funding the data preparation; and to Trinity College, Carmarthen, for sponsoring the analysis.

REFERENCES

Argyle, M. and Beit-Hallahmi, B. (1975), *The Social Psychology of Religion*, London: Routledge and Kegan Paul.

Brown, L. B. (1987), *The Psychology of Religious Belief*, London: Academic Press.

Department of Education and Science (1989), *The Education Reform Act 1988: religious education and collective worship*, London: DES, circular 3/89.

Francis, L. J. (1978), 'Attitude and longitude: a study in measurement', *Character Potential*, Vol. 8, pp 119-130.

Francis, L. J. (1982a), *Youth in Transit*, Aldershot: Gower.

Francis, L. J. (1982b), *Experience of Adulthood*, Aldershot: Gower.

Francis, L. J. (1987a), 'The decline in attitudes towards religion among 8-15 year olds', *Educational Studies*, Vol. 13, pp 125-134.

Francis, L. J. (1987b), *Religion in the Primary School*, London: Collins Liturgical Publications.

Francis, L. J. (1989a), 'Drift from the churches: secondary school pupils' attitudes towards Christianity', *British Journal of Religious Education*, Vol. 11, pp 76-86.

Francis, L. J. (1989b), 'Monitoring changing attitudes towards Christianity among secondary school pupils between 1974 and 1986', *British Journal of Educational Psychology*, Vol. 59, pp 86-91.

Francis, L. J. (1989c), 'Measuring attitude towards Christianity during childhood and adolescence', *Personality and Individual Differences*, Vol. 10, pp 695-698.

Francis, L. J. (1990), 'Theology of education', *British Journal of Educational Studies*, Vol. 38, pp 349-364.

Francis, L. J., Gibson, H. M. and Fulljames, P. (1990), 'Attitude towards Christianity, creationism, scientism and interest in science among 11-15 year olds', *British Journal of Religious Education*, Vol. 13, pp 4-17.

Francis, L. J., and Thatcher, A. (eds) (1990), *Christian Perspectives for Education: a reader in the theology of education*, Leominster: Fowler Wright Books.

Hay, D. and Heald, G. (1987), 'Religion is good for you', *New Society*, Vol. 80 pp 20-22.

Lazenby, D. (1991), 'The Christianity in RE programme', *Journal of Beliefs and Values*, Vol. 12, No. 1, pp 14-15.

Lealman, B. (1988), *Words into Action*, London: CEM.

Likert, R. (1932), 'A technique for the measurement of attitudes', *Archives of Psychology*, Vol. 140, pp 1-55.

Mark, T. J. (1982), 'A study of religious attitudes, religious behaviour, and religious cognition', *Educational Studies*, Vol. 8, pp 209-216.

24

Popular Religious Television and Adolescent Attitudes towards Christianity

LESLIE J. FRANCIS AND HARRY M. GIBSON

INTRODUCTION

Religious broadcasts have played an important part in Sunday programme scheduling within England and Wales for both the BBC and
the ITV channels. The practice has been for many years to make a
clear distinction between the morning programmes, typically a televised church service, and the evening programmes, typically involving personal comment and informal hymn singing. Since 1984 the
ITV network has broadcast on Sunday evenings *Highway* against the
BBC's long established *Songs of Praise*.

The television rating figures, which monitor the number of viewers, demonstrate that the Sunday morning religious broadcasts appeal to a minority interest audience. During February 1988 0.8 million
people watched *Morning Service* on ITV and 0.3 million watched the
comparable programme on BBC. The Sunday evening religious broadcasts appeal to a much broader audience, with 7.8 million watching
Highway and 6.9 million watching *Songs of Praise*. Indeed, more than two-
thirds of the people watching one of the four broadcast channels at this
time on Sunday (about one-in-three of the UK population) had opted for
these religious programmes, rather than the alternatives, including the
Winter Olympics on BBC2 (Svenning, Haldane, Spiers and Gunter,
1988). The television rating figures also show that *Highway* and *Songs of
Praise* appeal more to women than men, more to older viewers than to
younger viewers and more to those who express other interests in religion
than to those who do not value religion.

Since a larger number of people appear to watch *Highway* or *Songs of Praise* on a Sunday than attend church services (Brierley, 1991), it seems likely that these programmes may now be playing a central role in shaping some viewers' perceptions of the character of the Christian worshipping community. Although a sequence of studies under the auspices of the Independent Broadcast Authority and its predecessor the Independent Television Authority (ABC Television, 1964; Independent Television Authority, 1970; Svenning, Haldane, Spiers and Gunter, 1988) has set out to map viewers' perceptions of religion on television, little attempt has been made to model the role played by popular religious television programmes in shaping or sustaining religiosity. While little is known about the correlates of popular religious television programmes among adults, even less is known about these among children and young people. Indeed, even the television rating figures quoted in relation to *Highway* and *Songs of Praise* by Svenning, Haldane, Spiers and Gunter (1988) provide age profiles only for those aged sixteen years and over.

Although research has generally not concentrated on the impact of religious television programmes on young people, a number of studies has explored the effects of other types of broadcasting, including the news (Cairns, 1990; Furnham and Gunter, 1985; Phillips and Carstensen, 1986), advertisements (Adler *et al.*, 1980; Collins, 1990; Tan, 1979), cartoon programmes (Davidson, Yasuna and Tower, 1979; Sprafkin, Gadow and Grayson, 1983, 1988), drama (Collins, Wellman, Keniston and Westby, 1978; Newcomb and Collins, 1979), situation comedy (Tidhar and Peri, 1990), game shows (Potter, 1990) and science programmes (Ormerod, Rutherford and Wood, 1989). It is the aim of the present study to open the correlates of popular religious television programmes to similar scrutiny.

At the same time, a series of recent studies has attempted to construct a detailed profile of the correlates of religious attitudes during childhood and adolescence. Specific studies have mapped sex differences and age trends during primary and secondary schooling (Greer, 1981), and generational differences between the early 1970s and the late 1980s (Francis, 1989a). The influence of Church of England and Roman Catholic schools on pupils' religious attitudes has been studied at primary level (Francis, 1987) and secondary level (Francis and Carter, 1980). The influence of different religious education syllabuses has been studied by Kay (1981a). The relationship between home background and religion has been studied in terms of social class (Gibson, Francis and Pearson, 1990), marital happiness (Kay, 1981b), denominational identity (Francis, 1990) and

Sunday school attendance (Francis, Gibson and Lankshear, 1991). The influence of religious experience has been studied by Francis and Greer (1992b) and conversion by Kay (1981c).

The relationship between personality and religion has been charted in terms of extraversion (Francis, Pearson and Kay, 1983), neuroticism (Francis, Pearson, Carter and Kay, 1981) and psychoticism (Kay, 1981d). Studies concerned with the relationship between religion and other individual differences include impulsivity (Pearson, Francis and Lightbown, 1986), empathy (Francis and Pearson, 1987), openness (Greer, 1985), moral values (Francis and Greer, 1992a), lying (Pearson and Francis, 1989), school subject preferences (Kay, 1981e), interest in science (Francis, Gibson and Fulljames, 1990) and creationism (Francis, Fulljames and Gibson, 1992).

In order to develop an integrated picture, all of the above studies have agreed on employing the same measure of religiosity, the Francis scale of attitude towards Christianity (Francis, 1989b). The aim of the present study is to model the relationship between popular religious television programmes and adolescent religiosity, using the same scale of attitude towards Christianity. In developing this model, it is recognized from the cumulative findings of the previously cited corpus of studies that key factors in predicting adolescent attitudes towards Christianity include age, sex, social class, parental religious behaviour and personal church attendance. After taking these factors into account, the model tests two hypotheses. The first hypothesis suggests that the overall amount of time spent watching television is unrelated to adolescent attitude towards Christianity. In other words, television itself neither promotes nor detracts from the religiosity of young people. The second hypothesis suggests that popular religious broadcasting helps to reinforce a positive attitude towards Christianity. In other words, young people who choose to view popular religious television programmes are likely to have their religiosity supported and maintained by this experience.

METHOD

A total of 5,432 pupils between the ages of eleven and fifteen years, attending twelve non-denominational and three Roman Catholic state maintained secondary schools in Dundee, completed the Francis scale of attitude towards Christianity (Francis, 1989b). At the same time the pupils rated the frequency with which they watched a range of listed television programmes, including *Highway* and *Songs of Praise*, on a three point scale: often, sometimes and never. The overall amount of time spent watching television was measured by two questions: the number of days on which television was watched during the previous week and the number of hours on which television was watched during the previous day.

Mother's church attendance, father's church attendance and each pupil's personal church attendance were all measured on a five point scale: never, once or twice a year, sometimes, at least once a month, and weekly. Social class was assessed according to the five point categorization proposed by the Office of Population, Censuses and Surveys (1980) applied to reported paternal occupations.

The questionnaires were administered by teachers within the schools according to a standardized procedure, emphasizing confidentiality and anonymity. The data were analysed by means of the SPSSX package (SPSS Inc., 1988), using the multiple regression and path analysis techniques (MacDonald, 1977; Keeves, 1988).

RESULTS

The data show that only a very small proportion of the pupils watch popular religious television programmes often. Overall *Songs of Praise* is watched often by 1% of the boys and 2% of the girls, while *Highway* is watched often by 3% of the boys and 5% of the girls. On the other hand, a considerable proportion of the pupils, nearly one in three (32%), watches one or other of these programmes from time to time. Table 1 presents the proportions of pupils who watch *Songs of Praise* and *Highway* at least sometimes, by age and sex.

Table 1   Proportion of pupils who watch popular religious television at least sometimes, by age and sex

age	Songs of Praise		Highway		either or both	
	male %	female %	male %	female %	male %	female %
11 years	18	31	19	39	29	50
12 years	19	29	25	29	32	43
13 years	17	26	23	30	29	41
14 years	10	21	17	25	21	34
15 years	9	19	16	21	20	31

The correlation matrix presented in table 2 (see Appendix) explores the bivariate relationships between watching popular religious television, the total time spent watching television, age, sex, social class, father's church attendance, mother's church attendance, personal church attendance and attitude towards Christianity. These correlations confirm seven characteristics associated with watching popular religious television. First, girls are more likely to watch popular religious television than boys. This is consistent with the more general finding that adolescent girls are more likely to pray (Francis and Brown, 1991), attend church (Francis, 1984) and hold positive attitudes towards Christianity (Francis, 1989b). Second, the tendency to watch popular religious television significantly declines between the ages of eleven and fifteen years. This is consistent with the general decline in adolescent religiosity reported over this age span (Greer, 1981; Mark, 1982; Francis, 1989b). Third, there is a slight tendency for pupils from lower social class backgrounds to watch more popular religious television than pupils from higher social class backgrounds. This is consistent with the general finding that children from lower social class backgrounds hold a more positive attitude towards religion, although they are less inclined to attend church (Gibson, Francis and Pearson, 1990; Francis, Pearson and Lankshear, 1990). Fourth, there is a positive relationship between the pupil's church attendance and the likelihood of watching popular religious television. This is consistent with the general finding that church attendance is a central predictor of other pro-religious attitudes and behaviours (Francis, 1989b). Fifth, parental church attendance also emerges as a significant predictor of the tendency to watch popular religious television. This is consistent with the findings of a number of studies concerned with the nature of parental influence on adolescent religiosity (Hoge and Petrillo, 1978; Kieren and Munro, 1987). Sixth, no relationship emerges between the overall time spent watching television and the tendency to watch popular religious programmes. Other studies concerned with adolescent television viewing preferences have tended to demonstrate a positive relationship between the overall time spent watching television and entertainment programmes, but a negative relationship with news and current awareness programmes (Rubin, 1979; Francis and Gibson, 1992). The present data suggest that heavy viewers may have a tendency to switch off or change the channel when popular religious programmes are broadcast, but are less likely to do so consistently than when current affairs or news programmes are broadcast.

Finally, the correlation matrix also demonstrates a significant positive relationship between adolescent attitude towards Christianity and popular television, as well as a significant negative relationship with the overall time spent watching television. However, given the significant relationships of sex, age, social class, father's church attendance, mother's church attendance and personal church attendance with attitude toward Christianity, as well as with the tendency to watch popular religious television programmes, it is not possible to discover from this correlation matrix the precise nature of the relationship between popular religious television and attitude towards Christianity. Similarly, given the significant relationships of sex, age and social class with attitude towards Christianity, as well as with overall television watching time, it is not possible to discover from this correlation matrix the precise nature of the relationship between overall television watching time and attitude towards Christianity. Table 3 and figure 1 (see Appendix), therefore, display and test the significance of a set of hypothesized causal paths, designed to explore the potential influence of both overall television watching time and popular religious television on adolescent attitude towards Christianity.

This path model elicits two additional important conclusions from the data. First, it demonstrates that, after controlling for the influence of age, sex and social class, there is no significant relationship between overall television watching time and attitude towards Christianity. This finding suggests that there is no evidence to support the views that television per se either promotes or detracts from the development of positive attitudes towards Christianity among eleven- to fifteen-year-olds. Second, the path model demonstrates that, after controlling for the influence of age, sex, social class, parental church attendance and personal church attendance, there is a significant positive relationship between watching popular religious television programmes and attitude towards Christianity. This finding suggests that adolescents who watch popular religious television programmes, at least from time to time, hold a more positive attitude towards Christianity than adolescents of the same sex and age, from the same social class background, with the same level of parental religious support and with the same practice of church attendance who do not watch popular religious television programmes, at least from time to time. In this sense, popular religious television programmes seem to help to reinforce a positive attitude towards Christianity among the young people who view them.

CONCLUSION

This study has found that nearly one in three (32%) of eleven- to fifteen-year-olds within the state maintained schools in Dundee watch *Songs of Praise* or *Highway*, as examples of popular religious television, at least from time to time. These programmes are more likely to be viewed by girls than by boys, by younger adolescents than by older adolescents, by pupils from lower social class backgrounds than by pupils from higher social class backgrounds, by young people who attend church and whose parents attend church than by young people who have no contact with the churches and whose parents have no contact with the churches. Path analysis suggests that, while the overall time spent watching television neither promotes nor depresses adolescent religiosity, popular religious programmes help to reinforce a positive attitude towards Christianity among the young people who view them.

These findings indicate that popular religious television programmes, like *Songs of Praise* and *Highway* appear to make a helpful contribution towards promoting a positive image of the Christian churches and Christianity among young people in today's society and certainly do not contribute towards undermining the attractiveness of religion. Further research is now needed to explore the impact of popular religious television both among adolescents in other parts of the United Kingdom and among a wider age range of young viewers, and also to examine the impact of other forms of religious broadcasting more generally among children and young people.

ACKNOWLEDGEMENT

The specific data analyses undertaken for this paper were sponsored at Trinity College, Carmarthen, by Channel Four Television.

REFERENCES

ABC Television (1964), *Television and Religion*, London: University of London Press.
Adler, R. P., Lesser, G. S., Meringoff, L., Robertson, T. S., Rossiter, J. R. and Ward, S. (1980), *The Effects of Television Advertising on Children*, Lexington: Lexington Books.
Brierley, P. (1991), *'Christian' England*, London: MARC Europe.
Cairns, E. (1990), 'Impact of television news exposure on children's perceptions of violence in Northern Ireland', *Journal of Social Psychology*, Vol. 130, pp 447-452.
Collins, J. (1990), 'Television and primary school children in Northern Ireland: the impact of advertising', *Journal of Educational Television*, Vol. 16, pp 31-39.
Collins, W. A., Wellman, H., Keniston, A. H. and Westby, S. D. (1978), 'Age-related

aspects of comprehension and inference from a televised dramatic narrative', *Child Development*, Vol. 49, pp 389-399.

Davidson, E. S., Yasuna, A. and Tower, A. (1979), 'The effects of television cartoons on sex-role stereotyping in young girls', *Child Development*, Vol. 50, pp 597-600.

Francis, L. J. (1984), *Teenagers and the Church*, London: Collins.

Francis, L. J. (1987), *Religion in the Primary School*, London: Collins Liturgical Publications.

Francis, L. J. (1989a), 'Monitoring changing attitudes towards Christianity among secondary school pupils between 1974 and 1986', *British Journal of Educational Psychology*, Vol. 59, pp 86-91.

Francis, L. J. (1989b), 'Measuring attitude towards Christianity during childhood and adolescence', *Personality and Individual Differences*, Vol. 10, pp 695-698.

Francis, L. J. (1990), 'The religious significance of denominational identity among eleven year old children in England', *Journal of Christian Education*, Vol. 97, pp 23-28.

Francis, L. J. and Brown, L. B. (1991), 'The influence of home, church and school on prayer among sixteen year old adolescents in England', *Review of Religious Research*, Vol. 33, pp 112-122.

Francis, L. J. and Carter, M. (1980), 'Church aided secondary schools, religious education as an examination subject and pupil attitudes towards religion', *British Journal of Educational Psychology*, Vol. 50, pp 297-300.

Francis, L. J., Fulljames, P. and Gibson, H. M. (1992), 'Does creationism commend the gospel? a developmental study among 11-17 year olds', *Religious Education*, (in press).

Francis, L. J. and Gibson, H. M. (1992), 'The influence of age, sex, social class and religion on television viewing time and programme preferences among 11-15 year-olds', (in press).

Francis, L. J., Gibson, H. M. and Fulljames, P. (1990), 'Attitude towards Christianity, creationism, scientism and interest in science among 11-15 year olds', *British Journal of Religious Education*, Vol. 13, pp 4-17.

Francis, L. J., Gibson, H. M. and Lankshear, D. W. (1991), 'The influence of Protestant Sunday Schools on attitude towards Christianity among 11-15-year-olds in Scotland', *British Journal of Religious Education*, Vol. 14, pp 35-42.

Francis, L. J. and Greer, J. E. (1992a), 'Catholic schools and adolescent religiosity in Northern Ireland: shaping moral values', *Irish Journal of Education*, (in press).

Francis, L. J. and Greer, J. E. (1992b), 'The contribution of religious experience to Christian development: a study among fourth, fifth and sixth year pupils in Northern Ireland', *British Journal of Religious Education*, (in press).

Francis, L. J. and Pearson, P. R. (1987), 'Empathic development during adolescence: religiosity the missing link?', *Personality and Individual Differences*, Vol. 8, pp 145-148.

Francis, L. J., Pearson, P. R., Carter, M. and Kay, W. K. (1981), 'The relationship between neuroticism and religiosity among English 15- and 16-year-olds', *Journal of Social Psychology*, Vol. 114, pp 99-102.

Francis, L. J., Pearson, P. R. and Kay, W. K. (1983), 'Are introverts still more religious?', *Personality and Individual Differences*, Vol. 4, pp 211-212.

Francis, L. J., Pearson, P. R. and Lankshear, D. W. (1990), 'The relationship between social class and attitude towards Christianity among ten and eleven year old children', *Personality and Individual Differences*, Vol. 11, pp 1019-1027.

Furnham, A. and Gunter, B. (1985), 'Sex, presentation mode and memory for violent and non-violent news', *Journal of Educational Television*, Vol. 11, pp 99-105.

Gibson, H. M., Francis, L. J. and Pearson, P. R. (1990), 'The relationship between social class and attitude towards Christianity among fourteen- and fifteen-year-old adolescents', *Personality and Individual Differences*, Vol. 11, pp 631-635.

Greer, J. E. (1981), 'Religious attitudes and thinking in Belfast pupils', *Educational Research*, Vol. 23, pp 177-189.

Greer, J. E. (1985), 'Viewing "the other side" in Northern Ireland: openness and attitude to religion among Catholic and Protestant Adolescents', *Journal for the Scientific Study of Religion*, Vol. 24, pp 275-292.

Hoge, D. R. and Petrillo, G. H. (1978), 'Determinants of church participation and attitudes among high school youth', *Journal for the Scientific Study of Religion*, Vol. 17, pp 359-379.

Independent Television Authority (1970), *Religion in Britain and Northern Ireland*, London: Independent Television Authority.

Kay, W. K. (1981a), 'Syllabuses and attitudes to Christianity', *Irish Catechist*, Vol. 5, No. 2, pp 16-21.

Kay, W. K. (1981b), 'Marital happiness and children's attitudes to religion', *British Journal of Religious Education*, Vol. 3, pp 102-105.

Kay, W. K. (1981c), 'Conversion among 11-15 year olds', *Spectrum*, Vol. 13, No. 2, pp 26-33.

Kay, W. K. (1981d), 'Psychoticism and attitude to religion', *Personality and Individual Differences*, Vol. 2, pp 249-252.

Kay, W. K. (1981e), 'Subject preference and attitude to religion in secondary schools', *Educational Review*, Vol. 33, pp 47-51.

Keeves, J. P. (1988), 'Path analysis', in J. P. Keeves (ed), *Educational Research, Methodology, and Measurement: an international handbook*, Oxford: Pergamon Press, pp 723-731.

Kieren, D. K. and Munro, B. (1987), 'Following the leaders: parents' influence on adolescent religious activity', *Journal for the Scientific Study of Religion*, Vol. 26, pp 249-255.

MacDonald, K. I. (1977), 'Path analysis', in C. A. O'Muircheartaigh and C. Payne (eds), *The Analysis of Survey Data*, volume 2, New York: John Wiley and Sons, chapter 3.

Mark, T. J. (1982), 'A study of religious attitudes, religious behaviour, and religious cognition', *Educational Studies*, Vol. 8, pp 209-216.

Newcomb, A. F. and Collins, W. A. (1979), 'Children's comprehension of family role portrayals in televised dramas: effects of socio-economic status, ethnicity, and age', *Developmental Psychology*, Vol. 15, pp 417-423.

Office of Population Censuses and Surveys (1980), *Classification of Occupations 1980*, London: HMSO.

Ormerod, M. B., Rutherford, M. and Wood, C. (1989), 'Relationships between attitudes to science and television viewing among pupils aged 10 to 13+', *Research in Science and Technological Education*, Vol. 7, pp 75-84.

Pearson, P. R. and Francis, L. J. (1989), 'The dual nature of the Eysenckian lie scales: are religious adolescents more truthful?', *Personality and Individual Differences*, Vol. 10, pp 1041-1048.

Pearson, P. R., Francis, L. J. and Lightbown, T. J. (1986), 'Impulsivity and religiosity', *Personality and Individual Differences*, Vol. 7, pp 89-94.

Phillips, D. P. and Carstensen, L. L. (1986), 'Clustering of teenage suicides after television news stories about suicide', *New England Journal of Medicine*, Vol. 315, pp 685-689.

Potter, W. J. (1990), 'Adolescents' perceptions of the primary values of television programming', *Journalism Quarterly*, Vol. 67, pp 843-851.

Rubin, A. M. (1979), 'Television use by children and adolescents', *Human Communication Research*, Vol. 5, pp 109-120.

Sprafkin, J., Gadow, K. D. and Grayson, P. (1983), 'Effects of viewing aggressive cartoons on the behaviour of learning disabled children', *Journal of Child Psychology and Psychiatry*, Vol. 28, pp 387-398.

Sprafkin, J., Gadow, K. D. and Grayson, P. (1988), 'Effects of cartoons on emotionally disturbed children's social behaviour in school settings', *Journal of Child Psychology and Psychiatry*, Vol. 29, pp 91-99.

SPSS Inc (1988), *SPSSX User's Guide*, New York: McGraw-Hill.

Svenning, M., Haldane, I., Spiers, S. and Gunter, B. (1988), *Godwatching: viewers, religion and television*, London: John Libbey and IBA.

Tan, A. S. (1979), 'TV beauty ads and role expectations of adolescent female viewers', *Journalism Quarterly*, Vol. 56, pp 283-288.

Tidhar, C. E. and Peri, S. (1990), 'Deceitful behaviour in situation comedy: effects on children's perceptions of social reality', *Journal of Educational Television*, Vol. 16, pp 61-76.

APPENDIX

Table 2 Correlation matrix

	sex	age	social class	father's church	mother's church	pupil's church	TV time	religious TV
attitude to Christianity	+0.1673 .001	-0.1904 .001	-0.0335 .05	+0.3676 .001	+0.4000 .001	+0.5606 .001	-0.0531 .001	+0.3013 .001
religious TV	+0.1352 .001	-0.1162 .001	+0.0277 .05	+0.1019 .001	+0.1211 .001	+0.1871 .001	+0.0023 NS	
TV time	-0.0613 .001	-0.0582 .001	+0.1641 .001	-0.0831 .001	-0.0894 .001	-0.0797 .001		
pupil's church	+0.1095 .001	-0.0883 .001	-0.1141 .001	+0.5576 .001	+0.6604 .001			
mother's church	+0.0234 .05	-0.0276 .05	-0.1656 .001	+0.6015 .001				
father's church	+0.0030 NS	-0.0177 NS	-0.1971 .001					
social class	+0.0315 .05	-0.0301 .05						

Figure 1 : Path Model

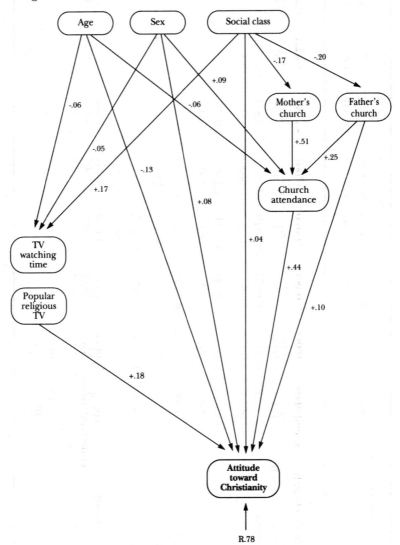

R.78

Table 3 Multiple regression significance tests

criterion variables	predictor variables	R^2	Increase R^2	F	P<	Beta	T	P<
father's church	social class	.0383	.0383	146.0	.001	-.1957	-12.1	.001
mother's church	social class	.0294	.0294	111.3	.001	-.1716	-10.5	.001
church attendance	sex	.0110	.0110	42.4	.001	+.0897	+7.7	.001
	age	.0186	.0076	29.7	.001	-.0620	-5.3	.001
	mother's church	.4502	.4316	2993.3	.001	+.5097	+35.3	.001
	father's church	.4907	.0405	303.3	.001	+.2527	+17.4	.001
	social class	.4909	.0002	1.4	NS	-.0149	+1.3	NS
TV time	sex	.0025	.0025	9.4	.01	-.0588	-3.7	.001
	age	.0059	.0034	13.2	.001	-.0541	-3.4	.001
	social class	.0361	.0302	119.6	.001	+.1741	+10.9	.001
attitude to Christianity	sex	.0281	.0281	110.4	.001	+.0833	+6.5	.001
	age	.0629	.0348	141.5	.001	-.1268	-10.0	.001
	church attendance	.3563	.2934	1738.0	.001	+.4471	+25.2	.001
	mother's church	.3586	.0023	13.5	.001	+.0253	+1.4	NS
	father's church	.3636	.0049	29.5	.001	+.0955	+5.8	.001
	social class	.3650	.0015	9.0	.01	+.0365	+2.8	.01
	TV time	.3653	.0004	2.1	NS	-.0168	-1.3	NS
	religious TV	.3963	.0309	195.0	.001	+.1820	+14.0	.001

25

A Survey of Bible Reading Practice and Attitudes to the Bible among Anglican Congregations

ELIZABETH FISHER, JEFF ASTLEY AND CAROLYN WILCOX

THE SAMPLE

Four hundred and forty-five adult lay people from ten parishes in one Anglican diocese completed a self-administered questionnaire about their Bible reading habits and attitudes to the Bible in the autumn of 1988. For some it was on Bible Sunday. It was made clear that the questionnaires were to be distributed on Sunday and that, whilst help could be given over the meaning of questions, the respondents were otherwise to complete them unaided. Most congregations filled them in during or after the service. One clergyman gave out his copies at a Mothers' Union meeting, arguing that as his congregation was elderly and female in any case the sample was not unrepresentative. In another parish the curate gave out copies to a mid-week congregation after the incumbent had refused to take part in the survey. One other clergyman distributed them at a mid-week service. These factors may help to explain why the results of the survey show a high level of church attendance on the part of the respondents. This paper therefore summarizes the views of a sample of *regular* Anglican worshippers.

Age/Sex
Of the 445 responses from those aged 15 and over we found people in every age group (see Appendix 2). 118 of the sample were male and 308 were female (a further nineteen respondents gave no details). Nearly 45% were aged 60 or over. This distribution is not markedly atypical of Anglican church congregations.[1]

Church Attendance

Nearly three-quarters of the respondents attend church weekly. A further 11% attend fortnightly, and 4% attend once a month. Only slightly more than 5% attend less than once a month; twenty-four gave no answer. When one considers the age of many of the respondents this is a remarkable degree of commitment. Had the questionnaire been distributed at Christmas or Easter the figures would have been different, with many more casual attenders.[2] But the Church of England has a core of very regular attenders, and it is their use of and attitudes to the Bible that we have researched.

Educational Background

It seemed appropriate to ask about the educational qualifications of the respondents. Ninety-three people had left school with, or were later awarded, an 'O' level, CSE, GCSE or school certificate as their highest paper qualification. This figure represents 20.9% of the sample. A further 6.3% had left school with, or were later awarded, an 'A' level, ONC or HNC qualification. Just over a quarter (27.6%) have a higher education certificate (eg Teachers' Certificate), diploma, first degree or higher degree. This represents a higher proportion than is true of the population as a whole, indicating that our sample includes a substantial educationally well-qualified group.[3] Nevertheless, two hundred and one (45.2%) of the sample have no formal paper qualifications.

THE USE OF THE BIBLE IN CHURCH

A substantial minority did not know the number and nature of the readings at the eucharistic services which most of them attended. Sixty-five of the two hundred and twenty-four respondents from one deanery (ie 29%) failed to make a correct response. 19.8% of the total sample failed to do so. Many did not know that the readings came from the ASB (the *Alternative Service Book*, in general use in the Church of England since its publication in 1980).

THE USE OF THE BIBLE AT HOME

Owning and Reading

The 445 people between them own 1099 Bibles. In only one of the ten parishes were there fewer Bibles in total than respondents. The most numerous version owned is the Authorised Version (AV), with 297 copies. The second most popular is the New English Bible (NEB), with 212 copies declared. The next most popular version is the Good News Bible (GNB), originally intended for those who use English as a second language (199 copies). The Revised Standard Version (RSV), which many still regard as the translation closest to the original texts, is owned by one hundred and twenty-three respondents. 118 copies of the Jerusalem Bible were declared, and 47 copies of the (more recently published) New International Version. Interestingly seventeen lay people in our sample own a Greek New Testament. 73 'Children's Bibles' and 14 Revised Versions complete the tally.

Respondents were asked to nominate which version of the Bible they used 'most often' for private reading. The most frequently-used version is the GNB: 25.8% of the total number of respondents chose this version. But this figure is closely followed by the very different AV (24.9%). The next most popular version is the NEB (17.1%). The RSV was rated as the version used most often by only fifty-one churchgoers (ie 11.5%).

Bible Reading Habits

Of the four hundred and forty-five respondents only eighty-one (18.2%) claim to read their Bibles daily ('at least once a day'). A further 16.6% claim to read it 'about once a week'. Thus one hundred and fifty-five (34.8%) read their Bibles at least once a week at home. These figures are not likely to be underestimates. A further 7.6% read their Bible about once a month, and a staggering two hundred and twelve (47.6%) confessed to reading their Bibles only 'occasionally'. Thirty admitted that they *never* read the Bible at home, and fourteen gave no answer (together these two groups make up nearly 10% of the sample). Thus a total of 256 (57.5%) read their Bibles less than once a month. The only real exception to this pattern was one parish where the predominantly evangelical congregation seems to have developed habits of sustained personal Bible reading. In this parish over 60% of the sample claim to read the Bible daily, and 84.6% read it at least once a week. There was no association between the frequency of Bible reading and either the age or the sex of the respondents.[4]

We asked when the Bible was usually read at home, and the length of time spent on such reading. Sixty-three claim never to read the Bible or offered no answer (this compares with forty-four who responded similarly to the earlier question). Many respondents usually read their Bibles (when they do!) in the evenings (21.8%) or at bedtime (28.3%). However 24.7% claim that they do their reading at 'any time', or ticked more than one time of the day. The morning (7.6%) and the afternoon (3.6%) were less popular options.

It appears that the majority of these regular Anglican worshippers have lost the habit of Bible reading, if they ever had it. This claim is strengthened when we come to see how long these committed churchgoers spend on personal Bible reading 'at one sitting'. Fifty-six (about a ninth) gave no answer, a further sixteen said 'no time'. 15.2% of the sample replied that they read the Scriptures for 5 minutes or less, and 48.8% reported between 5 and 10 minutes. A further 17.3% claim to read at one session between 10 and 30 minutes, and 2% claim to read for an hour or more. These figures should be considered in conjunction with the finding that only about a third of our sample read with any disciplined regularity. Any regular thirty minute television programme is given a greater time commitment by most of these churchgoers than the foundation document of the Christian faith.

Bible Reading Aids
Over 60% of the sample never use 'an aid or commentary' when reading the Bible. Only 18.2% of the sample said that they 'usually' used such an aid, and a further 12.6% said that they 'occasionally' did so. The Bible Reading Fellowship notes were the most popular aids selected for use.

Books about the Bible
To give some further insight into Anglican reading habits with regard to the Bible, we asked the respondents to tell us how many books about the Bible they owned and had read. We did not ask for specific categories (eg commentaries), only a general question about 'books on the Bible'. 20.9% own no such books. When added to those who gave no answer this amounts to over a quarter of the sample. A surprising 58.2% of the sample own between 1 and 5 books; 7.4% own between 6 and 10 books; 7.8% own more than 10.

It is one thing to have books on shelves, it is another thing to have read them — and of course one can read books without owning them. 18.4% have read no books on the Bible. A further 50.3% claim to have read between 1 and 5 books. 7.6% have read between 6 and 10. 12.1% have read more than 10 books. Forty-five people gave no answer. If we add these 'no' respondents to the eighty-two who have done no reading, we produce a figure of one hundred and twenty-seven, or 28.5%.

ATTITUDES TO THE BIBLE

The respondents were asked to indicate their views on several questions relating to their understanding of and attitude to the Scriptures. First they were asked to indicate their opinions with regard to various claims on a five-point scale from 'agree strongly' through 'neither agree nor disagree' to 'strongly disagree'. Alternatively they could record that they did not know what attitude to adopt about the claim in question. A Chi^2 test was carried out on the frequency data to determine whether these attitudes were influenced by the age or sex of the respondents (see Appendix 2).

Accurate History?

The first statement presented for consideration was: '*The Bible is not always accurate when it describes history*'. Eighty-nine neither agreed nor disagreed, and a further fifty-seven (32.8% in all) did not know. Fifty-three (11.9%) disagreed, nine of them strongly. Two hundred and forty-six (55.3%) agreed, of whom fifty did so strongly (11.2%). Neither the age nor the sex of the respondents had a significant influence on the opinions expressed in this area.

Accurate Science?

When asked their views on the statement: '*The Bible is not always accurate when it talks about scientific matters*', ninety-eight (22%) neither agreed nor disagreed and seventy-three did not know, together making 38.4% of the sample. This represents an even larger figure than the 'don't knows' and 'can't says' that we noted with regard to the *historical* claims of the Bible. This is rather suprising; the science-versus-the-Bible controversy clearly remains unresolved for many adults.[5] Just over a tenth disagreed with the statement (forty-six in all), registering a view held or strongly held that the Bible *is* always accurate when it talks about scientific matters. Sixty (13.5%) strongly held the view that the Bible is not always accurate in this area, a further one hundred and sixty-eight (37.8%) 'agreed' with the statement. Again age had no significant influence on opinion, but the sex of the respondent did make a difference to how they answered this question. Women were more likely than men to be unsure how to respond, or to disagree strongly with the statement. They were less likely to agree strongly with it.

Accurate Theology?

The third statement was as follows: *'The Bible is not always accurate when it talks about God, God's acts and God's will for humans'.* This time a rather smaller number could give no opinion: 15.1% neither agreed nor disagreed, and 14.2% of the sample did not know. We expected that this question was one that adult Christians in general would feel that they *could* answer. We were not expecting, however, that as many as one hundred and twenty-one (27.2%) would agree with the statement, with twenty-five of these doing so strongly. One hundred and ninety-four (43.6%) disagreed, of whom sixty-two did so strongly (13.9%). In one congregational sample of twenty-six, sixteen disagreed strongly and the total number who disagreed represented 84.6% of that church. This group knew where they stood on the question as to whether the Bible is a secure foundation for theology.

In the overall sample, both sex and age were significant factors in the patterns of response to this question. Women were on the whole more likely to agree (or agree strongly) with the statement than were male respondents; and over 27% of the men strongly disagreed with the claim compared with 12.3% of the women. (Males below the age of 40 were particularly likely to reject the statement.) On the whole in the churches sampled it was the group of older people, particularly those over 60, that was the one most likely to express doubts about the theological veracity of the Bible. This is an interesting fact, and readers may like to speculate on the possible explanations for it, particularly in the light of the findings of the next section.

Accurate Ethics?

In order to discover something about churchgoers' views on the Bible's ethical teaching we offered them this statement: *'The Bible is always accurate when it talks about how people should behave'.* Here only a fifth could give no opinion: forty-six of them neither agreed nor disagreed and forty-three did not know. Slightly more (one hundred and two, or 22.9%) disagreed with the claim, of whom eleven did so strongly. For them the Bible was not to be trusted as an ethical source-book. One hundred and sixty-nine (nearly 38%) took the opposite view, agreeing with the statement, and a further eighty-five (19.1%) strongly agreed with it. The percentage of those who responded positively was thus over 57%, a figure that represents an even stronger vote of confidence than was expressed for the Bible as an accurate *theological* text. In the particular evangelical parish mentioned in the last section, 88.5% expressed agreement with the claim about the

Bible's ethical accuracy and half of that parish's entire sample did so strongly. In another parish 80% agreed with the statement.

In the total sample the sex of the churchgoers was not a significant influence on the response patterns but the age variable was. In this case those over 60 were the ones most likely to agree (or agree strongly) with the statement, whereas the group below 40 included the most substantial proportion of those who rejected the claim.

Relevant Today?

When asked to indicate their opinion about the claim that '*the Bible is not very relevant to us today*' the number who could offer no view fell to eighty-three (18.7%). Forty-seven agreed (10.6%) with the claim, and three hundred and fifteen (70.8%) disagreed, nearly 30% disagreeing strongly. In one particular parish 88.5% disagreed with the statement, with those who disagreed strongly making up 73.1% of that congregational sample. In another village parish forty-eight out of fifty-five members of the congregation expressed disagreement (87.3%). But this vote of confidence in the Bible's relevance (however minimal) should be balanced by the fact that nearly 30% of the total sample either thought that the Bible was *not* very relevant, or were uncertain what to think about it. Both age and sex were significant in the pattern of responses here, with age being a highly significant factor in the case of women. Women over 60 were more likely than any other group to agree with the statement. Taking the figures overall, men were more likely to disagree with the claim than were female respondents.

A Spectrum of Views

The questionnaire sought further clarification of the respondents' attitudes to the Bible by asking them to consider five possible positions and to indicate the one that was closest to their own.[6] Some found this a difficult exercise and either left it blank or gave multiple responses. These null returns account for seventy-two respondents in all (just over a sixth). Five (1% of the sample) ticked '*The Bible is an ancient book and has no relevance today*', an extreme rejectionist view of the Scriptures. These responses should however be taken together with the 10.6% of the sample who thought that the Bible 'is not very relevant to us today' (see above). Only a further fifteen (3.4%) ticked the position at the other end of the spectrum: a fundamentalist claim that '*The Bible was dictated by God to the people who wrote it and it contains no errors*'.[7] Eighty-six (19.3%) preferred the conservative — but not necessarily fundamentalist — position that *'The Bible contains all that is necessary for salvation. We must believe what we read there'.* One hundred and eighteen (26.5%) ticked one of the more 'central' positions, one of the two that may be appropriately designated as 'liberal' views of the Scriptures, ie *'The Bible is the book in which we read of God's dealings with his people. He still uses it to reveal himself today but not everything in it is true'.* Interestingly enough the largest number (one hundred and forty-nine, ie 33.5%) ticked another liberal view as nearest to their own. This represents a position with a more relativist — or 'perspectivist' — emphasis, but without a 'not-everything-in-it-is-true' clause, ie *'The Bible is indispensable to Christianity but the meaning of its contents is conditioned by the culture in which the story was first written'.* Thus altogether nearly 60% of the sample ticked one or other of the liberal responses on offer.

Age and sex were both relevant here, with the modal choice for women being the first of the liberal views described above, whereas the figures for the male respondents showed two modes: they were more equally divided between the two liberal options. More women over 60 ticked the conservative option than any other: this group represents more than half of all those in both sexes and any age group who chose this position.

What is particularly noticeable in this exercise is the number of people who failed to tick any box, or who found the task confusing and gave a multiple answer (16.2% in all). In some instances the combinations of multiple responses were logically impossible. In one parish three people ticked four positions in this section, with some of their responses clearly ruling out others. This fact, taken with the large proportion of the sample who said that they 'did not know' or could 'neither agree nor disagree' with the opinions about the Bible expressed in the earlier exercises (ranging from nearly 19% to over 38%), suggests that many of these highly committed Anglicans found it difficult to identify or articulate their own attitudes to the Bible. Perhaps this inability is of more significance than the particular positions adopted by those who do know their own minds. Should this be a cause for concern for adult Christian education?

CONCLUSIONS

It seems, then, that many Anglicans have no consistent understanding of the Bible, and many have lost (if they ever had) the habit of reading the Bible in a disciplined way. Was there ever a time when Bible reading had a high priority among Anglicans, and when all such churchgoers had a clear view of what they thought about the Scriptures? Or is that just another myth about the 'good old days' of the church and Christian education that needs to be exploded? The only exception to our general assessment is provided by one evangelical parish where the respondents consistently revealed a conservative (but not a fundamentalist) attitude to the Bible, and where the majority of them read it daily. Does that attitude go hand-in-hand with this commitment? Or can more liberal Christians be persuaded to think about, become clear about, and actually *read* the Scriptures?

In our sample we have a number of highly committed people who attend church very regularly. But many of them do not undergird that churchgoing commitment by Bible reading at home. Is that just because they are too busy? Is it because the Bible is now regarded as too difficult, or too confusing? Do they fear the psychological 'pain of new learning' which might be involved in seriously studying the Scriptures, perhaps especially in the light of modern scholarship?[8] Or is it because they are just not interested in the Bible any more? It is true that in some traditions within Anglicanism emphasis is placed elsewhere, perhaps with a resulting depreciation of Bible reading. It would be interesting to test this out through further research. Clearly Christian education, however effective it has been in other areas, has not created a Bible reading congregation in most of the churches that we have surveyed. Many of our respondents surely represent the 'educated lay people' of whom publishers sometimes fondly speak. But the Bible largely remains a closed book, even to such folk. They have sometimes read *about* it, but they only occasionally read it for themselves.

One may speculate on other possible contributory causes of this state of affairs. Has the introduction of the ASB, with its own collection of readings, rendered Bible reading an irrelevant activity for many Anglicans? Has the growth in pew leaflets, which often include the weekly lections, actually discouraged the *handling* of Bibles? Has the very success of the parish communion movement, and the phasing out of the offices of Morning and Evening Prayer in which lessons from Scripture are much longer and more prominent, contributed to the current situation?

All these questions spring from data which cannot answer them. But from their own experience the authors would stress the need to encourage lay people in many cases actually to buy a modern version (for so much of the Authorised Version is incomprehensible, even when read so nicely on the BBC), to take up the habit of reading it in a disciplined way, and to begin to address — with the help of educators and written aids — those issues of contemporary life on which the Bible has a bearing. People need encouragement to do this, not guilt-engendering preaching. They need to be shown the riches of the biblical tradition, and its relevance. And — *we* would claim — they can best be given this encouragement in the context of a critical approach to the Bible: an approach to which many of them are clearly sympathetic, at least in principle. Unless we succeed in these tasks the gap between pulpit and pew will grow even wider.

NOTES

1. The English Church Census gave the following figures for Anglican churchgoers: ratio of the sexes — 61% women, 39% men; proportion of churchgoers (aged 15 or over) who are 65 or over — 29.7%. See P. Brierley (ed), *Prospects for the Nineties: All England*, London: MARC Europe, 1991, p 39.

2. As a percentage of the population (aged 15 or over), the figure for Anglican Sunday attendances in 1988 was given as 2.4%, which compares with a figure of over 4% for Easter or Christmas communicants. See *The Church of England Year Book*, London: CIO, 1991, p 401.

3. The equivalent national figure for persons aged 16 or over is 16.2% (including a nursing qualification as a higher education qualification). See Office of Population Censuses and Surveys, *General Household Survey 1987*, London: HMSO, 1989, p 175.

4. In a general survey (ie not just of churchgoers) in Scotland it was shown (i) that women were much more regular readers of the Bible than men, and (ii) that the proportion of elderly people who read their Bible at least once a week was very much higher than the proportion of those in the 'young' or 'middle-aged' groups. See Church of Scotland Board of Social Responsibility, *Lifestyle Survey*, Edinburgh: Quorum Press, 1987, pp 50, 79.

5. In a related study of nearly 300 'A' level Religious Studies students, Elizabeth Fisher discovered that they were fairly evenly divided on the question of the Bible's accuracy on *historical* matters (with slightly more questioning its accuracy than confirming it, and nearly 36% remaining neutral on the question). But when it came to the accuracy of the Bible on *scientific* matters, over 44% denied this compared with less than 5% who accepted it. In this case only 28% were neutral on the question and a further 7% were 'don't knows'.

6. The positions were based on those described in D. H. Kelsey, *The Uses of Scripture in Recent Theology*, London: SCM, 1975, and E. Farley and P. C. Hodgson, 'Scripture and Tradition', in P. C. Hodgson and R. H. King (eds), *Christian Theology*, Philadelphia: Fortress, 1982.

7. According to a survey in 1986 the national figure for those *in the general population* who accept that the Bible is 'the actual Word of God and is to be taken literally' is very much higher — ie 14%, with 18% of the general population accepting that it is 'certainly true' that the miracles in the Bible really happened. See M. Svennevig *et al.*, *Godwatching: Viewers, Religion and Television*, London: John Libbey, 1988, pp 35f. The Scottish *Lifestyle Survey* asked a forced choice question about the Bible in response to which 14.3% of the males in the general population and 21.8% of the females accepted as closest to their own position the view that the Bible is 'God's word — true in every detail'. The other options were: 'Written by men who were inspired by God and therefore must be interpreted' (56.7% of the men, 57.3% of the women),

'Contains much vision but God has not affected it specially' (10.6% men, 7.3% women), 'A normal book' (5.7% men, 2.9% women), and 'no opinion' (12.8% men, 10.7% women). See *Lifestyle Survey*, p 87. However these questions are not strictly comparable with those asked in our survey. We should note too that fundamentalism, while claiming that the Bible is inerrant, does not commit itself to the different position that it is all to be taken 'literally'. See J. Barr, *Fundamentalism*, London: SCM, 1981, ch 3.

8. See J. M. Hull, *What Prevents Christian Adults from Learning?*, London: SCM, 1985, ch 3.

APPENDIX 1: CLERGY RESPONSES

It is never easy either to devise a questionnaire for clergy, or to analyse those responses that are eventually returned. Eleven clergy, representing eight of the parishes of our sample, returned their (specially designed) version of this Bible questionnaire.

Many of the questions for clergy were intended as a check to help us to interpret the lay responses. We asked, for example, about the versions of the Bible used in worship in the parish, and how many readings there were at the eucharist. In addition we asked for a list of Christian education activities in the parish, and whether or not the clergy thought that groups should be lay-led. We also asked if there was a bookstall or parish library in church, and if any particular forms of Bible aid were recommended for lay people to read.

Much energy is put by clergy into the area of what can loosely be described as Christian education. Seven respondents said that Lent groups were available in their parish, and seven mentioned confirmation groups. Four indicated groups created for baptism preparation. In addition five clergy reported the existence of Bible study groups in their parishes, and a further two have discussion groups. Six of the eleven respondents preferred groups to be lay-led; one other clergyman stated that he would like the groups to be lay-led but such a policy had not proved feasible. Four said that they prefer clergy to be *members* of such groups, but a further five opined that clergy should not even attend them.

When we look at the attitudes of the clergy themselves to the Bible an interesting picture emerges. All the respondents agreed with the statement that '*The Bible is not always accurate when it describes history*' (four agreed strongly). Nor did anyone disagree with the claim that '*The Bible is not always accurate when it talks about scientific matters*' (six agreed). Only one disagreed with the claim that '*The Bible is not always accurate when it talks about God, God's acts and God's will for humans*', whereas four agreed strongly with it. With regard to the claim that '*The Bible is always accurate when it talks about how people should behave*', two agreed, one neither agreed nor disagreed, six disagreed, and a further two strongly disagreed with the statement. No one agreed with the view that '*The Bible is not very relevant to us today*' (eight disagreed strongly with it).

Of the eleven clerical responses to the spectrum of positions on the Bible, no one ticked either extreme view as representing the view nearest to his own. Two felt that the view that '*The Bible is indispensable to Christianity but the meaning of its contents is conditioned by the culture in which the story was first written*' was nearest to their own, and a further three ticked this *as well as* the view that '*The Bible is the book in which we read of God's dealing with his people. He still uses it to reveal himself today but not everything in it is true*'. Six ticked only this latter position. Thus all the clergy surveyed adopted some sort of liberal stance to Scripture.

Only two of the clergy responses indicated that there is a bookstall or parish library with aids to the Bible available in their churches, although another indicated that one was about to be set up. If, as our study suggests, there is a need for the promotion of serious study and reading of the Bible, with aids that enable people to grow both in their own faith and in a critical understanding of the text, the lack of provision of suitable materials is a matter of concern. If the churches do not make them available, why should the secular bookshops? Perhaps there also needs to be some sort of oversight of the lay leadership that is offered in the Christian education groups of these parishes to ensure that the best sorts of materials and methods are in fact being used, and a lively interest in the Bible engendered. Clergy are often enthusiastically in favour of lay leadership in the Christian education, study or discussion that takes place in their parishes, and rightly so. But they still bear a responsibility themselves to ensure that the educational content and methods used by such people is realizing the intended goals.

APPENDIX 2:   TABLES OF SELECTED DATA, LAY RESPONSES

TABLE A
Breakdown according to Age and Sex

15-19		20-29		30-39		40-49		50-59		60-69		70 or over		N/A
M	F	M	F	M	F	M	F	M	F	M	F	M	F	
5	12	9	17	11	28	29	53	16	49	31	72	17	77	19

TOTAL SAMPLE = 445

TABLE B
Q13 Attitudes to the Bible

The respondents were asked to indicate their opinions of the following claims:

Agree Strongly	Agree	Neither Agree Nor Disagree	Dis-agree	Strongly Disagree	Don't Know

a. 'The Bible is not always accurate when it describes history'

| 50 | 196 | 89 | 44 | 9 | 57 |

b. 'The Bible is not always accurate when it talks about scientific matters'

| 60 | 168 | 98 | 38 | 8 | 73 |

c. 'The Bible is not always accurate when it talks about God, God's acts and God's will for humans'

| 25 | 96 | 67 | 132 | 62 | 63 |

d. 'The Bible is always accurate when it talks about how people should behave'

| 85 | 169 | 46 | 91 | 11 | 43 |

e. 'The Bible is not very relevant to us today'

| 6 | 41 | 39 | 182 | 133 | 44 |

Agree Strongly	Agree	Neither Agree Nor Disagree	Dis-agree	Strongly Disagree	Don't Know

TABLE C
Chi² values

Question		Age Chi^2	Sex Chi^2
Q6	Frequency of reading Bible	15.2 (NS) df = 8	0.6 (NS) df = 4
Q13a	Historical accuracy of Bible	14.8 (NS) df = 8	5.4 (NS) df = 4
Q13b	Scientific accuracy of Bible	6.3 (NS) df = 8	15.3 (**) df = 4
Q13c	Bible accurate about God	34.6 (***) df = 8	13.8 (**) df = 4
Q13d	Bible accurate about people's behaviour	21.6 (**) df = 8	3.5 (NS) df = 4
Q13e	Bible not very relevant today	51.6 (****) df = 8	15.7 (**) df = 4

**   significant at 1% level
*** significant at 0.1% level
**** significant at less than 0.1% level

26

Learning and Believing in an Urban Parish

GUY BUCKLER AND JEFF ASTLEY

The present paper represents an interim report on an ongoing project based in a large urban, predominantly working-class, Anglican parish (population 26,000) in northern England.[1] Work to date has centred on four main areas:

(i) A 'parish audit' survey which included the mapping of significant features of the parish and the analysis of small area statistics from the national census.

(ii) Interviews with a sample of 221 residents of the local community during which a questionnaire was administered to gather data about their community involvement and feelings regarding the area, their educational background and attitudes to learning, and their religious beliefs and practice.

(iii) A self-administered questionnaire to churchgoers. One hundred and sixty-six of these were returned, representing 70-80% of the average adult attendance at the main Sunday services of the three churches in the parish. This questionnaire focused on the respondents' involvement in church activities, their educational background and attitudes to Christian learning.

(iv) A parish weekend to report on the work of the project to eighteen lay representatives of the three churches, and to raise awareness of the need for churches to develop appropriate methods and materials for Christian learning. The weekend included an intensive study of a range of Christian education materials and methods.

(v) A follow-up day eight months later, with the same lay representatives, to reflect on the outcomes of the parish weekend and to begin preparations for the final stage of the project. The day included an exercise in which the participants were asked to rate the value of different ways of promoting the use of a variety of Christian education materials and methods.

VARIETY IN THE SAMPLES

Our research has begun to identify the variety that exists within what, on a superficial view, may be regarded as a monochrome 'urban, working-class' parish. Much of this will be touched on in other sections of this paper, but some comments are apposite at this stage.

The parish studied covers traditional (former docklands) industrial/residential areas and council estates dating mainly from the 1930s and 1960s, with some more recent housing including privately-built areas. In our sample of 221 residents of the local community, 70% said that they have lived in the area for 20 years or more, and over 90% said that they enjoyed living there. The sample was entirely white (which reflects the make-up of the community as a whole). Over half were in employment; two thirds of these were in full-time employment (98% of the employed males, but only 41% of the employed females). In our churchgoers sample, however, people in full-time employment were greatly under-represented, as were the unemployed; whereas part-timers and retired people were over-represented and together made up nearly half of the worshipping community. This may be mirrored in other congregations and should be taken into account when encouraging churchgoers to reflect on 'theology-at-the-workplace' issues.

Within the congregations themselves the 'traditional' pattern of weighting by age and sex shows through the figures: 80% are female (compared with 58% of our local community sample who were female), and 42% are 60 years of age or over (compared with 28% in our local community sample). There were no males at all between 18 and 23 in our churchgoers sample. These are very significant factors for those reflecting on the context and nature of Christian education in the churches. However, nearly 40% of the churchgoers were aged between 18 and 45, and men — if under-represented — *were* there. It is worth noting that the occupational class variable showed a similar range within the sample of churchgoers to that exemplified in the local community at large, but with a significantly higher proportion of white collar and blue collar workers, and a much smaller proportion of manual workers. The mode for the churchgoers sample was 'routine non-manual', whereas in the local community sample a twin mode of 'skilled manual' and 'routine manual' was revealed. (But only 21% of churchgoers were in full-time employment anyway.) But no similar disparity was revealed when we compared the age of completing full-time education in the community and congregational samples: both surveys showed that over 60% of the sample had left school before the age of sixteen, and only 8% at eighteen or over. Most of our worshippers were married (69%), but nearly a third were not (16% widowed, 11% single, 4% divorced or separated). Only 39% of the married churchgoers have a spouse who usually attends church with them. Any assumptions based on a picture of congregations of 'churchgoing couples' clearly require some qualification.

A BELIEVING/PRACTISING PEOPLE?

Church Affiliation and Attendance
Our local community sample showed the familiar willingness of the English to confess and call themselves Christians. Only 2 out of 221 people interviewed declared that they had no religion. 96% claimed to belong to one or another Christian church or fellowship: 66% 'Church of England', 21% 'Roman Catholic', 4% 'Methodist', 1% 'URC', 2% 'other'. This follows the pattern of other surveys, with slightly more Catholic representation being shown in the parish when compared with the national average.[2] 97% had been baptized (although 10% of the 18-29 year olds had not — a growing trend even in the religiously conservative North of England) and 42% had been confirmed. 78% had been married in church, but there appeared to be no significant association between this fact and their churchgoing practice. Three-quarters of our sample had attended Sunday school and most had enjoyed the experience (enjoyment seemed to be positively associated with churchgoing, with churchgoers being more likely than non-churchgoers to have enjoyed the experience). But although 89% of those over 60 had attended, the proportion declined to 52% of the 18-29 age group. Formal Christian education for the young is clearly on the decline.

Despite these figures, only 22% of our local community sample said that they attend a local church, with only 15% of the sample attending at least once a month. These figures are rather smaller than those revealed in national survey results.[3] 43% of our 'Catholics' go to church, but only 15% of our 'Anglicans' do so — and only half of this latter group attend at least once a month. Nevertheless our sample enables us to distinguish between 'churchgoers' and 'Christian non-churchgoers' in our analysis of the data provided by this survey of the general community, as well as to compare both of these groups with the churchgoers we surveyed in the Anglican congregations of the parish.

Some Religious Beliefs

What do they believe? We offered the local community sample a range of christological positions in a format in which they could choose more than one option. 54% of those interviewed were willing to describe Jesus as the Son of God, 20% thought of him as 'just an ordinary man', and 23% as 'a very good man'. These figures are similar to those shown by other research, although revealing more of a pattern of orthodox belief.[4] Women were more likely than men to adopt a higher christology. A substantial proportion of 'Christians' in the general population seem to embrace a low christology. Many of them can also be classified as 'religious relativists', with 47% of all those interviewed saying that they believe that all religions are equally true. Only 16% *in toto* said that only one religion can be true, whereas 27% adopted the intermediate position that 'some religions are closer to the truth than others'. Among the 4% who regarded all religions as *false* we found 6 people who claimed to be members of the Church of England and one who claimed to attend church! Churchgoers (50%) were only marginally more likely than non-churchgoers (46%) to say that all religions are equally true.

59% of the local community sample believe that there is a life after death.[5] Women are more likely than men to believe this (68% of women, compared with 48% of the men, do so).[6] Over three-quarters of those who believe in a life after death believe that everyone will experience it, and over half think that it will be better than this life. Interestingly a person's age group has no significant influence on whether or not he or she believes in life after death. But churchgoers are more likely to believe in a life after death than non-churchgoers (78% compared with 53%).

Some Religious Practices

What about religious practice? We have already reviewed the church-going activities of our local community sample. Prayer is a more popular form of religious practice than public worship. 31% of those interviewed said they prayed regularly and 75% answered 'Yes' to the more general question, 'Do you ever pray?'.[7] Women were far more likely than men to say that they prayed: in our sample 90% of the women said 'Yes', compared with only 55% of men. Older respondents were more likely to say that they prayed: 84% of those over 45, compared with 62% of those aged 18-29.[8] As one would expect, churchgoing tends to be associated with praying regularly. 96% of those who go to a local church said that they pray, and 55% that they pray regularly; the equivalent figures for non-churchgoers are 68% and 23% respectively.

Of those in the total local community sample who pray at all, 58% said that their prayers were sometimes answered (49% of the non-churchgoers and 80% of the churchgoers), and an amazing 16% that their prayers were 'always answered'.

Do people still own and read Bibles? 80% of those interviewed have a Bible at home, but 54% of these do not read it at all. Only 11 out of 221 people (6% of those with a Bible at home) say that they read it 'regularly'. Of this last group, 6 were over sixty years of age, 3 were non-churchgoers, and 9 were female. The percentage of non-churchgoers who identified themselves as Christian and who claim to read their Bibles regularly is only 2% compared with 12% of churchgoers who fall into the same category. The corresponding figures for occasional reading are 23% of the non-churchgoers and 37% of the churchgoers. Nevertheless the percentage of the total sample who read their Bibles either regularly or occasionally (31%), which is exactly the same as the percentage who pray regularly, is higher than the percentage who attend church (22%). There is a significant pattern of relationship between advancing age and the likelihood of a person being engaged in Bible reading.[9]

'Non-churchgoing Christians'

In principle our sample should be open to further categorization, as sub-categories within the large group of 'non-churchgoing Christians' could be distinguished. These are all Christians by their own lights: ie they describe themselves as members of a particular Christian denomination. If within this category there were a group of people who claimed both to pray 'regularly' *and* to read their Bibles 'regularly', we could distinguish them (somewhat paradoxically) as 'non-churchgoing, practising Christians'. We might do this despite the quite proper protests of those for whom Christian practice involves much more than Bible reading and prayer, whether that 'more than' is restricted to worship or extends beyond that (or even denies its relevance) to various expressions of Christian love and care. In fact in our sample of 221 there were only 3 of these 'non-churchgoing, practising Christians', which represents a little over 1% of the population and nearly 2% of the non-churchgoing Christians. (But note that only 10% of the *churchgoing* members of the community both prayed regularly and read their Bibles regularly.)

We might then try to separate out various degrees of *'non-church-going, occasional practising Christians'*. Thus in our survey people who pray only occasionally *and* read their Bibles only occasionally represented 9.5% of the community sample and nearly 13% of the non-churchgoing Christians. Other categories may be distinguished, showing different degrees of religious practice, until we pared the sample down to wholly *'secular Christians'* who neither attend church at all, nor pray at all, nor ever read the Bible, but still describe themselves as Christians (in our sample some 22.5% of the non-churchgoing Christians).

Our data will not allow us to discriminate more clearly between the beliefs and attitudes of these different groups, but a larger sample study might reveal significant differences. What we can say is that the percentage in our population (urban, mainly working-class) who go to church is less than the percentage who pray regularly, and less than the percentage who read the Bible at least occasionally, by a figure of about 10%. There clearly therefore exists a group of *'threshold Christians'* akin to the God-fearers who clustered around the synagogues in the Judaism of the first century. This is a group of non-churchgoers who share some of the practices (and, as the earlier data show, many of the beliefs) of the churchgoers, but who have not taken the extra step of churchgoing-commitment.[10] Most Christian evangelists and educators view them as potential full 'converts' or 'disciples', and aim to encourage them over the threshold into the main body of the church. But some would argue that we may speak of, and that we have a responsibility for, their Christian discipleship and its formation even though they may never become more regular churchgoers. Perhaps Christian education with such a group does not need to include among its aims the increase of their churchgoing practice and should be aimed solely at increasing their Christian believing, valuing, lifestyle etc 'where they are'? This is a claim worthy of discussion by Christian educators.

A LEARNING PEOPLE?

Formal, Explicit Learning

Only a small proportion of this local community and its congregations had experienced higher education (6% of the congregation, 4% in the local community). But 38% of the population of the local community, and a massive 61% of the churchgoers, said that they had been involved in some further education (daytime or evening classes) since leaving school. The significantly higher proportion of churchgoers with this experience indicates that such congregations may be more open to programmes of formal Christian education than many clergy suppose. Those clergy for whom 'post-school education' is synonymous with higher education at college or university can too easily ignore the fact that very many people do have experience of formal education outside the walls of the school, but that this is the rather different experience of the further education class. The likelihood of respondents having experienced further education decreases with increasing age.

We asked both church attenders and 'ordinary' members of the parish which secular subjects they would most like to learn about. 56% of the local community sample and 28% of the churchgoers sample did not respond (and only a quarter of those churchgoers who did respond did so positively). This general lack of interest in *further* further education prepares us for the fact that when asked if there was any particular aspect of the Christian faith and life that respondents would like to learn more about in the next twelve months, 25% of the churchgoers sample did not answer this question and a further 54% answered in the negative. Thus only 21% of these regular churchgoers said that there was some particular aspect of the Christian faith or life that they would like to learn more about (this compares with 17% who positively responded to the similar question about secular subjects). Although in one sense their past experience should have made them more open to formal education, most churchgoers are clearly just not interested in doing so, even in the area of Christian education. We believe that further research needs to be done to discover the reasons for this reluctance. Those who did respond positively to the question about further Christian study asked for courses on doctrine, the Bible, other faiths, other Christian denominations, church history, women in the church, and Christianity and change, as well as more practical topics such as church organization, prayer and healing, pastoral skills and dealing with life situations.

These figures should also be interpreted in the light of the fact that 53% of respondents said that they had at some time since confirmation been a member of a study, discussion or prayer group (ie a *church-based* learning/activity group). We found that those who had attended such groups were more likely than others to have at least half their friends or social contacts as members of the church.

Also those who attend church *regularly* are more likely to have been a member of such a group. Those who attend more church services (eg Sunday morning *and* evening services, or a Sunday morning service *and* a weekday service) are more likely to be or to have been group members. It may be that formal Christian education groups have an important effect on increasing a sense of commitment to the worship and fellowship of the church, and/or that those who are already committed are more likely to attend such groups.

We asked both the churchgoing and the local community respondents about their preferred '*learning environment*'. When we asked the churchgoers about learning methods for Christian education, in a question allowing them to tick more than one response, 57% of those who answered (48% of the sample) said they would be happy to learn with others in a small group; 28% (23% of the sample) 'on my own with specially prepared books etc'; and 24% (20% of the sample) 'in a class with a teacher'. 17% did not answer this question.[11] These figures compare with responses to similar questions about general formal further education in our local community questionnaire where 70% of the sample replied 'with a small group', 16% on their own 'with specially prepared books', 13% on their own 'with a teacher'. In this sample the age of respondents was not a significant factor, but those who had completed their full-time education after the age of sixteen were more likely to be happy to learn in a class with a teacher than those who had left before that age. Interestingly, those who said they had *not* enjoyed school were more positively disposed to learning on their own than those who had (40% compared with 26%). Those who had attended evening/day classes since leaving school were less likely than others to favour learning on their own. The option of learning in a small group in someone's home was not much welcomed in our survey of the general population: preferred locations were all outside the home (local school, pub, community centre, etc).

Sixty-three percent of our sample of churchgoers said that they would be happy to learn with people from their own church, and forty percent said that they would be happy to learn with people from other churches: female respondents divided 66%/39% over this question, whereas male respondents divided 48%/44%.[12]

With regard to the *length* of a learning programme, 42% of those who answered the question from the congregations (35% of the sample) said that they would be happy to learn 'in short stretches' of about six weeks; 15% (13% of the sample) in twelve week stretches; and 26% (21% of the sample) regularly throughout the whole year.[13]

Younger people and those in full-time employment were more likely than those from other groups to respond positively to this last option.

With regard to the *times* for learning, 67% of those who answered (52% of the churchgoers sample) regarded a weekday evening as a 'convenient' time, 26% (20% of the sample) so regarded Saturday evening — although few in full-time employment did so, and 16% (12% of the sample) thought that Sunday evening would be convenient. Only 6% (5% of the sample) ticked weekday daytime, 13% (10% of the sample) Saturday afternoon, 11% (8% of the sample) Sunday afternoon. (In this question a multiple response was allowed.) In the local community survey, as well as in a related diocese-wide survey that sampled lay people already involved in a formal Christian education course, a majority also rated weekday evening as the most convenient time for learning.

Explicit, formal Christian education can often best be organized in existing church groups, rather than through more *ad hoc* groupings that have been specially set up for the purpose of learning. Interestingly 62% of the congregational respondents said that they have at some time belonged to some organization or committee in the church, 28% having been at some time a member of the parochial church council or a district church committee. (Those who have been on the PCC/DCC are more likely than others to have friendship and social contacts among church members. Church committee members are also more likely to have continued in school beyond the age of 16 compared with the whole sample.) 19% of female respondents have been members of the Mothers' Union, and a further 24% of female respondents have been members of some other church women's group, making 43% *in toto*. This compares with 33% of male respondents who recorded membership of a church-related men's group. The potential for Christian education channelled through such groups is clearly considerable.

Informal, Implicit Christian Learning

Many Christian educationalists will be less interested in data relating to the setting up of explicit Christian education programmes than in making some assessment of the many implicit pathways and experiences that lead to Christian learning, but are rarely labelled as such (see chapter 10 of this volume). Our congregational questionnaire listed some ten ways in which people might be helped to understand more about Christianity: some of these may be described as implicit learning experiences, whereas others are more explicit (eg sermons). Respondents were invited to rate these on a scale of 1-5. Categories with a median rating of 5 ('very helpful') were: public worship, receiving holy communion, and private prayer; those with a median rating of 4 ('helpful') were Christian literature and books, preaching/talks, belonging to a group, reading the Bible, sharing with another Christian, and talking with a member of the clergy. No one rated radio and television programmes at 4 or 5 (their median rating was 3).

It has to be admitted that these facts need to be qualified by the suppositions that experiences that are not widely shared are likely to be rated as 'least helpful' — and that all churchgoers attend worship! But our survey also shows that 81% of our churchgoers watch religious TV programmes,[14] and therefore that the lower rating of these experiences by comparison with prayer and worship may not be insignificant.

Follow-up research in which a small group of congregational respondents rated a wider range of church-related experiences on their helpfulness in promoting an understanding of Christianity showed that worship (particularly eucharistic worship) was again rated very highly, as was the singing of hymns. The fellowship of the community before and after worship was rated highest of all.

In that later survey those features of church life that were regarded on the whole as 'unhelpful' in promoting Christian understanding included the way in which churches made their decisions, the activities of the church councils, and the financial arrangements of the church.

(Of course 'Christian learning' should be taken much more widely than 'understanding more about Christianity', but we have not yet attempted to make any assessment of the self-perceived changes in Christian attitudes, values, lifestyle-behaviour etc that may result from different learning experiences.)

MATERIALS AND METHODS

Returning to a consideration of the organization of formal, explicit Christian learning experiences, the authors felt that they should try to discover more about which resources and methods ought to be used in this area. Patently this is a very big question and includes theological as well as pedagogical ('androgogical') factors. Some points may be made by way of introduction. In our local community sample we noted that 68% of the population owned a video player and 71% read at least one book a year. (As many as 39% read more than 10 books a year, although admittedly only 10% of the general population admitted to enjoying reading books about *religion*.[15]) Seventy-five percent of the general population of the parish read a newspaper daily, with 91% doing so at least once a week. (Fifty percent of those who attend church in this sample read tabloid newspapers, as compared with fifty-eight percent of those who do not. In this area the most widely read paper is a locally-edited broadsheet covering both national and local news stories.) The ready availability of video players and the substantial proportion of the population who are doing some reading suggests that, in this area at least, these are media that may be exploited for the purposes of Christian education.

Although our evaluation of learning materials and methods is still at an early stage, we feel that some of the indications that we have so far are worth recording. The opinions of a group of 18 churchgoers were surveyed in some detail at the parish weekend and during a subsequent Saturday study day. This small sample of men and women was structured so as to include representation across the age groups. It represents nearly 9% of the regular Sunday congregation. At the weekend we tried out on them various Christian education materials and methods, all of which related to the subject of prayer.

These exercises have convinced the authors of the importance of taking more seriously the learners' *own* evaluation of Christian education materials. Too often such material is evaluated by the teacher in terms of what he/she 'likes', 'approves of', etc (doubtless for educationally significant reasons). But the evaluations of the learners may be very different, and they are surely not irrelevant — especially in Christian education.

Video and tape/slide
Short sections of five videos and two tape/slide presentations were shown to the respondents who were asked to complete individual evaluation sheets giving the material a mark out of ten in order 'to help a church committee decide which one to buy'. Respondents were also invited to add any comments on content or style.

The most professionally produced video ('The Seven Circles of Prayer') was, as expected, well received by almost all respondents; but surprisingly the rather amateur acting and direction of another video, which we (along with other Christian educators) had been prepared to dismiss out of hand, did not prevent the majority of our respondents giving it a similar high score (median 7, mode 8, mean 6.5;

compare the figures for the 'Seven Circles of Prayer' — median 8, mode 8, mean 7.4). From their comments it would appear that the respondents were more concerned — in both cases — with the content rather than the style or presentation of the videos (insofar as these can be separated). This particular 'amateurish' video had something to say, and said it; most people liked that. If it is important to start where people are in education, then we must recognize that very often people want content: as they often put it, 'the basics'. Perhaps Christian educators attempt too often to 'tell it slant' when learners often want to hear it (or at least something) 'straight'?

The most noteworthy result from the exercise, however, was the great range of evaluations offered. The video which received the highest median, mode and mean scores still only managed one mark of 10 and came in with ratings of 2 and 4 from other respondents; whereas the video that had the lowest overall scores (a diocesan-produced, episcopal 'talking head': median 5, mode 5, mean 6.2) could boast three 10s to its credit, whereas its lowest marks were 3 and 4! Clearly different people appreciate different things. As Christian educators we can never assume that any congregation or group is monochrome. People are very different one from another, and there is no one set of Christian education materials that will appeal to everybody.

It would appear from the comments made, and from later discussion with respondents, that people say that they approve of 'well-presented' videos, but that they mean by this that the presenters concerned should be at ease with the material and present it honestly, rather than that the presentation has to be up to the professional standards of television. Indeed some commented that one, professionally produced, video was 'too slick' and 'too much like an advert'. The medium is very much the message in this field and, at least for *churchgoers*, Christian education videos that are made to look like adverts, pop videos or party political broadcasts may well be rejected (and resented).

A video that used local people and scenes was not as well received as we had expected. Was it too local? In producing Christian education material for local churches we may have to recognize that sometimes people do not appreciate an emphasis on a local context and a local accent. We recall that Tyne Tees Television moved away from using presenters with local accents after surveying the opinions of their viewers. There is a real ecclesiological question here about how 'local' the local church is or wants to be — or should be encouraged to be.

Audio Tapes

Extracts from seven audio cassettes of talks on prayer were played to our respondents in small groups. Once again each person filled in an evaluation sheet, scoring the material for interest and ease of understanding. After hearing all the extracts the group were then encouraged to make general comments on the tapes and their value for Christian education.

The general opinion of respondents was that it is easy in a group to listen to, and concentrate on, a cassette. However it is important to ensure that there are no distractions when a cassette is being used in a group situation: the setting is vital if the most is to be made of this medium. The point was also made that some cassettes may be more suitable for use by a group than others which may be better suited to individual use. Interestingly, there appeared to be no relationship between the respondents' perception of the *difficulty* of a piece and how *interesting* they found it.

Two extracts proved to be particularly popular: those from David Watson and Frank Topping. These represent two very different approaches. David Watson offers a clear, logical exposition of Christian teaching on the Holy Spirit; Frank Topping makes a point by telling an amusing story. Several people said that the *voice* is an important element in determining whether or not a cassette is worth listening to; they felt that both David Watson and Frank Topping had good voices. One person described David Watson's as 'very clear and authoritative'. (Again the authors perceived matters rather differently.) Another comment was that it is the voice rather than the content that determines whether or not the cassette is a 'success', which rather goes against the group's comments about videos. Another point that came up in discussion was that if the speaker is a person whose name is known to the listener, then it is easier for the cassette to attract attention. Again, however, a well-known ecclesiastical figure in one of the videos was not particularly well received. Perhaps different criteria are being applied to these two media?

The least popular audio tape extracts were those from Peter Baelz and Michael Hollings. Half the respondents found Peter Baelz's contribution 'a little difficult to understand', and just under half found it 'not very interesting' or 'boring'. Respondents found Michael Hollings' talk easier to understand — over 75% said it was 'very easy'; but nearly half found it 'not very interesting' or 'boring'. The authors would have rated both these pieces much more highly.

As to the content of such talks, over three-quarters of the

respondents found Frank Topping's story 'very helpful', and 60% found David Hope's illustration from personal experience 'very helpful'. Less than a third, however, thought that Michael Hollings' illustrations from the Bible were 'very helpful', although 60% said they were 'quite helpful'.

Evaluation of Written Materials
Short passages from various Christian education booklets and courses were provided, some of them including exercises, for people to respond to individually (three to five items per respondent).[16] Participants were given evaluation sheets on which they rated each item on a 'difficult-easy' scale and a 'boring-interesting' scale, answered specific questions about the style or content of the material, and were then invited to add other 'good' or 'bad' comments about it. They were then asked to mark each item out of 10 'to help a church committee decide which one to buy', and to say which of the pieces particularly changed how the respondent 'thought or felt about prayer'. An opportunity was also given for the respondent to record further thoughts about the group of pieces evaluated, and in some cases further general questions were asked about all of them. Each item was rated by a number of respondents.

Again we noted the *variety* of responses, with regard to interest level, perception of difficulty, whether the material was regarded as 'helpful' or not, and in people's 'voting choices'. This should encourage us to see that different people appreciate different things, and to try to provide a greater range of materials for people's own learning. Clearly this is difficult in group work, but that is perhaps one of the *disadvantages* of Christian education in a group.

We noted that passages that used short sentences or a 'concise style' were generally regarded as easy to understand, eg the note form in Montefiore's *Confirmation Notebook*; whereas the long sentences in one other selection seemed to contribute to its more mixed response. An item that presented material in a very abbreviated note form was commended for its separate sections by a number of respondents.

One respondent commented on D'Arcy-Berubé's *Someone There* that it was 'easy to read: short passages with no complicated words'. The use of 'mood pictures' (as in *This Prayer Called Life*) did not seem to most respondents to 'add anything to the text'. Where pictures were closely related to the text, almost like comic illustrations (à la Rupert Bear?), people tended to feel that they did 'add something', although in the case of the *Someone There* material the pictures probably also contributed to the comments that the material was 'a bit childish'. The Venn-type diagrams in one item were regarded as helpful.

Averaging out the ratings out of 10 (the score given to help a church committee decide which item to purchase) indicates that Mountford's *Newness of Life* came out highest, with a score of 9, along with Montefiore's *Confirmation Notebook*. These were closely followed by Herbert's *Ways into Prayer* and Winjgaard's *Seven Circles of Prayer*. Rankin's *Looking at Worship* (designed for classroom use) rated lowest, with an average of 3.5.[17]

Three items were considered together. These were items in which people had to do writing exercises on the sheet provided. On the whole people found these helpful, although one indicated that 'there was not enough space to write in'. All the materials in this test were written for adolescent confirmation candidates, but the level of writing and of the exercises was found to be acceptable by most of these adult respondents. Jones's *Praying with Jesus* scored highly on most criteria.

Various other points are worth making about the material. We asked a number of respondents to comment on Allen's *Signposts on the Way*, as it contained several cartoons that we felt were rather witty. Three people felt that the cartoons added nothing to the material, four were positive about them, and two unsure. The style of Herbert's *Ways Into Prayer* was regarded by all reviewers as helpful. This was a piece of work with short sentences; a clear, but not unpoetic, repetitive style; and proclaimed itself as beginning 'right at the very beginning'. The newspaper style (with sub-headings) used in Mountford's *Newness of Life* was evaluated as 'clear and easily understood', and seemed to contribute to a positive response to this piece.

The Jonah Dialogue

Small groups of lay people were also introduced to a more experiential form of Christian learning. Each group was asked to tell the story of Jonah as far as they could remember it. They then followed an exercise in which people were asked to write a dialogue between themselves and the part of them which runs away from God, continuing until the dialogue came to some sort of conclusion.[18] They were then asked in pairs to share with one another their feelings about what they had written (they were not required to share the dialogue itself).

Eighteen people took part in this exercise and filled in the evaluation sheets. They were asked to say how difficult and how interesting they found this type of 'participatory Bible study', and also to assess what they had learned from the exercise. Two people commented that the exercise was very difficult to begin with but then got easier, only one person found it very difficult without any qualification. Four found it a little difficult and the remaining eleven found it either 'quite easy' or 'very easy'. No one classed the exercise as boring, although two people felt that it wasn't very interesting. Six classed it as 'quite interesting' and ten as 'very interesting'.

Responses to this piece of experiential learning were on the whole positive, therefore, but the experience provoked as great a variety of comments as any other method/medium. Because of the nature of the exercise, the learning here seemed to be happening at a much deeper level than with other methods, and thus gave rise to strong feelings. Comments on the experience varied from 'made me think much deeper...than I ever done before' and 'very revealing, almost frightening', to 'waste of time' and 'embarrassing'. Such experiential work needs to be in the hands of a skilled facilitator (as it was in this case, with the help of a diocesan adult adviser). In normal Christian education, of course, a facilitator can wait for the 'golden moment' (although not everyone reaches this at the same time), and preparatory and follow-up work is possible, so the weekend context left a great deal to be desired. But there is no doubt that this learning experience was the deepest of the weekend, but also the most controversial.

Other Research

At the Saturday learning day the same eighteen respondents discussed in groups of two or three their assessments of various ways of promoting the different materials and methods for Christian learning that they had experienced at the weekend conference. They were asked to give each of these a mark to indicate 'how useful' on a scale of 1 to 5 they would find it, if it were to be provided by the church. The mean, mode and median of these marks were then computed to give some indication of the preferred options.

In the *'reading* area' respondents on the whole favoured the provision of a good church library and (a little less popular) the provision of a good bookstall (especially if books were made available at less than their full cost). Providing reviews and recommendations about books, and setting up reading groups for people to discuss a book, scored nearer to the middle of the 'most useful' to 'least useful' scale.

Respondents on the whole rated highly the setting up of groups using *videos* to stimulate discussion and (rather less so) the provision of a video library for home borrowing. The making of parish-based videos for Christian education, however, and the borrowing of videos from other agencies both received low scores.

The provision of regular *Bible* study groups, including participatory Bible study such as the Jonah exercise, was rated very highly. Special talks/lectures on the Bible were also regarded as useful (and as more useful than providing Bible study notes for daily use). But the provision of notes on the Sunday readings was not regarded as particularly useful.

The idea of a parish *audio cassette* library was nearly as popular as that of a video library, but the church groups using audio cassettes were not thought to be quite as useful as those using video cassettes. Again the actual making of 'local' audio cassettes, and a scheme to encourage people to borrow cassettes from other agencies, were not popular options.

Various kinds of *talks* were consistently scored highly, with mean, mode and median scores higher than four. Even higher scores were attracted by the *small group* suggestion: almost identical marks being given for a group studying one particular 'Christian topic/issue' over 6-8 weeks as for 'a group whose primary aim is to help members to explore their own experience'. But respondents rated as less useful a group following 'a course of study spread over one year or longer', albeit in 6-8 week 'terms'.

One of the lowest scores (with a mode and median of only 2) was given for the idea of promoting *individual learning*, with people following a course of study on their own using specially prepared materials. Such 'Open University-type' learning, at whatever level it is pitched, finds little favour with these Christians. An even lower score (mode 1, mean 2.1, median 1.5) was given to *sermons* of 20 minutes or longer. But clergy may be relieved to note that sermons of up to 10-12 minutes were rated very highly (mode 5, mean 4.2, median 4.5). Very little enthusiasm was shown for the provision of notes to accompany sermons; but courses of sermons on a particular topic attracted a stronger vote, as did the use of visual aids in sermons (mean 3.7, median 4). Another very highly rated option was the provision of regular *learning days* for adults, either within or (particularly) away from the parish. The idea of all-age days within the parish also scored highly.

FURTHER REFLECTIONS

Our experience of this project has made us realize much more clearly than when we started that the aim of providing adult Christian education in a parish is not likely to be realized by producing one single 'appropriate' course of Christian learning, or one set of Christian education materials. We must, rather, plan a *variety* of learning opportunities that will respect the variety that exists within the parish and its congregations.

This paper has indicated some of the areas uncovered by our research that will need to be addressed in the future. For example, we need to consider the significant proportion of retired people in our congregations: to what extent are such people in the minds of those who plan learning and produce educational materials? Do current learning opportunities and materials seem irrelevant (even oppressive) to retired and elderly people? Again we need to take greater account of those issues that are of concern to the large number of women in our congregations: to what extent do we deal in our parishes with their particular concerns? Do those with responsibility for adult education in a parish (usually men) always know what these issues are?

We have referred to the existence in the parish of 'threshold Christians', and posed the question of what is the responsibility of the adult Christian educator to this significant group 'beyond' the church.

Another area which requires further research is the apparent reluctance of churchgoers to engage in formal, explicit Christian education. If we are concerned to ensure that the worshipping people of our churches are at the same time people who are learning and growing, we must both discover more about the reasons for this reluctance and ways in which it might be overcome, *as well as* paying greater attention to those informal, implicit ways of learning ('the hidden curriculum') through which the values, beliefs, and behaviour-dispositions of churchgoers are being formed.

Our testing of existing methods and materials for adult Christian education has revealed just how important it is to consult potential learners before presenting them with pre-selected methods and materials. The adult educator must not only be aware of the wide range of methods and materials that exist, but must also be prepared to negotiate with the learners themselves before the final selection is made.

We conclude with some more general comments from our research project that suggest additional lines of enquiry. As with the above remarks, none of these comments is restricted in its application to this particular parish, or to 'urban working-class' congregations.

Variety of Intentions for Learning

In conversations with individual lay people and groups of lay people, we have gained some impression of the variety of intentions for learning among laity. For example, some have expressed a strong desire to be 'taught the basics of Christian belief and church member-ship'; others have expressed a desire for some form of training which will equip lay people to share in the ministry of the church; others see learning activities as opportunities for mutual support between Christians; others, rather, view Christian education as a way of 'edu-cating non-churchgoers into church membership and Christian com-mitment'. It would be illuminating to see how far the intentions of those clergy and others who provide programmes of Christian learning differ from the intentions of the laity who are the potential 'consumers'.

Variety of Views of the Church and the Christian Life

The results of the group discussion at the parish weekend of four 'models' of the church indicate that, among lay people, there is *both* (a) a variety of ideas about priorities for Christian ministry and mission; *and* (b) a variety of ideas about the kind of Christian forma-tion that is required for this mission and ministry — eg deepening of personal spirituality, improving skills for ministry, gaining further knowledge or the ability to work alongside other agencies. In all discussion about the nature of Christian education it is imperative to clarify how both learners and educators understand Christianity and the nature of the church before any real progress can be made in the planning of appropriate contexts, experiences and educational meth-ods/materials for Christian formation and church education.

Variety of Language

In some preliminary studies for future in-depth research into the belief patterns of lay people in the parish we have gathered descriptors of God, Jesus, and the church both from 'ordinary churchgoers' here and from a panel of more 'theologically-articulate' Christians (includ-ing scholars, clergy and bishops, and Christian educationalists). It has become very clear to us through pilot studies using these descriptors that the everyday parlance of the latter group is very often unfamiliar to, and sometimes misunderstood by, the members of the congrega-tion. This would not matter if it were not also the case that a great deal of this obscure or misunderstood language is to be found in the texts of the Sunday liturgy, in Bible readings and in sermons. Its use there makes many in our congregations feel 'ignorant'. Some are embarrassed and slightly guilty about this, and perhaps they eschew further Christian education so as to avoid revealing their ignorance. Churchgoers often feel at the edge of the church, even if it is a church which they have attended all their lives, because they feel excluded by the 'technical' vocabulary (or behaviour patterns). How can we create Christian education materials that help church attenders to feel that they are not gate-crashing their own church? This 'language gap' deserves further study, and may prove to be a very real problem in the promotion of a Christian learning that is properly 'understanded of the people'.

NOTES

1. The authors wish to express their thanks to the Trustees of St Hild and St Bede for funding this project, and to Mme Sophie Baillarguet, the Project's Research Assistant, for considerable help with the survey work.

2. The national figures are variously given as 13% who claim to be Roman Catholic, 65% Church of England (or Church of Scotland etc), 7% Free Church, 5% other Christian churches (Eric Jacobs and Robert Worcester, *We British: Britain Under the MORIscope*, London: Weidenfeld & Nicholson, 1990, p 78), and 11% Catholic, 37% Anglican, 5% Presbyterian, 11% other Christian churches (Roger Jowell *et al.*, *British Social Attitudes: the 7th Report*, Aldershot: Gower, 1990, p. 185; but this survey found that 34% regarded themselves as having 'no religion').

3. The national MORI figures are 17% claiming to attend at least once a fortnight and a further 22% attending 'occasionally' (Jacobs and Worcester, *loc. cit.*). A figure of 23% attending church monthly is given by Mark Abrams *et al.*, *Values and Social Change in Britain*, Basingstoke: Macmillan, 1985, p 61.

4. In a forced choice format, the Leeds Religious Research Project found 43% adopting the description 'the Son of God', 30% 'an ordinary human being', and 12% 'a prophet'. Helen Krarup, *Conventional Religion and Common Religion in Leeds: Interview Schedule, Basic Frequencies by Question*, Leeds: University of Leeds, 1982 (survey date), p 48.

5. Comparative national figures are somewhat lower: 49% in Jacobs and Worcester, *op. cit.*, p 80; 45% in Abrams, *op. cit.*, p 60.

6. The MORI poll reveals 57% of the women and 39% of the men holding this view (*op. cit.*, p 57). The figures from a national survey in Scotland show a similar significant difference between the sexes on this question: see Church of Scotland Board of Social Responsibility, *Lifestyle Survey*, Edinburgh: Quorum Press, 1987, p 86. That survey supports our findings that 'no significant association exists between age and individuals' belief in life after death' (p 54).

7. The Leeds figures were 35% who pray several times a week, and 71% who pray 'at all' (*op. cit.*, pp 64f).

8. The Scottish *Lifestyle Survey* figures are similar (*op. cit.*, pp 50, 79).

9. The claim that being older and being female is positively associated with a greater frequency of Bible reading is shown in the Scottish *Lifestyle Survey*, pp 50, 79.

10. Cf Jean Bouteiller, 'Threshold Christians: A Challenge for the Church', in W. J. Reedy (ed), *Becoming a Catholic Christian*, New York: Sadlier, 1979, pp 67f.

11.   Comparative figures from a 1987/88 survey of 'congregation members interested in Christian learning' by the Theological Education by Extension Forum (TEEF) showed that 59% would like to do their learning in a small group, 27% in a class, and 34% alone (Mike Butterworth *et al., Christian Learning,* no date, p 13).

12.   Comparative TEEF figures showed 37% who would like to do their learning with people from their own congregation, and 38% who would like to learn with those from other congregations (*loc. cit.*).

13.   This contrasts with TEEF figures from churchmembers who were described as interested in Christian learning. In that sample 31% said that they would like to do their learning in six week stretches, 22% 'over a term or more', and 44% 'regularly throughout the year' (*loc. cit.*). In a related study with churchgoers who were already engaged in a formal course of Christian education (in the same diocese as the parish studied in this paper), the most popular length for such a course was between two and six sessions (48%), followed by a length of seven to twelve sessions (24%), the remainder preferring the life of a group or course to be longer than twelve sessions or responding that 'any period' was acceptable. (We are grateful to Mrs Carolyn Wilcox for providing this information from her survey data.)

14.   This compares with 44% of the community sample overall, and with the 62% declared in the IBA's survey as having watched at least one religious programme in February 1988. The proportion of the general population who watch religious programmes increases significantly with age according to our figures (24% in the 18-19 age group, 79% in the 65+ age group). The IBA's figures are similar: see Michael Svennevig *et al., Godwatching: Viewers, Religion and Television,* London: John Libbey, 1988, ch 5.

15.   There are two libraries in the parish; 25% of those from this community who were interviewed use one or other of them — those younger than 45, or older than 59, being more likely to do so. About half of the number of respondents who said that they 'ever' read books *buy* books, a slightly smaller percentage *borrow* them from friends. Fiction was the most popular category of books read, followed by biography/autobiography, history and travel in that order.

16.   The materials tested were selected from eighteen different publications. Details of those mentioned in the paper are as follows: Marjorie Allen, *Signposts on the Way,* Derby: Church House, 1991; John Bernard, *This Prayer Called Life,* Minneapolis: Winston Press, 1972; Francoise D'Arcy-Berubé and John Paul Berubé, *Someone There,* Indiana: Avé Maria Press, 1986; Christopher Herbert, *Ways into Prayer,* London: Church House, 1987; James Jones, *Praying with Jesus,* London: BRF, 1988; Hugh Montefiore, *Confirmation Notebook,* London: SPCK, 1973; Brian Mountford, *Newness of Life,* Oxford: Mowbray, 1984; John Rankin, *Looking at Worship,* Cambridge: Lutterworth, 1981; John Wijngaards, *Seven Circles of Prayer,* Great Wakering: McCrimmon, 1987.

17.   This is a school text written as an objective account of what Christians do. Three out of four people said that they did not like the approach taken in this material, and two of them wrote that it was 'too technical' or had a 'lot of jargon which may be difficult to understand'.

18.   Chris Peck, 'Bringing the Bible Alive: Jonah', Method 6 'Internal Dialogue', in *Bringing the Bible Alive: Introducing Participatory Bible Study,* Liverpool: Southwark Lay Training Team/Liverpool Department of Development for Mission, 1990.

Contributors

The Revd Dr Jeff Astley is founding Director of the ecumenical North of England Institute for Christian Education, and honorary lecturer in the Department of Theology and the School of Education of the University of Durham. He was formerly Principal Lecturer and Head of Religious Studies at Bishop Grosseteste College, Lincoln. He has published articles on theological and Christian education topics in a number of journals, including *The Journal of Theological Studies, Theology* and *Religious Education.* He is principal author of *How Faith Grows: Faith Development and Christian Education,* co-editor of *Christian Perspectives on Faith Development,* and author of *The Philosophy of Christian Religious Education* (forthcoming).

Canon Dr Edward I. Bailey is Rector of Winterbourne, Honorary Convenor of the Network for the Study of Implicit Religion, and Associate Editor of *Sociological Analysis.* In addition to articles in sociological journals, journals on the study of religion, and various collections, he has contributed to *A Dictionary of Religious Education* and written a book entitled *Belief.* He is currently engaged in preparing a full summary of the data on implicit religion from his researches, and their implications for the church.

Dr Stephen Barton lectured at Salisbury and Wells Theological College before taking up a post as Lecturer in New Testament in the Department of Theology of the University of Durham. His articles have appeared in *New Testament Studies, Theology* and *Jahrbuch für Antike und Christentum.* He is the author of *The Spirituality of the Gospels* (forthcoming).

The Revd Guy Buckler is Parish Priest in the team ministry of the Anglican parish of Willington on Tyneside, having previously served at St Thomas's, Parkside, near Luton. He is also part-time chaplain at North Tyneside College of Further Education.

David Day is Senior Lecturer in Religious Education, University of Durham School of Education. He was previously Senior Lecturer in

Theology and Religious Studies at Derby Lonsdale College of Higher Education, and is currently Chair of the Durham County Council Standing Advisory Council on Religious Education. He is the author of articles in *Spectrum* and the *British Journal of Religious Education*, and of the study *Jeremiah: Speaking for God in a Time of Crisis*. He is co-author of *Teenage Beliefs*.

Elizabeth Fisher was formerly Assistant Director and Institute Project Officer at the North of England Institute for Christian Education, and Director of Studies of the North East Ordination Course. She is an Anglican, a member of the General Synod and a Ministerial Training Consultant. She is author and editor of a series of adult Christian education course booklets and has published in the journal *Christian*.

The Revd Professor Leslie J. Francis is currently D.J. James Professor of Pastoral Theology and Mansel Jones Fellow at Trinity College, Carmarthen and St David's University College, Lampeter. In addition to academic appointments, he has been non-stipendiary priest in charge of parishes in the Dioceses of Gloucester and of St Edmundsbury and Ipswich. He is the author and co-author of a large number of articles in the psychology and sociology of religion, as well as on Christian education issues, including papers in the *Review of Religious Research, Journal for the Scientific Study of Religion* and *British Journal of Religious Education*. He has authored and edited a number of books, most recently *Churches in Fellowship, Christian Perspectives for Education* and *The Country Parson*.

The Revd Dr Harry M. Gibson is a Church of Scotland minister, currently Minister of The High Kirk, Dundee. He has previously served in the parishes of Carmunnock and of Aberfeldy and Amulree. He is a member of the Church of Scotland's Adult Christian Education Committee. His doctoral dissertation is entitled 'Attitudes to Religion and Communication of Christian Truth' (University of St Andrews, 1989). He has contributed to the journals *Education Research, British Journal of Religious Education* and *Journal of Empirical Theology*.

The Revd Dr David Heywood is Team Vicar, St Antony's, Sanderstead, and a member of the Support and Training Committee of the Southwark Diocesan Board of Ministry and Training. He spent three years researching a Ph.D. thesis entitled 'Revelation and Christian Learning' (University of Durham, 1989) under the supervision of Dr Jeff Astley at NEICE. He has published articles in the *British Journal of Religous Education*.

Professor John M. Hull is Professor of Religious Education and Dean of the Faculty of Education and Continuing Studies in the University of Birmingham. He is the Editor of the *British Journal of Religious Education* and General Secretary of the International Seminar on Religious Education and Values. He is the author of many articles in educational and theological journals, including the *British Journal of Educational Studies, Educational Review* and the *Scottish Journal of Theology*. His books include *What Prevents Christian Adults from Learning?*, *Mishmash: Religious Education in Multi-Cultural Britain, a Study in Metaphor* and *Touching the Rock: An Experience of Blindness*. He describes his denominational allegiance as 'Church of England and United Reformed Church'.

Professor Edward Hulmes is Spalding Professorial Fellow in World Religions, Department of Theology, University of Durham. He was formerly William Belden Noble Lecturer at Harvard University and Director of the Farmington Institute, Oxford. He is a Roman Catholic layman. In addition to articles in the *Scottish Journal of Theology, The Tablet* and other religious journals, he has published *Commitment and Neutrality in Religious Education* and *Education and Cultural Diversity*.

Robin Minney is Lecturer in Religious Education at the University of Durham School of Education. He was formerly Principal Lecturer in Religious Education at the College of St Hild and St Bede, Durham. His articles have appeared in a number of journals including the *British Journal of Educational Studies, Religious Studies* and *Curriculum*. He has written a classroom text, *Christianity for GCSE*, and is the author of the book *Of Many Mouths and Eyes* and co-author of *Awe and Wonder in the Classroom*.

Monsignor Kevin Nichols is Parish Priest at the Church of the Holy Family, Darlington. He was formerly Head of Education at Christ's College, Liverpool, and later National Adviser for Religious Education, Catholic Bishops Conference of England and Wales. He was recently Visiting Professor at the Catholic University of America, and Visiting Pastoral Theology Lecturer in the University of Durham. He has published in *The Tablet* and *Lumen Vitae*, and his books include *Cornerstone* and *Orientations*. He is the editor of *Voice of the Hidden Waterfall*.

Father Jim O'Keefe is the Administrator for Catholic Care North East and Assistant Priest at St Aloysius Parish, Hebburn, Tyne & Wear. He was formerly Director of Pastoral Theology and Communications at Ushaw College, the Roman Catholic Seminary. He is a member of the Management Committee of CAFOD. In addition to articles in *Priest* *and People, The Furrow* and the *CAFOD Journal,* he is the author of a number of publications for Catholic Care North East, including *I'll Tell you a Secret* and *How is it For You?*

The Revd Martyn Percy studied theology at Bristol University and trained for the Anglican ministry at Cranmer Hall, Durham. He is now curate at St Andrew's, Bedford, and a member of St Alban's Diocesan Synod. While at Durham University he began his doctoral studies which he is now continuing as a research student at King's College, London.

The Revd Dr W. S. F. Pickering was formerly Senior Lecturer in Sociology at the University of Newcastle upon Tyne. He has published in *Revue Française de Sociologie* and *Archives de Sociologie des Religions.* His books include *Durkheim's Sociology of Religion* and *Anglo-Catholicism: A Study in Religious Ambiguity.* He was co-editor of *Sociology and Theology: Alliance and Conflict.* He is currently involved in setting up the British Centre for Durkheimian Studies at the Institute of Social and Cultural Anthropology of the University of Oxford.

The Revd Dr Peter H. Sedgwick lectured at Birmingham University prior to taking up the post of Theological Consultant to the North East Ecumenical Group. He is now Lecturer in Theology at the University of Hull, and Adviser in Industrial Affairs to the Archbishop of York. He chairs the Urban Theology Committee of the House of Bishops of the Church of England. In addition to articles in *Modern Churchman, Theology* and *Crucible,* he is the author of *Mission Impossible?: A Theology of the Local Church,* and co-editor of *The Weight of Glory: The Future of Liberal Theology.*

Dr Elmer J. Thiessen teaches philosophy at Medicine Hat College, Alberta, Canada. He was formerly lecturer in philosophy at Waterloo Lutheran University, Ontario. He is a Mennonite. In addition to articles in the *Journal of Philosophy of Education, Interchange* and *Religious Education,* he is the author of *Humanities in Alberta Post-Secondary Technical-Vocational Education,* guest editor of a special issue of *Ethics in Education* devoted to the ethics of religiously-based schools, and has recently completed a manuscript tentatively entitled *Teaching for Commitment: Liberal Education, Indoctrination and Christian Nurture.*

Dr Elizabeth Varley is Adult Education Adviser of the Diocese of Durham. She was formerly Fieldwork Secretary to the Community and Race Relations Unit of the British Council of Churches. She has published in *Crucible* and *Education in Church Today,* and has a forthcoming book entitled *The Last of the Prince Bishops: William Van Mildert and the High Church Movement of the Early Nineteenth Century.*

Carolyn B. Wilcox is Research Fellow at the North of England Institute for Christian Education. She was formerly Research Officer to the Medical Research Council, and Research Associate at the Human Development Unit of Newcastle Education Authority. She has co-authored various articles reporting research in medical journals (including *The Lancet*) and has a paper in the collection *Longitudinal Studies in Child Psychology and Psychiatry.*

Richard Zipfel gained his teaching experience in secondary schools in the USA. He is currently Secretary to the Committee for Community Relations, Catholic Bishops Conference of England and Wales. He is co-author of *From Barriers to Community: The Challenge of the Gospel for a Divided Society.*

Acknowledgments

The editors are grateful to the publishers and editors of the following journals for permission to re-publish in this volume material published by them in earlier versions:

Spectrum (for Elmer Thiessen's article, 'Christian Nurture, Indoctrination and Liberal Education', in Vol. 23, No. 2, Summer 1991);

Lumen Vitae (for Kevin Nichols's paper, 'The Logical Geography of Catechesis', in Vol. XLI, No. 3, 1986).

Index